ARNOLD READERS IN HISTORY

TITLES IN THE
ARNOLD READERS IN HISTORY SERIES

THE STALINIST DICTATORSHIP

Edited by
CHRIS WARD

*Lecturer in Slavonic Studies and
Fellow of Robinson College,
University of Cambridge*

A member of the Hodder Headline Group
LONDON • NEW YORK • SYDNEY • AUCKLAND

First published in Great Britain in 1998 by
Arnold, a member of the Hodder Headline Group
338 Euston Road, London NW1 3BH

http://www.arnoldpublishers.com

Co-published in the United States of America by
Oxford University Press Inc.,
198 Madison Avenue, New York, NY 10016

British Library Cataloguing in Publication Data
A catalogue entry for this book is available from the British Library

Library of Congress Cataloging-in-Publication Data
A catalog entry for this book is available from the Library of Congress

ISBN 0 340 70641 4 (pb)
ISBN 0 340 70640 6 (hb)

Production Editor: Rada Radojicic
Production Controller: Helen Whitehorn
Cover Designer: Terry Griffiths

Composition by J&L Composition Ltd, Filey, North Yorkshire
Printed and bound in Great Britain by MPG Books Ltd, Bodmin, Cornwall

Contents

Acknowledgements

The editor and the publisher would like to thank the following for permission to use copyright material in this volume:

Leon Trotsky: Selections from *The Revolution Betrayed* (Faber & Faber Ltd, 1937) Copyright © 1937, 1972 Pathfinder Press. Reprinted by permission; Theodore H. von Laue: 'Stalin in Focus', from *Slavic Review* 42 (3, 1983) pp. 373–89. Reprinted by permission of the American Association for the Advancement of Slavic Studies; Robert C. Tucker: Selections from *Stalin as Revolutionary 1879–1929*. Copyright © 1973 by Robert C. Tucker. Reprinted by permission of W. W. Norton & Company Inc.; Dimitri Volkogonov: Selections from *Stalin: Triumph and Tragedy*, trs. Harold Shukman (Weidenfeld & Nicolson, 1991). Reprinted by permission of The Orion Publishing Group; Isaac Deutscher: Selections from *Stalin: A Political Biography* (2nd ed., 1967). Copyright © Oxford University Press 1967; copyright © 1949, 1966 by Oxford University Press, Inc. Reprinted by permission of Oxford University Press and Oxford University Press, Inc.; J. Arch Getty: 'The politics of repression revisited', in J. Arch Getty and R. T. Manning (eds) *Stalinist Terror: New Perspectives* (Cambridge University Press, 1993). Reprinted by permission of Cambridge University Press and the author; Moshe Lewin: 'Society, state, and ideology during the First Five-Year Plan', in Sheila Fitzpatrick (ed.) *Cultural Revolution in Russia 1928–1931* (Indiana University Press, 1976). Reprinted by permission of the author; Lynne Viola: 'Bab'i bunty and peasant women's protest during collectivization', from *Russian Review* (Vol. 45, No. 1, Jan 1986) pp 23–42. Reprinted by permission of Ohio State University Press; Lewis H. Siegelbaum: 'Stakhanovites in the cultural mythology of the 1930s', from *Stakhanovism and the Politics of Productivity in the USSR 1935–1941* (Cambridge University Press, 1988). Reprinted by permission of Cambridge University Press and the author; Gabor T. Rittersporn: 'The omnipresent conspiracy: on Soviet imagery of politics and social relations in the 1930s in Nick Lampert and Gabor T. Rittersporn (eds), *Stalinism:*

Its Nature and Aftermath, Essays in Honour of Moshe Lewin (M. E. Sharpe, 1991). Reprinted by permission of M. E. Sharpe Inc. and Macmillan Press Ltd; Sheila Fitzpatrick: 'How the Mice Buried the Cat: Scenes from the Great Purges of 1937 in the Russian Provinces', from *The Russian Review*, Vol. 52, No. 3 (July 1993) pp. 299–332. Reprinted by permission. © 1993 by the Ohio State University Press. All rights reserved; Nicholas S. Timasheff: Selections from *The Great Retreat: The Growth and Decline of Communism in Russia* (E. P. Dutton & Co. Inc, 1946) © 1946 by E. P. Dutton. Used by permission of Dutton Signet, a division of Penguin Books USA Inc.; Vera S. Dunham: Selections from *In Stalin's Time: Middleclass Values in Soviet Fiction* (Duke University Press, 1990) © 1990 Duke University Press, Durham, N.C. Reprinted with permission.

Every effort has been made to trace copyright holders. Any rights not acknowledged here will be acknowledged in subsequent printings if notice is given to the publisher.

Glossary

Russian words and phrases explained in the text or footnotes have been excluded. Items in square brackets indicate alternative forms.

Apparatchik (*pl.* apparatchiki)
'Apparatus man'. Functionary in the administrative apparatus of the government or party (q.v.).

Artel' (pl. arteli)
In agriculture the predominant form of collective farm in which peasants retained some livestock and a family plot.

Brigadir
Head of work brigade.

Central committee
[CC, TsK] Elected by the party congress (q.v.). The central committee was the party's governing body between congresses, though in practice the Politburo (q.v.) came to dominate the central committee.

Central control commission
[TsKK] A department of the central committee (q.v.) which investigated complaints by party members against the party apparatus (1920–34).

Chastushka
Popular rhyming ditty on a topical or humorous theme.

Cheka
[VCHEKA] Extraordinary Commission for Combating Counter-Revolution, Sabotage, Speculation and Misconduct in Office (secret police 1917–22).

Chistka (pl. chistki)	'Cleansing'. Loosely a party purge. More accurately the expulsion of inactive or undesirable members.
Comintern	[Komintern, Communist International] Communist or Third International. The organization of foreign communist parties based in Moscow (1919–43).
Council of People's Commissars	*See* Sovnarkom.
Ezhovshchina	'The time of Ezhov' (pejorative). The 'Great Purge' of the 1930s named after Nikolai Ezhov, then head of the NKVD (q.v.).
Former people	[*Byvshie liudi*] A term current in the 1920s and 1930s used to describe the remnants of tsarist social classes deemed neutral or hostile to the regime.
Gensek	General Secretary.
Glasnost'	The policy of 'openness' associated with Mikhail Gorbachev.
Glauk	Chief committee; central directorate.
Gosplan	State General Planning Commission, based in Moscow (1921 onwards).
GPU	State Political Administration (secret police 1922–23).
Grubost'	Rudeness.
Guberniia (pl. gubernii)	Province.
Gulag	[GULag] Chief Administration for Corrective Labour Camps (1930 onwards). In popular parlance the Soviet labour camp system in general.
KGB	Committee for State Security (secret police 1953 onwards).
Kolkhoz (*pl.* kolkhozy)	A collective farm in which the produce was divided between kolkhozniki (q.v.) after obligatory deliveries had been made to the state.

Kolkhoznik (pl. kolkhozniki)	Peasant in a kolkhoz (q.v.).
Komsomol	[Comsomol] Young Communist League. The party's youth wing (1918 onwards).
KPK	*See* Party control commission.
Kraikom	District committee.
League of Communist Youth	*See* Komsomol.
Muzhik (pl. muzhiki)	A peasant (slightly pejorative).
Narkomtiazhprom	People's Commissariat for Heavy Industry.
Некультурная	Uncultured, ignorant (feminine adjective).
NEP	*Novaia ekonomicheskaia politika* (New Economic Policy), 1921–c. 1927/28.
NKVD	People's Commissariat for Internal Affairs (interior commissariat 1917–34, combined secret police and interior commissariat 1934–43, interior commissariat 1943–46).
Obkom	Oblast' (q.v.) committee of the party (q.v.).
Oblast' (pl. oblasti)	Administrative region of the USSR.
Obmen	The 'exchange of party cards' (1936).
OGPU	United State Political Administration (secret police 1923–34).
Okrug (pl. okrugi)	Territorial division of the USSR.
ORS	Department of Workers' Supply.
Party	[CPSU, KPSS, RKP(b), RSDRP(b), VKP(b)] The Bolshevik party.
Party congress	Theoretically the party's sovereign body. Delegates elected by party members.
Party control commission	[KPK] Successor to the central control commission (q.v). A department of the

	central committee (q.v.) responsible for checking the fulfilment of central decisions (1934 onwards).
People's Commissar	Minister of the Soviet government (1917–46).
Plenum	A full meeting of an organization.
Politburo	[Politbureau] Political Bureau. The body elected by the central committee (q.v.) responsible for making political decisions on behalf of the central committee and the party congress (q.v.) (1917 and 1919–52).
Prazdnik	Holiday.
Proverka	The 'verification' of party documents (1935).
Raion (pl. raiony)	Administrative district of the USSR.
RSFSR	Russian Soviet Federated Socialist Republic. The Russian state (1918 onwards).
RTsKhIDNI	Russian Centre for the Preservation and Study of Recent Documents. Successor to TsPA IML (q.v.).
Secretariat	The body elected by the central committee (q.v.) responsible for drawing up agendas for the Politburo (q.v.) and the general management of lower party organizations (1919 onwards).
Sel' sovet	Village soviet (q.v.).
Soviet	A council. The primary organ of elective government after October 1917.
Sovkhoz (pl. sovkhozy)	A farm run by the state in which the workforce received a wage.
Sovkhoznik (pl. sovkhozniki)	Worker in a *sovkhoz* (q.v.).
Sovnarkom	[SNK] Council of People's Commissars, based in the capital. The apex of the formal system of government between 1917–41 and 1945–46.

TsGAOR	Central State Archive of the October Revolution. The chief repository of primary sources pertaining to the state in the Soviet period.
TsPA IML	Central Party Archive of the Institute of Marxism–Leninism attached to the Central Committee of the Communist Party of the Soviet Union. The chief repository of primary sources pertaining to the party in the Soviet period.
Twenty-five thousander	One of the first 25 000 urban volunteers who went out to help collectivize the countryside.
Vozhd'	'Leader', 'chief' or 'boss'. A term applied, unofficially, to Stalin.
VTsSPS	All-Union Central Council of Trade Unions.
Zhdanovshchina	'The time of Zhdanov' (pejorative). The drive for ideological purity following the 1941–45 War, named after Andrei Zhdanov, then a secretary of the central committee (q.v.).

Introduction

This book is divided into three sections. The first, *Approaching Stalin*, tackles the meanings ascribed to Stalin by focusing on his background, interpretations of his character and investigations of those factors which have generally been advanced to explain his rise to power. Here, as with all the extracts, I have chosen articles and chapters which seem to me to be seminal and representative: seminal because they originated a debate or affected the terms of a debate; representative because they reveal something of the distinctive manner in which historians of twentieth-century Russia imagine their subject. I make no apology for ceding a good deal of space to extracts containing meditations on Stalin's personality, here and throughout the book, because this is precisely how so many academics have tried to understand what happened in Russia between the late 1920s and early 1950s. Whether or not any of this is plausible is another matter, but no one who thinks about Soviet history can avoid Stalin: somehow or other we must deal with the everlasting puzzle of the relationship between events and personality, between individual volition and impersonal forces.

Like the first section, the second, *Approaching Stalinism*, is split into two. Historians have always debated Stalin's role within the Soviet Union, and until quite recently most were content to accept that some kind of coherent system existed in the USSR. After noting its existence many then assigned pride of place to the General Secretary's actions and predilections – by delineating Stalin and then looking *through* him they hoped to see Soviet reality, or at least understand the functioning of the governmental machine. Some are still looking and hoping, although increasingly researchers are inclined to view Stalin as only one part (albeit an important one) of a complex and evolving culture of politics and administration, not as the *primum mobile* of a fixed system.

On the issue of Stalinism I have avoided writers whose primary concern is political theory. While it is true that for many years totalitarian models determined images of the Soviet Union, historians also characterized

Stalinism as a set of practices. Indeed, in a way this has been the central issue dividing the profession for half a century or more; on the one side stood those who accepted *a priori* definitions of Stalinism and read the past through totalitarian spectacles, on the other stood academics who viewed Stalinism more or less as that which happened during Stalin's tenure as General Secretary. Frequently both tendencies struggled within the same individual, sometimes with fruitful results. Though often derided nowadays, totalitarian interpretations still command the attention of many historians, and it is worth bearing in mind that without totalitarianism there could have been no revisionism, and that explorations of Soviet history would have taken quite different forms.

The final section veers away from debates about Stalin, the coherence of the political and economic system or the general nature of Stalinism, although, of course, these themes inflect all the extracts assembled under the rubric Living Stalinism. Here I have given the floor to academics who have dealt with the ways in which the Soviet people 'handled' socialism. Whether or not this has anything to do with Stalin personally is not really at issue: what these researchers have tried to show is how policy (Stalinism, if you like) functioned on the ground – what the regime's actions and ideology meant to people, how they responded and how things worked out in practice.

In each of these sections the biggest problem I faced was deciding who to leave out. I reluctantly excluded some important historians on the grounds that their work, although influential, is relatively uncontroversial. Others I put aside simply because they do not readily lend themselves to extraction or summary. E. H. Carr, Robert Conquest, R. W. Davies and Roy Medvedev are among the most obvious omissions here.[1] But if any number of fine historians deserved a place three cohorts disqualified themselves from the outset. If good history is always influential (although not always immediately and not in the way one might expect), not all influential history is good. In the first instance I therefore ruled out a huge swath of popular books about Stalin's Russia. Usually inaccurate, often boring, always prone to reflect rather than confront ingrained prejudices, their main fault lies in their complete failure to say anything new or add to a debate. Examples can be found in any university library. The same is true of the overwhelming bulk of Soviet monographs which, of course, suffer from another defect: until the Gorbachev years Soviet historians could not write anything original even if they wanted to. With the exception of Volkogonov, I therefore have included no extracts at all from material published in the USSR. This does not mean that I have ignored Marxist historiography or avoided writers whose lives were in some way involved with Stalinism. Far from it. But Soviet Marxism had been a living corpse long before the USSR's demise, and thoughtful Russian or East European Marxists published in exile, not inside the Soviet Union or the satellite states.

At first glance, the third group – contemporary Russian researchers – looked more promising, but most post-Soviet monographs are organized under the sign of totalitarianism or revisionism, and there seems no good reason to include extracts which are derivative of Western models and approaches just because they come from Russia. Russian academics are still trying to absorb new (and often not so new) theoretical developments across a whole range of disciplines, and, for better or worse, Soviet history continues to be driven forward by Western practitioners and Western thought, not by Russians.

A final point: of necessity this book mirrors rather than challenges debates about Stalin's Russia, and its contents reflect my personal view of what is stimulating and important about research into the period *c.* 1929–53. Other editors might well have chosen very different extracts, but they would, I think, have tackled roughly the same broad range of topics. The five years or so after 1928 witnessed Stalin's conclusive defeat of his rivals, forced collectivization, the launch of a nationwide planned industrialization drive, the elimination of private enterprise, the burgeoning of the Gulag system and massive social and cultural change. Nothing like this had ever happened before. The 'Great Breakthrough into Socialist Construction' astonished contemporaries and it continues to fascinate historians today. For the past half century virtually every researcher has characterized the period not just as Stalinism's defining moment but also as the epicentre of a series of vast detonations which echoed down the decades: purging, the transformation of the party-state, the birth of a new society and the elaboration of new cultural forms – all are seen as in some way inscribed in the period 1928–32. This is why most of the extracts relate primarily to the 1930s, and it also explains why I have disregarded several other topics – pre-war foreign policy, nationality, ethnicity, religion, the Nazi–Soviet War or the origins of the Cold War, for example. Though each has attracted scholarly attention, to date none has excited the same level of controversy or pushed the study of Soviet history forward in quite the same way. But the present keeps telling us what the past is about, and in a few decades the history of the Stalin period might well look very different.

Note

1 R. W. Davies, the world's leading economic historian of Soviet Russia, and the late E. H. Carr, the founding father of Soviet History in Great Britain, have written extensively on the period *c.* 1917–33. Robert Conquest has given us classic totalitarian readings of Stalin, Stalinism and the purges. Roy Medvedev's *Let History Judge: The Origins and Consequences of Stalinism* (New York: Alfred A. Knopf), translated into English by C. Taylor in 1971, was the most impressive work on Stalinism to emerge from the Soviet Union before glasnost'.

SECTION

I

APPROACHING STALIN

Commentary

Stalin bestrode twentieth-century Europe like few other men, but he has no really satisfactory biography. In part, this is because biography is a very difficult form. Historians dislike speculation and conjecture, but tied to the evidence as they are they nevertheless introduce themselves into their texts. How could it be otherwise? A life is never reconstructed from evidence alone, from documents, photographs, films, memoirs and reminiscences. Biographers endeavour to pierce the external and enter the core of a personality. Each must therefore discuss character, motivation and the human predicament in general – matters where opinion intrudes and evidence is often of little help. Moreover, the past is always shaped by the tyranny of the present, by the unconscious assumptions sustaining what we fondly imagine to be our own singular hopes, joys, fears and beliefs. Every biography is a tangle of subject, author and time which cannot be unravelled. Each might in some way be plausible, though none can be definitive or true. Each signals to a part of us, or falls silent, or recedes, or disappears, or becomes implausible as our concerns mutate, until some become so remote that we read them not for what they tell us about their subject but for the light they cast on the writer and his or her milieu. Every age and every writer fabricates a different life for the living and the dead to inhabit.

This is where we start from with all biographies, but Stalin presents us with further difficulties. In the first place Stalin, Stalinism and the twentieth century are inextricably mixed: the man, the times, the Soviet system and beyond form a single subject, and so his authors also write political, social and economic narratives in which the excesses and enormities of the Soviet regime saturate readings of his personality. Additionally, historians must negotiate the grim legacies of systematic falsification, obsessive secrecy and the 'cult of personality', all of which effaced Stalin as individual and created instead Stalin as icon: omniscient, omnipotent, immutable. We therefore have comparatively few indications of a complex inner life or range of interests beyond the compass of his official concerns. Evidence on his private life is meagre. We know hardly anything about his first marriage, for example, and can only guess at the effect of his second wife's suicide in 1932 or his eldest son's death in 1943.[1] Stalin seems one-dimensional, unreal, elusive, a cipher: a *tabula rasa* upon which we are invited – compelled almost – to inscribe a personality. His whole being seems to have been subsumed in administration and politics. Trotsky spoke to this condition in 1937 when wrestling with the problem of Stalin's relationship to the bureaucracy: 'In Stalin each one easily finds himself. But Stalin also finds in each one a small part of his own spirit. Stalin is the personification of the bureaucracy. That is the substance of his political personality.'[2]

Chapter 1: Situating Stalin

Like the other representations discussed below, Trotsky's Stalin cannot, of course, be true: you might not even find him plausible, but he is significant. Not only did Trotsky anticipate much scholarship on the socio-economic factors underpinning Stalin's ascendancy and the nature of the regime by more than half a century, he also profoundly influenced a generation of Western historians, whether or not they shared his Marxist assumptions [Reading 1].

There is no need to rehearse Trotsky's career in detail. He was instrumental in establishing Soviet power and subsequently fought against Stalinism, in the Soviet Union and in exile. As an historian he viewed human affairs through the lens of classical Marxism.[3] 'Men make their own history', wrote Marx in 1852, 'but they do not make it just as they please; they do not make it under circumstances chosen by themselves, but under circumstances directly encountered, given and transmitted from the past.'[4] With this Trotsky wholly concurred: Stalin's rise to power, the emergence of the dictatorial one-party state, his image of Stalinism and the factors which kept the entire system in being are all expressed as necessary outcomes of the dialectical tension between subjective and objective factors.

In examining these contingencies he elaborated three themes repeatedly discussed by later historians: Stalin's personality, to be sure, but much more importantly the world environment and factors specific to Russia. Trotsky believed that socialism must be international, that it could arise only in advanced capitalist economies and that without European revolution peasant Russia would remain backward. The years after 1917 threw these theoretical considerations into sharp relief. As the economy collapsed and hostile powers intervened in the civil war the coercive state grew alarmingly. Never more than a small minority of the population, Russia's proletariat disintegrated, robbing the Bolsheviks of their class support. Those that did not die on the battlefields perished from hunger or disease, fled to the countryside or were absorbed into the burgeoning party-state apparatus cobbled together to deal with a plethora of emergencies. In the struggle to defeat enemies soviet democracy soon disappeared, and when discontent resurfaced inside Bolshevism the 1921 X party congress abrogated intraparty democracy too.

With the war's end thousands of demobilized soldiers flooded into the civilian administration, bringing with them authoritarian habits learned in the barracks. Inevitably, given the context of endemic poverty, the result of Russia's backwardness and isolation, the bureaucracy ossified into a privileged group confronting society and seized the opportunities offered by the NEP to insulate itself from the hungry masses. By the mid-1920s 'Thermidorian reaction' – Trotsky had in mind events in France in 1794 when moderates overthrew Robespierre and the Jacobins – was in the making. Come the times, comes the man: Stalin's personality mirrored exactly the new ruling stratum's aspirations and prejudices. Finally, rather than mitigating the tensions and inequalities generated by the NEP, collectivization and industrialization only exacerbated them. Want, scarcity and the impatience of the masses stimulated the bureaucracy to gather ever more power to itself while propelling the General Secretary to new heights. According to Trotsky by the mid-1930s Stalinism, Stalin's personality and the totalitarian state formed an unholy trinity, blighting socialism, destroying Bolshevism and deforming the regime.

If Trotsky's Stalin is the dialectic made flesh, von Laue's is catastrophe personified [Reading 2]. Best known for his study of late-Imperial modernization,[5] like Trotsky, von Laue places Stalin, Stalinism and the USSR squarely within the context of Russian and European history, but he also characterizes each as a function of something much wider – the vast tragedy of the modern world, the dimensions of which the Anglo-American historical community has signally failed to appreciate.

Stalin's ambitions, avers von Laue, were formed *for* him, not *by* him. Like many late-nineteenth century revolutionaries Stalin believed that politics alone could refashion human existence. Like all, he grew up with the anxieties engendered by imperialism, industrialism and global Westernization and in a world haunted by the spectre of final solutions. In the Great War these spectres became realities. Not only did the monstrous slaughter teach that political ends justify any means, the threat posed by German imperialism could hardly have been greater. By 1918 the Russian state seemed on the point of extinction; all authority disappeared, all structures disintegrated and all power centres fell apart. In the maelstrom of war and revolution only the Bolsheviks kept their drive, but dreams of a world made safe through socialism, reinforced by an unconscious Russian messianism born of a pervasive sense of inferiority, were hopelessly at variance with a catalogue of harsh realities. Because after 1917 no state institutions remained and no mediating organizations existed to curb political ambition, the ruling elite exercised unlimited power based solely on personal will. In addition, von Laue believes that Russians lacked habits of peaceful intercourse, the foundation of civil society developed in the West over many centuries. Next, industrialization, which nourished a series of negotiations between individuals and groups, fostering compromise and cohesion, was weakly developed in Russia. Further, unlike Western Europeans and North Americans, Russians rarely associated concepts of freedom with restraint and responsibility. Finally, Russia's geographical situation, forever exposing regime and society to foreign aggression, had always frustrated the development of liberty and consensus. Instead for four hundred years or more an overmighty state born of necessity bullied a sullen and refractory people into submission in a desperate attempt to overcome the country's backwardness.

Insecure, wary and power hungry, the leaders grouped around Lenin therefore faced an appalling prospect. Their attempt to realize a New Jerusalem was immensely complicated by circumstance, history and Russian culture – even, speculates von Laue, reflecting the linguistic preoccupations of contemporary thought, by the patterns and registers of the Russian language. For a while Lenin was able to reconcile socialist dream with harsh realities and contain the colossal frustrations wracking the party and beyond, but with his illness and death Bolshevism began to fracture. Henceforward the times favoured a man who instinctively understood intrigue, brute force and all that would be required to make Russia strong. Given the forces arraigned against the Soviet Union little would change in Stalin's lifetime.

Chapter 2: Stalin's personality

Though no historian can fail to situate his life, nearly all studies of the USSR move from positioning Stalin to emphasizing the importance of his character in shaping events. Robert Tucker's 1973 essay in psychohistory represents one of the most sophisticated attempts to locate in Stalin's personality the source of all the horrors which afflicted those who fell under Soviet rule [Reading 3].

Small-minded, vengeful, chauvinistic, malicious and pathologically jealous, Tucker's Stalin presented a clear danger to the regime and to all around him, but a fatal deficiency in the Bolshevik mentality blinded colleagues to his faults. Marxists generally dismissed the personal factor in politics, judging adversaries and allies instead on the basis of their opinions, so he deflected criticism and confused opponents by recasting personal attacks as political opposition. According to Tucker this was not necessarily a matter of conscious duplicity. Stalin viewed the world through his cultural heritage. Key personality traits – self-dramatization, role playing, pronounced asocial tendencies and a thirst for enemies – sprang from his Georgian background, and the adolescent Stalin found satisfying parallels between Lenin's uncomplicated narrative of class war, the Leninist conception of the party and the clan myths of his homeland. By the mid-1920s he saw himself as a revolutionary knight in the tradition of his childhood folk heroes and a genius second only to the dead leader. But though he had risen high in the party-state apparatus there was much to offend his *amour propre:* few Bolsheviks took him seriously, his plebeian origins and Georgian identity elicited condescension rather than respect, his record in the revolution and Civil War was not without blemishes and, most devastatingly of all, Lenin had attacked him from his deathbed.

Thereafter, using categories borrowed from analytical psychology, Tucker intuits the evolution of Stalin's personality through middle age. As he emerged onto the national stage he struggled to become Russian and camouflaged his massive ego with displays of modesty and humility. Driven to maintain his identity by rejecting failings and inflating successes he unconsciously responded to anything which contradicted his self-image with a mixture of repression, denial and projection. But he needed constant praise because the facade of perfection disguised a gnawing insecurity (a factor which accounts for the rise of Beria, who was only too willing to flatter the dictator). Neurotic, vainglorious and hypersensitive, Stalin never forgot an insult and never forgave those who challenged him. He imagined pretence in others because his entire personality was pretence. Since his mask of perfection could never be allowed to slip he struggled to unmask others, and since he could neither separate the personal from the political nor admit that he might be wrong attacks on Stalin became attacks on socialism. Enemies – projections of his fantasies – surrounded him, and by extension enemies of Stalin became enemies of the people. Eventually, once he had achieved supreme power, he was free to lash out at them all in a series of lethal mass purges.

Reading Stalin's personality as the demiurge of history invites consideration of those qualities which made it possible for him to overpower rivals of seemingly far greater ability and stay at the helm of the party-state for nearly a quarter of a century. In the mid-1920s he began to assemble a library. It is this which provided Dmitri Volkogonov, a retried KGB General who had privileged access to Soviet archives in the 1980s, with a starting point for his depiction of Stalin's mind [Reading 4].

Stalin chose books according a precise scheme which reflected his political preoccupations. At the library's core stood the classics of Marxism, history texts and materials on the Russian social democratic movement. In addition he paid particular attention to anything connected with his enemies or with the lives of emperors and tsars. Over the years he returned again and again to Lenin's works – extant volumes once in his possession are heavily underscored – and he was no less obsessed with the writings of his chief opponent, Trotsky. During brief breaks in the working day he was forever correcting novels, plays and pamphlets which caught his eye, but his comments were invariably jejune and always coloured by narrow political exigencies. Stalin viewed everything that came his way through the prism of a dogmatic, vulgar Marxism. Volkogonov thinks that this was at once a strength and a weakness. On the one hand the mass of party members responded with alacrity to his simple formulations – more subtle intellects were always disadvantaged when he posed as Lenin's champion and defender. On the other he could never get to grips with Marxism's intricate abstractions: attempts by party theoreticians to explain Hegel or the dialectic ended in disaster, and his unfortunate teachers paid the price of their failure in the purges. His greatest assets, displayed most clearly in the Nazi–Soviet War, were a strong will, a phenomenal memory, the ability to process enormous masses of information quickly and efficiently and a talent for grasping the essence of a situation at lightning speed.

Far from being the party's 'outstanding mediocrity' therefore, a judgement of Trotsky's which has echoed down the century, Volkogonov maintains that it was not just chance or circumstance that made him one of Lenin's chief lieutenants during and after the revolution. Stalin possessed an exceptional intellect. But, adds Volkogonov, it belonged to a man who had no inkling of his own limitations and no moral sense at all.

Notes

1 Stalin married Ekaterina Svanidze around 1904 when she was only sixteen years old. She died in 1910, two years after the birth of their son Iakov. He married

Nadia Alliluieva in 1918. There were two children: Vasilii (1921–62) and Svetlana (born 1926).

2 L. D. Trotsky, *The Revolution Betrayed. What is the Soviet Union and Where is it Going?* trans. M. Eastman (London, Faber & Faber, 1937), p. 262.

3 Studies of Trotsky's thought abound. For a comprehensive treatment see B. Knei-Paz, *The Social and Political Thought of Leon Trotsky* (Oxford, Clarendon Press, 1978).

4 K. Marx, 'The Eighteenth Brumaire of Louis Bonaparte', in *Karl Marx and Fredrick Engels: Selected Writings* (London, Lawrence & Wishart, 1970), p. 96.

5 T. H. von Laue, *Sergei Witte and the Industrialization of Russia* (New York, Columbia University Press, 1963).

Chapter 1 Situating Stalin

Reading 1 *The Soviet Thermidor*

L. D. TROTSKY

Why Stalin triumphed

[. . .] It is sufficiently well known that every revolution up to this time has been followed by a reaction, or even a counter-revolution. This, to be sure, has never thrown the nation all the way back to its starting point, but it has always taken from the people the lion's share of their conquests. The victims of the first reactionary wave have been, as a general rule, those pioneers, initiators, and instigators who stood at the head of the masses in the period of the revolutionary offensive. In their stead people of the second line, in league with the former enemies of the revolution, have been advanced to the front. Beneath this dramatic duel of 'coryphées' on the open political scene, shifts have taken place in the relations between classes, and, no less important, profound changes in the psychology of the recently revolutionary masses.

Answering the bewildered questions of many comrades as to what has become of the activity of the Bolshevik party and the working class – where is its revolutionary initiative, its spirit of self-sacrifice and plebeian pride – why, in place of all this, has appeared so much vileness, cowardice, pusillanimity and careerism – Rakovsky referred to the life story of the French revolution of the eighteenth century, and offered the example of Babeuf, who on emerging from the Abbaye prison likewise wondered what had become of the heroic people of the Parisian suburbs. A revolution is a mighty devourer of human energy, both individual and collective. The nerves give way. Consciousness is shaken and characters are worn out. Events unfold too swiftly for the flow of fresh forces to replace the loss. Hunger, unemployment, the death of the revolutionary cadres, the removal of the masses from administration, all this led to such a physical and moral impoverishment of the Parisian suburbs that they required three decades before they were ready for a new insurrection.

The axiomlike assertions of the Soviet literature, to the effect that the laws of bourgeois revolutions are 'inapplicable' to a proletarian revolution, have no scientific content whatever. The proletarian character of the October revolution was determined by the world situation and by a special correlation of internal forces. But the classes themselves were formed in the barbarous circumstances of tzarism and backward capitalism, and were anything but made to order for the demands of a socialist revolution. The exact opposite is true. It is for the very reason that a proletariat still backward in many respects achieved in the space of a few months the unprecedented leap from a semifeudal monarchy to a socialist dictatorship, that the reaction in its ranks was inevitable. This reaction has developed in a series of consecutive waves. External conditions and events have vied with each other in nourishing it. Intervention followed intervention. The revolution got no direct help from the west. Instead of the expected prosperity of the country an ominous destitution reigned for long. Moreover, the oustanding representatives of the working class either died in the civil war, or rose a few steps higher and broke away from the masses. And thus after an unexampled tension of forces, hopes and illusions, there came a long period of weariness, decline and sheer disappointment in the results of the revolution. The ebb of the 'plebeian pride' made room for a flood of pusillanimity and careerism. The new commanding caste rose to its place upon this wave.

The demobilization of the Red Army of five million played no small role in the formation of the bureaucracy. The victorious commanders assumed leading posts in the local Soviets, in economy, in education, and they persistently introduced everywhere that regime which had ensured success in the civil war. Thus on all sides the masses were pushed away gradually from actual participation in the leadership of the country. [. . .]

The degeneration of the Bolshevik party

The Bolshevik party prepared and insured the October victory. It also created the Soviet state, supplying it with a sturdy skeleton. The degeneration of the party became both cause and consequence of the bureaucratization of the state. It is necesary to show at least briefly how this happened.

The inner regime of the Bolshevik party was characterized by the method of *democratic centralism*. The combination of these two concepts, democracy and centralism, is not in the least contradictory. The party took watchful care not only that its boundaries should always be strictly defined, but also that all those who entered these boundaries should enjoy the actual right to define the direction of the party policy. Freedom of criticism and intellectual struggle was an irrevocable content of the party democracy. The present doctrine that Bolshvism does not tolerate factions is a myth of the epoch of decline. In reality the history of Bolshevism is a history of the struggle of factions. And, indeed, how could a genuinely revolutionary organization, setting itself the task of overthrowing the world and uniting under its banner the most audacious iconoclasts, fighters and insurgents, live and develop without intellectual conflicts, without groupings and temporary factional formations? The farsightedness of the Bolshevik leadership often made it possible to soften conflicts and shorten the duration of factional struggle, but no more than that. The Central Committee relied upon this seething democratic support. From this it derived the audacity to make decisions and give orders. The obvious correctness of the leadership at all critical stages gave it that high authority which is the priceless moral capital of centralism.

The regime of the Bolshevik party, especially before it came to power, stood thus in complete contradiction to the regime of the present sections of the Communist International, with their 'leaders' appointed from above, making complete changes of policy at a word of command, with their uncontrolled apparatus, haughty in its attitude to the rank and file, servile in its attitude to the Kremlin. But in the first years after the conquest of power also, even when the administrative rust was already visible on the party, every Bolshevik, not excluding Stalin, would have denounced as a malicious slanderer anyone who should have shown him on a screen the image of the party ten or fifteen years later.

The very center of Lenin's attention and that of his colleagues was occupied by a continual concern to protect the Bolshevik ranks from the vices of those in power. However, the extraordinary closeness and at times actual merging of the party with the state apparatus had already in those first years done indubitable harm to the freedom and elasticity of the party regime. Democracy had been narrowed in proportion as difficulties increased. In the beginning, the party had wished and hoped to preserve freedom of political struggle within the framework of the Soviets. The civil war introduced stern amendments into this calculation. The opposition parties were forbidden one after the other. This measure, obviously in conflict with the spirit of Soviet democracy, the leaders of Bolshevism regarded not as a principle, but as an episodic act of self-defense.

The swift growth of the ruling party, with the novelty and immensity of its tasks, inevitably gave rise to inner disagreements. The underground oppositional currents in the country exerted a pressure through various channels upon the sole legal political organization, increasing the acuteness of the factional struggle. At the moment of completion of the civil war, this struggle took such sharp forms as to threaten to unsettle the state power. In March 1921, in the days of the Kronstadt revolt, which attracted into its ranks no small number of Bolsheviks, the tenth congress of the party thought it necessary to resort to a prohibition of factions – that is, to transfer the political regime prevailing in the state to the inner life of the ruling party. This forbidding of factions was again regarded as an exceptional measure to be abandoned at the first serious improvement in the situation. At the same time, the Central Committee was extremely cautious in applying the new law, concerning itself most of all lest it lead to a strangling of the inner life of the party.

However, what was in its original design merely a necessary concession to a difficult situation, proved perfectly suited to the taste of the bureaucracy, which had then begun to approach the inner life of the party exclusively from the viewpoint of convenience in administration. Already in 1922, during a brief improvement in his health, Lenin, horrified at the threatening growth of bureaucratism, was preparing a struggle against the faction of Stalin, which had made itself the axis of the party machine as a first step toward capturing the machinery of state. A second stroke and then death prevented him from measuring forces with this internal reaction.

The entire effort of Stalin, with whom at that time Zinoviev and Kamenev were working hand in hand, was thenceforth directed to freeing the party machine from the control of the rank-and-file members of the party. In this struggle for 'stability' of the Central Committee, Stalin proved the most consistent and reliable among his colleagues. He had no need to tear himself away from international problems; he had never been concerned with them. The petty bourgeois outlook of the new ruling stratum was his own outlook. He profoundly believed that the task of creating socialism was national and administrative in its nature. He looked upon the Communist International as a necessary evil which should be used so far as possible for the purposes of foreign policy. His own party kept a value in his eyes merely as a submissive support for the machine.

Together with the theory of socialism in one country, there was put into circulation by the bureaucracy a theory that in Bolshevism the Central Committee is everything and the party nothing. This second theory was in any case realized with more success than the first. Availing itself of the death of Lenin, the ruling group announced a 'Leninist levy'. The gates of the party, always carefully guarded, were now thrown wide open. Workers, clerks, petty officials, flocked through in crowds. The political aim of this maneuver was to dissolve the revolutionary vanguard in raw human material, without experience, without independence, and yet with the old habit of submitting to the authorities. The scheme was successful. By freeing the bureaucracy from the control of the proletarian vanguard, the 'Leninist levy' dealt a death blow to the party of Lenin. The machine had won the necessary independence. Democratic centralism gave place to bureaucratic centralism. In the party apparatus itself there now took place a radical reshuffling of personnel from top to bottom. The chief merit of a Bolshevik was declared to be obedience. Under the guise of a struggle with the Opposition, there occurred a sweeping replacement of revolutionists with *chinovniks*.[1] The history of the Bolshevik party became a history of its rapid degeneration. [. . .]

Of party democracy there remained only recollections in the memory of the older generation. And together with it had disappeared the democracy of the soviets, the trade unions, the co-operatives, the cultural and athletic organizations. Above each and every one of them there reigns an unlimited hierarchy of party secretaries. The regime had become 'totalitarian' in character several years before this word arrived from Germany. 'By means of demoralizing methods, which convert thinking communists into machines, destroying will, character and human dignity', wrote Rakovsky in 1928, 'the ruling circles have succeeded in converting themselves into an unremovable and inviolate oligarchy, which replaces the class and the party'. Since those indignant lines were written, the degeneration of the regime has gone immeasurably farther. The G.P.U. has become the decisive factor in the inner life of the party. If Molotov in March 1936 was able to boast to a French journalist that the ruling party no longer contains any factional struggle, it is only because disagreements are now settled by the automatic intervention of the political police. The old Bolshevik party is dead, and no force will resurrect it.

Parallel with the political degeneration of the party, there occurred a moral decay of the uncontrolled apparatus. The word 'sovbour' – soviet bourgeois – as applied to a privileged dignitary appeared very early in the workers' vocabulary. With the transfer to the NEP bourgeois tendencies received a more copious field of action. At the 11th Congress of the party, in March 1922, Lenin gave warning of the danger of a degeneration of the ruling stratum. It has occurred more than once in history, he said, that the conqueror took over the culture of the conquered, when the latter stood on a higher level. The culture of the Russian bourgeoisie and the old bureaucracy was, to be sure, miserable, but alas the new ruling stratum must often take off its hat to that culture. 'Four thousand seven hundred responsible communists' in Moscow administer the state machine. 'Who is leading whom? I doubt very much whether you can say that the communists are in the lead . . .' In subsequent congresses, Lenin could not speak. But all this thoughts in the last months of his active life were of warning and arming the workers against the oppression, caprice and decay of the bureaucracy. He, however, saw only the first symptoms of the disease.

Christian Rakovsky, former president of the Soviet of People's Commissars of the Ukraine, and later Soviet Ambassador in London and Paris, sent to his friends in 1928, when already in exile, a brief inquiry into the Soviet bureaucracy, which we have quoted above several times, for it still remains the best that has been written on this subject. 'In the mind of Lenin, and in all our minds', says Rakovsky, 'the task of the party leadership was to protect both the party and the working class from the corrupting action of privilege, place and patronage on the part of those in power, from *rapprochement* with the relics of the old nobility and burgherdom, from the corrupting influence of the NEP, from the temptation of bourgeois morals and ideologies . . . We must say frankly, definitely and loudly that the party apparatus has not fulfilled this task, that it has revealed a complete incapacity for its double role of protector and educator. It has failed. It is bankrupt'.

It is true that Rakovsky himself, broken by the bureaucratic repressions, subsequently repudiated his own critical judgements. But the seventy-year-old Galileo, too, caught in the vise of the Holy Inquisition, found himself compelled to repudiate the system of Copernicus – which did not prevent the earth from continuing to revolve around the sun. We do not believe in the recantation of the sixty-year-old Rakovsky, for he himself has more than once made a withering analysis of such recantations. As to his political criticisms, they have found in the facts of the objective development a far more reliable support than in the subjective stout-heartedness of their author.

The conquest of power changes not only the relations of the proletariat to other classes, but also its own inner structure. The wielding of power becomes the specialty of a definite social group, which is the more impatient to solve its own 'social problem', the higher its opinion of its own mission. 'In a proletarian state, where capitalist accumulation is forbidden to the members of the ruling party, the differentiation is at first functional, but afterward becomes social. I do not say it becomes a class differentiation, but a social one . . .' Rakovsky further explains:

> The social situation of the communist who has at his disposition an automobile, a good apartment, regular vacations, and receives the party maximum of salary, differs from the situation of the communist who works in the coal mines, where he receives from fifty to sixty rubles a month. [. . .]

The social roots of Thermidor

We have defined the Soviet Thermidor as a triumph of the bureaucracy over the masses. We have tried to disclose the historic conditions of this triumph. The revolutionary vanguard of the proletariat was in part devoured by the administrative apparatus and gradually demoralized, in part annihilated in the civil war, and in part thrown out and crushed. The tired and disappointed masses were indifferent to what was happening on the summits. These conditions, however, important as they may have been in themselves, are inadequate to explain why the bureaucracy succeeded in raising itself above society and getting its fate firmly into its own hands. Its own will to this would in any case be inadequate; the arising of a new ruling stratum must have deep social causes.

The victory of the Thermidorians over the Jacobins in the eighteenth century was also aided by the weariness of the masses and the demoralization of the leading cadres, but beneath these essentially incidental phenomena a deep organic process was taking place. The Jacobins rested upon the lower petty bourgeoisie lifted by the great wave. The revolution of the eighteenth century, however, corresponding to the course of development of the productive forces, could not but bring the great bourgeoisie to political ascendancy in the long run. The Thermidor was only one of the stages in this inevitable process. What similar social necessity found expression in the Soviet Thermidor? We have tried already in one of the preceding chapters to make a preliminary answer to the question why the gendarme triumphed. We must now prolong our analysis of the conditions of the transition from capitalism to socialism, and the role of the state in this process. Let us again compare theoretic prophecy with reality. 'It is still necessary to suppress the bourgeoisie and its resistance', wrote Lenin in 1917, speaking of the period which should begin immediately after the conquest of power, 'but the organ of suppression here is now the majority of the population, and not the minority as has heretofore always been the case . . . In that sense the state *is beginning to die away*'. In what does this dying away express itself? Primarily in the fact that 'in place of special institutions of a privileged minority (privileged officials, commanders of a standing army), the majority itself can directly carry out' the functions of suppression. Lenin follows this with a statement axiomatic and unanswerable: 'The more universal becomes the very fulfillment of the functions of the state power, the less need is there of this power'. The annulment of private property in the means of production removes the principal task of the historic state – defense of the proprietary privileges of the minority against the overwhelming majority.

The dying away of the state begins, then, according to Lenin, on the very day after the expropriation of the expropriators – that is, before the new regime has had time to take up its economic and cultural problems. Every success in the solution of these problems means a further step in the liquidation of the state, its dissolution in the socialist society. The degree of this dissolution is the best index of the depth and efficacy of the socialist structure. We may lay down approximately this sociological theorem: the strength of the compulsion exercised by the masses in a worker's state is directly proportional to the strength of the exploitive tendencies, or the danger of a restoration of capitalism, and inversely proportional to the strength of the social solidarity and the general loyalty to the new regime. Thus the bureaucracy – that is, the 'privileged officials and commanders of a standing army' – represents a special kind of compulsion which the masses cannot or do not wish to exercise, and which, one way or another, is directed against the masses themselves.

If the democratic soviets had preserved to this day their original strength and independence, and yet were compelled to resort to repressions and compulsions on the scale of the first years, this circumstance might of itself give rise to serious anxiety. How much greater must be the alarm in view of the fact that the mass soviets have entirely disappeared from the scene, having turned over the function of compulsion to Stalin, Yagoda and company. And what forms of compulsion! First of all we must ask ourselves: what social cause stands behind this stubborn virility of the state and especially behind its policification? The importance of this question is obvious. In dependence upon the answer, we must either radically revise our traditional views of the socialist society in general, or as radically reject the official estimates of the Soviet Union.

Let us now take from the latest number of a Moscow newspaper a stereotyped characterization of the present Soviet regime, one of those which are repeated throughout the country from day to day and which school children learn by heart:

> In the Soviet Union the parasitical classes of capitalists, landlords and kulaks are completely liquidated, and thus is forever ended the exploitation of man by man. The whole national economy has become socialistic, and the growing Stakhanov movement is preparing the conditions for a transition from socialism to communism
>
> (*Pravda*, April 4, 1936.)

The world press of the Communist International, it goes without saying, has no other thing to say on this subject. But if exploitation is 'ended forever', if the country is really now on the road from socialism, that is, the lowest stage of communism, to its higher stage, then there remains nothing for society to do but to throw off at last the straitjacket of the state. In place of this – it is hard even to grasp this contrast with the mind! – the Soviet state has acquired a totalitarian–bureaucratic character.

The same fatal contradiction finds illustration in the fate of the party. Here the problem may be formulated approximately thus: why, from 1917 to 1921, when the old ruling classes were still fighting with weapons in their hands, when they were actively supported by the imperialists of the whole world, when the kulaks in arms were sabotaging the army and food supplies of the country – why was it possible to dispute openly and fearlessly in the party about the most critical questions of policy? Why now, after the cessation of intervention, after the shattering of the exploiting classes, after the indubitable successes of industrialization, after the collectivization of the overwhelming majority of the peasants, is it impossible to permit the slightest word of criticism of the unremovable leaders? Why is it that any Bolshevik who should demand a calling of the congress of the party in accordance with its constitution would be immediately expelled, any citizen who expressed out loud a doubt of the infallibility of Stalin would be tried and convicted almost as though a participant in a terrorist plot? Whence this terrible, monstrous and unbearable intensity of repression and of the police apparatus?

Theory is not a note which you can present at any moment to reality for payment. If a theory proves mistaken we must revise it or fill out its gaps. We must find out those real social forces which have given rise to the contrast between Soviety reality and the traditional Marxian conception. In any case we must not wander in the dark, repeating ritual phrases, useful for the prestige of the leaders, but which nevertheless slap the living reality in the face. We shall now see a convincing example of this.

In a speech at a session of the Central Executive Committee in January 1936, Molotov, the president of the Council of People's Commissars, declared: 'The national economy of the country has become socialistic (applause). In that sense [?] we have solved the problem of the liquidation of classes (applause)'. However, there still remain from the past 'elements in their nature hostile to us', fragments of the former ruling classes. Moreover, among the collectivized farmers, state employees and sometimes also the workers, 'petty speculators'[2] are discovered, 'grafters in relation to the collective and state wealth, anti-Soviet gossips, etc'. And hence results the necessity of a further reinforcement of the dictatorship. In opposition to Engels, the workers' state must not 'fall asleep', but on the contrary become more and more vigilant.

The picture drawn by the head of the Soviet government would be reassuring in the highest degree, were it not murderously self-contradictory. Socialism completely reigns in the country: 'In that sense' classes are abolished. (If they are abolished in that sense, then they are in every other.) To be sure, the social harmony is broken here and there by fragments and remnants of the past, but it is impossible to think that scattered dreamers of a restoration of capitalism, deprived of power and property, together with 'petty speculators' (not even *speculators*!) and 'gossips' are capable of overthrowing the classless society. Everything is getting along, it seems, the very best you can imagine. But what is the use then of the iron dictatorship of the bureaucracy?

Those reactionary dreamers, we must believe, will gradually die out. The 'petty speculators' and 'gossips' might be disposed of with a laugh by the super-democratic Soviets. 'We are not Utopians', responded Lenin in 1917 to the bourgeois and reformist theoreticians of the bureaucratic state, and

> by no means deny the possibility and inevitability of excesses on the part of *individual persons*, and likewise the necessity for suppressing *such* excesses. But . . . for this there is no need of a special machine, a special apparatus of repression. This will be done by the armed people themselves, with the same simplicity and ease with which any crowd of civilized people even in contemporary society separate a couple of fighters or stop an act of violence against a woman.

Those words sound as though the author had especially foreseen the remarks of one of his successors at the head of the government. Lenin is taught in the public schools of the Soviet Union, but apparently not in the Council of People's Commissars. Otherwise it would be impossible to explain Molotov's daring to resort without reflection to the very construction against which Lenin directed his well-sharpened weapons. The flagrant contradiction between the founder and his epigones is before us! Whereas Lenin judged that even the liquidation of the exploiting classes might be accomplished without a bureaucratic apparatus, Molotov, in explaining why *after* the liquidation of classes the bureaucratic machine has strangled the independence of the people, finds no better pretext than a reference to the 'remnants' of the liquidated classes.

To live on these 'remnants' becomes, however, rather difficult since, according to the confession of authoritative representatives of the bureaucracy itself, yesterday's class enemies are being successfully assimilated by the Soviet society. Thus Postyshev, one of the secretaries of the Central Committee of the party, said in April 1936, at a congress of the League of Communist Youth: 'Many of the sabotagers . . . have sincerely repented and joined the ranks of the Soviet people'. In view of the successful carrying out of collectivization, 'the children of kulaks are not to be held responsible for their parents'. And yet more: 'The kulak himself now hardly believes in the possibility of a return to his former position of exploiter in the village'. Not without reason did the government annul the limitations connected with social origin! But if Postyshev's assertion, wholly agreed to by Molotov, makes any sense it is only this: not only has the burearucracy become a monstrous anachronism, but state compulsion in general has nothing whatever to do in the land of the Soviets. However, neither Molotov nor Postyshev agrees with that immutable inference. They prefer to hold the power even at the price of self-contradiction.

In reality, too, they cannot reject the power. Or, to translate this into objective language: the present Soviet society cannot get along without a state, nor even – within limits – without a bureaucracy. But the cause of this is by no means the pitiful remnants of the past, but the mighty forces and tendencies of the present. The justification for the existence of a Soviet state as an apparatus of compulsion lies in the fact that the present transitional structure is still full of social contradictions, which in the sphere of *consumption* – most close and sensitively felt by all – are extremely tense, and forever threaten to break over into the sphere of production. The triumph of socialism cannot be called either final or irrevocable.

The basis of bureaucratic rule is the poverty of society in objects of consumption, with the resulting struggle of each against all. When there is enough goods in a store, the purchasers can come whenever they want to. When there is little goods, the purchasers are compelled to stand in line. When the lines are very long, it is necessary to appoint a policeman to keep order. Such is the starting point of the power of the Soviety bureaucracy. It 'knows' who is to get something and who has to wait.

A raising of the material and cultural level ought, at first glance, to lessen the necessity of privileges, narrow the sphere of application of 'bourgeois law', and thereby undermine the standing ground of its defenders, the bureaucracy. In reality the opposite thing has happened: the growth of the productive forces has been so far accompanied by an extreme development of all forms of inequality, privilege and advantage, and therewith of bureaucratism. That too is not accidental.

In its first period, the Soviet regime was undoubtedly far more equalitarian and less bureaucratic than now. But that was an equality of general poverty. The resources of the country were so scant that there was no opportunity to separate out from the masses of the population any broad privileged strata. At the same time the 'equalizing' character of wages, destroying personal interestedness, became a brake upon the development of the productive forces. Soviet economy had to lift itself from its poverty to a somewhat higher level before fat deposits of privilege became possible. The present state of production is still far from guaranteeing all necessities to everybody. But it is already adequate to give significant privileges to a minority, and convert inequality into a whip for the spurring on of the majority. That is the first reason why the growth of production has so far strengthened not the socialist, but the bourgeois features of the state.

But that is not the sole reason. Alongside the economic factor dictating capitalistic methods of payment at the present stage, there operates a parallel political factor in the person of the bureaucracy itself. In its very essence it is the planter and protector of inequality. It arose in the beginning as the bourgeois organ of a workers' state. In establishing and defending the advantages of a minority, it of course draws off the cream for its own use. Nobody who has wealth to distribute ever omits himself. Thus out of a social necessity there has developed an organ which has far outgrown its socially necessary function, and become an independent factor and therewith the source of great danger for the whole social organism.

The social meaning of the Soviet Thermidor now begins to take form before us. The poverty and cultural backwardness of the masses has again become incarnate in the malignant figure of the ruler with a great club in his hand. The deposed and abused bureaucracy, from being a servant of society, has again become its lord. On this road it has attained such a degree of social and moral alienation from the popular masses, that it cannot now permit any control over either its activities or its income.

The bureaucracy's seemingly mystic fear of 'petty speculators, grafters, and gossips' thus finds a wholly natural explanation. Not yet able to satisfy the elementary needs of the population, the Soviet economy creates and resurrects at every step tendencies to graft and speculation. On the other side, the privileges of the new aristocracy awaken in the masses of the population a tendency to listen to anti-Soviet 'gossips' – that is, to anyone who, albeit in a whisper, criticizes the greedy and capricious bosses. It is a question, therefore, not of specters of the past, not of the remnants of what no longer exists, not, in short, of the snows of yesteryear, but of new, mighty and continually reborn tendencies to personal accumulation. The first still very meager wave of prosperity in the country, just because of its meagerness, has not weakened, but strengthened, these centrifugal tendencies. On the other hand, there has developed simultaneously a desire of the unprivileged to slap the grasping hands of the new gentry. The social struggle again grows sharp. Such are the sources of the power of the bureaucracy. But from those same sources comes also a threat to its power.

Notes

1 Professional governmental functionaries.
2 Spekulantiki.

Reading 2 *Stalin in focus*

T. H. VON LAUE

> As a writer, I would like to examine what kind of soil the personality cult arose from, what social causes produced it. After all, one cannot explain everything in terms of Stalin's individual peculiarities. The philosophers ought to give an explanation.
>
> Elizar Maltsev (quoted in Roy Medvedev's *Political Diary)*[1]

Parading under an innocuous title, this essay intends to disarm some of the extreme tensions that still surround the image of Stalin. The disarming, as Elizar Maltsev suggested, has to take a philosophical turn, reaching from the political and biographical data of the specialists into the larger issues of politics and morality that agitate an age of global interdependence and escalate the nuclear arms race. In times like the present, scholarship and a broad concern for the drift of events should overlap. Put differently, this essay tries to enlist the philosophical and historical faculties necessary to examine – and to do so humanely – the harsh context in which Stalinism operated.

The purpose here is not to justify political terror; it is merely to place it into a context in which overweening ambition and vast human sacrifice for political ends have been accepted as legitimate policy. The author hopes that the explanations here offered will persuade the reader to reconsider basic assumptions of past and present politics and, more important, to take a more realistic and complete – a more tragic and moral – view of the age in which we live. Such reconsideration may help to change attitudes and eventually even policies, so that Stalinism can be laid to rest as an ominous symptom of an age that did not understand what it was doing. These considerations set wide boundaries for a mere essay. But do not Stalinism and the untold millions of its victims call for ever renewed impulses of healing imagination?

We begin with a bit of theoretical history, with the far-reaching generalizations which, like an improvised bridge, help us to cross over a profound cognitive abyss into an alien political culture. We reach out from the security of an American scholarly study and from the limited resources of the English language into the Russian world of Stalin and the Soviet Union as it existed over half a century ago – into realms of individual and collective experience happily unexplored on this side of the Atlantic. Lacking the experiential foundations for understanding and fair judgement, we have to use substitutes: constructs of the mind, enlarged visions of interdependence, extended frameworks of political and moral interaction, and a higher level of abstraction into which to fit the available evidence.

Starting in this manner we disavow any claim to speak to the condition of Soviet citizens; they have to come to terms with Stalin and his heritage in their own way. Yet as we try from our American perspectives to assess Stalin, we still have a right to do likewise with his Soviet critics. As outsiders we are concerned with the far-flung circumstances that produced both Stalin and anti-Stalinists.[2]

In the light of our theoretical considerations we will attempt appropriate moral conclusions.

Our first consideration of theory (or enlarged vision) has to do with the outermost context for our assessment of Stalin. To begin with the dimensions of power into which Bolshevik imagination was set and to state the obvious: the framework for Stalin's ambition was not of his own making. It was defined for him (through Lenin and through German nationalists) by the scope of *Weltpolitik* established in the late nineteenth century. The pacesetter and model of global power for ambitious patriots everywhere was the world-spanning British Empire, controlling one quarter of the world's land surface and taking the lead in what one might call the world revolution of westernization (and now of modernization). As Lord Lytton, Viceroy of India from 1874 to 1880, proclaimed: 'We have placed, and must perpetually maintain, ourselves at the head of a gradual but gigantic revolution, the greatest and most momentous social, moral, and religious, as well as political revolution which, perhaps, the world has ever witnessed'.[3] The affectation of modesty expressed by his 'perhaps' merely underscored the magnitude of Britain's leadership in the world.

Consider next Lord Rosebery's imperious contention of 1893: 'We have to remember that it is part of our responsibility and heritage to take care that the world, so far as it can be moulded by us, shall receive the Anglo-Saxon and not another character'.[4] Remember also Cecil Rhodes's memorable maxim: 'Expansion is everything'. Seen in this context Bolshevik ambition was merely of the 'catch-up-and-surpass' variety (with more emphasis on catching up and with a Russian twist).

When Lenin grew up, nationalists in the major European states copied another important British concern, expressed by Disraeli in a much-quoted speech of 1872 at the Crystal Palace; it set the perspectives for a new age of final solutions. The issue, Disraeli told his listeners, is

> whether you will be content to be a comfortable England, modelled and moulded upon continental principles and meeting in due course an inevitable fate, or whether you will be a great country, an imperial country, a country where your sons, when they rise, rise to paramount positions, and obtain not merely the esteem of their countrymen, but command the respect of the world.[5]

That Social Darwinist either/or of being a world power or nothing at all was combined by the turn of the century with a widespread sense of living at a major turning point in history. The Marxists shared the excitement, expecting the locomotive of history to race forward into a superior stage of social existence. Nations, classes, cultures were in flux – the whole world was on the move. It was as if the dimensions of human existence had suddenly been widened out to near-infinitude. For the prewar generation the scale of political power and also of individual and collective ambition had been globalized and, thanks to the keen historical interest of the time, vastly extended chronologically as well, looking backward and forward in terms of centuries or whole historical eras.

World War I raised that ambition for world domination to a new pitch; henceforth political power was to shape not only political boundaries but the forms of state and society as well. In 1917 Woodrow Wilson stepped forward with the American ambition to make the world – the whole world – safe for democracy. In the same year Lenin went Wilson one better with the Bolshevik claim to make the world still safer through Soviet socialism. Russians had traditionally reacted with characteristic hyperbole to any external presumption of superiority, claiming a higher status for themselves, as the Third Rome under Vasilii III, as an empire under Peter I, as an advanced polity in the name of Orthodoxy, Autocracy, and Nationality under the last tsars. Throughout history the scope of Russian ambition has been defined outside the country. It has been reactive and therefore inclined to one-upmanship, no matter how ludicrous in the light of reality.

A second set of considerations follows from the first. Russia has long felt the revolutionary effects of westernization – the paradigm of a 'developing' country with a keen political ambition. Since the seventeenth century it has suffered the torments of 'modernization' so evident around the world now. Viewed in this all-inclusive perspective, Russia's historical evolution originated in the interaction between internal conditions and the external threat – and not, as is often assumed in discussions of Russian history or Stalinism, in the internal dynamics of Russian state and society alone. For the past four hundred years Russian history has recorded the Russian response to a superior West, a dialectic resulting from Western stimuli and indigenous responses – a process in which the initiative always came from what Russians called 'the West'.[6]

The revolutionary impact of Western power assumed different forms. Superior military force was the most obvious one. Foreign invasion, defeat in war, and the perpetual fear of both have cast a deep shadow over Russian history; they have also given brute force a permanent priority in Russian statecraft. The most humiliating defeat in modern times came in 1917. The strains of World War I led to a national catastrophe of the utmost severity. Imperial Russia collapsed, its institutions repudiated by revolution, its army dissolved, and the very survival of Russia as a state called into question. It was indeed a time of final solutions. The lesson was obvious: more military power was needed if the country was to survive at all.

Western power made itself felt in yet another crucial way: it subverted the credibility of indigenous authorities and foisted institutional and even cultural imitation upon unprepared and disoriented people. Certainly since Peter the Great the basic pattern of government revolved around the deliberate mobilization of the country's material and human resources to meet a superior Western challenge. Since the French Revolution especially, Russian autocracy has deliberately countered the revolution of westernization – a sort of counterrevolution paradoxically promoted through an indigenous revolution of westernization of its own, carried by a small governmental elite into the ranks of a reluctant and resentful population. The aims of that revolution from above were characteristically ambiguous. They were both Western and anti-Western, adapting Western ways, and foremost the instruments of power, to Russian conditions in order to safeguard and underline the country's non-Western identity – in vain. In the process Russian traditions were eroded; yet Russia's backwardness persisted. The revolution of westernization could not be contained.

Comparison with a forever superior West was always at Russia's expense. Any government that assumed responsibility for the country continued to be subjected to this humiliating comparison. As part of the paradoxical permanent indigenous revolution of westernization, the government was therefore compelled to combat invidious comparison by any

means at hand, however contradictory: by military power, by extravagant
political visions of superiority, and by importation of Western skills and
accomplishments. The regime of Nicholas I furnished an excellent pre-
Soviet model of the confused dynamics of Russian statecraft under the
Western impact; it has stood as godfather to the Soviet model.

By 1918 the Western impact was devastatingly triumphant. The country
faced dissolution, its partition by Germany having been prevented only by
Germany's defeat on the western front. The external disaster coincided
with a domestic populist revolution repudiating all governmental authority and all forms of modernization carried out by the privileged classes,
whether tsarist or liberal. The orgy of revulsion against unwanted change
was accompanied by an unprecedented tide of violence arising from a
population already brutalized by nature and tsarist rule, a tide made
more vicious yet by the succession of war, revolution, and civil war
followed by famine.

At the end of World War I the social and political catastrophe of Russia
was infinitely more searing and dehumanizing than any crisis in the history
of any Western country, let alone the Western liberal democracies. It was
imprinted in the subconscious of the Bolshevik leaders, the only group that
had managed both to retain a measure of control over the tides of anarchy
and to take a global view of Russia's predicament. Like the French after
1871, they felt no need to talk about that blow to their patriotic pride, nor
even to document it. Their class-oriented Marxism (unlike the old discredited nationalism) allowed little opportunity for rational analysis or
public documentation of Russia's plight. What counted, far more tempes-
tuously than in the minds of Frenchmen after 1871, was their effort to wipe
out the ignominy with whatever resources came to hand in time for the
next round of trials.

Yet, suspended between their exalted vision of making the world safe for
communism and the utter chaos of their country, how could the Bolsheviks
make the extremes meet? How could they build up a polity capable of at
least preventing a recurrence of the recent disaster? Our search for understanding the Soviet answer to that question prompts another recourse to
theory.

Before preceeding, however, we must first settle a moral question (considerations of morality inevitably intrude into any discussion of Soviet
policy). Who or what was responsible for the collapse of the Old Regime,
for the ensuing revolution, and for the monstrous Bolshevik ambition to
make Russia the jumping-off point for a communist world revolution
superior to the world revolution of westernization?

If the foregoing observations on the dynamics of Russian history are
accurate, the answer is simple. The impetus, the ambition, and even the
example of using force regardless of the human price came from without,
from the West, from the sum total of the ambitions that had sustained four

years of unprecedented slaughter in the war just ended. Whatever the consequences of that war for Russia, they came as a response and not as an original initiative. The response, admittedly, drew on the lessons of Russian history.

Seen in this light, the moral responsibility for the Soviet system thus lies as much with the West as with the communists. Those who furnished the model for political behavior and possess the power to prove its superiority share the blame for the results wherever the model sets the pace. Soviet Russia was the child of the world revolution of westernization, born at the height of a monstrous war among the Great Powers of Europe, a war that had consumed, on the first day of the battle of the Somme, some sixty thousand soldiers and, all told, had taken the lives of millions. The lesson of legitimating vast human sacrifice for political ends struck a familiar chord in Lenin who had watched the war from Zurich and in the Russian soldiers who returned from the front to take part in the revolution. In a time of final solutions, what did the individual count?

Thus back to our theoretical considerations and to the problems of state building under extreme adversity. How is the power of states produced?

More specifically: how was state power produced in the model states of the West, the 'capitalist' democracies (which offer the sharpest contrasts)?[7] Equipped with an answer we can then carry the question back into the Russian setting as it existed after March 1917 and ask: how could Russians construct a matching state power under the conditions prevailing in the country?

In trying to determine how Western state power was produced, we discover no ready-made answers. State power had always been taken for granted. Of course, national unity had been forever a concern of domestic politics; during the war it had required additional mobilization. But at the beginning of the war millions of men had been ready to fight and die for their countries; workers labored overtime. Before the war compulsion had been minimal, especially in the case of Great Britain, the paragon of both empire and government by consensus. What made possible the social discipline that supported the spontaneous cohesion of the nation-states which provided the model of power?

There is no space here for a full explanation. What we need is not political theory as traditionally defined, but a cultural anthropology and sociology of power, a structuralist study of the infinite filigree of invisible linkages between individuals – the 'covenants of every man with every man' in Hobbe's terms[8] – under a common government; of popular attitudes, values, habits, unspoken assumptions; of notions of selfhood and society; of widely practiced ways of controlling individual wills and libido; of the general capacity for cooperation in impersonal institutions;

of socialization. We also need to study the network of power relations between the sexes, parents and children, teachers and students, masters and servants, rich and poor, rulers and ruled. State power also involves the relations between human beings and their environment, their mechanical aptitudes, their command over nature, their docility toward their tools (including machines), their patience and openness in dealing with inert substances; their scientific training.

The production of state power is an infinitely complex cultural process developed over centuries (if not millenia) and carried on for the most part below the threshold of awareness; even its visible aspects are not commonly related to state power. It grows from an unending management and manipulation of human relations at all levels, each relationship concerned with some form of power through persuasion, mutual accommodation, or constraint. The production of state power begins within the family; it extends through school, job, community action; it is interwoven with the way people earn their living and sustain their material life; it draws on a complex web of communications and on extended communities of trade and commerce, of government agencies and representative bodies. It is upheld by religious sanction, spiritual awareness, and aesthetic sensibility; by activities as diverse as philosophizing and competing in sports. Politics merely covers the surfaces of power; political institutions are merely the handles by which we try to shape or control the invisible substructures of power ranging from the psychic universe within to the sociocultural universe without.

Viewed in this fashion, power is a huge cooperative enterprise, integrating individual egos through a thousand covenants with public needs as defined in peace and war. As the structuralist philosopher Michel Foucault has written: power

> traverses and produces things, it induces pleasure, forms knowledge, produces discourse. It needs to be considered as a productive network which runs through the whole social body, much more than as a negative instance whose function is repression.[9]

What he calls 'the economy of power' is a tight weave of minute social and cultural relationships. Marx sensed some of the essential linkages, though one-sidedly; Max Weber traced the connecting threads between Calvinist spirituality and capitalist enterprise; Foucault himself has isolated other filaments in regard to deviancy or sexuality. One could lay bare infinitely more of those criss-crossing fibers of sociopolitical – or even cultural – bonding, all of them contributing to the production of state power.

Let us merely stress here the essential point. In what we call Western society (admittedly idealized by liberal theory), peaceful intercourse among the ladders of social and political institutions has been taken for granted; such intercourse constituted no challenge for deliberate action that might upset the existing order. It has been marked by minor violence, but examples of the use of physical compulsion on a large scale have been rare in recent history. The body politic has been held together largely by its own cement of good will and cultural conditioning. When it came to war, the Western belligerents (unlike the Russian government) could count on the collective skills of their peoples to provide the military power that justified their status as Great Powers.

Considering the emphasis commonly placed on Stalin's monstrous will to power, we need to add some reflections about the nature of individual political ambition and power. The essential point here is the relative impersonality of the power of a prime minister or American president. Nobody could be formally more powerful than, for instance, Woodrow Wilson at the end of World War I; he was both president and commander-in-chief of the mightiest nation on earth. Yet his authority was not of his own making; it was based on the many intermediary channels of power built into the machinery of American presidential elections. Thanks to that institutional support presidential power was wielded by consensus; Wilson was the most powerful contemporary statesman by virtue of being Mr. President.

At the same time he was known as an able and ambitious individual who had prevailed over other presidential candidates under time-honored rules. Under these rules personality counted; political ambition mattered even more – a massive ego is essential for success in any political system.[10] In Western democratic practice, fortunately, personal ambition has always been socialized through many constitutionally-derived institutions. What would happen in a country where no such support structures existed while the needs of the times cried out for the exercise of power as far-reaching as that of an American president?

Besides government authority and political leadership, a third factor of Western state power needs to be considered: industrialism. Like the network of governmental power, industrialism is based on an immense diversity of intermediary covenants between the individual and a highly productive industrial economy. These covenants arise in part from the relationship between people and their machines, complex machines in factories and mills which are tied to the organizations that make up the institutional fabric of an industrial society. Consider merely the tension between workers and their machines. The operators mastermind the functioning of the machines and are responsible for their performance and output. The machines in turn command the operators' bodily motions, their thoughts and attitudes. In the dialog either party may get the upper hand. The operators may proudly think of their machines as their obedient slaves; or they may feel enslaved by their machines. In the West the former response prevailed; during the industrial revolution in England much mechanical ingenuity originated among the lower classes.

Even in the West, however, the socialization of workers in factories and mills was not easy. Yet despite perennial industrial unrest, industrialism prospered, tightening its grip on the individual. Command over the machines was associated with a variety of related skills: more precise accounting of time, more refined personal attention to detail in complex work, an ever more subtle division of labor and specialization of function, popular mechanics and literacy – all the interlacing ingredients of an advanced industrial culture. Inside and outside the workshops the solidarity of industrialism was combined with the civic loyalty that cemented the state. In tandem they produced the unity of tens of millions of people in urban-industrial society under the common government of a nation-state.

The external order of state and industry is buttressed by even less visible supports originating within the individual. Civic docility is based on the collective subconscious, on an intrapsychic order as complex and structured as the external setting. In the internal household of the individual subconscious, as yet totally unexplored in intercultural comparison, we find (apart from the myriad personal variations) a wide range of appropriate physiological responses supporting the external civic discipline. Each word in popular speech sets off a corresponding psychosomatic reaction. Compare, for a superficial example, the relaxed physiological response to the term 'government' or 'law' in England and the United States with the cardiovascular tenseness occasioned in Russia by the term 'vlast'. Our entire speech – our whole set of social relations – constitutes a vast keyboard: a single word can touch off socially and culturally tuned (and therefore predictable) psychosomatic vibrations. Our very subconscious is programmed to support the production of state power. It has been the good fortune especially of the English-speaking West that the internal physiological tuning and the external order were generally in agreement; 'soul' was not opposed to civic duty. Out of this happy union of the internal and external realms rose the liberal sense of freedom.

A word then about freedom, as crucial an issue as that of morality in the comparisons between Russia and the West. The essence of freedom is the subliminal acceptance of the dense fabric of restraints that make the production of state power possible. Lying below the threshold of awareness, these restraints constitute no limitation in human creativity; on the contrary, they are the precondition for the liberating opportunities which prosperity, good government, and power in the world afford. Cultural outsiders, visiting Russians for instance, have always resented the customs and mores of Western (or 'bourgeois') Europe as a hated strait jacket. Yet the great majority of Western Europeans and Americans freely accepted it as a comfortable cultural uniform for serving their world-wide pre-eminence.[11]

Finally, a comment about the geographical givens in the production of state power. Considering the paragons of democratic government, England and the United States, which provide the model in East–West comparisons, we cannot overlook their traditional insular security. They possessed gratis (or at a low price) the most essential ingredient of state power: comparative freedom from external attack. They suffered little pressure to mobilize either human values or the institutions of government against an external threat and were thus saved from any major conflict between ends and means in statecraft. That priceless boon has become part of the ways of thinking embodied in the English language, in liberal democratic political theory, and in the analyses of modern social science; it has profoundly influenced even Marxist thought. The relative peace of domestic politics derived from the unmatched external security – or, put differently, from the balance between high ethical–moral standards and the need for brute state power – was responsible for the emergence of government by consensus and the legal safeguard protecting what has come to be known as 'human rights'.

To sum up: imperial pre-eminence, government by consensus, industrialism, the sensibilities of the English language, human rights – all are inseparable parts of the cultural package now loosely called 'the West'. They define the range of Western insight into the production of state power; they also limit Western capacity to understand differently structured cultures. Judging the world by their own immensely privileged conditions, English-speaking observers have always practiced what we might call 'cognitive imperialism', annexing the non-Western world to their own historical experience. Cognitive imperialism has been an integral part of the world revolution of westernization; its foremost victim has always been Russia – Russia as it has been judged by Western standards.[12]

With these considerations in mind, let us turn to Russia after the overthrow of the tsarist regime. How could the Bolsheviks, the most alert and experienced in the politics of chaos among the claimants for the succession, match Western state power with the material and human resources at their disposal? What, to start with, were the conditions they faced?

The condition of the country was bleak indeed. The Revolution, carried forward by soldiers, workers, and peasants as well as by the non-Russian minorities – by the masses – had repudiated the entire superstructure of the state built up for centuries, together with its bureaucracy, its army, and its social base. It had also dislodged the Orthodox church, and with it the moral sanctions upholding the old order. Gone too were the influence and power of the liberal elements in industry, finance, and the professions, the most westernized segment of the population.

The Revolution, culturally conservative or even reactionary, had brought a massive anti-Western liberation of the accumulated popular resentment against autocracy and the changes it had foisted on uncomprehending and rebellious people. Now that the country was no longer held together by force, the long-feared eruption from below was inevitable. It had disastrous consequences. Trade and industry came to a virtual halt, the trains stopped running. The country fell apart into its historic constituent units, the social and political – the civic – awareness of its inhabitants shrank to a raw libidinous selfishness. Thus the question of how a new state order and an all-inclusive civic awareness could arise from the ruins assumed a special urgency. Was *any* government possible under the circumstances?

For an answer we need to attempt, at least in outline, an anthropology of power in the Russian setting. There is no dearth of suitable material for such study. We find it in literary works as diverse as Sholokhov's novels on the Don Cossacks, Pasternak's *Dr. Zhivago*, E. E. Dwinger's account of the experiences of German prisoners of war in Siberia called *Zwischen Weiss und Rot*, Gor'kii's novels and especially his essay (1922) on the Russian peasants, Nadezhda Mandel'shtam's reminiscences, or Solzhenitsyn's documentary on Gulag.

The evidence submitted by these works leads to an obvious conclusion: Russia found itself in a brutish state of nature, in a war of all against all incited by the soldiers fresh from the fronts, their rifles still cocked, their anger readily taken up by workers and peasants. Under the strains of civil war even the family, the primary unit of social existence, fell apart; villagers too were at each other's throats. Throughout the country life was predatory and without regard for human rights. In many cases people delighted in torture for its own sake, men of hardened will hacking away at other men equally spiteful. The political dissension caused by the collapse of the old order was aggravated by moral disorientation; prewar morality was discredited or even discarded.

The Revolution, many revolutionized intellectuals proclaimed, created its own morality – at the point of the bayonet. It held out an exalted vision of democracy or socialism, for the sake of which much blood could be spilled, as in the recent war or more apocalyptically for world revolution. Besides the new creeds, atavistic memories of ancient blood feuds and times of troubles were revived.

In the aftermath of the war a novel political phenomenon arose: mass politics. The war had brought a new political awareness to people hitherto nonpolitical and quiescent who constituted no experienced democratic electorate. Their sights raised as never before by war propaganda and by the sudden new visions of an earthly paradise, their greed aroused by their suffering, they carried their stock of prejudice and bitter memories into the elemental disorders of the postwar years as their only preparation for citizenship. Short-tempered, violent, unstable and unpredictable, they formed an explosive political force. Few members of Russia's educated classes had looked closely into the hidden recesses of popular political culture. The masses revealed their character through action in revolution and civil war, in Russia as in other parts of Europe.

From their midst a new breed of leaders emerged. Cast in the common mold and raw like their followers, they represented the wide variety of ethnic traditions and cultural levels within their countries, thereby drawing on untapped resources of vitality and heroic folklore. Marginal, insecure, aware of the opportunities of mass politics and power-hungry, they were suddenly confronted with world war, world revolution, global politics, and with the task of producing effective state power out of utterly unsuitable human material under conditions of utter material want. Thus rose Mussolini, Hitler, and Stalin. Stalin, a perceptive German communist observed, '*das ist Hitler plus Asien*'.[13] The Bolsheviks were the foremost practitioners of the Russian – the 'Asian' – variant of mass politics, the most extreme in Europe. Was it a wonder that they turned out to be monsters?

In Russia the Revolution and the civil war stirred up an immense need for leadership, in party cells, army units, factories, local soviets, and even in the countryside. American scholarship is just beginning to probe into the many local revolutions scattered through European Russia, turning up evidence of a militant crop of local organizers representing the mood and the wishes of their constituents.[14] The new leaders could count on a minimal consensus in the common outlook of people of peasant stock. That consensus, however, was restricted to local affairs and by all accounts rather brittle. It did not extend across the whole country or rise to a grasp of the larger world which, at the end of World War I, determined the fate of the country. Obviously, it did not reach upward into the superstructure of government; there was neither government nor a substructure on which, as in the West, an effectual government could be constructed. Yet there also existed, amid the near-universal urge for having one's way at last, a vague contrary yearning for stability and order at any price, dredged up, as always in times of crisis, from the deepest folk memories.

It is no exaggeration to argue – following Sun Yat-sen's characterization of the Chinese people – that Russian society constituted 'a sheet of sand', or, more prosaically, a collection of mutually repellent human atoms, unsocialized by any of the myriad covenants of power on which authority in Western states was founded. Admittedly, tiny nuclei of slightly enlarged social awareness existed, the breeding ground for the new leadership. Yet each of these local power centers was riddled by factionalism. Even the Bolsheviks, although disciplined by party rules, suffered from incessant intrigue and personal feuds. What cohesion the Bolsheviks possessed derived largely from the personal ascendance of one man, Lenin, who battled against the intelligentsia's notorious splintering individualism. By 1922 he was incapacitated and out of touch with the harsh conditions of governing the country.

Under these circumstances the production of state power capable of meeting the urgent needs of postwar reconstruction and long-range mobilization could proceed only in one way: by force and compulsion. The many invisible intermediary covenants of power in Western political practice had to be artificially and deliberately recreated by organization and outright command. Lenin had indicated the basic process – the substitution of deliberate controls for the invisible promptings of custom and culture – when he observed: 'What is to a great extent automatic in a politically free country [he was thinking of German Social Democrats] must in Russia be done deliberately and systematically by our organization'.[15] From the structuralist perspective Soviet totalitarianism is but a form of contrived large-scale substitutionism.

Yet substitution still left unanswered the central question of power: who was to be in charge? In this respect, too, Western practice did not apply. In the absence of a constitutional ladder for the advancement of leadership, the rise to the top was possible only for the most energetic and ruthless men by an assertion of individual will. They could take nothing for granted; everything depended on their own resources, on their mastery of political forces, on their capacity to mold the human raw material to their designs. In a pulverized, brutalized polity, state power could be built only around the person of the leader, a leader who had to be even more ruthless than his followers. Personal power and state power thus became identical. The legitimacy of that power had to be established by any means at hand.

It may be objected now that Russians were also capable of exceptional kindness, meek, long-suffering, and of profound spiritual depth, as shown, for instance in Solzhenitsyn's story 'Matrena's House'. But these qualities had always been the recessive strain, the soft underside of the Slavic temperament evident, among unappreciative neighbors, only as private virtues in personal relations and always on the losing side; they never reached into the superstructure of state power. After the Revolution a small number of people, including the poet Osip Mandel'shtam, stuck to their humaneness. Most highminded intellectuals were political innocents, however; they had no effective answers to the problems of the Russian body politic in an age of world wars and mass politics. How could they lead the aroused masses? Like many Western liberals they expected state and society to provide them with a stable or even civilized environment for their work (yet, to paraphrase Solzhenitsyn, even the Western city did not stand on righteousness alone; its relative humaneness was premised on insular security and superior might). That was one of the tragedies of a Russia greatly different from the West: even people of goodwill contributed to the anarchy that throughout Russian history has been both the cause and the product of autocratic state-building.

After 1917, as so often before, kindness and soul were in short supply. In their absence, the intermediary covenants of social cohesion, like state power itself, could only be built on the basest human motivations: selfishness, greed, and the raw desire to live and, if possible, to reap the benefits of the new opportunities presented by mass politics. The character of the new Sovereign, if one was to arise out of chaos, could hardly be found in Hobbes's civilized and legalistic political theory. The Soviet Leviathan was an inarticulate brute; he took his cues from the brutes with whom he had to work. 'Where did this wolf-tribe appear from among our people? Does it really stem from our own roots? Our own blood?' Devastatingly Solzhenitsyn answered: 'It is our own', thereby underlining the absurdity of applying the standards and practices of liberal democracy to revolutionary Russia.[16]

Even this ex post facto theorizing imposes a foreign pattern upon Russian developments. It represents a calm historical reconstruction of events which is rational only from a Western perspective. Those in the midst of battle interpreted these events with the equally valid reasons of inarticulate instinct and private passion, or, if they attempted a more sophisticated analysis, of ideology. Western observers may question the rationality of Marxism, or even Marxism–Leninism, as applied to the course of events in Russia. Yet by putting Hobbes and Hobbesian structuralism above Marx, we disregard the necessity for an instrumental theory that could support state-building in the chaotic Russian setting.

An updated Russian Leviathan had to provide not only a transethnic source of social solidarity (no matter how fictitious) but also a promise of a glorious and globally preeminent future (no matter how utopian) as spiritual cement for the projected political superstructure. Emancipated from the Orthodox church, the 'wolves' required taming by a secular creed that still carried the trappings of religion and projected forward the old vision of Russian superiority while also catering to the aroused material ambitions of the masses. In this sense Marxism–Leninism as a disguised nationalist mobilization theory was a highly relevant creed, even though its thought patterns created a false consciousness. It submerged the memory of the recent defeat and prevented, among observers both inside and outside, an adequate understanding of the necessities facing the country, leading to endless hypocrisy and intellectual deceit.

But let us complete our theoretical history. Thus far we have merely dealt with the necessities of state building. More was required for stemming the revolution of westernization that had just led to the near-extinction of the Russian state. A powerful Russia capable of holding its own required industrialization; it had to copy the industrial skills of the 'capitalist' West. Industrialization, unfortunately, imposed an even greater burden than a Hobbesian rebuilding of the state. It called for nothing less than a drastic reculturation of the entire population.

Obviously, the intermediary 'covenants' between the individual and a highly productive industrial economy did not exist. Lacking the subliminal uniformity of Western life, Russian 'broad nature' was infinitely more wide-ranging in emotions, more variable, more unpredictable, and therefore more free. That deeply cherished freedom, however, was a poor preparation for industrialism. By its very nature, rather than by any special Russian application, industrialism was a source of repression. How then could that industrial component of state power be reproduced under the conditions prevailing in Russia at the end of World War I?

In the 1930s Westerners delighted in telling stories about Russian peasants beating a stalled tractor as though it were a horse. What then could a Russian Leviathan bent on industrialization before the next great crisis do but whip a population of peasants through several centuries of cultural evolution and transform them into equivalents of their Western contemporaries (or rather into their betters, since they now lived under 'socialism')? Born before the turn of the century, a Russian Leviathan himself was bound to be entirely ignorant of industrial culture; he merely knew the superior works of Western industrialism, above all its weapons. Yet in response to the humiliation which defeat had brought to his country, he had to become an industrial superboss, undertaking a revolution from above prompted not by indigenous initiative or skills, but imposed from without under sentence of collective political death.

Reculturing a Russian into an 'industrial man' was infinitely more difficult than transforming him into a citizen. He had been pressed into citizenship before. Stubborn and resentful as he was toward all uncomprehended innovation, he now had to become even more perfectly socialized not only with his fellows, but also with inanimate objects possessing a built-in mechanical will of their own.[17] In Russia industrialization meant reculturation of a whole people at the core of their individual wills; it meant 'a new man' beaten into shape by an ignorant and brutish Leviathan; it meant an extreme version of totalitarian substitutionism, and even a war against the toiling masses carried out in their own name – another example of the paradoxes created by the transformation of Marxism into a theory of mobilization for backward countries.[18]

Industrialism imposed by a Leviathan barely able to hold the state together, however, contained a fatal contradiction. Not Hobbes but John Locke provided the civic theory for what we call the industrial revolution; not compulsion but willing cooperation generated, and still generates, the creative impulses of industrialism. Yet what could a boorish Russian Leviathan do in the face of that contradiction? Surrender was not in his nature. His only escape lay in muddling through, whatever the costs – the costs always measured against the costs of lost political sovereignty. He would give no thought to the long run. The instincts set loose by the lost war and its aftermath riveted his attention to the most immediate necessities.

When did people in the West ever face similar conditions? What practical advice could they offer from their own experiences? More important, what moral justifications could they derive from their favored circumstances for judging the application of their institutions under adverse conditions which they unwittingly had made even worse? The reproduction of the fullness of Western state power in an alien and hostile setting was bound to be an utterly exhausting, uncertain experiment, repulsive and yet inevitable. Future generations would be made to pay for Stalin's policy of letting the post-World War I generation barely escape political extinction, maimed and crippled, yet at least alive and free of direct foreign domination.[19]

What, in summary, should be our answer to Elizar Maltsev? What, in the enlarged historical-philosophical perspectives, were the causes of Stalin and Stalinism?

Stalin can be understood only in the full context of global power politics, as viewed from the all-inclusive perspective and with the impartial detachment befitting an interdependent world. In this light he should be seen as one of the most remarkable products of the world revolution of westernization, as a generic symptom rather than as a unique individual to be judged on his personal merits.[20] He reflected the monstrous political ambitions unleashed in Western Europe at the end of the nineteenth century and spread into an unprepared Russia during World War I. Stalin lived in an age of final solutions conceived before 1914 as grandiose and legitimate human ventures and put into practice during and after the first large-scale slaughter in modern history. In 1929 Hitler was not yet in power, but *Mein Kampf*, as a straw in the winds of change, pointed to yet further escalation of the struggle for world power.

The final solution envisaged by the imperial German army command in 1918 threatened the very existence of the Russian empire as a polity; the memory of this solution dominated Stalin's revolution. That revolution was designed to assure survival – always under the pressure of a superior 'capitalist' West, always forcing government and people to change their ways according to an alien pattern, drastically reculturing the country and imposing a form of state and society requiring far greater social discipline than tradition provided. Reculturation had to be carried out in the face of an elemental nativist rebellion among aroused, embittered, and brutalized people, under the novel conditions of mass politics. It favored a leader close to the masses by temperament and style, exceptionally energetic and driven by an ambition as great as the chaos in the country and the scope of *Weltpolitik*.

Considering the extreme tensions in the age of final solutions, the Soviet counterrevolution of self-assertion through reculturation had to be carried out in great haste in the panicky remembrance of a lost war, pitting the human costs against the price of ever-dreaded foreign domination. In the absense of any prior experience it had to proceed by trial and error, under the guidance of a master who craved legitimacy and therefore deified himself while yet remaining all too human, taking his vengeance as a means of sustaining the psychic burden of his responsibility. Whatever his faults – and they matched his ambition – he remained dedicated even in senility to enhancing the country's security, allowing himself little private indulgence and always keeping on guard as master in the eye of a sociopolitical storm more devastating than any humanity had ever witnessed before. The storm center has now passed, but basic adversities continue to confront his successors, keeping the seeds of Stalinism alive.[21]

High-altitude historical analysis of Russian events furnishes only one-half of the explanation. The other half lies in the abysmal ignorance among most participants in the global revolution of westernization. How many of them have yet understood the causes behind the course of events or even their own actions?

Russian rulers had traditionally been inarticulate about their methods of governance. Autocracy evolved no political theory relating governmental practice to the conditions of the country. If it had, its realism would have shocked the public both inside and outside the country, discrediting the authorities; however desirable, political realism was politically inexpedient. Thus neither rulers nor ruled gave themselves a clear account of the problems of government in Russia; administrative practice and official explanations (or official ideology) remained far apart.

Under Soviet rule after 1917 the predicaments grew worse. Marxism–Leninism, though useful in other respects, imposed an even more extreme false consciousness; it too allowed no realistic and all-inclusive assessment of the problems of governance. Yet as before, realism (as shown for instance in this essay) would have been politically counterproductive. It would have laid bare the extent of Russian backwardness, thus undercutting the Soviet claim of superiority with all its morale-building effects.

The political opposition in Russia also lacked a liberating realism. Under both tsars and Soviets it was given to utopian expectations derived from inapplicable Western models or idealized tradition. Deprived of political responsibility and misguided by official ideology, it devised its own escapist remedies. Moreover, by endowing its ignorance with moral superiority, it made government by consensus even more difficult, hardening attitudes and inciting discontent. If, as in the case of the Bolsheviks, an opposition party assumed the responsibilities of government, the adjustment to reality caused further disunity; mentally many Old Bolsheviks continued to live in tsarist Russia even after 1917.

Ignorance was, and still is, equally widespread and dangerous in the West. Who has explored the consequences of Lord Lytton's remark about the world revolution of westernization? Who is aware of the inhuman burden imposed upon unprepared peoples at the fringes of Europe and beyond by the extension of the Western instruments and organizations of power? Who makes the mental and spiritual effort to see the world from the angle of the men charged with responsibility for external security and civic continuity in countries outside the West, and especially in Russia? Who in the United States, or in the democratic West generally, realizes the vastness of power that resides in the challenges thrust by the most favored countries at the rest of the world? Are historians and political scientists willing to stretch their perspectives to the full length of interaction between the Western peoples and the rest of the world? Are they ready to abandon the prevailing moral parochialism in favor of full account-ability for all the consequences of the world revolution of westernization, including even Stalin?

Any answers to these questions – all central to the philosophical expla-nations desired by Elizar Maltsev – prompt a scaling down of our claim to understand the world in which we live. In this age the chief moral and intellectual challenge for our studies of non-American and non-Western cultures lies in fathoming the legitimacy of the incomprehensible and the outrageous. Only in that manner can we hope to uncover the hidden forces at work in our world and, by learning how to control them, escape the drift toward catastrophes worse than Stalinism.

Notes

1 Quoted in Stephen F. Cohen (ed.), *An End to Silence. Uncensored Opinion in the Soviet Union from Roy Medvedev's Underground 'Political Diary'* (New York, 1981), p. 108.
2 Two Soviet critics of Stalin, A. Antonov-Ovseenko and R. Medvedev, are reviewed from the perspectives set forth here in my essay 'Stalin Reviewed', to appear in *Soviet Union/Union Soviétique* (1984). It should be read as a compa-nion piece to the present essay; it furnishes additional documentation.
3 Quoted in A. J. Thornton, *Doctrines of Imperialism* (New York, 1965), p. 178.
4 Quoted in R. J. Sontag, *Germany and England, Background to Conflict, 1848–1894* (New York, 1938), p. 309.
5 Quoted from *Selected Speeches of the Late Right Honorable the Earl of Bea-consfield*, ed. T. E. Kebbel (London, 1889), p. 534.
6 The foregoing characterization of Russian history runs counter to most inter-pretations by Russian and Western historians writing in the traditional mold of national histories. Critically reexamined in the total context, Russian history – like the history of all other countries – assumes a different shape more readily suited to comparative studies. For the nature of some overlooked aspects of Western power over Russian life, see my articles 'Die Revolution von aussen als erste Phase der russischen Revolution von 1917', *Jahrbücher für Geschichte Osteuropas*, July 1956, and 'Imperial Russia at the Turn of the Century: The Cultural Slope and the Revolution from Without', *Comparative Studies in Society and History*, July 1961.
7 The term 'the West' (originally a Russian concept denoting indiscriminately all

of Europe west of the country) is used here to characterize essentially the 'capitalist' democracies, England, and, to a lesser extent in the period under discussion, the United States (which of course is the inevitable experiential reference point for American students of Stalin). Great Britain, it is assumed, served as a universal model to continental Europe (and much of the world) even where it was formally repudiated. Continental states deviated from that model to the degree to which they could not match the voluntarist civic cooperation that characterized the democratic regimes. In order to highlight the theoretical problems of comparison, the present analysis deals with ideal types at opposite poles; it is England and the U.S. versus Russia. France, Germany, Italy occupy intermediary stages on this scale, all 'Western' from the Russian perspective and all favored by a higher degree of civic voluntarism. In the years under discussion Japan, of course, did not count.

8 Thomas Hobbes, *Leviathan* (London, 1914), p. 89.

9 Michel Foucault, *Power/Knowledge: Selected Interviews and Other Writings, 1972–1977* (New York, 1980), p. 119. I am much indebted to Hugh Ragsdale for his advice on structuralism and to Jonathan Bordo for his help with Foucault's philosophy.

10 Compare Stalin with Lyndon Johnson as described by his recent biographer Robert A. Caro, who wrote that Johnson had a 'hunger for power not to improve the lives of others but to manipulate and dominate them, to bend them to his will in a hunger so fierce and consuming that no consideration of morality or ethics, no cost to himself – or to anyone else – could stand before it'. *The Path to Power. The Years of Lyndon Johnson* (New York, 1982,), p. xix.

11 Admittedly, since Rousseau the tyranny of civilization has been a common theme among romantic intellectuals, the most outspoken the further east we look. Germany and Eastern Europe occupied an intermediary position between the English-speaking West and Russia.

12 Cognitive imperialism, of course, is a world-wide phenomenon among high and low alike; all people assess outsiders from their own limited inside perspectives. But it causes greater damage when practiced by the mighty. As this essay tries to prove, it can be counteracted.

13 A. Antonov-Ovseenko, *The Time of Stalin* (New York, 1980), p. 255. The term 'Asia' has come to denote in Russian and even in German usage the sum total of the cultural traits that run against the grain of the comparatively more subtly structured sensibilities of Western-oriented intellectuals. Yet 'Asian' promptings (or values) possess their own subtle structures, 'primitive' by Western standards, but as legitimate in their natural settings as those of the West. Any effective intercultural historical analysis must take these invisible promptings as objective given factors.

14 See for instance Donald J. Raleigh's article 'Revolutionary politics in provincial Russia: the Tsaritsyn "Republic" in 1917', *Slavic Review*, 40, no. 2 (June 1981): 194–209, and the forthcoming book by Rex A. Wade; also Robert Service, *The Bolshevik Party in Revolution* (New York, 1979), which, however, does not take into account the larger circumstances shaping party policy and the evolution of leadership.

15 V. I. Lenin, 'What is to be Done?' in R. C. Tucker (ed.), *The Lenin Anthology* (New York, 1975), p. 83.

16 Aleksandr Solzhenitsyn, *The Gulag Archipelago* (New York, 1973), 1: 160. Solzhenitsyn here refers to the Bluecaps but intimates a wider application,

citing himself as an example. See also the evidence cited by Valery Chalidze, *Criminal Russia* (New York, 1977), in chapters 1–3 especially.

17 As for factories, Friedrich Engels pointed out ('On Authority') that 'the automatic machinery of a big factory is much more despotic than the small capitalists who employ workers'.

Industrial discipline in Russia on the eve of World War I has, to my knowledge, hardly been studied. On the incidence of violence among Russian workers see the recent article by Daniel Brower (*Slavic Review*, 41, no. 3 [Fall 1982]: 417–31). Yet the larger questions remain: how was industrial discipline affected by the continued influx of raw rural labor? What resources of technical training and mechanical craftsmanship were available? What were the workers' attitudes toward factories? The crucial evidence, it would seem, comes from the years of liberation between 1917 and 1921. What spontaneous industrial cooperation was left then among the workers? How disciplined were the Factory Committees? Consider also Lenin's assertion that Russian workers lagged behind their German counterparts in the essentials of industrial productivity.

18 As perceptive readers will have noticed by now, the structuralist approach here attempted implies a bias in favor of cultural determinism. It argues that there exists a great variety of crucial but invisible factors determining policy and political behavior. The illusion of free options is understandable when insiders deal with their own affairs within the limits of the possible; they can take the invisible substructures for granted. If, however, we are engaged in intercultural comparisons we have to account for the full range of factors, visible and invisible, at work in a given historical era. If we do so, we find that human beings have their hands and their minds tied right and left. Structuralist attention to the invisible substructures of human action inevitably encourages cultural determinism: it enlarges enormously the complexity of causation. It should be clear, however, that such determinism limits human freedom as little as does the physical law of gravity. In knowingly submitting to the given necessities, we learn to control them and thereby to exercise our freedom. In our present understanding of political systems, of course, we have not yet reached the stage of Newtonian physics, with disastrous results in cross-cultural relations.

In the structuralist perspective, incidentally, the much-discussed differences between Lenin and Stalin, the availability of more humane solutions, or the relevance of the Marxist vision cease to be meaningful topics. Based largely on wishful thinking, they have been disregarded in the present essay.

19 The foregoing considerations may help to bring some intelligibility to hitherto obscure aspects of early Soviet life that have puzzled some distinguished students of Soviet affairs writing in Sheila Fitzpatrick (ed.), *Cultural Revolution in Russia, 1928–1931* (New York, 1982). See for instance David Joravsky's comment that there is no rational explanation for the 'wild irrationality' of Soviet policy toward science (p. 128); or Moshe Lewin's bafflement over the change of an optimistic Marxist creed into a dark and deeply pessimistic attitude to people and culture (p. 69).

It is worth noting in this context that the terms 'rational' and 'rationality' have no meaning in intercultural comparisons. As there are reasons of the heart that the intellect does not know, so the rationality of one culture appears irrational to another. By this perspective the application of the values of the West to Russia appears irrational, and Stalin's seeming irrationality entirely rational (although deplorably inarticulate). The present essay, obviously, attempts to establish the rationality of Stalinism – in Western terms which only partially do justice to the other side.

20 Stalin's personal merits are discussed in Von Laue, 'Stalin Reviewed'.

21 The basic domestic and external insecurities persist. In addition we still find Stalinist attitudes in Soviet popular culture, even among stout anti-Stalinists. For evidence see Von Laue, 'Stalin Reviewed'.

Chapter 2 Stalin's personality

Reading 3 *The decisive trifle*

R. C. TUCKER

As others saw him

Apart from their attitude toward Lenin, Bolsheviks were not generally inclined to attach much importance to the personal factor in politics. To their Marxist-trained minds, what mainly mattered about a comrade was not his personality but his political beliefs, his ideological commitment, the rightness or wrongness of his positions in party councils. Lenin was taking account of this ingrained assumption when he wrote in the post-script to the testament that the question of Stalin's personal qualities 'may seem an insignificant trifle'. And he was taking issue with it when he went on to contend that in this instance the personality trifle might prove of *decisive* historical significance.

In later years some other party leaders came around to his view under the pressure of their own further experiences with Stalin, but they, too, found it hard to overcome the Bolshevik tendency to deprecate the role of personality. Stalin made it even harder by maintaining that oppositionist attacks impugning him on personal grounds were a red herring. We have seen, for example, that in his confrontation with Trotsky in October 1927 he dismissed the personal factor as something of no real conse-quence – one of those 'petty questions' that had to be cleared away before coming to the serious substance of the dispute. Again, in addres-sing the Central Committee in April 1929 on his conflict with the Bukharin group, which had accused him of lusting after despotic power, he began by saying:

> Comrades, I shall not touch on the personal factor, although it played a rather conspicuous part in the speeches of some comrades of Bukharin's group. I shall not touch upon it because it is a trifle, and it is not worthwhile dwelling on trifles.

The personal accusations, he said, were only a cheap trick designed to 'cover up the underlying political basis of our disagreements'.[1] And in the lengthy speech that followed, Stalin presented the conflict strictly in terms of fundamental differences over party policy. Although these differences existed, Stalin owed part of his success to the Central Committee's will-ingness to view the personal factor as the 'trifle' that he said it was.

Lenin, albeit tardily, realized that Stalin's personality very much mattered. But neither he nor others who later arrived at the same realization succeeded in supporting this insight with anything like an adequate analysis of Stalin's character. Lenin, as we have seen, became alarmed about Stalin's rudeness; his administrative peremptoriness; his Great Russian nationalism; his tendency to give animosity free rein in official conduct; and his lack of tolerance, loyalty, and considerateness toward others. It was a weighty catalogue of politically significant character defects, but not a reasoned analysis. The others, too, even as their horror of Stalin deepened, stood somehow mentally paralyzed before the enigma of the man's personality. Krestinsky, for example, described him privately as 'a bad man with yellow eyes'.[2]

Trotsky, in whose writings we find very many valuable observations on Stalin as an individual, took the position that he was important not in his own right but only as a personification of the Thermidorean bureaucracy. As he summed up his view in *The Revolution Betrayed*, 'Stalin is the personification of the bureaucracy. That is the substance of his political personality'.[3] Even Stalin's personal traits, such as the notorious rudeness, seemed significant to Trotsky primarily as manifestations of a social phenomenon: the characteristics of the new bureaucratic ruling stratum as a group.[4] So the problem of Stalin as a personality was partially set aside by the one man who combined a wealth of pertinent knowledge and recent observation with full freedom to communicate his thoughts in writing during the years that remained to him after he was deported from Russia in 1929. And the full-scale biography of Stalin in which he was trying finally to come to grips with the personal factor remained in raw and unfinished condition when the assassin sent by Stalin struck him down in 1940.

Bukharin was more inclined to consider the personal factor in its own terms. He enjoyed excellent opportunities to observe Stalin at close range over a long period of years, and it appears that even after his fall in 1929 he continued, on occasion, to be a summer guest of the Stalins at Zubalovo.[5] We have seen the importance that he attached to Stalin's theory of 'sweet revenge'. Along with others in high Soviet circles, he came to believe that a motivating mainspring of Stalin's personality was the need for a vindictive triumph over those whom he regarded as his enemies. But what aroused his vindictive feelings, and whom did he regard as his enemies? It was in offering a clue to the answer to this crucial question that Bukharin made his best contribution to a deeper understanding of Stalin. Briefly, he saw that Stalin was psychologically driven to feel enviously vengeful toward all who surpassed him in qualities or capacities in which he considered *himself* to be pre-eminent. 'Stalin's first quality is laziness', Bukharin told Trotsky on one occasion. 'And his second is an implacable jealousy of anyone who knows more or does things better than he'.[6]

Fate gave Bukharin an opportunity to express this view of Stalin to persons living abroad, who preserved it for posterity. In early 1936 he was sent to Paris as the head of a three-man Soviet delegation to negotiate for the purchase of Marx archives belonging to the German Social Democratic party. These archives had been sent from Berlin to Paris and Copenhagen in 1933 by Boris Nicolaevsky, editor of the émigré Menshevik *Sotsialisticheskii vestnik* (Socialist Herald). Nicolaevsky and a colleague, the prominent Menshevik Fyodor Dan, were intermediaries in the negotiations and saw Bukharin frequently over a period of about two months.[7] One day he appeared unexpectedly and unaccompanied at the Dans' apartment and stayed for several hours, during which he spoke at length of Stalin. Perhaps he wanted to take advantage of a unique opportunity to say something for the historical record on a subject concerning which the world remained very largely in the dark. Dan, who had known Stalin a little in earlier years, found Bukharin's characterization of him not only disturbing but surprising. In a memoir published years later, after both Bukharin and Dan were dead, Mrs. Dan revealed it.

In one of the early negotiating sessions with Dan and Nicolaevsky, Bukharin had said jocularly that the Bolsheviks were so interested in everything pertaining to Marx that they would even be willing to buy his remains for transfer to Moscow. If that were to happen – he now remarked in private to the Dans – a monument to Marx would be erected on the spot. But it would not be a very tall one, and beside it would be built a taller monument to Stalin. He would be shown reading *Capital*, with pencil in hand in the event he should find it necessary to make some marginal corrections in Marx's book. Elaborating, Bukharin went on:

> You say you don't know him well, but we do! He is unhappy at not being able to convince everyone, himself included, that he is greater than everyone; and this unhappiness of his may be his most human trait, perhaps the only human trait in him. But what is not human, but rather something devilish, is that because of this unhappiness he cannot help taking revenge on people, on all people but especially those who are in any way higher or better than he. If someone speaks better than he does, that man is doomed! Stalin will not let him live, because that man is a perpetual reminder that he, Stalin, is not the first and the best. If someone writes better, matters are bad for him because *he*, Stalin, has to be the premier Russian writer. Marx, of course, no longer has anything to fear from him, save possibly to appear small to the Russian worker in comparison with the great Stalin. No, no Fyodor, he is a small-minded, malicious man – no, not a man, but a devil![8]

Future history was to provide abundant corroboration of Bukharin's words. For all its emotionalism, his characterization pointed to a fact of cardinal importance for an understanding of Stalin: his sense of himself as a very great man and his imperative need to have his greatness acknowledged by others.

How Stalin became in early life the kind of person who has to be 'the first and best' has been shown in a previous chapter. Now we must take up the inner story again, as it was unfolding during his middle years.

As he saw himself

To comprehend the mental world of Stalin, we must be aware that those who peopled it fell into two classes: friends, whom one could trust, and enemies, whom one must fight against and strive to overcome. There was hardly any possibility of escaping this dichotomy. If a given individual was neither friend nor foe, he was still *potentially* the one or the other, and for Stalin this was always a fact of cardinal significance about him.

Character and culture coalesced and reinforced each other in this way of perceiving other people. A gifted and unusually sensitive child suffered bad early experiences, including his father's brutality toward himself and his mother, and emerged as a hardened, vigilant youngster with a self-idealizing tendency, on the one hand, and a vengeful streak and indomitable will to fight and to win, on the other. The Georgian social setting and its Russifying overseers offered him a ready-made hostile division of people into friends and enemies, together with such cultural traditions as the blood feud and such dramatizations of the situation as the Koba story. As a youth in the seminary he immersed himself in the Marxian revolutionary sub-culture; what particularly appealed to him in that, as we have seen, was the ideological symbolism that split the social universe into two great warring classes of oppressed and oppressors: friends and enemies on the scale of all mankind and all recorded history. Within the sub-culture he gravitated unerringly to the militant version of the ideology that Lenin presented. As has been noted earlier, Lenin's was an angry Marxism, replete with invective and imagery that projected the class enemy as irremediably evil and hostile. Stalin found in his writings a wealth of material that he wrought into his own image of the enemy. Moreover, Lenin's notion of the revolutionary party as a comradely band of fighters for the people, united in mutual trust, defined for him an idealized conception of what it would – or should – mean to have friends.

Implicit in this discussion is a further fact of great importance in understanding Stalin. The distinction between 'personal' relationships and 'political' ones, something we may take for granted, was foreign to his mind. Of course, the personalizing of political relationships, and the politicalizing of personal ones, is a familiar phenomenon in revolutionary movements and perhaps in political life generally. What may have been somewhat peculiar to Stalin was the extreme form that this merger took in his case. His political life was as intensely personal in its meaning to him as his personal life was absorbed in the political realm. One of the contributing factors was his early background in a traditional society, the Georgian, where the distinction between private and public relationships was undeveloped as a cultural pattern. Another was the pronounced asocial tendency that we have observed in him, the small number of personal ties outside the political milieu. But not least among the explanations was the highly political character of his personal self-concept as Stalin. As we shall now try to make clear, because of the terms in which he defined *himself*, he could never exclude the play of personal passion from his relations with political associates, particularly other party members.

But how did Stalin define himself in his middle years? We are fortunate in having a statement that represents in a way his own answer to this question. In June 1926, while on a visit to Tiflis, Stalin gave a sketch of his revolutionary biography as he liked to view it. Replying to acclaim from workers of the local railway shops, he chided them for flattery. It was quite an unnecessary exaggeration, he said, to picture him as a hero of the October Revolution, a leader of the party and the Communist International, a legendary warrior-knight, etc. That was how people usually spoke at the graveside of departed revolutionaries – and he had no intention of dying yet. The true story of his revolutionary career, he explained, was one of apprenticeship, of learning from worker–teachers first in Tiflis, then in Baku, and finally in Leningrad. In 1898, when he was put in charge of a study-circle of workers from the Tiflis railway yards, older comrades like Djibladze, Chodrishvili, and Chkheidze, who perhaps had less book learning than he but possessed more experience, had given him practical instruction in propaganda activity. That was his first 'baptism' in the revolutionary struggle. Here, among his first teachers, the Tiflis railroaders, he had become an 'apprentice of revolution'. Then, in the years 1907 to 1909, spent in Baku, where he had learned to lead large masses of workers in the oil-fields, he had received his second baptism in the revolutionary struggle and become a 'journeyman of revolution'. And in Leningrad in 1917, operating among the Russian workers and in direct proximity to the great teacher of the proletarians of all countries, Lenin, in the maelstrom of class war, he had learned what it means to be one of the leaders of the party. That had been his third revolutionary baptism. In Russia, under Lenin's leadership, he had become a 'master-workman of revolution', said Stalin, and concluded: 'Such, comrades, without exaggeration and in all conscience, is the true picture of what I was and what I became'.[9]

This revealing essay in revolutionary autobiography laid the ground-work for a full biography of Stalin by his assistant, Tovstukha. Prepared for a special volume of the *Granat entsiklopediia* containing the autobio-graphies or authorized biographies of some 250 leading Soviet figures, the Tovstukha biography was also published in 1927 as a separate pamphlet in an edition of fifty thousand copies. Reading this account of Stalin's pre-1917 years, and comparing it with the careers of other prominent Bolshe-viks recounted in the same biographical volume, one is struck by several distinctive features of Tovstukha's treatment. True, it followed a general stylization that was visible in this Bolshevik 'lives of the revolutionaries'. In substance it was a laconic listing of revolutionary actions participated in, conferences attended, punishments suffered, etc. What distinguished it from the others was not simply that it modified historical reality in a number of subtle ways flattering to its subject. More than that, it showed a solemnity of tone, a reaching for superlatives, and even an occasional grandiloquence that deviated from the volume's general tendency to under-statement. Thus Stalin did not simply move to Baku. Rather, 'From 1907 commences the Baku period in the revolutionary activity of Stalin'. His arrival in Petersburg in 1911 marked the beginning of 'the Petersburg period in the revolutionary activity of Stalin'. Here, with some revision, is the three-stage progress to 'master-workman of revolution' which Stalin had set forth to the Tiflis railroaders. We sense that a revolutionary biography is being recast in retrospect according to certain canons of drama.[10]

From this and other evidence we may infer that the psychological forces which impelled the younger Djugashvili to form a heroic revolu-tionary identity for himself as 'Koba Stalin' remained active in the older Djugashvili, and prevented him from accepting himself on any other terms. As a man in his forties he continued to believe in the vision of himself as a leader and fighter of genius. His life appeared to him in retrospect as a realization of his youthful dream of playing Koba to Lenin's Shamil. Such was the message of the dramatic sketch of his political biography that he gave in 1926. He presented it as a saga of one man's rise to revolutionary greatness alongside Lenin, and his concluding expres-sion of gratitude to the Russian workers and Lenin conveyed a sense of himself as the latter's chosen continuator and heir: 'Permit me to extend my sincere comradely gratitude to my Russian teachers and to bow my head before the memory of my great teacher – Lenin'.

Stalin's accomplishments, it must be granted, were sufficient to encou-rage him in his *hubris*. By all wordly tests, his career up to the mid-twenties was a dazzling success story. He had come out of nowhere, a son of poor and illiterate parents living in a provincial corner of one of the non-Russian borderlands of the Empire. Yet, by the time of his arrest on the eve of the World War he had risen to a leading position in the

Bolshevik party and was in direct collaborative association with Lenin, who entrusted him with the treatment of one of the movement's most important theoretical problems. He had returned from exile in March 1917 to join the leadership of the party that then carried off one of the stunning revolutionary feats of history. He had gone on to play an active part in the Civil War and in organizing the institutions of the Soviet state. Finally, he was now emerging as the party's new supreme leader in succession to Lenin. Surely he had gone very far toward realizing his 'bright hope' of rising 'higher than the great mountains'. What more was needed to prove that he was a political man of genius?

On the other hand, Stalin had failed in many ways to fulfill the demands of his heroic revolutionary persona. He had not become a leader of renown second only to Lenin's. For all his formidable talents and commitment to the party's cause, he lacked the extraordinary qualities needed to make him a star of the first magnitude on the Russian revolutionary horizon. Not only Lenin but many of the other major Bolshevik figures eclipsed him in one way or another. Not even in his native Caucasian milieu had he been a notable success as a revolutionary. His poor performance during the March days of 1917 was so notorious in the party that he had felt constrained to apologize publicly for it, and the remainder of his record in the Revolution was spotty. If he became a 'masterworkman of revolution' in 1917, this fact failed to impress itself upon the party mind.

Far from starring in the Civil War, he had created difficulties at Tsaritsyn, carried on a feud with Trotsky, and disgraced himself by his insubordination in the futile effort to capture Lvov. Not he but Trotsky had risen to the heights of glory as Lenin's right-hand man in the Revolution and the Civil War. A former non-Bolshevik had thus enacted the role that the young Stalin had foreseen for himself, and as if in mockery of his vision of linking his own name with Lenin's in history, that party had become known as that of 'Lenin–Trotsky'. To make matters worse, the dying Lenin had turned against him and advised the party to remove him from his position of power. No event could have been more cruelly incongruent with the younger Stalin's life-scenario.

There was, similarly, a discrepancy between Stalin's acquired sense of Russian self-identity and the fact of his being Georgian. All his 'true-Russianness' could not erase from people's minds, his own included, the fact of his Georgian nationality. It was obvious in his appearance, in his generally known family name, and in his speech. Despite the fluency of his Russian, the traces of a Georgian accent were as ineradicable from his speech as those of his childhood smallpox were from his face. He could never really pass for a Russian. He was in the position of continually reminding others, if not also himself, that Stalin was Djugashvili.

Dealing with discrepancies

But chastening experience did not cause him to question his idealized image of himself. Nor did his political victories of the post-Lenin period incline him toward realistic retrospection concerning himself and his career. Rather, they fortified him in his grandiosity. Instead of scaling down his self-estimate in the face of clear evidence of disparity between the man he had aspired to be and the man he actually was, he took the opposite path of rejecting the evidence. Extremely powerful feelings drove him to do this. From all that we know concretely of him on the one hand and his general personality type on the other,[11] it appears that any failure to measure up to his lofty standards and self-expectations was unbearably painful to him. Violation of the norms of achievement implicit in his revolutionary self-concept would arouse, or threaten to arouse, shame, self-accusation, and self-hatred. To guard against such tormenting experiences, he employed a number of internal security operations familiar to students of modern depth psychology, notably repression, rationalization, and projection.

In repression, he would ignore, deny, or forget the potentially disturbing fact, thrust it out of conscious awareness. In rationalization, he would subject the fact to an interpretation that made it consistent with his self-image. An example of Stalin's use of rationalization is provided by his concluding speech to the Fourteenth Congress in 1925. In a passage criticizing Zinoviev's 'The Philosophy of an Epoch', he mentioned that Molotov had sent him a copy of this article while he was away on a trip and that he had reacted rudely and sharply. 'Yes, comrades', he went on, 'I am forthright and rude, that is true and I don't deny it'. But then: 'I sent back a rude criticism, *because it is intolerable that Zinoviev should for a whole year systematically ignore or distort the most characteristic features of Leninism in regard to the peasant question. . . .'*[12] The final phase transmuted the offensive rudeness into a manifestation of zeal for preserving the purity of Leninist doctrine.

Stalin returned to the question of his rudeness in his speech of October 23, 1927, quoting the postscript to Lenin's testament and acknowledging the justice of the charge that Lenin had brought against him. But he did this in a special way, saying: 'Yes, I am rude, comrades, *toward those who rudely and treacherously smash and split the party.* I have not concealed this and do not do so now. It may be that a certain softness should be shown toward splitters. But it doesn't come off with me'.[13] This was to emasculate Lenin's accusation in the act of pleading guilty to it. What had worried Lenin was Stalin's tendency to antagonize party comrades and potential political allies (like the Georgians) by his *grubost*. In Stalin's speech, and doubtless in his mind as well, that grave personal defect was now transformed into a forgivable fault: hardness toward *enemies* of the party. An excess of such hardness could even be seen as a virtue in a Bolshevik. In all probability, it was by means of just this rationalization that Stalin learned to live with the memory of the postscript to Lenin's testament. Even so, however, he preferred to forget – that is, he repressed – the episode. Thus, the text of the postscript was omitted from the speech of October 23, 1927, as later reprinted in Stalin's collected works, of which Stalin himself was the chief editor.[14] And, as noted earlier, the decision of the Fifteenth Congress to publish the testament was never carried out.

Stalin's attempt to repress awareness of his Georgian nationality was shown even in his manner of speech. 'He could read Georgian but used to say that he had largely forgotten the language', reports his daughter.[15] He spoke Russian in a low, monotonous voice, which he sometimes softened further at points where the Georgian accent would be most audible. An Old Bolshevik who heard him speak at the Sixth Congress in 1917 later wrote: 'He had on a gray modest jacket and boots, and was speaking in a low, unhurried, completely calm voice. I noted that Nogin, sitting in the same row as I, could not suppress a slight smile when the speaker uttered a certain word *in a somehow especially soft tone with his special accent*'.[16] Further, Stalin expunged from his family life most of what might recall his Georgian origins. His daughter describes him as a man who in certain of his living habits remained Georgian all his life. He liked, for example, to conduct business while sitting at the dinner table with his associates and sipping Georgian wines. But she makes clear that he was a person who thought of himself – and wanted to be thought of – as Russian. He did not, for example, bring up the two children of his second marriage, Vasily and Svetlana, to think of themselves as partly Georgian or to take pride in the Georgian side of their ancestry. Observing that 'in general, Georgian ways were not cultivated in our home – father was completely Russified', Svetlana recalls a day in 1931 or so when Vasily said to her: 'You know, our father *used to be* a Georgian once'. In another passage, Svetlana writes that because of her mother and grandparents, Georgia remained a living presence in their home. But this had nothing to do with her father: 'He was the one, I think, who cared about it least. It was Russia that he loved. He loved Siberia, with its stark beauty and its rough, silent people'. And elsewhere: 'I know no other Georgian who had so completely sloughed off his qualities as a Georgian and loved everything Russian the way he did'.[17]

Stalin's attitude toward Yakov, the son of his early marriage, shows how painful it was for him to be confronted with the fact that he himself was Georgian. After being brought up by his mother's sister in Georgia and attending school there, Yakov came to Moscow during the twenties at the insistence of his uncle, Alexander Svanidze, and joined his father's household. Since he not only was Georgian in appearance and upbringing but at first found it hard to learn to speak Russian, he was a living reminder of his father's Georgianness. Doubtless on this account Stalin disapproved of his coming and of everything about him. So great was his contempt that when Yakov shot himself in 1928 or 1929, in despair over his father's hostility, Stalin ridiculed him for bungling the suicide attempt, exclaiming: 'Ha! He couldn't even shoot straight!' After that Yakov went to Leningrad to live with the elder Alliluyevs.[18] Later he became a Red Army officer and was one of the thousands captured by the invading Germans in the early period of the Soviet–German war. Stalin rejected a German offer to trade him for some German prisoners in Russian hands. He died in the Sachsenhausen concentration camp, reportedly by making a suicidal escape gesture after the fact was broadcast over the camp's radio that his father had said in reply to a foreign correspondent's question that there were no Russian prisoners-of-war in Hitler's camps, only Russian traitors who would be done away with after the war, and: 'I have no son called Yakov'.[19]

Violent rages for which there seems small cause commonly express feelings about oneself that are turned outward against others. There is reason to believe that the anger with which Stalin reacted to Yakov's appearance in Moscow was really anger against himself. It is very likely, in other words, that the arrival upon the scene of an unmistakably Georgian son activated Stalin's intense but normally repressed feelings of shame and self-contempt about being a Georgian himself, feelings that he could not bear to experience in relation to himself and therefore experienced as contempt for Yakov. This turning outward – or projection – of self-recriminatory feelings aroused by lapses from his self-ideal or violations of his standards of accomplishment was a cardinal characteristic of Stalin's. He could not tolerate in himself any deviation from his idealized self-image. But, on the other hand, neither could he help registering them unconsciously, and he habitually experienced the resulting rage against himself and self-accusations as rage and accusations against others. Here, it may be added, is part of the explanation for the moodiness, irascibility, and outbursts of ill temper which were frequent with Stalin.

Failure to perceive one's own flaws and shortcomings is a common human trait. What made Stalin's case an extreme one was his intolerance of anything short of perfection in himself. He totally identified himself with the ideal Stalin of his imagination, and became oblivious of everything in himself that detracted from this picture. Not only gross defects but any departures from the self-ideal, any failings in the revolutionary biography, were censored. Since the internal censorship became habitual and automatic, Stalin developed an extraordinary blindness to his own blemishes. This made it possible for him to read moral lectures to others without any apparent realization of their applicability to himself.

For example, speaking in 1929 to a group of American Communist leaders gathered in Moscow, he declared that the Comintern was not a stock market but the 'holy of holies of the working class', and went on:

> *Either* we are Leninists, and our relations one with another, as well as the relations of the section with the Comintern, and vice versa, must be built on mutual confidence, must be as clean and pure as crystal – in which case there should be no room in our ranks for rotten diplomatic intrigue; *or* we are not Leninists – in which case rotten diplomacy and unprincipled factional struggle will have full scope in our relations. One or the other. We must choose, Comrades.

An American present on that occasion recalled later that Stalin put the tip of his thumb and index finger together when he spoke the words 'clean and pure as crystal', and said them with a straight face. Knowing how far Stalin himself was from being the 'angel of purity' that he affected to be, the American viewed the statement as 'rank hypocrisy'.[20] This not unreasonable interpretation overlooked the inner complexity of Stalin, his capacity for self-deception. Because of his imperative need to be perfect (in accordance with his own special definition of perfection) and the associated habit of not taking cognizance of his faults and deficiencies, Stalin could believe in himself as a paragon of political virtue while behaving like any other factional politician. What appeared to others as rank hypocrisy could thus be unconscious duplicity. Cynical about much in life, Stalin was a true believer where he himself was concerned, and as such he was prey to illusions. Lenin may have had an inkling of this when he remarked to Krupskaya toward the end of his life that Stalin was 'devoid of the most elementary honesty, the most simple human honesty'.[21]

All this underlines the significance of the self-dramatizing tendency that we have observed in Stalin at a number of points in his career. Others, too, including some who observed him close up, were struck by a certain theatricality in his nature. Former American Ambassador in Moscow George F. Kennan has described him as 'a consummate actor'.[22] Milovan Djilas, to whom we owe a vivid character sketch of Stalin drawn from life, found him to be a role-player for whom the roles were real, a person with whom 'pretence was so spontaneous that it seemed he himself became convinced of the truth and sincerity of what he was saying'. As Djilas saw him, Stalin had a 'passionate and many-sided nature – though all sides were equal and so convincing that it seemed he never dissembled but was always truly experiencing each of his roles . . . .' The Yugoslav visitor also noted, while attending one of the after-dinner movie showings which were a regular feature of life in Stalin's Kremlin, that 'throughout the showing Stalin made comments – reactions to what was going on, in the manner of uneducated men who mistake artistic reality for actuality'.[23] It should be mentioned in this context that Stalin showed a strong liking for dramatic productions on stage and screen, including historical dramas like *Lenin in October*, in which he himself figured as a character. Yuri Yelagin, one of our sources on this point, recalls from his own experience an occasion when Stalin appeared at Moscow's Vakhtangova Theatre for a special Lenin anniversary showing of the last act of the heroic revolutionary drama *Man with a Rifle*. In it Lenin stands on the Smolny steps greeting the Red Guards as they march off to battle, and Stalin appears at his side. Yelagin, who was playing the drum in the orchestra that evening, observed Stalin seated in his special box, applauding Ruben Simonov in the role of Stalin and evidently deriving great pleasure from the performance.[24]

Stalin gave sensitive observers like Djilas the impression of being a role-player because, at bottom, that is what he was: a person whose life was dedicated to the enactment of a role of historical glory. It started with his early hero-identification with Lenin, which gave rise to the conception of himself as the Lenin II of Bolshevism. An element of unconscious acting is inevitably involved in the psychological process of identification, for the identifying person is patterning himself on someone else. Role-playing was therefore integral to Stalin's political personality from the outset. In later years he did not outgrow it. Rather, the original role of being Bolshevism's second Lenin evolved into a whole cluster of hero-roles that he believed himself to have played or to be playing in the still unfolding drama of party history, Russian history, and world history. The word to be emphasized here is *belief*. Of course, Stalin was also capable of conscious play-acting when political situations called for it, although even at such moments, as Djilas perceived, he actually experienced the role he was playing. But underlying the surface displays of expedient histrionic behavior was the serious drama of a personality whose chosen role of greatness was a life-long identity-commitment. To understand Stalin we must see him as a person for whom '*genial'ny* Stalin'[25] – a phrase that the Soviet media regularly applied to him after the mid-thirties – represented his fundamental belief about himself.

The need for affirmation

When an individual is driven to repress many facts concerning himself in order to maintain a façade of perfection in his own mind, he becomes inwardly insecure. So it was with Stalin. Despite his characteristic show of complete self-confidence, he was not a genuinely self-confident person. His repressed thoughts lived on at the subconscious level, and so did the self-doubts, self-recriminations, and self-accusations that they provoked. His resulting insecurity was manifested, among other ways, in the extreme touchiness that we have repeatedly had occasion to note in him, his 'un-Georgian' inability to take a joke.

One illustration is an episode out of *Pravda*'s history near the end of the twenties. The prominent cartoonist Boris Efimov submitted a friendly caricature of Stalin for publication in the paper's picture magazine, *Prozhektor* (The Searchlight). It showed him in a characteristic pose, with one arm thrust inside his jacket and the other held behind his back, smoking his pipe, and wearing exaggeratedly big boots polished to a gleam. As Efimov told the story in reminiscences published after Stalin's death, the editors sat there looking the sketch over and scratching their heads. They remembered how heartily Lenin, Gorky, and others had laughed when they saw comparable cartoons of themselves in *Pravda*. Still, something about the saturnine figure of Stalin gave them pause. So, instead of deciding the matter on their own, they sent the drawing to Stalin's office with a request for permission to publish it. Next day it came back with Tovstukha's reply: 'Not to be printed'.[26]

Nor did subsequent success ease Stalin's painful sensitivity about being seen humorously. In his year of supreme triumph, 1945, when Roosevelt confided to him over a dinner table at Yalta that he and Churchill between them called him 'Uncle Joe', Stalin showed genuine pique. Churchill's personal interpreter, Mr. Hugh Lunghi, who observed that scene, grew convinced from six years of close watching of Stalin at such meetings that he had a 'basic inferiority complex'. One of the signs of it was his way of jockeying for a position on a step higher than anyone else when photographs were being taken. A further expression of the uneasiness that he evidently felt because of his short stature was his habit of wearing shoes with built-up heels which were only just revealed by his wide and sharply creased trousers.[27]

Bukharin put his finger upon the source of Stalin's insecurity when he observed in his conversation with Fyodor Dan that Stalin was unhappy at not being able to convince everyone, 'himself included' that he was greater than everyone. In other words, Stalin was nagged by an undercurrent of suspicion that he might not really be the unblemished hero figure that he took himself to be. This in turn made him highly dependent upon the attitudes of others, no less so after he attained the pinnacle of power than before. To assuage his underlying uncertainty and doubts, his suppressed awareness of not always fulfilling the dictates of his pride, he thirsted for others' admiration and devotion, their recognition of him as a great man, their affirmation of his view of himself as the *genial'ny* Stalin. Some close associates grew uncomfortably aware of the compulsive strength of this need in Stalin. Thus, Yenukidze complained of him in a private conversation of the mid-twenties: 'I am doing everything he has asked me to do, but it is not enough for him. He wants me to admit that he is a genius'.[28] Having been brought up by a mother who lavished praise and admiration upon him, Stalin now needed more of the same to bolster his unconsciously shaky ego.

In the post-revolutionary years his immediate social milieu was both satisfying and unsatisfying from this viewpoint. On the positive side, he had a wife who at first rendered him not only wifely devotion but glowing admiration as one of the great figures of the Revolution. At the time of her marriage to Stalin, Nadya Alliluyeva was seventeen and he was forty. In the eyes of this ardent daughter of the Revolution, he represented the ideal of the revolutionary New Man.[29] In time, his brusque and inconsiderate manner sorely tried her feeling for him, and at the beginning of the thirties a political estrangement occurred as well. Once in 1926, after a quarrel provoked by some act of rudeness on his part, she took the children and went off to Leningrad to live with her parents. A conciliatory phone call from him led her to relent and return, however, and life resumed its normal pattern.[30]

As mentioned earlier, the Stalins at Zubalovo received a constant flow of guests from among their relatives and friends. The guests, along with the children and the children's friends, stayed in the rooms downstairs, while Nadya and Stalin occupied the upper story. The elder Alliluyevs; Nadya's brothers, Fyodor and Pavel, and their wives; and her sister, Anna, and Anna's husband, Stanislav Redens, were frequent visitors, as were the relatives of Stalin's first wife: her sisters, Alexandra and Mariko; her brother, Alexander Svanidze, and his wife, Maria. Among the friends whom Svetlana recalls as house guests were the Ordzhonikidzes, who would stay for long stretches; the Bukharins, who would often come for the summer; and Sergei Kirov, who in addition to being a close personal friend of Stalin's had friendly ties with the Alliluyevs dating from pre-revolutionary days. Guests on family social occasions or companions of the Stalins on the summer trips to the Black Sea resort of Sochi that became their custom during the twenties included Yenukidze (who was Nadya's godfather as well as Stalin's old party comrade), the Molotovs, the Voroshilovs, the Mikoyans, and Budenny.[31]

The people of the Stalins' circle, most of them Old Bolsheviks, were pursuing a wide variety of public careers. Stalin's factional associates each had a sphere of leadership in the Soviet system: Ordzhonikidze as head of the Transcaucasian party organization and later of the Party Control Commission; Kirov as chief of the Leningrad party organization; Yenukidze as secretary of the Central Executive Committee of the Soviets; Molotov as Stalin's deputy in the Central Committee Secretariat; Voroshilov as war commissar; Mikoyan as trade commissar. The relatives, too, were involved in public affairs. Nadya's father was active in electric power plant construction. Alexander Svanidze served in Soviet financial posts abroad, and his sister Mariko worked as Yenukidze's secretary. Pavel Alliluyev, a soldier by profession, served on the General Staff and in the Military Academy. Redens, a one-time colleague of Dzerzhinsky's in the Cheka, was a secret police official. These people contributed a wealth of knowledge and experience to the conversations at Zubalovo and were inclined to speak their minds freely. 'In this house', writes Svetlana, 'my father was neither a god nor a "cult" but just the father of a family'.[32]

That judgment calls for a certain qualification. At Zubalovo in the later twenties Stalin was living in an atmosphere of friendly recognition of him, if not deference to him, as a man not only of great power but of merited authority, an atmosphere of esteem for his positive strengths and talents as a leader as well as for his services to the party's cause on the revolutionary road to power. In addition to esteem, there existed in the circle – first of all among such men as Ordzhonikidze and Yenukidze who had known Stalin long and well – an awareness of his need for affirmation and his extreme sensitivity to anything he perceived as a slight. Although constitutionally incapable of paying fulsome tribute to his genius (as the earlier-quoted remark by Yenukidze attests), such men must have taken care not to offend his pride and not to appear overly critical of him. Subordinates like Molotov and Voroshilov must have done likewise, probably with less effort.

Still, it is true that Stalin was not a cult figure in the Zubalovo circle before the end of the decade, and this helps to explain why a man like Lavrenti Beria was becoming significant in his life. A Georgian twenty years Stalin's junior, Beria had joined the Cheka during the turbulent post-1917 period in the Transcaucasus. He was suspected by some leading Bolsheviks involved in the protracted Transcaucasian revolution of having played a double game as the fortunes of competing Bolshevik and anti-Bolshevik forces rose and fell. He also became known in those circles as a despicable, wholly unscrupulous character. By around 1930 he had become head of the Transcaucasian secret police administration. Just when he and Stalin first met is not known, but it was probably before the end of the twenties.[33] He was hated by the Svanidzes, the Redenses, and others of the Zubalovo circle who knew about his past. Much later Stalin told his daughter that Nadya had 'made scenes' and had insisted, as early as 1929, that 'that man must not be allowed to set foot in our house'. He recalled:

> I asked her what was wrong with him. Give me facts. I'm not convinced. I see no facts! But she just cried out, 'What facts do you need? I just see he's a scoundrel! I won't have him here'. I told her to go to hell. He's my friend. He's a good Chekist.[34]

What attracted Stalin to Beria was not just the fact that he saw in him a useful tool as a 'good Chekist'. Sensing Stalin's craving for admiration, Beria won a place in his good graces through flattery, an art in which he excelled. 'He flattered my father with a shamelessness that was nothing if not Oriental', states Svetlana. 'He praised him and made up to him in a way that caused old friends, accustomed to looking on my father as an equal, to wince with embarrassment.'[35] Whether these recollections refer to the time of which we are writing or to a later period, we may be sure that Beria employed these deferential devices from the start in his relations with Stalin. His future services as one of the architects of the personality cult must have been prefigured in the worshipful attitude that he assumed toward Stalin even then.

The fact that he tolerated Beria's extravagant praise bespoke Stalin's receptivity to it. For a long time, however, this hankering for adulation was something that he felt constrained to conceal, particularly from the party at large. Personal vanity was frowned upon in Bolshevik circles, and Lenin's freedom from it was well known. One of Trotsky's disadvantages in the succession contest had been the suspicion in many party minds that he was a vain and ambitious man. In *Revolutionary Silhouettes* Lunacharsky dismissed the suspicion as groundless, but contrasted Lenin's and Trotsky's attitudes toward themselves. Lenin, he wrote, was a man who never contemplated himself, never looked at himself in the mirror of history, and never even considered what posterity would say of him, but simply did his work, actuated by an enormous confidence in his own rightness combined with a certain inability to see things from his opponent's point of view. Trotsky, on the other hand, was one who without doubt frequently contemplated himself, valued his role in history, and would make any personal sacrifice, even life itself, to remain wreathed in mankind's memory as a true revolutionary leader.[36] Given such a climate of opinion in the party, it was contrary to Stalin's interest to be seen as another who liked to view himself in the mirror of history. So he carefully avoided conveying such an impression. He cultivated a public image of himself as a simple, modest, unassuming man, devoid of vanity like Lenin; a man whose whole being was selflessly absorbed in the party's political affairs, the concerns of Communism as a movement.

In his talk to the Kremlin cadets in January 1924, for example, he invoked the memory of Tammerfors, where Lenin had set him an instructive example of the simplicity and modesty characteristic of a true proletarian *vozhd'*. Earlier, in his speech at the meeting for Lenin's fiftieth birthday, he had singled out 'the modesty of Comrade Lenin' as his special theme and illustrated it with two examples of the courageous way in which 'this giant' admitted his mistakes. The emphasis on modesty as a Bolshevik virtue recurred in his statements of subsequent years, as when he saluted a deceased Civil War leader of his acquaintance as 'the bravest among our modest commanders and the most modest among the brave'.[37] In keeping with this, he portrayed himself as Lenin's disciple and insistently ascribed his views to Lenin even when, as in the case of the doctrine of socialism in one country, they were essentially post-Leninist. When a participant in the party discussions of early 1927 described the slogan of a 'worker-peasant government' as 'Comrade Stalin's formula', Stalin replied that he was only repeating Lenin, and then pedantically proved his point by giving the page references to thirty passages in Lenin's works where the formula appeared.[38] The purpose of showing that the formula was Leninist merged with that of presenting himself as Lenin's self-effacing disciple. His simple style of dress accentuated the impression. As a result of all this, Stalin's enormous egocentricity remained hidden from general view. Probably very few persons outside the narrow circle of close associates realized what a swollen and sensitive self-esteem lurked behind the pipe-smoking *gensek*'s gruff, unassuming exterior.

The vindictive response

The other side of his swollen self-esteem was Stalin's painful sensitivity to whatever he interpreted as a slight or aspersion. If the surest way of pleasing him was to affirm his idealized version of himself, the surest way of incurring his displeasure or wrath was to negate it. For the same reason that adulation was balm to his insecurity, anything resembling disparagement aggravated it. If the disparagement was justified, Stalin would have to plead guilty before his inner tribunal and accept its condemnatory judgment. That being intolerable, he had to assume that the disparagement was unmerited, in which case the person who failed to give him due recognition and deference must be intentionally maligning him, and Stalin characteristically responded by striking out in anger against the maligner.

There were many occasions during Stalin's time of post-Lenin struggle and triumph when fellow party members behaved toward him in ways that impugned his exalted self-concept. One section of the party, the Left opposition, not only failed to recognize him as a great leader but fought his policy views, rejected his theoretical argumentation as un-Leninist and invalid, and let it be known that they considered him a mediocrity. Kamenev rose before the Fourteenth Congress in 1925 to contest his credentials for becoming the new *vozhd'*. As the intra-party battle reached its climax in October of the following year, Trotsky depicted Stalin as a man whose leadership threatened ruination of the Revolution. Before very long, accusations of comparable gravity were coming from leaders of the embattled Right opposition. There were instances, too, in which old revolutionaries treated Stalin condescendingly not because they were active in the oppositions but simply because they were unable to take him seriously in the role of Bolshevik supreme leader or Marxist theoretician. Finally, there were a great many in the party who, whatever they said openly, entertained a view of Stalin greatly at variance with his own. He had not, as we have seen, become one of the legendary figures of Bolshevism. Not even on the tenth anniversary of October did he figure in Soviet publicity as its co-leader. Although Trotsky's name was now rapidly being expunged from the record, everyone still knew that he was 'the second great leader of the Russian Revolution', as Lunacharsky had written in *Revolutionary Silhouettes*[39] – in which, as noted earlier, there was no 'silhouette' of Stalin. This was but one of numerous instances in which Stalin was confronted by *non*-affirmation of his self-concept inside the party.

Unable to question his fundamental beliefs about himself in the light of all this, Stalin questioned the motives and the political character of the people who were – as he saw it – underestimating his revolutionary services, disparaging his abilities, maligning his policies, and generally vilifying *him*. He reacted with resentment, anger, and the resolve to gain a vindictive triumph over those who did not affirm his view of himself. It was not always politic for him to voice such feelings openly, but they came to the surface in various ways. Trotsky points out, for example, that Stalin found a subtle means of expressing his resentment against Lunacharsky for omitting him from *Revolutionary Silhouettes*. He did it by alluding, in a speech of 1925, to Lunacharsky's less than courageous conduct while in police custody in Petrograd in July 1917.[40] On some occasions, he reacted with an explosion of wrath. When Trotsky dramatically pointed to Stalin during a stormy Politburo session of 1926 attended by many Central Committee members and exclaimed: 'The first secretary poses his candidature to the post of gravedigger of the Revolution!'[41] Stalin 'turned pale, rose, first contained himself with difficulty, and then rushed out of the hall, slamming the door'. Soon afterwards Piatakov, one of the Central Committee members who had been present at the meeting, arrived pale and shaken at Trotsky's apartment:

> He poured out a glass of water, gulped it down, and said: 'You know I have smelt gunpowder, but I have never seen anything like this! This was worse than anything! And why, why did Lev Davidovich say this? Stalin will never forgive him until the third and fourth generation!' Piatakov was so upset that he was unable to relate clearly what had happened. When Lev Davidovich at last entered the dining room, Piatakov rushed at him asking: 'But why, why have you said this?' With a wave of his hand Lev Davidovich brushed the question aside. He was exhausted but calm. He had shouted at Stalin: 'Gravedigger of the revolution'. . . . We understood that the breach was irreparable.[42]

In this instance everyone realized instinctively that no matter how ill-disposed Stalin might have been toward Trotsky hitherto, his will to vengeance would now be utterly implacable. The challenge that Trotsky had flung down was so flagrant that Stalin could never desist from the quest for revenge. What remained far less clear at the time was that he would respond in the same basic manner to incomparably less serious provocations than Trotsky's terrible epithet. Any statement or omission that appeared derogatory to himself – and this meant anything that detracted from the image of the *genial'ny* Stalin – could call forth his vengeful anger. It was not necessary to directly impugn one or another of his claims to greatness. Simply by taking issue with him on a theoretical problem or point of party history, and particularly by persisting in one's position after he had once argued its erroneousness, one could implicitly disparage his picture of himself as a pre-eminent Marxist thinker and evoke the vindictive response.

Stalin's correspondence with one S. Pokrovsky in 1927 is an illustration. In a first exchange, Pokrovsky contested and Stalin upheld the view that in 1917 the party had dropped its previous strategic slogan of 'alliance *with the whole* peasantry' in favor of a new one calling for 'alliance *with the poor* peasantry'. An important issue of current peasant policy was implicit in this historical debate, but that would not explain the emotional outburst that Pokrovsky provoked from Stalin by writing him a second letter in which, while retreating on the slogan question, he asserted that he had been guilty only of a 'verbal' inaccuracy and then taxed Stalin with 'having given no reply' on the matter of neutralizing the middle peasants. Stalin began his second and final letter, which remained unpublished for twenty-one years, by saying that he had thought he was dealing with someone in search of the truth, but that now, after Pokrovsky's second letter, he could see that he was corresponding with a conceited, insolent man who placed the interests of his ego higher than those of truth. A terrible tongue-lashing followed, replete with epithets like 'you and many other political philistines' and language such as the following:

> Carried away by the 'artistry' of your own pen and conveniently forgetting your first letter, you assert that I have failed to understand the question of the *growing over* of the bourgeois revolution into the socialist revolution. That is indeed a case of laying one's own fault at another's door!

Stalin ended:

> Conclusion: one must possess the effrontery of an ignoramus and the self-complacency of a narrow-minded equilibrist to turn things upside down as unceremoniously as you do, esteemed Pokrovsky. I think the time has come to stop corresponding with you. *I. Stalin.*[43]

A similar episode, which also remained private for many years, occurred in 1930 when a party member responded to one of Stalin's public speeches by writing him a note in which he apparently said something about contradictions between the proletariat and the kulaks. In Stalin's reply, which as later published in his collected works identified the correspondent only as 'Comrade Ch-e', Stalin said that the note reflected a confusion. The speech had been concerned only with resolvable contradictions between the proletariat and the mass of working peasants. 'Plain? I think so', remarked Stalin, ending his reply: 'With Communist greetings'. Whereupon Comrade Ch-e made the mistake of continuing the discussion in a second letter. Stalin, now infuriated, took him to task in his own second reply for playing a 'game of words' instead of honestly admitting his mistake. The diplomatic blurring over of the difference between the two sorts of contradictions was highly characteristic of Trotskyist–Zinovievist thinking, he said. 'I did not think you were infected with this disease, but now I have to reckon with this too', ran the ominous conclusion.

> Since I do not know what kind of a game you will play next and I am devilishly overburdened with current work, in view of which I have no time left for games, permit me to say good-bye to you, Comrade Ch-e.

This time there were no Communist greetings.[44]

There were many other such episodes in which party members unwittingly wounded Stalin's pride. They were acting in the tradition of sanctioned intra-party discussion, remembering how Lenin had respected the right of Bolsheviks to disagree with him on questions of party policy. Stalin's very insistence upon his faithful discipleship to the master, his assurances that the Leninist style of leadership was his model, afforded them encouragement in this. For these reasons, the widespread acceptance of Stalin as the party's new supreme leader did not bring automatic acquiescence in all his views. Many went on voicing opinions at variance with his, only to discover later that they had been acting as 'enemies'. For this was his characteristic conclusion concerning those who aroused the vindictive response.

Stalin's daughter has given a graphic description of him in the act of drawing such conclusions. If he was told that someone 'has been saying bad things about you' or 'opposes you', and that there were facts to prove this, a 'psychological metamorphosis' would come over him. No matter how long and well he had known the person concerned, he would now put him down as an enemy. According to Svetlana,

> At this point – and this was where his cruel, implacable nature showed itself – the past ceased to exist for him. Years of friendship and fighting side by side in a common cause might as well never have been. . . . 'So you've betrayed me', some inner demon would whisper. 'I don't even know you anymore'.[45]

In an individual who had thus incurred his vindictive hostility Stalin was compelled to see not simply a personal enemy but also an enemy of the Soviet cause. The Bolshevik political culture provided a strong foundation for this in its conception of the class struggle as a continuing phenomenon in Soviet society and as a fact of international life in a world divided into two hostile camps. This doctrine, in both of its aspects, found no more fervent exponent among the party leaders than Stalin, who summed it up in a 1928 speech by saying: 'We have internal enemies. We have external enemies. This, comrades, must not be forgotten for a single moment'.[46] In expounding the two-camp theory, moreover, his reasoning was more schematic and his rhetoric more violent than Lenin's. 'The world has split decisively and irrevocably into two camps', he wrote in 1919. 'The struggle between them is the entire axis of contemporary life, the whole substance of the internal and external policies of the leaders of the old world and the new'.[47] In another article of that time he showed his tendency to highlight anything stealthy, devious, or conspiratorial in the class enemy's behavior. The imperialist camp, he said, was 'not dozing'. Its agents were 'on the prowl through all the countries from Finland to the Caucasus, from Siberia to Turkestan, supplying the counter-revolutionaries, hatching criminal conspiracies, organizing a crusade against Soviet Russia, and forging chains for the peoples of the West'.[48] Elsewhere he wrote that the Entente, having failed in its open intervention against Soviet Russia, was now going over to a new policy of 'disguised' or 'masked' intervention involving the use of Rumania, Poland, Galicia, Finland, and Germany for counter-revolutionary operations.[49] Although these statements were not devoid of some factual basis, it is worth noting here that the conspiracy theme, which would be one of the hallmarks of Stalinist thinking, was making its appearance in Stalin's writings of the revolutionary era.

He did not necessarily harbor any great personal animosity against people who by definition fell in the category of class enemies – heads of foreign states, for example. But the converse did not hold true. When his personal animosity was aroused against persons in his own milieu, he had to see them as class enemies rather than simply as party critics or opponents of Stalin. This ominous inference was necessitated, first, by the fact that it provided justification for voicing and acting upon his rage against these people, his urge to take revenge upon them. For if they were class enemies, they fully deserved to be mercilessly exposed and harshly punished. But equally important, the categorizing of his critics as class enemies was for Stalin a necessary way of rationalizing their derogatory attitudes toward him. He thereby warded off any need to confront himself in a self-questioning way and accept the painful possibility that these attitudes had some foundation.

It was out of the question for him to regard such an individual – we may call him X – as an honorable anti-Stalin Bolshevik. For this would be an implicit admission that a party person in good standing could conceivably find some political failing or imperfection in Stalin, which in turn would threaten to arouse Stalin's latent self-doubts and suppressed self-condemnatory feelings. So, he identified X as an anti-*party* person, an enemy of the Bolshevik *cause*. Now he could take full account of X's critical or unfriendly view without a twinge of self-questioning, *or even construe it as an indirect confirmation of his idealized image of himself*. For if X was an enemy of the Bolshevik cause, then he would naturally and necessarily be opposed to a Stalin who was the best of Leninists and the principal defender of that cause. He would be critical of Stalin's ideas and policies precisely *because* they were in the interests of Communism. He would belittle Stalin's revolutionary past and disparage him as a political personality precisely *because* he perceived his historic merits and his genius as a Marxist–Leninist leader. Far from expressing X's real opinion of Stalin, the belittlement and disparagement would be his way of trying to tear Stalin down in the eyes of the party, to keep the younger generation from realizing what a great revolutionary Stalin had been, to discredit Stalin as the foremost figure of the movement after Lenin, and thereby to hurt the movement.

By this logic, the very attributes of personal and political greatness which made Stalin an outstanding party leader would make him also, inevitably, the chief target of hatred and opposition on the part of all deviationists, ill-wishers of the party, and the like; they were against him precisely *because* he was the man of genius that he conceived himself to be. Here, then, was a line of reasoning that made it possible for him to interpret anti-Stalin attitudes as evidence in favor of his heroic self-image. As a result, the picture of his detractors as enemies of the party and people became an integral part of his identity structure. Instead of having a restraining effect upon his self-estimate, the unflattering view that many in the party took of him only made him all the more adamantly insistent upon its validity, and all the more avid for others' affirmation that they saw him as he saw himself. And having rationalized opposition to himself as a twisted kind of tribute to his genius, he could welcome attacks on the part of those he had put down as 'enemies'; they were flattery in disguise. Let the Trotskyists attack me to their hearts' content, he said in his speech of October 23, 1927, in the Central Committee. They rightly choose me as their main target, for I am the one who best sees through them and their machinations. And consider the abuse that Trotsky once poured on Lenin! Is it any wonder that one who disparaged Lenin as he did in his letter of 1913 to Chkheidze should now be vilifying Stalin?

Stalin's way of rationalizing derogatory attitudes was not lost upon perceptive persons around him. *Pravda*'s leading article for his fiftieth birthday on December 21, 1929, which must have been written under the direction of his former assistant Mekhlis, who was now the editor, said:

> Stalin stands at the head of the Leninist Central Committee. Therefore he is invariably the object of savage abuse on the part of the world bourgeoisie and the Social Democrats. All the oppositions

inside the party always aim their arrows at Comrade Stalin as the most unbending, the most authoritative Bolshevik, the most implacable defender of Leninism against any and all perversions.

To cite a further example, G. Krumin observed in his birthday article on Stalin's merits as a theoretician that 'countless enemies of the party' were *right*, from their own point of view, in denying these merits. Not for nothing, he went on, did the world bourgeoisie and the Social Democratic press assail Stalin with such malice and bestial hatred, and heap filthy slander upon him. And by the same token, attacks on Stalin were the telltale sign of each new opposition arising in the party under the influence of hostile elements and classes. 'For the enemies of the party know that a blow against Stalin is a blow against the party, a blow against the most faithful disciple and confederate of Lenin. . . .'[50]

But if the maligners of Stalin were enemies of the party, they would not admit to being such. If it was hostility toward the Bolshevik cause that made them hate Stalin and strive to besmirch him, the hostility was concealed. Derogatory attitudes toward Stalin were strongest, after all, in Old Bolshevik circles. Although Trotsky and some of his colleagues had not joined the Bolshevik organization until 1917, many members of the Left as well as the Right opposition, and still others who were not friendly to Stalin, had illustrious Bolshevik records going as far back as Stalin's or farther. Ostensibly they had been and remained loyal party men and good Leninists, and they purported to be acting as such when they attacked, opposed, criticized, and belittled Stalin. As enemies of the party, therefore, they must be *covert* enemies operating behind the masks of friends. Their Bolshevism must be a masquerade. That such was the trend of Stalin's thinking would become abundantly clear in the thirties, but this was beginning to be apparent still earlier, as was his general readiness, noted above, to perceive class enemies as conspiratorial in their conduct. The word 'mask', for example, came readily to his lips or pen. Thus, in his furious final letter to S. Pokrovsky he commented, apropos Pokrovsky's point that his earlier letter had not dealt with the question of neutralizing the middle peasant: 'One or the other: either you are too naïve or you are deliberately putting on a mask of naïveté for some purpose that is by no means scientific'.[51] In his Central Committee speech of April 1929, he accused Bukharin of trying to 'mask' his treacherous position toward the party with talk about collective leadership. Moreover, he said, Bukharin had talked in the same way when, as leader of the Left opposition against the Brest agreement in 1918, he 'conspired' with the Left SR 'enemies of our party', who for their part had intended to arrest Lenin and carry out an anti-Soviet coup.[52]

Before his final victory in the post-Lenin power struggle, Stalin was beginning to manifest his tendency to view Bolsheviks hostile toward him as enemies who had spent much of their lives wearing a mask of loyalty and conspiring against the very party to which they claimed to be totally dedicated. This being the direction of his thinking, it is no wonder that a 'psychological metamorphosis' would come over him when he concluded that one whom he had considered a friend was really an enemy. In general, no enemy is so evil and dangerous, so important to expose and so deserving of harsh treatment, as one who has worn the mask of a friend. Stalin therefore grew mercilessly hostile toward any individual whom he had come to see in this light, regardless of how long and close their association had been. As his daughter has further testified, years of friendship and common struggle meant nothing to him in these circumstances. Once his condemnatory judgment had been pronounced, he could not retract it:

> Once he had cast out of his heart someone he had known a long time, once he had mentally relegated that someone to the ranks of his enemies, it was impossible to talk to him about that person anymore. He was constitutionally incapable of the reversal that would turn a fancied enemy back into a friend. Any effort to persuade him only made him furious.[53]

Stalin's inability to reverse the judgment of condemnation is understandable. For if someone had been an enemy in disguise all along, then his manifestations of loyalty and good will must have been feigned; and the greater the false show of friendship had been, the more evil and depraved an enemy he must be. Naturally, it was hopeless under these conditions to appeal to Stalin with reminders of the past record of friendly association. For him, that very record now stood as evidence of the unmasked individual's perfidy.

In Stalin's mind, then, the hero-image of himself was in symbiosis with a villain-image of the enemy. Counterposed to the picture of himself as a great revolutionary and Marxist, the truest of Lenin's disciples and his rightful successor at the head of the movement, was a picture of the enemy inside the party as would-be betrayer of it and the Revolution. The enemy was everything that the *genial'ny* Stalin was not: an opponent of Lenin, a disguised counter-revolutionary, a military bungler, a pseudo-Marxist in theory, and a saboteur of the construction of a socialist society in Russia. Because he was all these things, the enemy was also, necessarily, a vicious hater and maligner of Stalin. In addition, he was morally loathsome in his duplicity and his willingness to resort to the most devious, underhanded, conspiratorial means in pursuit of his anti-party ends. Such was Stalin's generic view of those party comrades whom he mentally classified as enemies. He was willing to admit that individual cases differed from one another, but ultimately the differences seemed inessential. The crucial question was whether a given person belonged to the category of 'friend' or that of 'enemy'. Those Bolsheviks who by word or deed convinced

Stalin that his image of the enemy applied to them did so at their peril and, in a great many instances, to their subsequent sorrow.

The projected Stalin

Stalin has gone down in history with a merited reputation for being, among other things, a fighter without scruples, a Machiavellian power-seeker, a master at double-dealing, and a cynical realist in politics. He showed this side of himself in small ways as well as large. Duplicity was second nature to him. He used coarse language at times and was given to obscenity in private conversations with associates. The esteem in which he held the physical realities of power was later to be immortalized in his question: 'How many divisions has the Pope?' Many biographers have stressed these qualities of Stalin. Trotsky, who came by his knowledge of them through harsh experience, was planning to entitle an unfinished chapter of his biography '*Kinto* in Power'. *Kinto*, in Georgian, was a slang term referring to the tough, sly street youth of old Tiflis. Trotsky recalled Makharadze saying of Stalin at some point in the twenties: 'He's a — *kinto!*'[54]

While keeping the *kinto* side of Stalin clearly in view, we should take care not to assume that it was part of Stalin's self-image: the evidence presented in these pages testifies that it was not. His self-consciousness was focused upon the attributes and exploits of genius that made up the lofty paragon-self. Insofar as he could not help being aware of such elements of his nature as rudeness, underhandedness, duplicity, meanness, and cruelty, he attempted to reconcile them with the idealized image of himself by rationalization. As shown above, by rationalization he trans-muted the rudeness for which Lenin had faulted him into, in one instance, a zeal for preserving the purity of Leninist doctrine and, in another, a hardness toward enemies of the party. In both cases the offensive trait underwent a metamorphosis and emerged as something Stalin could prop-erly take pride in; indeed, as an attribute of his heroic revolutionary persona.

In yet another episode of rationalizing, Stalin justified an unbecoming course of conduct by reference to the final goals of the Revolution. A certain Shinkevich wrote to him in protest against a party decision to reopen the vodka trade as a governmental monopoly. In old Russia vodka had served as the common man's consolation for a grim life, and many revolutionaries – including Lenin, whom Shinkevich now quoted – had denounced the state vodka trade as an evil. In his reply to Shinkevich, dated March 20, 1927, but first published twenty-five years later, Stalin admitted that this had been Lenin's position but explained that in 1922 Lenin had agreed with members of the Central Committee that it was necessary to re-introduce the vodka monopoly. Had the Genoa conference of that year (at which economic problems were discussed by Soviet Russia and the major European powers) resulted in a large foreign loan or long-range credits, such a decision would not have become necessary. As it was, however, vodka remained the only possible source of funds for industrial development. Stalin went on:

> Which was better: enslavement to foreign capital or the introduction of vodka? This was how the question stood before us. It is clear that we came down on the side of the vodka because we believed and continue to believe that *if we have to dirty our hands a little bit* for the sake of the final victory of the proletariat and the peasantry, *we will go to this extreme for the sake of the interests of our cause.*[55]

In this instance the action being rationalized was one taken by the party Central Committee, though evidently with Stalin's strong concurrence. Undoubtedly, however, 'the interests of our cause' was a formula by which he also rationalized many actions of his own that involved the dirtying of hands.

But there was much in Stalin's character, conduct, and past career that did not easily lend itself to rationalization by reference to the Revolution's goals or the need to resort to foul means in combating foul enemies. Here, as already indicated, repression played a great role in his mental life, helping him to hold on to his pride system and preserve his rigidly self-righteous posture in spite of everything. He kept the *genial'ny* Stalin in clear focus by censoring out or blurring discordant aspects of himself. Repression operated as a defense mechanism, however, in tandem with projection. Facts thrust out of awareness because of their inconsistency with the self-concept tended to re-appear in his perceptions of others; and then he could and would give vent to the self-recriminatory feelings that these discordancies aroused in him as *recriminatory feelings toward these others.* So projection performed the cathartic service of permitting him not only to admit painful or embarrassing facts into consciousness but also to give uninhibited expression to the emotions associated with them.

Let us consider his characteristic way of coming to terms with his mistakes and the blame for them. Sooner or later the mistakes would be attributed to and blamed on others. Of course, politicians under all forms of government have an interest in shifting responsibility for their own mistakes onto others, preferably their opponents. But in Stalin this went along with an intense psychological aversion to admitting errors and being blamed, an aversion arising from the incompatibility of blameworthy mistakes with the paragon-self. If he was truly the *genial'ny* Stalin, he could hardly have taken a whole series of wrong stands in the revolutionary politics of 1917. He could not have considered even hypothetically the possibility of Lenin's volunteering to appear before a court of the Provisional Government. He could not have been recalled from the south-western front in 1920 for costly insubordination. But it was not sufficient for him to shut these and other transgressions out of awareness; he had to go further and impute them to others, upon whom he could then heap the blame that he found it intolerable to take upon himself. The others may in fact have committed mistakes of the type ascribed to them, or they may not have. Kamenev, for example, had taken some stands similar to Stalin's in 1917, whereas there was no basis for accusing Bukharin, as would one day be done, of advocating Lenin's surrender for trial by the Provisional Government. Or for casting Trotsky in Stalin's historical role as a political commissar who had to be recalled from the front during the Civil War because of military failures, although this was beginning to be done in Soviet writings by 1929.

If Stalin was under inner pressure to impute his own mistakes and failings to others and then to visit upon them the self-accusations and self-punitive feelings that these mistakes and failings caused in him, the most suitable targets – although not the only possible ones – were people already identified in his mind as enemies of the Revolution. They, after all, were in many instances the people for whom he already harbored vindictive hostility as a result of some sin of commission or omission against his pride. Since they were already objects of his hatred, the projection of his self-hatred upon them only intensified an established enmity and reinforced his conviction that those people deserved whatever punishment he might inflict upon them. Moreover, who but his enemies were the logical repository of all that he felt enmity toward in himself?

So it was that the villain-image of the enemy came to represent, as was suggested above, everything that Stalin rejected and condemned in himself. All that belonged to the rejected evil Stalin – the errors, flaws, and elements of villainy that had no place in his hero-image of himself – tended to be incorporated into his picture of the enemy, especially the picture of the internal enemy as villain of party history. Whatever he inwardly censored from the record of his past deeds and misdeeds was likely to re-appear in characterizations of his enemies. Further, Stalin had a remarkable propensity for seeing and condemning in enemies the qualities that he condemned *without seeing* in himself. We can infer from his idealized version of himself as an extremely modest man that one of the qualities he unconsciously rejected and condemned in himself was his monstrously inflated self-esteem, his arrogance. Accordingly, it comes as no surprise to find him ascribing 'swollen pretentiousness' in the field of theory to Bukharin, who was actually the soul of modesty as well as the recognized chief theorist of Bolshevism, or to find him berating the hapless Pokrovsky for placing the 'interests of his ego higher than those of truth'. Or, finally, to be accusing this same Pokrovsky of doing precisely what he,

Stalin, was doing in these and very many other instances – 'laying one's own fault at another's door'.

One further facet of the projected Stalin especially merits mention at this point. Stalin, we have seen, was acting out in life a role of historical greatness. Fully identified in his own mind with the revolutionary persona, he experienced himself as the Lenin II of Bolshevism. In a great many ways, however, the persona made demands that the real Stalin simply could not fulfill; the role was too much for him. He was in the position of attempting throughout life to be something that he was not, yet of never being able to face this fact. Consequently, there was unconscious pretense in him, which may explain the histrionic impression that he made on sensitive observers like Kennan and Djilas. Symbolizing as it did his ultimate incapacity to carry out his life-project, this pretense was supremely unacceptable to him, hence most stringently in need of repression and projection. This made Stalin prone to perceive pretense all around him. One of the telltale signs was his above-mentioned tendency to see those hostile to him as people wearing masks. To wear a mask means, of course, to put on an alien identity, to pretend to be something that one is not. Stalin's mental world was full of enemies wearing masks. External enemies were wont to wear masks, which they themselves took off. 'Following the Nanking events', said Stalin in 1927, 'imperialism is throwing aside unctuous speeches, non-intervention, the League of Nations, and any other mask. Now imperialism stands before the world in all its nakedness as an open predator and oppressor'.[56] The masks of internal enemies, on the other hand, always had to be ripped off in order for them to be revealed in all their nakedness. Stalin's passion for vindictive exposure of internal enemies who, he thought, had lived lives of pretense behind masks of Bolshevism would become horrifyingly evident in the coming decade of the thirties.

Owing to the habit of projecting his unacceptable traits and self-accusations upon others, Stalin's accusations were very often self-revelatory. The villain-image of the enemy became a sort of dumping-ground for the rejected evil Stalin. The personal and political shortcomings, biographical blemishes, lapses, failures, mistakes, scandals – all the facts and memories that Stalin had to repress because there was no place for them in the *genial'ny* Stalin – could be emptied into his image of the enemy and by this means mentally projected onto real persons in the environment whom he identified as enemies. Then he could admit the incriminating facts and memories into consciousness as facts and memories that related not to him but to them. In the same way, feelings too painful to be consciously felt with reference to himself could be felt with reference to enemies 'out there', Stalin could feel his own guilt as theirs, his own self-condemnation as condemnation of them, his own self-accusations as accusations against them. In addition, he could act upon the feelings thus admitted into consciousness. He could expose the guilty ones and inflict punishment upon the accused.

Finally, the mechanism of projection made it possible for Stalin to experience certain particularly inadmissible feelings as enemy feelings toward himself. This is how he appears to have dealt with his unconscious hatred and contempt of himself for not measuring up to his standards of perfection. One piece of evidence is the fact that the villain-image envisaged the enemy as a terrible hater of Stalin. There were, of course, Bolsheviks who disliked him intensely, and some who loathed him. But the savage, slow-burning, anti-Stalin fury that he imputed to 'enemies of the party' bore a strange resemblance to his own special way of hating. By projecting his self-hatred not only as hatred of them but also, in part, as *their hatred of him*, he could consider himself all the more justified in repaying them in kind. He could take the offensive against them in the belief that he was acting in self-defense. He could more freely turn others into the objects of his self-destructive rage.

'We are surrounded by enemies – that is clear to all', said Stalin to a party congress in 1923. 'The wolves of imperialism who surround us are not dozing. Not a moment passes without our enemies trying to seize some little chink through which they could crawl and do harm to us'. But it was not only the world beyond the Soviet borders that Stalin saw in this way. Inside Russia, too, and even within its Communist party, he felt himself to be in a besieged fortress. He was driven by unconscious needs and drives to people the party world around him with Stalin-hating enemies who pretended to be loyal Bolsheviks while watchfully waiting for an opportunity to strike a blow against the Communist cause and against him as its leader. Were such enemies lacking in sufficient numbers, he would have to invent them. And invent them he did.

Notes

1 I. V. Stalin, *Sochineniia* (Moscow, 1946–53), XII pp. 1–2.
2 L. Trotsky, *My Life* (New York, 1930), p. 449.
3 L. Trotsky, *The Revolution Betrayed* (New York, 1945), p. 277.
4 In his speech in the Central Committee session of October 23, 1927, on the motion for his expulsion, Trotsky said: 'The rudeness and disloyalty of which Lenin wrote are no longer mere personal characteristics. They have become the character of the ruling faction . . .' (*The Real Situation in Russia* [New York, 1928], p. 7).
5 Svetlana Alliluyeva, *Twenty Letters to a Friend* (New York, 1967), p. 31.
6 Trotsky, *My Life*, p. 450. Trotsky evidently agreed with at least the latter part of the statement, for he himself spoke here (p. 477) of Stalin's 'enormous envy and ambition'. Elsewhere he wrote that the mainspring of Stalin's personality, besides love of power, was 'ambition, envy – active, never-slumbering envy of all who are more gifted, more powerful, rank higher than he'. And further, that

'he tirelessly schemed, with people and circumstances, in order to push aside, derogate, blacken, belittle anyone who in one way or another eclipsed him or interfered with his ambition' (Trotsky, *Stalin: An Appraisal of the Man and His Influence* [New York, 1967], pp. 237, 336).

7 For Boris Nicolaevsky's account of Bukharin's stay in Paris, see his *Power and the Soviet Elite* (New York 1965), pp. 3–7.

8 Lydia Dan, 'Bukharin o Staline', *Novy zhurnal*, No. 75 (1964), pp. 181–182.

9 *Stalin*, VIII, pp. 173–175.

10 I. P. Tovstukha, *Iosif Vissarionovich Stalin, Kratkaia biografia* (Moscow, 1927).

11 His form of personality development corresponds closely to that delineated by Karen Horney in her work *Neurosis and Human Growth* (New York, 1950). See in particular chs. 1, 4, and 8, esp. pp. 197–212.

12 *Stalin* VII, p. 375. Italics added.

13 *Stalin* X, p. 175. Italics added.

14 Robert H. McNeal, *Stalin's Works: An Annotated Bibliography* (Stanford, 1971), p. 129. The speech, with the text of Lenin's postscript included, appeared in *Pravda* on November 2, 1927.

15 Svetlana Alliluyeva, *Only One Year* (New York, 1969), p. 379.

16 I. G. Korolev, in *Voprosy istorii*, No. 2 (1956), pp. 12–13. Italics added. See also Alliluyeva, *Twenty Letters*, p. 31, where reference is made to Stalin's habit of speaking in a low monotone.

17 Alliluyeva, *Twenty Letters*, pp. 31, 32, 67, 119–120.

18 Alliluyeva, *Twenty Letters*, pp. 101, 158–159. Svetlana explains her father's contempt for Yakov on the basis of temperamental difference, suggesting that 'Yakov's gentleness and composure were irritating to my father, who was quick-tempered and impetuous, even in his later years'. The feelings that caused Stalin to reject his son were no doubt numerous as well as complex.

19 Alliluyeva, *Only One Year*, p. 370.

20 Benjamin Gitlow, *I Confess: The Truth about American Communism* (New York, 1929), p. 15. For the text of Stalin's statement, see *Stalin's Speeches on the American Communist Party* (New York, n.d.), p. 15.

21 Trotsky, *Stalin*, p. 375. Trotsky learned of the remark directly from Krupskaya after Lenin's death.

22 George F. Kennan, *Russia and the West under Lenin and Stalin* (Boston, 1960), p. 248. According to Erving Goffman, a 'performer' may or may not believe in his own act. 'At one extreme, one finds that the performer can be fully taken in by his own act; he can be sincerely convinced that the impression of reality which he stages is the reality' (*The Presentation of Self in Everyday Life* [Garden City, 1959], p. 17). As an actor Stalin falls into the latter category.

23 Milovan Djilas, *Conversations with Stalin* (New York, 1962), pp. 69–70, 97, 103.

24 Iu. Elagin, *Ukroshchenie iskusstv* (New York, 1952), p. 381. (English translation: Jury Jelagin, *The Taming of the Arts* [New York, 1951], pp. 287–288).

25 Since English lacks the adjectival form of 'genius' ('genial' having another meaning), the closest translation would be 'Stalin the genius'. To avoid that clumsy phrase, I will employ the Russian word *genial'ny*.

26 M. I. Ulianova *Sekretar' 'Pravdy'*, ed. Z. D. Bliskovski *et al.* (Moscow, 1965), pp. 199–200.

27 Hugh Lunghi, 'Stalin Face to Face', *The Observer Weekend Review*, February 24, 1963, p. 25.

28 Trotsky, *Stalin*, p. 389. The remark was made to Trotsky's good friend Serebriakov.

29 Alliluyeva, *Twenty Letters*, p. 105.
30 Alliluyeva, *Twenty Letters*, p. 103. Svetlana Alliluyeva learned these facts from her Aunt Anna, after Stalin died.
31 Alliluyeva, *Twenty Letters*, pp. 24–36, 138.
32 Alliluyeva, *Twenty Letters*, pp. 24, 35–36, 39.
33 Roy A. Medvedev suggests that it was in the summer of 1931, when, as he also reports, Stalin went south for a rest cure and Beria took personal charge of his bodyguard. But Medvedev's position is internally inconsistent on this point, for he also reports that later in 1931, when a deputation of Transcaucasian party officials called on Ordzhonikidze in Moscow to protest Stalin's intention to promote Beria to second secretary of the Transcaucasian Party Committee, Ordzhonikidze said: 'For a long time I've been telling Stalin that Beria is a crook, but Stalin won't listen to me, and no one can make him change his mind' (*Let History Judge: The Origins and Consequences of Stalinism* [New York, 1971], p. 243).
34 Alliluyeva, *Twenty Letters*, pp. 19–20. The author writes that this conversation with her father took place when she was grown up.
35 Alliluyeva, *Twenty Letters*, p. 137.
36 A. V. Lunacharskii, *Revoliutsionnye siluety* (Moscow, 1923), pp. 26, 27.
37 *Stalin*, VIII, p. 99. The statement was made in 1926.
38 *Stalin*, IX, p. 180.
39 *Revoliutsionnye siluety*, p. 27.
40 Trotsky, *Stalin*, pp. 389, 394.
41 Isaac Deutscher, *The Prophet Unarmed: Trotsky, 1921–1929* (London, 1959), p. 296. For Trotsky's account of the episode, see *Trotsky's Diary in Exile, 1935* (New York, 1963), p. 69.
42 Deutscher, *The Prophet Unarmed*, pp. 296–297. The eyewitness account of the scene in Trotsky's apartment is quoted by Deutscher from Victor Serge, *Vie et mort de Trotsky* (Paris, 1951), pp. 180–181, some parts of which were written by Trotsky's wife, Sedova.
43 *Stalin*, IX, pp. 315–321.
44 *Stalin*, X, pp. 20–22.
45 Alliluyeva, *Twenty Letters*, p. 78.
46 *Stalin*, XI, p. 63.
47 *Stalin*, IV, p. 232.
48 *Stalin*, IV, pp. 181–182.
49 *Stalin*, IV, pp. 246–248.
50 *Pravda*, December 21, 1929.
51 *Stalin*, IX, p. 317.
52 *Stalin*, XII, pp. 100–101.
53 Alliluyeva, *Twenty Letters*, p. 59.
54 Trotsky, *Stalin*, p. 414.
55 *Stalin*, IX, pp. 191–192. Italics added.
56 *Stalin*, IX, pp. 198–199.

Reading 4 *Stalin's mind*

D. VOLKOGONOV

Trotsky's description of Stalin as 'an outstanding mediocrity' has been widely accepted as accurate, but is it really plausible? Could someone with so little mental ability have been a member of the party's top bodies from 1912, or deserve Lenin's description as one of the 'outstanding leaders', or emerged from the complex tangle of political contradictions of the 1920s as the victor over people with greater abilities than he had in many respects?

The fact is that his crimes, his cunning, his cruelty and his mercilessness towards those he regarded as his enemies, have come to dominate any assessment of his personality. These traits, however, highlight a man's moral character, not his intelligence. In this sense, Stalin's exceptional intellect – which I believe it to have been – has been framed by attributes than can only be defined as anti-human. Stalin's intellect in the moral sense has been all but nullified by being inextricably linked to manifestations of evil. One could say, in brief, that he had 'an exceptionally evil mind'. Any moral flaw in itself represents a huge gap in the intellect, creating a twilight zone in the mind, devoid of any scintilla of good. One may say that a moral gap in the personality can reduce even a powerful mind to the functions of a calculating machine, a logical mechanism to the level of a rational but pitiless apparatus.

Having frequently suffered from humiliating inadequacy in conversation with his opponents before the revolution, Stalin was determined not to play the part of an extra in future discussions and therefore did his utmost to broaden to the maximum the range of his political and theoretical knowledge. In addition to his enormous workload, he laboured to raise his intellectual level. The archives contain a very interesting document which, despite its length, deserves to be quoted extensively.

In May 1925 Stalin charged Tovstukha with assembling a good personal library for him. Hesitantly, his assistant asked what sort of books he had in mind. Stalin was about to begin dictating a list, when instead he suddenly sat down at his desk and, with Tovstukha looking on and almost without thinking, took ten to fifteen minutes to dash off the following list, writing in an ordinary school exercise book with a pencil:

Note to librarian. My advice (and request):
1 Books should be arranged according to subject, not author: a) philosophy; b) psychology; c) sociology; d) political economy; e) finance; f) industry; g) agriculture; h) cooperatives; i) Russian

history; j) history of other countries; k) diplomacy; l) foreign and domestic trade; m) military affairs; n) national question; o) Party, Comintern and other Congresses and Conferences, (with resolutions, without decrees and law codes); p) position of workers; q) position of peasants; r) Komsomol (everything there is in separate editions); s) history of the revolution in other countries; t) 1905; u) February revolution 1917; v) October revolution 1917; w) Lenin and Leninism; x) history of the RKP and Comintern; y) on discussions in RKP (articles and pamphlets); z) trade unions; aa) creative literature; ab) artistic criticism; ac) political journals; ad) scientific journals; ae) various dictionaries; af) memoirs.

2 Books to be removed from the above categories and shelved separately: a) Lenin; b) Marx; c) Engels; d) Kautsky; e) Plekhanov; f) Trotsky; g) Bukharin; h) Zinoviev; i) Kamenev; j) Lafargue; k) Luxemburg; l) Radek.

3 All other books are to be classified by author (except any textbooks, popular magazines, anti-religious pulp literature and so on, which are to be put to one side).[1]

Considering that this was scribbled down with virtually no forethought, and also given the state of the 'book culture' of the time, a certain breadth of vision was clearly at work here. At the top of the pyramid he placed the basic components of Marxism, history and a number of specific areas of knowledge directly connected with political activity and the struggle against the oppositions.

The application of ideas through action and behaviour provides a measure of a given intellect. Stalin's library, and the traces he left on it, therefore provide a certain amount of material in this respect.

Many of the books from the Kremlin, the dacha or the apartment, some of them bearing an *ex libris* label 'Library No . . . I. V. Stalin', contain annotations, markings and marginal comments. Lenin's *Collected Works*, for instance, are covered with underlinings, ticks and exclamation marks in the margins. Stalin evidently returned to certain items several times, for they are marked in red, blue and ordinary pencil. The topics that seem to have interested him most were Lenin's views on the dictatorship of the proletariat, his struggles with the Mensheviks and Socialist Revolutionaries, and his speeches at party congresses.

Of his contemporaries' writings, Stalin referred most frequently to Bukharin and Trotsky. For instance, Bukharin's pamphlet 'The Technique and Economy of Modern Capitalism', published in 1932, is covered with Stalin's red pencil marks, particularly what the author had to say about productive forces and production relations. M. Smolensky's book *Trotsky*, published in Berlin in 921, is underlined in those places which criticize his arch-enemy: 'Trotsky is prickly and impatient', he has 'an imperious nature which loves to dominate', 'he loves political power', 'Trotsky is a political adventurist of genius'.[2] From whatever source he could, Stalin sought ammunition against his rivals, e. g. Trotsky's 1920 pamphlet 'Terrorism and Communism', Zinoviev's 'War and the Crisis of Socialism', Kamenev's 'N. G. Chernyshevsky', A. Bubnov's 'The Main Stages in the Development of the Communist Party in Russia', I. Narvsky's 'On the History of the Struggle of Bolshevism with Luxemburgism', Jan Sten's 'On the Stabilization of Capitalism' and others. Anything concerned with 'struggle' seems to have caught his attention.

He maintained a lifelong interest in historical literature, above all the lives of emperors and tsars. He made a careful study of I. Bellyarminov's *Course of Russian History*, R. Vipper's *History of the Roman Empire*, Alexei Tolstoy's *Ivan the Terrible*, and a miscellany entitled *The Romanovs*. All the school and university textbooks that were collected for him in the 1930s and 1940s bear the marks of his close examination.[3] He evidently saw in Russian history, as interpreted by him, a means of forming the kind of public opinion that would accept his authoritarian rule.

His assistants drew his attention to whatever they thought might interest him in the serious journals, and during thirty- to forty-minute breaks that he took from working on official business, he would scan articles and leaf through the latest novels. Occasionally, he would be moved to press the bell for an assistant and ask to be connected with a writer or the head of one of the creative unions so that he could communicate his congratulations or comments personally. Sometimes he took up the pen himself. After reading Korneichuk's *In the Ukrainian Steppes* (1940), for instance, he at once wrote the following brief note:

Respected Alexander Yevdokimovich,
I have read your *In the Ukrainian Steppes*. It is a wonderful piece, artistically whole, joyful and merry. I'm only concerned that it is not a bit too merry. There is a danger that too much merriment in a comedy can distract the reader's attention from the content.
   Incidentally, I have added a few words on page 68. It makes things clearer.
   Greetings!
   I. Stalin

He had inserted the following:

1 'the tax would now be taken not on the basis of the number of livestock, but according to the area of kolkhoz land . . .'
2 'raise as many kolkhoz cattle as you like, the tax will remain the same . . .'[4]

Always on the lookout for practical opportunities, he had seized on Korneichuk's play to clarify a recent ruling of the Central Committee. Nor was he slow in commenting on what did not please him. After reading N. Erdman's play *The Suicide* (1931), he wrote to the producer, Stanislavsky:

> Respected Konstantin Sergeyevich,
> I don't think much of the play *Suicide*[5]. My closest comrades think it is empty and even harmful. I don't say the theatre will not achieve its aim. Kultprop[6] (i. e. Comrade Stetsky) will help you with this. There are comrades who know about artistic matters. I'm a dilettante in such things.
> Greetings
> 9.xi.31 I. Stalin[7]

Wishing to pass in artistic circles as a 'liberal', Stalin here flaunts his dilettantism, but in fact his judgements on plays, books, films, music and architecture were categorical in the extreme. Making utterances on practically everything, as first person in the state, he indeed became a universal dilettante, and this in turn worked to enhance his image as the omniscient leader.

Stalin also closely followed the literature that was being published abroad. Nearly everything about or by Trotsky was translated for him, in one copy. He also read the émigré editions. In December 1935, when B. Tal, the manager of the press and publications section of the Central Committee, requested the Politburo to say which of the following White émigré subscriptions should be taken out for 1936, *Poslednie novosti, Vozrozhdenie, Sotsialisticheskii vestnik, Znamya Rossii, Byulleten' ekonomischeskogo kabineta Prokopovicha, Kharbinskoe vremya, Novoe Russkoe slovo, Sovremennye zapiski, Illustrirovannaya Rossiya*[8] Stalin snapped, 'Order the lot!'[9]

He had a special cupboard in his study in which he kept a great deal of purely hostile émigré literature, including virtually all of Trotsky's works, heavily scored with underlinings and comments. Any interview or statement that Trotsky gave to the Western press was immediately translated and delivered to Stalin.

Whatever else one may say of him, his religious upbringing evidently had a lasting effect, as witness his attitude to anti-religious literature, which he flatly described as pulp, and also some of his speeches and writings, for instance, his dramatic speech on the radio on 3 July 1941, in which he addressed the Soviet people as 'brothers and sisters', not a formula they had been accustomed to hearing from him. After the celebration of his fiftieth birthday in 1929, he sent the following handwritten note of thanks to *Pravda*: 'Your congratulations and greetings I will bear on behalf of the great party of the working class which gave birth to me and which raised me in its own image and likeness'.[10]

In a conversation between Stalin and Churchill in Moscow in August 1942, the discussion turned to Lloyd George, who (like Churchill himself) had been one of the instigators of the Allied Intervention against the Bolsheviks during the civil war. Stalin fell silent and sighed, as if summing up all his memories of those distant times: 'All that is in the past, and the past belongs to God'.[11] No one would want to suggest that religious elements played a central part in Stalin's outlook, but his dogmatic cast of mind strongly suggests a religious origin. He loved formulae, definitions and fixed interpretations. In order to crush or shut up his opponents 'incontrovertibly', he would spend hours looking for the right word or expression in the Marxist classics. Thus, at the April 1929 joint Central Committee and Central Control Commission plenum, he accused Bukharin of 'not knowing his Lenin'.

At a meeting prior to the plenum, Bukharin had argued, quite rationally, that the transfer of excessive resources from agriculture to industry would impose an 'insupportable tribute' upon the peasantry. Stalin at once took note of the phrases 'military feudal exploitation of the peasants' and 'tribute' and spent a long time that evening, in his library with Tovstukha, scouring Lenin's works. After digging, he found what he was looking for – a whole array of 'murderous' arguments, so he thought. At the plenum he declared:

> Bukharin has destroyed himself here over the alleged fact that Marxist literature cannot tolerate the word 'tribute'. He was upset and surprised that the Central Committee and Marxists in general can permit themselves to use the word 'tribute'. But what is so surprising, if one can show that this word was granted civil rights long ago in the articles of no less a Marxist than Comrade Lenin? [Pause.] Unless Bukharin thinks Lenin does not satisfy the requirements of a Marxist?

Here Stalin cited 'On "Left Wing" Infantilism and Petty Bourgeois Mentality', 'On the Tax in Kind', 'Routine Tasks of Soviet Power', where Lenin used the term 'tribute' in a completely different context. A voice from the hall protested: 'But Lenin never applied the concept of "tribute" to the middle peasant'. Stalin calmly replied:

> Maybe you think the middle peasant is closer to the party than the working class? Then you're even a fake Marxist. If one can speak of 'tribute' in respect of the working class – the working class our party represents – then why can one not say the same about the middle peasant who is our ally, when all is said and done?[12]

The original question, on the use of the term 'tribute', was thus buried under a typical exchange about 'orthodoxy'.

The endless debates of the 1920s undoubtedly sharpened Stalin's intellect as a polemicist. To be sure, he commonly resorted to the device which trapped his opponents in a corner: he would present himself as Lenin's champion, arguing as if only he knew how to interpret Lenin correctly. In almost any argument, he would quickly find an appropriate quotation or expression of Lenin's, often from a totally different context. He had long ago realised that arming himself with quotations from Lenin would make him virtually invulnerable. Once, while discussing Comintern affairs, Zinoviev, whose relations with Stalin were already bad, snapped at him, 'You use quotations from Lenin like a certificate of your own infallibility. You should look for their meaning!' Stalin shot back, 'And what's wrong with having a "certificate" of socialism?'

In the end, his rigid thinking, aggressiveness, militancy and rudeness enabled Stalin to gain the upper hand over his opponents. It is strange, but the more subtle and often more cogent arguments made by Trotsky, Zinoviev, Kamenev and Bukharin found no support among the delegates in the hall, while Stalin's crude, often primitive and abusive invectives, tightly bound up with his claim to be 'defending Lenin', the general line of the party, the unity of the Central Committee and so on, were quickly absorbed by the party. Being of pragmatic mind, he did not bother too much, as Trotsky did, with an elegant style, or as Zinoviev did with rhetorical aphorisms, or Kamenev with intellectual rationality, or Burkarin with theoretical argument. Stalin's main weapon was to accuse them of wanting to revise Lenin while he defended him. And this became the official version from the early 1930s.

Stalin's way of thinking was schematic. As we have seen, he liked to have everything properly 'shelved', and he would predigest and popularize ideas almost to the point of primitive pastiche. If his opponents aired their ideas differently, he would castigate them for their 'un-Marxist approach', for 'showing petty-bourgeois tendencies' or 'anarchistic scholaticism'. His reports and speeches were always structured within a strict framework of enumeration, particulars, features, levels, directions, tasks. This is one reason why his works were popular, since they were accessible in their simplicity and people could grasp their meaning. But while this way of thinking may have facilitated the popularization of Stalin's ideas, it severely shackled the people's creative abilities, demanding no deep analysis or understanding of the complexity and interdependence of the world.

Perhaps Stalin had not thought, like Nero, that the study of philosophy 'was a hindrance to a future ruler', but he seems to have been intellectually incapable of achieving even the slightest grasp of that subject. The weakest spot in his intellect was his inability to understand dialectics. He was aware of this, for he spent a long time and devoted much effort trying to enrich his philosophical knowledge. On the recommendation of the directors of the Institute of Red Professors, in 1925 he invited Jan Sten, a leading philosopher among the Old Bolsheviks, to give him private lessons on the dialectic. Sten, who was the deputy head of the Marx–Engels Institute, and later an executive of the Central Committee apparatus, had been a delegate at several party congresses, was a member of the Central Control Commission, and a man of independent judgement. Appointed as Stalin's philosophy tutor, he devised a special programme which included the study of Hegel, Kant, Feuerbach, Fichte and Schelling, as well as Plekhanov, Kautsky and Bradley. Twice a week at a fixed hour he turned up at Stalin's apartment and patiently tried to eluciate to his pupil the Hegelian concepts of substantiation, alienation, the identity of being and thought. He tried in other words to give him an understanding of the real world as the manifestation of an idea. Abstraction irritated Stalin, but he controlled himself and sat listening to Sten's monotonous voice, occasionally losing his patience and interrupting with such questions as, 'What's all this got to do with the class struggle?' or 'Who uses all this rubbish in practice?'

Reminding his pupil that Hegel's philosophy, like that of the other German thinkers, had become one of the sources of Marxism, Sten carried on unperturbed. 'Hegel's philosophy', he declared, 'is in effect an encyclopedia of idealism. The dialectical method is developed in his metaphysical system with sheer genius. Marx said that Hegel had stood the dialectic on its head and that it was time to put it back on its feet in order to see it rationally'. Visibly irritated, Stalin cut in, 'But what's this got to do with the theory of Marxism?'

Again Sten tried patiently to boil down and explain Hegel's philosophical subtlety to his uncomprehending pupil, but despite his best efforts, Stalin could not master some of the basic notions in Hegel's philosophy, as his own 'philosophical works' show. All he seems to have gained from his lessons was hostility for his teacher. Together with N. Karev, I. K. Luppol and the other philosophers who were pupils of Academician A. M. Deborin, Sten was declared a theoretical 'lickspittle of Trotsky', and in 1937 he was arrested and executed. The same fate seemed to be in store for Deborin, who had been very close to Bukharin in the late 1920s and who in 1930 was labelled by Stalin a 'militant idealist Menshevik'. He was, however, spared, although he was prevented from doing any scientific or public work.

A meeting of the Communist Academy took place in October 1930 to discuss 'differences on the philosophical front'. It was in effect a lengthy condemnation of Deborin for his 'underestimation of the Leninist stage in the development of Marxist philosophy'. Deborin put up a stout defence, but Milyutin, Mitin, Melonov and Yaroslavsky 'established' his guilt, along with that of Sten, Karev and Luppol, for 'underestimating the materialistic dialectic'. Passions in the academy continued to seethe after this meeting. The academics could not accept the use of police methods in their work. Philosophy was probably the first victim of Stalinist 'scientific research'. Stalin made it perfectly clear that there was to be only one leader in the social sciences and that was the rôle of the political leader, i.e. himself.

Two months later, in December 1930, he spoke on 'the philosophical front' at the party bureau of the Institute of Red Professors, whose director was Abram Deborin. His speech is an eloquent example of his philosophical thinking, the level of his rationality and simply of his lack of tact. According to the minutes of the meeting, he said:

We have to turn upside down and dig over the whole pile of manure that has accumulated in philosophy and the natural sciences. Everything written by the Deborin group has to be smashed. Sten and Karev can be chucked out. Sten boasts a lot, but he's just a pupil of Karev's. Sten is a desparate sluggard. All he can do is talk. Karev's got a swelled head and struts about like an inflated bladder. In my view, Deborin is a hopeless case, but he should remain as editor of the journal[15] so we'll have someone to beat. The editorial board will have two fronts, but we'll have the majority.

Questions began to rain in as soon as Stalin stopped speaking: 'Can one link the struggle over theory with the political deviations?'

Stalin replied: 'Not only can one, but one absolutely must'.

'What about the "leftists"? You've dealt with the "rightists"'.

'Formalism is coming out under leftist camouflage', Stalin replied. 'It is serving up its dishes with leftist sauce. The young have a weakness for leftishness. And these gentlemen are good cooks'.

'What should the Institute concentrate on in the area of philosophy?'

'To beat, that is the main issue', Stalin replied. 'To beat on all sides and where there hasn't been any beating before. The Deborinites regard Hegel as an icon. Plekhanov has to be unmasked. He always looked down on Lenin. Even Engels was not right about everything. There is a place in his commentary on the Erfurt Programme about growing into socialism. Bukharin tried to use it. It wouldn't be a bad thing if we could implicate Engels somewhere in Bukharin's writings'.[14]

Thus, Stalin, who knew practically nothing about philosophy, 'instructed' the philosophers. The main thing was 'to beat'. As for Marxist philosophy, he explained what it should be in a special section of his *Short Course*. A series of short, sharp phrases divide philosophy up into a number of basic features, like so many soldiers lined up in ranks. Perhaps this 'philosophical alphabet', plus a few other sources, would do for the campaign against illiteracy, but after Stalin's works appeared, philosophy shrivelled up, as no one had the courage to write anything more on the subject. Within a month the Central Committee passed a special resolution about the journal *Pod znamenem marksizma*. Deborin's supporters, who were united around the editors of the journal, were dubbed 'a group of Menshevizing idealists'.

A. P. Balashov told me that Stalin absorbed a colossal amount of information in a day, including reports, telegrams, ciphers and letters, and that on almost every document he wrote his instructions or comments, tersely expressing his attitude and thus issuing a definitive decision on the most varied questions. Having read through a pile of letters and written his customary laconic comments, such as 'Thanks for your support', 'Help this man', 'Rubbish', he would often select one or two and write a substantial reply. For instance, in 1928, a veteran Bolshevik living in Leningrad wrote to ask about the danger of a restoration of capitalism and also whether there were any deviations in the Politburo. Stalin tore a sheet out of a big notepad and, in his large clear hand, wrote:

> Comrade Shneer,
> The danger of a restoration of capitalism does exist here. The right deviation underestimates the strength of capitalism. And the left deny the possibility of building socialism in our country. They propose to carry out their fantastic industrialization plan at the cost of a split with the peasantry.
> The Politburo has neither right nor left deviations.
> With comradely greetings.
> I. Stalin[15]

During the height of Stakhanovism[16] in the 1930s, the coal miners Stakhanov and Grant submitted a proposal to the government 'on the training of engineers and technicians', which would entail the release of Stakhanovites from work for one or two days of the six-day week in order to study. As it was both new and revolutionary, the idea was discussed in the press and gained a great deal of support. Stalin read the proposal and wrote tersely to Ordzhonikidze, 'This is not a serious matter'.[17]

It is difficult to trace the intellectual qualities that enabled Stalin to deal inventively with problems as they arose. He tried always to act in accordance with a plan, or a dogma or some postulate or preconceived notion. At the same time, he was capable of intuitive thinking and could see the point things would reach several stages ahead. At such times, his mental processes are hidden from view and only the result is visible, whether it be a decision, a generalization, a guess or a suspicion. The intuitive process bypasses logical thinking and produces an immediate 'output' in summary form. Of course, groundless suspicion often arises where there is a deficiency in moral awareness. Such was the case with Stalin. He could turn on one of his comrades and declare, 'You're trying not to look me in the eye!'

Pathological suspicion in this case was less a manifestation of intuitive thinking than of the fact that his suppositions lacked a basis in reality, and were rather an expression of a profoundly flawed, paranoid outlook which gave rise to a tendency to see potential enemies everywhere.

Knowledge enables a man to be competent, emotions may ennoble him, and will-power helps him to turn his convictions and initiatives into reality through action. The will is like the muscles of the mind, the motive force of the intellect. A strong will can make an intellect active and purposeful – the sort of intellect that may be found among military leaders. It is not surprising that it was they who were the first to notice that Stalin had a strong intellect.

For the purposes of describing his intellectual qualities, the testimony of two outstanding war leaders, Marshals G. K. Zhukov and A. M. Vasilievsky, both of whom worked closely with Stalin during the war, merit attention. Zhukov detected in Stalin 'an ability to formulate an idea concisely, a naturally analytical mind, great erudition and a rare memory'. He also had an enclosed, fitful character. Usually calm and rational, he was capable of lapsing into sharp irritation. At such times he would lose his objectivity, changing before one's eyes, he would go pale and his glance would become heavy and menacing.[18]

Recalling Stalin's traits, Marshal Vasilevsky singled out his phenomenal memory:

> I have never met anyone who could remember as much. He knew by name all the army and front commanders, of whom there were more than one hundred, and he even knew the names of some corps and divisional commanders . . . Throughout the war Stalin had the composition of the strategic reserves in his head and could name any formation at any time.[19]

Stalin's ability to grasp the essence of a situation quickly also made a deep impression on Winston Churchill: 'Very few people alive could have comprehended in so few minutes the reasons which we had all so long been wrestling with for months. He saw it all in a flash'.[20]

It seems indisputable that Stalin had considerable intellectual powers, in addition to his highly developed purposefulness and strong will, and that it was more than force of circumstance or mere chance that made of him one of Lenin's comrades-in-arms during the revolution and civil war. He was able to show these qualities at a time when they were most needed, and it was perhaps for that reason they became evident. Perhaps as a result Stalin came to believe in himself, and perhaps he was therefore able to do things that others found impossible. On the other hand, when Zhukov and Vasilevsky wrote about Stalin, there was still much they did not know and, more important, much they could not say.

While Stalin may be said to have had an exceptional intellect, he was far from being a genius. Nor was he at all realistic about his own capabilities, but made categorical judgements in almost every field of knowledge, from politics and economics to linguistics, lecturing film-makers and agronomists alike, and imposing peremptory opinions in military matters as readily as in the writing of history. For the most part, his views were those of an amateur, if not of an outright ignoramus, but the chorus of praise that greeted his every utterance raised those views to the rank of the highest revelation.

For instance, at the initiative of a group of architects (and according to a decision taken as early as 1922), Molotov and Kaganovich submitted a proposal to Stalin for the construction of a Palace of Soviets on the site of the superb cathedral of Christ the Saviour. Stalin quickly approved the plan, showing in full measure his utter lack of appreciation of a major monument of Russian culture. No one thought of asking the population of Moscow, who had contributed the money for the cathedral only fifty years earlier, what they wanted, and the edifice was duly blown up on 5 December 1931. When the explosions rang out, Stalin, in his Kremlin office, trembled and anxiously inquired: 'Where's the bombardment? What are those explosions?' Poskrebyshev explained that, in accordance with the July decision on the site for the Palace of Soviets, which Stalin had approved, the cathedral of Christ the Saviour was being demolished. Stalin relaxed and paid no further attention to the explosions, which went on for another hour, but returned instead to reading local reports on the progress of collectivization. He probably did not even know that the cathedral had been built with pennies contributed by ordinary folk, or that the interiors and sculptures had been done by Vereshchagin, Makovsky, Surkov, Pryanishnikov, Klodt, Ramazanov and other famous masters. The cathedral, built to stand for centuries, was demolished for 'atheistic and architectural reasons'.

The architect of the Palace of Soviets, B. Iofan, wrote of the event:

It was 1931. The cathedral of Christ the Saviour was still standing in the middle of a vast square on the Moscow River. Golden domed, huge and cumbersome, looking like a cake or a samovar, it overwhelmed the surrounding houses and the people in them with its official, cold, lifeless architecture, a reflection of the talentless Russian autocracy and the 'highly placed' builders who had created this temple for landowners and merchants. The proletarian revolution is boldly raising its hand against this cumbersome edifice which symbolizes the power and the taste of the lords of old Moscow.

Iofan ecstatically described the 'comments of genius' that Stalin had made on the plan for the Palace. His 'audacious' suggestions envisaged that the palace would rise to more than 1,200 feet, with a figure of Lenin 300 feet tall surmounting it, while the great hall was to have no less than 21,000 seats. Stalin's megalomania was well expressed in his comments on the project. Why is the podium raised so little above the hall? It must be higher! There must be no chandeliers, the illumination must come from reflected light. The chief artistic motifs should express the six parts of the oath that Stalin had taken after Lenin's death. He made it perfectly clear that this was not to be merely a Palace of Soviets, it was to be a monument glorifying him, the leader, for centuries. The whole grandiose civic structure was to express the 'idea of the creativity of the multi-million Soviet democracy. . .'[21] Some democracy, when everything from the shape of the building to its facing, the lighting, the height of the pylons, the subjects of its sculpture and mosaics, its very proportions and many other strictly professional matters were determined by one man who in his 'genius' thought it normal that he should be the one to give the final orders!

Politics always took priority when history, culture or art were under discussion. For instance, when Khrushchev announced at the February–March 1937 plenum that 'in reconstructing Moscow, we should not be afraid to remove a tree or a little church or some cathedral or other'[22] he received Stalin's silent approval. Cultural values were of secondary importance, and in any case he was the chief arbiter of what was valuable. The fate of many a work of art hung on his sole decision.

Stalin's mind lacked the embellishment of a single noble feature, a trace of humanitarianism, to say nothing of love of mankind. In July 1946, for instance, Beria reported that his corrective labour camps contained more than 100,000 prisoners who were completely incapable of further useful work and whose upkeep was costing the state a fortune. Beria recommended that the incurably ill and the mentally disturbed be released forthwith. Stalin agreed, but insisted that especially dangerous criminals and those serving hard labour, however sick, be kept in.[23]

Notes

1 TsPA IML. f. 558, op. 1, d. 2510.
2 TsPA IML. f. 558, op. 3, d. 461, 1. 9–21.
3 TsPA IML. f. 3, op. 1, d. 4674, 1. 1–3.
4 TsPA IML. f. 558, op. 2, d. 5374, 1. 1–3.
5 The name of the play is *The Suicide*, i.e. one who has committed suicide. Stalin calls it *Suicide*, meaning the act of suicide.
6 The department of culture and propaganda.
7 TsPA IML. f. 558, op. l, d. 5374.
8 All these newspapers were published in Berlin, Paris, New York, Prague and Harbin, by émigré groups ranging from the extreme right to conservative, liberal and socialist.
9 TsGASA, f. 33 987, op. 3, d. 273, 1. 36.
10 TsPA IML. f. 558, op. 2, d. 2898.

11 Churchill, W. S., *History of the Second World War* (Moscow, 1955), vol. 4, p. 443.
12 Stalin, I. V., *Sochineniia* (Moscow, 1946–52), vol. 12, pp. 53–54.
13 *Pod znamenem marksizma* ('Under the Banner of Marxism').
14 TsPA IML, f. 17, op. 120, d. 24, 1. 1–3.
15 Stalin, *Sochineniia*, vol. 11, pp. 239–240, 241.
16 A fake propaganda campaign, based on the record-breaking performance of a miner called Stakhanov, which was used to raise production by creating artificial working conditions.
17 TsPA IML, f. 558, op. 2, d. 4074, 1. 35.
18 Zhukov, G. K. *Vospominaniia i razmyshleniia*, 5th edn. (Moscow, 1963), vol. 2, p. 95.
19 Vasilevskii, A. M. *Delo vsei zhizni*. 3rd edn. Moscow, 1978, p. 501.
20 Churchill, W. S. *History of the Second World War* (Moscow, 1955), vol. 4., p. 434.
21 *K piatidesiatiletiiu so dnia rozhdeniia I. V. Stalina* (Moscow, 1940), pp. 268–274.
22 TsPA IML, f. 7, op. 2, d. 612, 1. 26.
23 TsGAOR, f. 9401, op. 2, d. 149, l. 108.

SECTION II

APPROACHING STALINISM

Commentary

When historians configure Stalin's personality they are at least talking about the same thing. There is someone to imagine, a man bounded by birth and death. Matters are otherwise when we shift our attention to Stalinism. What, after all, was it? At one extreme it could be envisaged as the totality of routines extant during and after Stalin's tenure as General Secretary. Imagined thus Stalinism arches across virtually the entire Soviet experience, takes in much of the history of post-Second-World-War Eastern and Central Europe and, it might be argued, lingers on in regions once under Soviet domination.

Broad readings such as this, concerned with political theory and comparative analysis rather than discrete events, are usually the preserve of social scientists. More narrowly Stalinism might be represented as a range of practices centred in the USSR – purging, collectivization, state directed industrialization, the elimination of the market, totalitarian control over society – and associated with Stalin during his lifetime, a definition which has generally attracted historians. At first glance this is appealing, but weaving the General Secretary's predilections into Soviet history only raises another difficulty: historians are left with the problem of deciding whether or not Stalin originated policy, controlled events, or even knew what was happening inside the country.

Chapter 3: Absence and presence

For Deutscher Stalin was the architect of the Soviet Union's transformation, but, though he invites comparison with earlier despots, in Stalin's case Deutscher finds a 'baffling disproportion' between events and personality [Reading 5]. Stalin oscillated between extremes, changing direction with astonishing rapidity and little regard for logic or consistency. He threw caution to the winds and initiated policies which drove millions into *kolkhozy*. Caught off balance by the ferocious opposition to the first, hectic phase of collectivization, in 1930 he suddenly retreated, lambasting others for his own excesses, though by the end of the decade he had managed to subdue the peasantry to his will. His gyrations over industrializa-tion were no less sensational. During the First Five-Year Plan he set targets which made even the most radical 'superindustrialists' of the mid-1920s seem models of restraint and circumspection.

By 1932, contends Deutscher, his extravagance had brought the country to its knees. Towns, villages and factories were in chaos, and rumour and discontent swept through the Central Committee, but within two years there were impress-ive achievements to his credit: the USSR was modernizing rapidly and his confla-tion of socialism in one country, Russian nationalism, Soviet patriotism and the 'Great Breakthrough into Socialist Construction' caught the imagination of millions. Thereafter the contours of a peculiar social order began to emerge. Its most novel component was the new technical intelligentsia; enthusiastic, optimistic and zealously committed to socialism. Less positively, a yawning chasm opened between bureaucrats, Stakhanovites and skilled workers on the one side, and the poor (collectivized peasants and unskilled labourers) on the other. In the lower depths, in shameful contrast to the hopes and dreams of 1917, multitudes of innocents suffered and died in forced labour camps.

Deutscher believed that not only did Stalin's tyranny defile socialism but that it also laid the foundations of Russia's might and power in the twentieth century. Much in his interpretation relates directly to his own life. Born in Krakow in 1907 into an orthodox Jewish family he became a Marxist in his teens and joined the Polish Communist Party in 1926, but he soon fell foul of the leadership. In 1932 he was expelled for leading an anti-Stalinist opposition group. Seven years later, just before war broke out with Nazi Germany, he left Poland for good and settled in England. 'Work on this book was to me a deeply personal experience', he confessed in 1949, 'the occasion for much silent heart-searching and for a critical review of my own political record. I belonged to those whom Stalin had cruelly defeated; and one of the questions I had to ask myself was why he succeeded.'[1] He comes therefore from a generation of ideologically committed historians profoundly touched by Stalinism, but unlike many writing while Stalin still lived he was not enamoured of the totalitarian paradigm. Though his Stalin is emphatically present in the regime's practices he shuns explanations which ignore the impact of political dissension, contingency or social constraints. Aspects of his work – his avowal of colour and complexity within Stalinism, for example – thus foreshadow something of what is loosely known as 'revisionism'.

Two decades after Deutscher's death totalitarianism came under sustained attack from historians determined to reinvent Stalinism by distancing themselves from what they dismissed as barren quarrels and Cold War formulations. Among the most important revisionists is the American John Arch Getty, who took issue with standard accounts of the origins of the 'Great Purge', or *Ezhovshchina*,[2] typified by Robert Conquest's *The Great Terror: Stalin's Purge of the Thirties*, first published in 1968, (London: Macmillan).

Standard accounts usually begin with the assassination of Kirov, Leningrad's party boss. The social and economic crises of 1932 convinced many that the time had come for a softer line. Hostility towards Stalin boiled over when Central Committee member Riutin circulated a document calling for his removal. Stalin pushed for Riutin's execution, but a moderate Politburo bloc headed by Kirov frustrated his will. At the XVIIth party congress held early in 1934 loud applause punctuated Kirov's speeches. On the final day he collected more votes than Stalin: the ballot was hurriedly rigged to cover up the scandal. Thoroughly alarmed, Stalin plotted with Leningrad's police chief to eliminate his rival. On 1 December 1934 Kirov's bodyguard was removed and one Leonid Nikolaev, previously supplied with a gun and passes, entered Smol'nyi and shot Kirov dead. According to the standard account the 'Kirov Affair' triggered a pre-planned terror. Stalin struck first at remnants of the Left Opposition and then at the party in general.

As the *Ezhovshchina* gripped the country most of the Old Bolsheviks died, along with a huge swath of the Red Army's officer corps and vast numbers of Soviet administrators and high-ranking Stalinists. The final prize was Bukharin, tried and executed in 1938. True to form, once his blood lust had been satisfied Stalin halted the carnage and blamed Ezhov for his own crimes.

Getty finds much here which is implausible, even derisory [Reading 6]. In any other field a spatchcock interpretation cobbled together from folklore, self-serving memoirs, fiction, spurious sources and speculations about what must have occurred would be 'laughable', but easier access to archives in the former Soviet Union has at last given researchers the chance to treat the subject professionally. For Getty the idea of a 'soft Kirov' was always hard to swallow. No policy differences separated him from Stalin and there is little to support accusations of ballot rigging at the XVIIth congress. Moreover, nothing conclusive has emerged to convict Stalin of Kirov's murder. Notions of a pre-planned terror are equally dubious because even after Kirov's death the Politburo, Stalin included, followed confused and contradictory policies.

Getty proposes three reasons to account for hesitations over purging. In the first place it is possible that Stalin affected liberalism while pursuing repression, but if this were so he would have appeared inconsistent when he threw his weight behind the hunt for enemies. Perhaps he was restrained by his cronies, but the problem here is the lack of any evidence for a moderate faction in the Politburo. A third interpretation therefore suggests itself. There is no doubt that he knew what was happening and personally participated in stimulating terror, and if his complicity in the Kirov Affair is not proven he still turned it to his own advantage. On the other hand he was not an 'omniscient and omnipotent demon'. For Getty, as for revisionists in general, Stalin emerges only fitfully in the regime's practices; a blurred, equivocal presence within Stalinism. But at crucial moments his ambitions temporarily coincided with those of others, and in the late 1930s this tipped the scales in favour of mass terror.

Chapter 4: Rationality and irrationality

If dispute surrounds the issue of Stalin's presence within Stalinism, division is no less marked over the coherence of Stalinism as a system. In the 1970s a significant controversy erupted amongst economic historians on the contribution of collectivization to industrialization and the wider economic rationality of the Great Breakthrough.

Most Western academics took for granted a scenario which characterized collectivization as in some way inevitable and rational. They arrived at this conclusion via a particular reading of the 'industrialization debate', the mid-1920s quarrel between the party's left and right wings. The quarrel started when the Soviet economist Evgenii Preobrazhenskii predicted that if the socialist sector (large-scale nationalized industry) failed to grow faster than the private sector (small-scale peasant farming and private trade), a general reversion to capitalism would follow. Progress could be achieved only by offering low grain prices to the peasantry, thereby 'pumping over' resources for industrialization. Bukharin countered that squeezing peasants would cause them to retreat into subsistence: this meant starving towns, industrial depression and the end of socialism. In 1927–28, confirming the worst fears of all concerned, grain marketings collapsed. Stalin cut the Gordian Knot by doing something no one had thought of; protecting socialism and the First Five-Year Plan by forcing peasants into collectives.

In James Millar's opinion this 'standard story' is wholly wrong [Reading 7]. Bukharin's fear of a calamitous retreat into subsistence was misplaced and Pre-obrazhenskii held that socialism would emerge from the NEP, not from the destruction of the market. As for the 1927–28 crisis, this was of the Stalinists' own making. Since grain prices were low and meat prices high peasants fed grain to their animals. The matter could have been resolved by equalizing prices. In addition, because collectivization triggered the mass slaughter of livestock the regime had to purchase agricultural machinery. Contrary to received opinion, the policy therefore made a 'negative' contribution to industrialization and resulted in the universal impoverishment of the Soviet people.

Alec Nove's response is to historicize Millar's critique [Reading 7]. Given ideological and historical constraints optimal outcomes existed only in a world of speculation. Bolsheviks distrusted market forces and naturally interpreted the grain crisis as a systemic failure of the NEP. In any event, fiddling with price mechanisms would have done no more than postpone conflict between regime and village; Russia's *jacquerie* had satisfied peasant aspirations, but the prevalence of antiquated farming methods made it very difficult to envisage a sustained increase in surplus production without a root and branch transformation of agriculture. Although undoubtedly cruel, wasteful and inefficient, collectivization was inscribed in Soviet conditions, and in some sense Stalinism was therefore 'necessary'. More-over, the policy did help industry: as resources were switched to capital projects rural consumption slumped and millions fled the famine to find work on the new construction sites.

As with many disputes between academics anywhere the Millar–Nove debate did more than air the narrow concerns of a few specialists; it encouraged further research, thus broadening the range of opinion on the efficacy, rationality and consequences of Stalinism in general. This is still more so in the case of Moshe Lewin's seminal article on the Great Breakthrough [Reading 8]. Revisionist explorations of Kremlin politics and recent accounts of the reception of Stalinism by various social groups probably owe more to Lewin than to any other historian. Indeed several of his metaphors – 'quicksand society', 'Caliban state', 'ruralization of the cities' – have entered the profession's lexicon and structured the architec-ture of Soviet history.

Stalinism intercepted Lewin's life in crucial ways, and like Trotsky and Deutscher before him this has undoubtedly affected his view of Russia's past. He was born in

Wilno in 1921 and became active in left-wing Polish politics. When the Nazis invaded he escaped to the Soviet interior and found work in a kolkhoz, a mine, and finally a steel mill. On the last day of the Nazi-Soviet War he was commissioned into the Red Army. In 1946 he returned briefly to Poland but soon left again, first for France and from there to Palestine and Israel, where he spent ten years on a kibbutz. In 1961 he embarked on yet another life, this time as a student at the Sorbonne. Subsequently he held senior academic positions in France, Britain and the USA.

Lewin incorporates his image of Stalinism within a generalized crisis of early twentieth century Russia. Revolution and civil war eliminated the upper ranks of the *ancien régime*, decimated cities and the working class, threw the entire course of late-Imperial modernization into reverse and fundamentally transformed the Bolshevik party. The aftershocks of this cataclysm had ominous consequences for the First Five-Year Plan and beyond. Bolshevik leaders presided over a lumpen party mass and a deformed and wounded society, both of which they were ill-equipped to understand. During the 'revolution from above' the state tried to substitute itself for the missing social elements, but for Lewin this was no planned, rational process. Massive social and geographical mobility disorientated millions and panicked the government into a range of woefully inappropriate measures: it struck out against the old technical intelligentsia, thereby depriving itself of precious expertise; it mistook peasant recalcitrance for class war, thus destroying enterprise and alienating putative allies; it unwittingly generated an inefficient, corrupt and bloated bureaucracy quite unable to manage the enormous, spontaneous flight to the cities and incited a cultural revolution which disappointed hopes of genuine change. Beset by crises on all sides, Stalin and his colleagues instinctively responded with a frenzied barrage of threats, punitive decrees and purges designed to impose central control.

Inside this pandemonium even the most energetic and ruthless commissar found it impossible to stem the flood of paperwork or discover what was happening in his bureaucratic empire. Repeated efforts to streamline the apparatus merely added further layers of red tape. As a result, Lewin believes that multi-centralism rather than centralism was obtained: a welter of competing agencies struggled and fought against each other for power and influence.

Outside, in the country at large, the population contrived defensive strategies which served only to whet the regime's appetite for violence: workers and peasants evaded responsibility, switched jobs and side-stepped regulation, while functionaries and enterprise bosses concealed mistakes, fabricated successes and elaborated 'family networks' to protect themselves from the arbitrary depredations of the secret police.

In Lewin's strikingly original representation Stalinism should not therefore be designated as a plan emanating from Moscow. Rather, it was a tumultuous array of events embodying numerous contradictory elements. If it certainly cannot be contained within the totalitarian paradigm (confusion and chaos were too much in evidence for that) then nor can it easily be described as a system, rational or otherwise: many actors and groups probably thought they were behaving rationally, but the overall motion of the 1930s – social, economic, political and cultural – was elemental, erratic and paradoxical. Like the sorcerer's apprentice the regime had conjured up forces which it could neither comprehend nor control, a bewildering phenomenon for participants and historians alike.

Notes

1 I. Deutscher, *Stalin: A Political Biography* (New York, Oxford University Press, 1967), p. x.
2 See J. Arch Getty, *Origins of the Great Purges: The Soviet Communist Party Reconsidered 1933–1938* (Cambridge, Cambridge University Press, 1985).

Chapter 3 Absence and Presence

Reading 5 *The 'Great Change'*

I. DEUTSCHER

IN 1929, five years after Lenin's death, Soviet Russia embarked upon her second revolution, which was directed solely and exclusively by Stalin. In its scope and immediate impact upon the life of some 160 million people the second revolution was even more sweeping and radical than the first. It resulted in Russia's rapid industrialization; it compelled more than a hundred million peasants to abandon their small, primitive holdings and to set up collective farms; it ruthlessly tore the primeval wooden plough from the hands of the *muzhik* and forced him to grasp the wheel of the modern tractor; it drove tens of millions of illiterate people to school and made them learn to read and write; and spiritually it detached European Russia from Europe and brought Asiatic Russia nearer to Europe. The rewards of that revolution were astounding; but so was its cost: the complete loss, by a whole generation, of spiritual and political freedom. It takes a great effort of the imagination to gauge the enormousness and the complexity of that upheaval for which hardly any historical precedent can be found. Even if all allowance is made for the different scales of human affairs in different ages, the greatest reformers in Russian history, Ivan the Terrible and Peter the Great, and the great reformers of other nations too, seem to be dwarfed by the giant form of the General Secretary.

And yet the giant's robe hangs somewhat loosely upon Stalin's figure. There is a baffling disproportion between the magnitude of the second revolution and the stature of its maker, a disproportion which was not noticeable in the revolution of 1917. There the leaders seem to be equal to the great events; here the events seem to reflect their greatness upon the leader, Lenin and Trotsky foresaw their revolution and prepared it many years before it materialized. Their own ideas fertilized the soil of Russia for the harvest of 1917. Not so with Stalin. The ideas of the second revolution were not his. He neither foresaw it nor prepared for it. Yet he, and in a sense he alone, accomplished it. He was at first almost whipped into the vast undertaking by immediate dangers. He started it gropingly, and despite his own fears. Then, carried on by the force of his own doings, he walked the giant's causeway, almost without halt or rest. Behind him were tramping the myriads of weary and bleeding Russian feet, an whole generation in search of socialism in one country. His figure seemed to grow to mythical dimensions. Seen at close quarters, it was still the figure of a man of very ordinary stature and of middling thoughts. Only his fists and feet contrasted with his real stature – they were the fists and the feet of a giant.

Our narrative of Stalin's life has reached the years 1925–6. Since then Stalin's Communist opponents have repeatedly described him as the leader of an anti-revolutionary reaction, while most anti-Communists have seen and still see the haunting spectre of communism embodied in his person. Yet, among the Bolshevik leaders of the twenties, he was primarily the man of the golden mean. He instinctively abhorred the extreme viewpoints which then competed for the party's recognition. His peculiar job was to produce the formulas in which the opposed extremes seemed reconciled. To the mass of hesitating members of the party his words sounded like common sense itself. They accepted his leadership in the hope that the party would be reliably steered along the 'middle of the road' and that 'safety first' would be the guiding principle. It might be said that he appeared as the Baldwin or the Chamberlain, the Harding or the Hoover of Bolshevism, if the mere association of those names with Bolshevism did not sound too incongruous.

It was neither Stalin's fault nor his merit that he never succeeded in sticking to the middle of any road; and that he was constantly compelled to abandon 'safety' for the most dangerous of ventures. Revolutions are as a rule intolerant of golden means and 'common sense'. Those who in a revolution try to tread the middle of the road usually find the earth cleaving under their feet. Stalin was repeatedly compelled to make sudden and inordinately violent jumps now to this now to that extreme of the road. We shall see him over and over again either far to the right of his right-wing critics or far to the left of his left-wing critics. His periodical sharp turns are the convulsive attempts of the man of the golden mean to keep his balance amid the cataclysms of his time. What is astounding is how well he has kept his balance – each of his many jumps would have broken the neck of any less resilient leader.

Thus, for all his inclination towards the reconciliation of conflicting Bolshevik viewpoints, he was no man of compromise. Apart from the fact that those viewpoints are mutually exclusive, his personal characteristics were not those of the conciliator. The only trait he had in common with any man of compromise was his distrust of extremes. But he lacked the suavity, the flair for persuasion, and the genuine interest in narrowing gaps between opposed views which make the political peacemaker. His temperament was altogether averse to compromise; and the conflict between his mind and his temperament underlay much of his behaviour. He appeared before the party with formulas, some parts of which he had borrowed from right-wing Bolsheviks and some from left-wing Bolsheviks. But these were strange compromise formulas: their purpose was not to bring the extremes together but to blow them up and to destroy them. He did not mediate between those who seemed to walk to the right or left of him; he annihilated them. He personified the dictatorship of the golden mean over all the unruly ideas and doctrines that emerged in post-revolutionary society, the dictatorship of the golden mean that could not remain true to itself, to the golden mean. [. . .]

The unpremeditated, pragmatic manner in which he embarked upon the second revolution would have been unbelievable if, during the preceding years, from 1924 until late in 1929, Stalin had not placed his views on record. Up to the last moment he shrank from the upheaval, and he had no idea of the scope and violence which it was to assume. In this he was not alone. Not a single Bolshevik group, faction, or coterie thought of an industrialization so intensive and rapid or of a collectivization of farming so comprehensive and drastic as that which Stalin now initiated. Even the most extreme of the left Bolsheviks conceived collectivization as a mild, gradual reform. The only man who had propagated the idea of a 'second revolution' in the country-side was Yuri Larin, a second-rate economist, once a right-wing Menshevik. He wrote about it as early as 1925; and Stalin then ironically treated his view as a cranky idea.[1] He fulminated against those Bolsheviks who thought of 'fanning class struggle in the country-side':[2] 'This is . . . empty chatter . . . old Menshevik songs from the old Menshevik Encyclopaedia'. When students of the Sverdlov University put to him the captious question, 'How can one fight against the *kulaks* without fanning the class struggle?', he replied in the same tone, brooking no contradiction, that the party 'was not interested in fanning class struggle' in the country-side and that that slogan was 'quite inappropriate'.[3]

Three years later, in May 1928, when the emergency measures against the *kulaks* were already in operation, he still insisted that the 'expropriation of *kulaks* would be folly'.[4] He did not expect more than a small fraction of agriculture to be reorganized on collective lines within the next four years.[5] The first five-year plan, approved by the end of the year, provided for the collectivization of, at the most, 20 per cent of all farms by 1933. Even in the spring of 1929, while he was already openly accusing the Bukharin group as the promotors of capitalist farming, Stalin still maintained that 'individual . . . farming would continue to play a predominant part in supplying the country with food and raw materials'.[6]

A few months later, 'all round' collectivization was in full swing; and individual farming was doomed. Before the year was out Stalin stated: 'We have succeeded in turning the bulk of the peasantry in a large number of regions away from the old capitalist path of development'.[7]

The Politbureau now expected that state-owned and collective farms would already supply half of all the food for the towns. In the last days of the year Stalin's orders for an all out 'offensive against the *kulak*' rang out threateningly from the Kremlin.

> We must smash the *kulaks*, eliminate them as a class . . . Unless we set ourselves these aims, an offensive would be mere declamation, bickering, empty noise. . . . We must strike at the *kulaks* so hard as to prevent them from rising to their feet again. . . .[8]

Far from denouncing expropriation of well-to-do farmers as folly, he now argued:

> Can we permit the expropriation of *kulaks* . . . ? A ridiculous question. . . . You do not lament the loss of the hair of one who has been beheaded. . . . We must break down the resistance of that class in open battle.[9]

A brief recapitulation of his crucial statements on industrialization reveals equally striking contradictions. In the middle twenties Russian industry, recovering to its pre-war condition, increased its output by 20 to 30 per cent per year.[10] The Politbureau argued over the rate at which output could be expanded after all the existing plants and factories had been made to operate to full capacity. Everybody agreed that once this point had been reached, the annual increases would be smaller. Zinoviev, Trotsky, and Kamenev thought that it would still be possible to raise output by somewhat less than 20 per cent a year. Stalin dubbed them 'super-industrializers'. When his opponents advanced the project for the Dnieprostroy, the great hydro-electrical power station on the Dnieper, he shelved it, allegedly saying that for Russia to build the Dnieprostroy would be the same as for a *muzhik* to buy a gramophone instead of a cow.[11] His report to the fifteenth congress, in December 1927, was full of contentment with the industrial condition of the country; but he already took a leaf from the opposition's book – and suggested that in the next few years industrial output should be increased at the annual rate of 15 per cent.

A year later his contentment with the condition of industry vanished; and he found that the Russian plants and factories were technically 'beneath all criticism'.[12] He now began to urge more rapid industrialization. Referring to a precedent in the minds of many of his listeners he argued:

> When Peter the Great, having to deal with the more advanced countries of the west, began feverishly to build factories and workshops, in order to supply his armies, . . . none of the old classes . . . could successfully solve the problem of overcoming the backwardness of the country.[13]

But the new structure of Russian society created incomparably better conditions for industrialization. Even now Stalin's projects were moderate. At a plenary session of the Central Committee he wrangled with the Commissar of Finance, Frumkin, who would not allocate in the budget more than 650 million roubles for capital investments. The Supreme Economic Council asked for 825 million roubles; and Stalin pleaded in favour of the higher appropriation.[14]

The actual investments in the next year, the first of the five-year plan, amounted to 1,300 million roubles, nearly 500 million more than Stalin's highest estimate. The radical and decisive turn towards industrialization occurred by the middle of 1929, when the appropriation for capital investments was suddenly raised to 3,400 million roubles, five times as much as the Commissar of Finance had allowed and four times as much as Stalin himself had demanded. Soon the Politbureau worked itself up into a real frenzy of industrialization. In June 1930 the sixteenth congress was dumbfounded by Stalin's triumphant statement: 'We are on the eve of our transformation from an agrarian into an industrial country'.[15] He predicted that in many branches of industry the plan would be fulfilled in three or even two and a half, instead of in five, years. He told the congress that in the current year industry was ordered to raise its output by nearly 50 per cent, an exertion which really belonged to the realm of superindustrial fantasy.[16]

He was now completely possessed by the idea that he could achieve a miraculous transformation of the whole of Russia by a single *tour de force*. He seemed to live in a half-real and half-dreamy world of statistical figures and indices, of industrial orders and instructions, a world in which no target and no objective seemed to be beyond his and the party's grasp. He coined the phrase that there were no fortresses which could not be conquered by the Bolsheviks, a phrase that was in the course of many years repeated by every writer and orator and displayed on every banner and poster in every corner of the country. [. . .]

––––––––

[. . .] Stalin was precipitated into collectivization by the chronic danger of famine in 1928 and 1929. Some of his opponents suggested that the danger might be averted if food were imported. But the means of payment were lacking; and the Government could not hope to obtain foreign credits – the financial boycott of Russia, which had started after the revolution, was virtually still on. Apart from this, if the scarce funds of foreign currency and gold were to be spent on foreign food, industry could not develop even on the modest scale on which it had progressed so far. Industrial stagnation was bound to entail an even graver food crisis and more dangerous tension between town and countryside later on.

The ransacking of the barns of the well-to-do peasants and the requisitioning of hidden stocks seemed to offer a simpler way out of the
predicament, one that was not necessarily more unfair than the threat of
starvation with which the country-side confronted the towns. But the
administration, even assisted by party and police, was hardly capable of
coping with the task. The peculiar gifts of peasants for evading regulations
and controls imposed upon them by a more or less remote urban administration is notorious. Such regulations and controls, let alone requisitions,
are most effective when they are enforced by a section of the rural population on the spot. Stalin therefore appealed to the poor peasants against the
well-to-do farmers. He could not turn to the mass of the poor *muzhiks*
empty-handed. He had to offer them tangible rewards for co-operation.
And what reward could be more alluring to the destitute *muzhik*, the
owner of a tiny plot, who tilled his land with a wooden plough (*sokha*),
who possessed neither horse nor cow and was constantly at the mercy of
the *kulak* and village usurer, what reward could be more tempting to the
multitude of such *muzhiks* than a collective farm, which the Government
promised to endow with some of the *kulaks'* agricultural implements and
cattle as well as with tractors?

It is not known exactly how many of the 25 million private farmers
belonged to that most destitute class. Their numbers were given as 5 to 8
millions – at least 5 millions of the smallest holdings were tilled with
wooden ploughs.[17] At the other end of the scale there were $1\frac{1}{2}$ or perhaps 2
million prosperous farmers. In between there were the 15 to 18 milions of
'middle peasants'. Thus, only a minority of the peasantry, though a very
substantial one, could be relied upon to welcome wholeheartedly the 'great
change'. If Stalin had limited the reform to the pooling of the poorest
holdings and to a moderate redistribution of wealth between the most
prosperous and the most destitute sections of the peasantry, the collectivization would hardly have become the bloody cataclysm which in the event
it did become. If the collective farms had, further, been endowed with tools
and machines, assisted by governmental credits and technical advice, if
they had then succeeded in visibly improving the living of their members,
they would probably have attracted many of the so-called middle peasants,
who in fact led a miserable existence on the shifting borderlines of poverty.

About the middle of 1929 Stalin was carried away by the momentum of
the movement. The beginning of collectivization was an indubitable success. As encouraging progress reports piled up on the desks of the General
Secretariat, Stalin began to press the collectivization beyond the limits
originally set. He dispatched thousands and thousands of agents to the
country-side, instructing them to 'liquidate the *kulaks* as a class' and to
drive the multitudes of reluctant middle peasants into the collective farms.
The spirit of his instructions can be recaptured from a speech he gave to
the party's rural agents in December 1929.[18] He used the bluntest words to

dispel the scruples of his listeners, who apparently felt that a revolution may and must deal ruthlessly with a handful of exploiters but not with millions of small proprietors. Stalin quoted with vague irony the following lines from Engels:

> We stand decisively on the side of the small peasant: we will do everything possible to make his lot more tolerable and to facilitate his transition to the co-operative, if he decides to take this step. If he cannot as yet bring himself to this decision, we will give him plenty of time to ponder over it on his holding.

Engels's 'exaggerated circumspection', Stalin told his listeners, suited the conditions of western Europe; but it was out of place in Russia. The small peasant was not to be given time to ponder over collectivism on his own holding. The *kulaks*, Stalin elaborated his point, must not only be expropriated; it was ridiculous to suggest, as some Bolsheviks did, that after they had been expropriated they should be allowed to join collective farms. He did not tell this audience what should happen to the two million or so *kulaks*, who with their families may have numbered eight or ten million people, after they had been deprived of their property and barred from the collective farms.

Within a short time rural Russia became pandemonium. The overwhelming majority of the peasantry confronted the Government with desperate opposition. Collectivization degenerated into a military operation, a cruel civil war. Rebellious villages were surrounded by machine-guns and forced to surrender.[19] Masses of *kulaks* were deported to remote unpopulated lands in Siberia. Their houses, barns, and farm implements were turned over to the collective farms — Stalin himself put the value of their property so transferred at over 400 million roubles.[20] The bulk of the peasants decided to bring in as little as possible of their property to the collective farms which they imagined to be state-owned factories, in which they themselves would become mere factory hands. In desperation they slaughtered their cattle, smashed implements, and burned crops. This was the *muzhik*'s great Luddite-like rebellion. Only three years later, in January 1934, did Stalin disclose some of its results. In 1929 Russia possessed 34 million horses. Only 16.6 millions were left in 1933 — 18 million horses had been slaughtered. So were 30 millions of large cattle, about 45 per cent of the total, and nearly 100 million, or two-thirds of all, sheep and goats.[21] Vast tracts of land were left untilled. Famine stalked the towns and the black soil steppe of the Ukraine.

The *tour de force* in farming impelled Stalin to attempt a similar *tour de force* in industry. Rapid mechanization of agriculture now became a matter of life and death. Large-scale farming demands a technical basis much higher than that on which small farming, especially that of the antediluvian Russian type, can exist. The tractor must replace the horse. Before the great slaughter of livestock, economists thought that complete collectivization would require at least a quarter of a million tractors and an enormous mass of other machinery. When the upheaval began only 7,000 tractors were available in the whole of Russia. By an extraordinary exertion Stalin secured nearly 30,000 tractors more in the course of 1929.[22] This was a drop in the ocean. Without machines and technical advice no rational organization and division of agricultural labour was possible. Many of the collective farms threatened to disintegrate and fall asunder as soon as they had been formed. It was now imperative that industry should, within the shortest possible time, supply fantastic masses of machinery, that the oil wells should produce the millions of tons of petrol by which the tractors were to be driven, that the country-side be electrified, that new power stations be built, and last, but not least, that millions of peasants be trained in handling and driving engines. But the plants and factories to produce the stuff did not exist. The output of coal, steel, oil, and other materials was desperately inadequate. And the men who were to teach the illiterate *muzhiks* to handle a tractor were not there either.

The whole experiment seemd to be a piece of prodigious insanity, in which all rules of logic and principles of economics were turned upside down. It was as if a whole nation had suddenly abandoned and destroyed its houses and huts, which, though obsolete and decaying, existed in reality, and moved, lock, stock and barrel, into some illusionary buildings, for which not more than a hint of scaffolding had in reality been prepared; as if that nation had only after this crazy migration set out to make the bricks for the walls of its new dwellings and then found that even the straw for the bricks was lacking; and as if then that whole nation, hungry, dirty, shivering with cold and riddled with disease, had begun a feverish search for the straw, the bricks, the stones, the builders and the masons, so that, by assembling these, they could at last start building homes incomparably more spacious and healthy than were the hastily abandoned slum dwellings of the past. Imagine that that nation numbered 160 million people; and that it was lured, prodded, whipped, and shepherded into that surrealistic enterprise by an ordinary, prosaic, fairly sober man, whose mind had suddenly become possessed by a half-real and half-somnambulistic vision, a man who established himself in the role of super-judge and super-architect, in the role of a modern super-Pharoah. Such, roughly, was now the strange scene of Russian life, full of torment and hope, full of pathos and of the grotesque; and such was Stalin's place in it; only that the things that he drove the people to build were not useless pyramids.

In his own mind he saw himself not as a modern Pharoah but as a new Moses leading a chosen nation in the desert. For the mind of this atheistic dictator was cluttered with biblical images and symbols. Among the few metaphors and images scattered in his dull and dreary writings, the phrase about the march 'to the promised land of socialism' recurred perhaps most frequently, even while he led only a few 'committee-men' of Tiflis or Baku. How much more real must that phrase have sounded in his own ears now. [. . .]

When Stalin put his programme before the people, demanding exertions and sacrifices, he could not simply explain it in terms of immediate economic needs. He tried to impart to it a more imaginative appeal. For the first time he now openly appealed to the nationalist as well as to the Socialist sentiments in the people. That double appeal had, it is true, been implied in the doctrine of socialism in one country; but so far he had refrained from openly stirring nationalist pride or ambition. Bolshevik hostility towards these sentiments had been fresh in the minds of the people; and any open departure from it would have been highly embarrassing to Stalin so long as he was exposed to criticism from his rivals. Nor is it certain that the nationalist train of thought was sufficiently crystallized in his own mind in earlier years. The new tone rang out with extraordinary force in one of his famous speeches to business executives, in February 1931. He was arguing interminably against those who pleaded for a slower tempo of industrialization; and he was explaining the international and national motives of his policy. Industrialization was essential for socialism; and the Soviet Government was in the eyes of the world proletariat in duty bound to build socialism. These international obligations, he said, he placed even higher than the national. But he spoke about the international Socialist aspect of the problem in clichés so lifeless that they make one feel clearly that the speaker's heart was not in them. His words began to pulsate with emotion and assumed colour only when he turned to the national, the purely Russian motives for his policy:

> No, comrades, . . . the pace must not be slackened! On the contrary, we must quicken it as much as is within our powers and possibilities. This is dictated to us by our obligations to the workers and peasants of the U.S.S.R. This is dictated to us by our obligations to the working class of the whole world.
>
> To slacken the pace would mean to lag behind; and those who lag behind are beaten. We do not want to be beaten. No, we don't want to. The history of old . . . Russia . . . she was ceaselessly beaten for her backwardness. She was beaten by the Mongol Khans, she was beaten by Turkish Beys, she was beaten by Swedish feudal lords, she was beaten by Polish-Lithuanian *Pans*, she was beaten by Anglo-French capitalists, she was beaten by Japanese barons, she was beaten by all – for her backwardness. For military backwardness, for cultural backwardness, for political backwardness, for industrial backwardness, for agricultural backwardness. She was beaten because to beat her was profitable and went unpunished. You remember the

words of the pre-revolutionary poet: 'Thou art poor and thou art plentiful, thou art mighty and thou art helpless, Mother Russia'.

. . . We are fifty or a hundred years behind the advanced countries. We must make good this lag in ten years. Either we do it or they crush us.[23]

Stalin's call for industrialization at first fired the imagination of the urban working classes. The younger generation had long cherished the dream of Russia becoming 'another America', a Socialist America. The schemes of Dnieprostroy and Magnitogorsk and a host of other ultra-modern, mammoth-like industrial combines conjured up before its eyes the vistas of a new civilization, in which man would subject the machine to his will instead of himself being subjected to the machine and its owner. Multitudes of young workers, especially members of the Komsomol, volunteered for pioneering work in the wilderness of remote lands. They ardently greeted the vision of the new world, even if that world was to be built on their own bones. Less idealistically minded people welcomed industrialization because it put an end to the unemployment that had harassed the Russian worker all through the period of N.E.P.

Here again Stalin was carried away by the momentum of the movement until he overreached himself to an extent to which no experienced economic administrator would have done. But, strange as this may seem, Stalin was still utterly inexperienced in economic matters. He was no economist by training, though the Marxist outlook gave him a closer grasp of economics than that possessed by average politicians. Under Lenin his part in framing economic policy was as insignificant as his role in the political administration was great. In addition, in those years the economic condition of Russia was so backward and primitive that there was no room for any really complex decisions. In later years he was immersed over his ears in marshalling the Bolshevik caucus against his rivals; and he had little opportunity and time to concern himself with more than the general direction of political affairs. He thus initiated an industrial revolution, being more or less unaware of the limits to which the national resources and the endurance of the people could be stretched without disastrous effects. All his experience had bred in him an excessive confidence in the power of a closely knit and ruthless administration. Had he not got rid of all his once so powerful rivals merely because he was able to turn that power against them? Had he not been able to tame a party, once so untameable, and to reduce it to a body of frightened and meek men always ready to do his bidding? Why then should he not succeed in dealing with the scattered, unorganized masses of *muzhiks* according to his ideas? Why should he not be able to make the directors of industry produce the quantities of coal, and steel, and machinery laid down in the plans? The main thing was that they should be subjected to ceaseless and relentless pressure from him and the Politbureau. He was unsurpassed at bringing that pressure to bear upon his subordinates and at making them convey it to all grades of the administration. He was the arch-intimidator, the arch-prodder, and the arch-cajoler in the whole business.

When at last he became aware of the results of the reckless drive in the country-side, he was anxious to appease the peasants and to free himself from the odium. On 2 March 1930 he tried to kill the two birds in a statement on 'Dizziness with Success'.[24] He threw the blame for what had happened on to over-zealous officials. He admitted that half the number of all the farms had already been collectivized; that in many cases force had been used; and that some of the collective farms were not viable. Three months before, while he was pressing the rural agents of the party not to allow the small peasants any more time to 'ponder' over collectivism 'on their own holdings', he himself gave his last unequivocal signal for forced collectivization. Now he intimated that his instructions had been misunderstood: 'Collective farms cannot be set up by force. To do so would be stupid and reactionary'. He railed at 'opportunists', 'blockheads', 'noisy lefts', 'timid philistines', and 'distortionists'; and he called for a halt to 'excesses'. His appearance in the role of the protector of the *muzhik* took the Politbureau and the Central Committee by surprise. He had not consulted them. He had made his appeal to the peasantry over the heads, as it were, of the men who had merely been his accomplices and whom he now made to appear as the main culprits.[25] Even the meek Central Committee of those days protested against being used in this way as the lightning conductor for popular anger. Stalin then issued another statement saying that his call for a halt to violence represented not his personal view but the attitude of the whole Central Committee.[26]

Whatever the truth of the matter, he put a powerful brake on the collectivist drive. In the next three years only 10 per cent more of all farms were pooled, so that by the end of the five-year plan six-tenths of all holdings were collectivized. The character, too, of the collective farm was altered. At first nearly all the farmer's belongings were declared collective property; and the members of the collectives were to receive for their labour no more than workmen's wages. In the early and middle thirties a whole series of 'Stalin reforms' made important concessions to the peasants' individualism. The *kolkhoz* was to be a co-operative (*artel*), not a commune. Its members shared in the farm's profits. They were allowed to own privately small plots of land, poultry, and some cattle. In the course of time a new social differentiation developed: there were 'well-to-do' and poor *kolkhozes* and 'well-to-do' and poor members in each *kolkhoz*. Authority came to favour the 'prosperous *kolkhozes*'. Stalin ordered the winding up of most state-owned farms (*Sovkhozes*) and made a gift to the collective farms of more than forty million acres of their land.[27] Thus a new, though not very firm, balance between private and

collective interests was created, which enabled the Government to collecti-
vize more slowly than at first nearly all the holdings without provoking
bitter resistance. The costly and bloody lesson of 1929 and 1930 was not
entirely wasted. In the late thirties the new social structure of rural Russia
achieved a measure of consolidation, despite all the shakiness of its
foundations at the beginning of the decade.

The ups and downs of the industrial revolution were not less abrupt and
violent. In 1930, it will be remembered, Stalin demanded that the output of
iron and coal be increased by nearly half within the year. The actual
increase was, as he himself admitted next year, only 6–10 per cent.[28]
The slow progress of mining hampered the manufacturing and engineering
industries. Stalin tenaciously pressed on with the development of new
gigantic and modern iron- and coal-mines in the Urals and in Siberia,
paying little or no heed to obstacles. 'In Magnitogorsk I was precipitated
into a battle', wrote an American eyewitness and participant. 'I was
deployed on the iron and steel front. Tens of thousands of people were
enduring the most intense hardships in order to build blast furnaces, and
many of them did it willingly, with boundless enthusiasm, which infected
me from the day of my arrival'. 'I would wager' [the writer concludes] 'that
Russia's battle of ferrous metallurgy alone involved more casualties than
the battle of the Marne'.[29]

Immense as was the waste of human life, energy, and of materials, the
achievement, too, was enormous. True, the targets of the first five-year
plan were not attained,[30] and never again, except in the years of the war
against Hitler, did Stalin demand from industry exertions like those to
which he had spurred it at first. In the second five-year plan the annual rate
of increase in industrial output was 13–14 per cent; and it was under that
more modest plan, in the years 1932–7, that the progress in industrialization was actually consolidated.[31]

Only an absolute ruler himself ruled neither by nerves nor by sentiments,
could persist in this staggering enterprise in the face of so many adversaries. There is something almost incomprehensible in the mask of
unruffled calmness which Stalin showed in those years. Behind that mask
there must have been tension and anguish. But only once did he seem to
have been on the point of breakdown. Throughout 1932 adversities and
frustrations piled up one upon another; and he sulked in his tent. His
popularity was at its nadir. He watched tensely the waves of discontent
rising and beating against the walls of the Kremlin. He could not fail to
catch gleams of hope mixed with anxiety in the eyes of his defeated
opponents, Bukharin, Rykov, Tomsky, Zinoviev, and Kamenev, whose
hands were stayed only by the perils threatening Bolshevism, in all its
shades and factions. The old division between the right and the left wings

of the party had almost gone, giving place to a common longing for change, which began to affect even some of Stalin's hard-bitten followers. Memoranda about the need to depose him circulated in his immediate entourage. They were signed by Syrtsov and Lominadze, two men who had helped him in defeating the Trotskyists and the Bukharinists – Syrtsov had even replaced Rykov as Premier of the Russian Soviet Socialist Republic.[32] A similar memorandum was signed by Riutin, chief of propaganda, and others. These men were charged with conspiracy and imprisoned. Strictly speaking, they had not engaged in any plot. They merely urged the members of the Central Committee to depose Stalin in a constitutional manner; and, nominally, Stalin never questioned the constitutional right of the Central Committee to depose its General Secretary. The Ukraine, too, was seething with despair and hidden opposition. One of Stalin's confidants, Postyshev, went there to purge the Ukrainian Government which had supposedly consisted of devoted Stalinists. The purge led to the suicide of Skrypnik, the Ukrainian Commissar of Education, a veteran Bolshevik.

As a climax to these developments, tragedy visited the dictator's own home. His own wife, Nadia Alliluyeva, the daughter of the workman Alliluyev, hitherto blindly devoted to her much older husband, began to doubt the wisdom and rightness of his policy. One evening, in November 1932, Stalin and his wife were on a visit at Voroshilov's home. Other members of the Politbureau were there too, discussing matters of policy. Nadia Alliluyeva spoke her mind about the famine and discontent in the country and about the moral ravages which the Terror had wrought on the party. Stalin's nerves were already strained to the utmost. In the presence of his friends he burst out against his wife in a flood of vulgar abuse. Nadia Alliluyeva left Voroshilov's house. The same evening she committed suicide.[33]

> The newspapers spoke about sudden and premature death [says V. Serge, a French ex-communist writer, who spent those years in Russia]. The story told by the initiated was that the young woman suffered because of the famine and the terror, because of her own comfortable life in the Kremlin and the sight of the pictures of the General Secretary covering whole buildings on the public squares. She was worn down by fits of melancholy . . .
>
> There was the man of steel, as he had called himself, . . . face to face with that corpse. It was about that time that he rose one day at the Politbureau to tender his resignation to his colleagues. 'Maybe I have, indeed, become an obstacle to the party's unity. If so, comrades, I am ready to efface myself . . .' The members of the Politbureau – the body had already been purged of its right wing – glanced at one another in embarrassment. Which of them would take it upon himself to answer: 'Yes, old man, that's that. You ought to leave. There is nothing better for you to do.' Which one? The man who would have

said such a thing, without being backed by others, would have risked a lot. Nobody stirred . . .. At last Molotov said: 'Stop it, stop it. You have got the party's confidence . . .' The incident was closed.[34]

This seems to have been the only instance in which Stalin's self-reliance broke down for a moment. A few weeks later, in January 1933, after months of sullen silence, he again addressed a plenary session of the Central Committee. His speech, though still apologetic in tone, testified to his regained confidence: 'The party whipped up the country and spurred it onwards. . . . We had to spur on the country. . . . It was a hundred years behind and faced with mortal danger. . . .'[35] He virtually admitted that the first five-year plan had not been fulfilled, but explained this on the ground that industry had had to switch over to the production of munitions, because of the threat of war in the Far East. These were the days of the Japanese conquest of Manchuria. It is doubtful whether Stalin himself had thought the danger of a Japanese attack on Russia so imminent as to call for a drastic remaking of economic plans. Now, at any rate, just on the eve of Hitler's coming to power, he assured the country that the danger was over and that there was no need for the exacting tempo of industrialization any longer. The task before Russia within the next two or three years was to consolidate her gains and to master industrial technique.

A few days later he was again on the platform, describing the dangers with which the situation in the country-side was fraught. He startled the party by saying that the collective farms might become even more danger-ous to the régime than private farming. In the old days the peasantry was scattered and slow to move; it lacked the capacity for political organiza-tion. Since the collectivization the peasants were organized into compact bodies which might support the Soviets but might also turn against them more effectively than the individual farmers could. To secure the party's close control over them, the rural Political Departments were established.[36] Parallel with these measures another amazing job was tackled. A year later Stalin reported to the seventeenth congress that two million *muzhiks* who had never handled a machine had in the meantime been trained to be drivers; that almost as many men and women had been trained in the administration of collective farms; and that 111,000 engineers and agro-nomists had been dispatched to the country-side. The number of illiterate people had dwindled to a mere 10 per cent.[37] This so-called cultural revolution was also carried through in feverish haste; and consequently it was extremely superficial. But it did mark the beginning of a momentous transformation in the outlook and habits of the nation.

The description of Stalin's role in the second revolution would be incom-plete without a mention of the new social policy which he inspired perhaps more directly than any other part of the 'great change'. It is in this field that the lights and the shadows of his policies contrasted most sharply. At the end of 1929 he initiated a new labour policy in terms so obscure and vague that their significance was almost entirely missed.[38] Under the N.E.P. labour policy had been characterized by a very high degree of *laisser faire*: workers had been free to choose their jobs, even though the scourge of unemployment made that freedom half-illusiory; managers had been more or less free to hire and fire their men. But rapid industrialization at once created an acute shortage of labour, and that meant the end of *laisser faire*. This was, in Stalin's words, the 'end of spontaneity' on the labour market, the beginning of what, in English-speaking countries, was later called direction of labour. The forms of direction were manifold. Industrial businesses signed contracts with collective farms, by which the latter were obliged to send specified numbers of men and women to factories in the towns. This was the basic method. It is an open question whether the term 'forced labour' can fairly be applied to it. Compulsion was used very severely in the initial phase of the process, when members of collective farms, declared redundant and deprived of membership, were placed in a position not unlike that of the unemployed man whom economic necessity drives to hire himself as a factory hand. Once in town, the proletarianized peasant was free to change his job. Stalin aimed at securing by decree the reserve of manpower for industry which in most countries had been created by the chronic and spontaneous flight of impoverished peasants to the towns.

Forced labour, in the strict sense, was imposed on peasants who had resorted to violence in resisting collectivization. They were treated like criminals and were subject to imprisonment. Here history played one of its malignant and gloomy jokes. Soviet penitentiary reforms of earlier years, inspired by humanitarian motives, viewed the imprisonment of criminals as a means to their re-education, not punishment. They provided for the employment of criminals in useful work. The criminals were to be under the protection of trade unions; and their work was to be paid at trade-union rates. As the number of rebellious peasants grew, they were organized in mammoth labour camps and employed in the building of canals and railways, in timber felling, and so on. Amid the famine and misery of the early thirties the provisions for their protection were completely disregarded. 'Re-education' degenerated into slave labour, terribly wasteful of human life, a vast black spot on the picture of the second revolution.

When Stalin then claimed that in Soviet Russia labour 'had from a disgraceful and painful burden been transformed . . . into a matter of glory, valour and heroism', his words sounded like mockery to the inmates of the labour camps. They did not sound so to those more fortunate workers to whom industrialization spelt social advance. Industrial labour and technical efficiency were surrounded by unusual glamour, which made them attractive to the young generation. Press, theatre, film, and radio extolled the 'heroes of the production front', the way famous soldiers or film-stars were exalted in other countries. The doors of technical schools of all grades opened to workers from the bench; and such schools multiplied with extraordinary rapidity. 'We ourselves', Stalin urged the Bolsheviks, 'must become experts, masters at our business.'[39] 'No ruling class has managed without its own intelligentsia.'[40] Throughout the thirties the ranks of that new intelligentsia swelled, until Stalin spoke of it as of a social group equal, or rather superior, in status to the workers and the peasants, the two basic classes of Soviet society. The cultural and political qualities of the new intelligentsia were very different from those of the old one, which had kindled the flame of revolution under the Tsars and guided the workers' and peasants' republic in its early days. The new intelligentsia was brought up to spurn political ambition. It lacked the intellectual subtlety and the aesthetic refinement of its predecessors. Its curiosity about world affairs was damped or not awakened at all; it had no real sense of any community of fate between Russia and the rest of the world. Its chief interest was in machines and technical discoveries, in bold projects for the development of backward provinces, in administrative jobs, and in the arts of business management. In all these fields, too, it showed a crudeness which sometimes made it the laughing stock of foreign experts. But it combined that crudeness with an extraordinary eagerness to learn, with great shrewdness and receptiveness of mind, the characteristics of pioneers. This was, indeed, the generation of Stalin's 'frontier men'.

At the same time the old intelligentsia suffered degradation. Stalin distrusted its critical mind and the cosmopolitan or internationalist outlook of many of its members. Old technicians and administrators viewed his project with cool scepticism and even open hostility. Some sided with the one or the other opposition. A few persisted in an attitude of defeatism which led them to obstruct or even to sabotage the economic plans. At first Stalin displayed towards the technicians and administrators of the older generation the exaggerated respect which is often so characteristic of proletarian new-comers to the business of government. Then, as his self-confidence grew and as he involved himself in clashes with economists and administrators, who were too strongly attached to their inert routine or too sober and realistic to keep pace with the industrial revolution, Stalin's respectful attitude towards them changed into its opposite. He scorned them and humiliated them. He used the offences or crimes of a few to surround them all with intense suspicion. A few demonstrative trials of 'wreckers' and 'saboteurs', at which scientists and academicians like Professor Ramzin and his associates were put in the dock, sufficed to make workmen and foremen look distrustfully upon their managers and technicians. The results were disastrous for industry. Moreover, the training of the new intelligentsia was dependent on the willing co-operation of the old one. In the end Stalin himself had to protect the members of the latter. His speeches on the subject bristled with contradictions which reflected his own phobias, vacillations, and belated attempts at retrieving the situation.

Perhaps the most important aspect of his social policy was his fight against the equalitarian trends. He insisted on the need for a highly differentiated scale of material rewards for labour, designed to encourage skill and efficiency.[41] He claimed that Marxists were no levellers in the popular sense; and he found support for his thesis in Marx's well-known saying that even in a classless society workers would at first be paid according to their labour and not to their needs. Nevertheless, a strong stand of equalitarianism had run through Bolshevism. Under Lenin, for instance, the maximum income which members of the ruling party, even those of the highest rank, were allowed to earn equalled the wages of a skilled labourer. That the needs of industrialization clashed with 'ascetic' standards of living and that the acquisition of industrial skill was impeded by the lack of material incentives to technicians, administrators, and workers can hardly be disputed. But it is equally true that, throughout the thirties, the differentiation of wages and salaries was pushed to extremes, incompatible with the spirit, if not the letter, of Marxism. A wide gulf came to separate the vast mass of unskilled and underpaid workmen from the privileged 'labour aristocracy' and bureaucracy, a gulf which may be said to have impeded the cultural and industrial progress of the nation as a whole, as much as the earlier rigidly equalitarian outlook had done.

It was mainly in connexion with Stalin's social policy that his opponents, especially the exiled Trotsky, denounced him as the leader of a new privileged caste. He indeed fostered the inequality of incomes with great determination. On this point his mind had been set long before the 'great change'. As early as 1925 he enigmatically warned the fourteenth congress: 'We must not play with the phrase about equality. This is playing with fire'.[42] In later years he spoke against the 'levellers' with a rancour and venom which suggested that in doing so he defended the most sensitive and vulnerable facet of his policy. It was so sensitive because the highly paid and privileged managerial groups came to be the props of Stalin's régime. They had a vested interest in it. Stalin himself felt that his personal rule was the more secure the more solidly it rested on a rigid hierarchy of interest and influence. The point was also so vulnerable because no undertaking is as difficult and risky as the setting up of a new hierarchy on ground that has just been broken up by the mighty ploughs of social revolution. The revolution stirs the people's dormant longings for equality. The most critical moment in its development is that at which the leaders feel that they cannot satisfy that longing and proceed to quell it.[43] They get on with the job which some of their opponents call the betrayal of the revolution. But their conscience is so uneasy and their nerves are so strained by the ambiguity of their role that the worst outbursts of their temper are directed against the victims of that 'betrayal'. Hence the extraordinary vehemence with which a Cromwell, a Robespierre, or a Stalin, each hit out against the levellers of his time.

It was only in the late thirties that the fruits of the second revolution began to mature. Towards the end of the decade Russia's industrial power was catching up with Germany's. Her efficiency and capacity for organization were still incomparably lower. So was the standard of living of her people. But the aggregate output of her mines, basic plants, and factories approached the level which the most efficient and disciplined of all continental nations, assisted by foreign capital, had reached only after three-quarters of a century of intensive industrialization. The other continental nations, to whom only a few years before Russians still looked up, were now left far behind. The industrial revolution spread from central and western Russia to the remote wilderness of Soviet Asia. The collectivization of farming, too, began to yield positive results. Towards the end of the decade agriculture had recovered from the terrible slump of the early thirties; and industry was at last able to supply tractors, harvester-combines, and other implements in great numbers and the farms were achieving a very high degree of mechanization. The outside world was more or less unaware of the great change and the shift in the international balance of power which it implied. Spectacular failures of the first five-year plan induced foreign observers to take a highly sceptical view of the results of the second and the third. The macabre series of 'purge' trials suggested economic and political weakness. The elements of weakness were undoubtedly there; and they were even greater than may appear when the scene is viewed in retrospect from the vantage point of the late forties. But the elements of strength were also incomparably greater than they were thought to be in the late thirties.

The achievement was remarkable, even if measured only by the yard-stick of Russian national aspirations. On a different scale, it laid the foundations for Russia's new power just as Cromwell's Navigation Act had once laid the foundation for British naval supremacy. Those who still view the political fortunes of countries in terms of national ambitions and prestige cannot but accord to Stalin the foremost place among all those rulers who, through the ages, were engaged in building up Russia's power. Actuated by such motives even many of the Russian White émigrés began to hail Stalin as a national hero. But the significance of the second revolution lay not only and not even mainly in what it meant to Russia. To the world it was important as the first truly gigantic experiment in planned economy, the first instance in which a government undertook to plan and regulate the whole economic life of its country and to direct its nationalized industrial resources towards a uniquely rapid multiplication of the nation's wealth. True enough Stalin was not the originator of the idea. He borrowed so much from Marxist thinkers and economists, including his rivals, that often he might well be charged with outright plagiarism. He was, nevertheless, the first to make of the abstract idea the practical business of government. It is also true that an important beginning in practical planning had been made by the German Government and General Staff in the First World War; and that Lenin had often referred to that precedent as to a pointer to future experiments.[44] What was new in Stalin's planning was the fact that it was initiated not merely as a wartime expedient, but as the normal pattern of economic life in peace. Hitherto governments had engaged in planning as long as they had needed implements of war. Under Stalin's five-year plans, too, guns, tanks, and planes were produced in great profusion; but the chief merit of these plans was not that they enabled Russia to arm herself, but that they enabled her to modernize and transform society.

We have seen the follies and the cruelties that attended Stalin's 'great change'. They inevitably recall those of England's industrial revolution, as Karl Marx has described them in *Das Kapital*. The analogies are as numerous as they are striking. In the closing chapter of the first volume of his work, Marx depicts the 'primitive accumulation' of capital (or the 'previous accumulation', as Adam Smith called it), the first violent processes by which one social class accumulated in its hands the means of production, while other classes were being deprived of their land and means of livelihood and reduced to the status of wage-earners. The process which, in the thirties, took place in Russia might be called the 'primitive accumulation' of socialism in one country. Marx described the 'enclosures' and 'clearings' by which the landlords and manufacturers of England expropriated the yeomanry, the 'class of independent peasants'.[45] A parallel to those enclosures is found in a Soviet law, on which Stalin reported to the sixteenth congress, a law which allowed the collective farms to 'enclose' or 'round off' their land so that it should comprise a continuous area. In this way the individual farmers were either compelled to join the collective farms or were virtually expropriated.[46] Marx recalls 'the bloody discipline' by which the free peasants of England were made into wage-labourers, 'the disgraceful action of the state which employed the police to accelerate the accumulation of capital by increasing the degree of exploitation of labour'.[47] His words might apply to many of the practices introduced by Stalin. Marx sums up his picture of the English industrial revolution by saying that 'capital comes [into the world] dripping from head to foot, from every pore, with blood and dirt'. Thus also comes into the world – socialism in one country.

In spite of its 'blood and dirt', the English industrial revolution – Marx did not dispute this – marked a tremendous progress in the history of mankind. It opened a new and not unhopeful epoch of civilization. Stalin's industrial revolution can claim the same merit. It is argued against it that it has perpetrated cruelties excusable in earlier centuries but unforgivable in this. This is a valid argument, but only within limits. Russia had been belated in her historical development. In England serfdom had disappeared by the end of the fourteenth century. Stalin's parents were still serfs. By the standards of British history, the fourteenth and the twentieth centuries have, in a sense, met in contemporary Russia. They have met in Stalin. The historian cannot be seriously surprised if he finds in him some traits usually associated with tyrants of earlier centuries. Even in the most irrational and convulsive phase of his industrial revolution, however, Stalin could make the claim that his system was free from at least one major and cruel folly which afflicted the advanced nations of the west:

> The capitalists [these were his words spoken during the Great Depression[48]] consider it quite normal in a time of slump to destroy the 'surplus' of commodities and burn 'excess' agricultural produce in order to keep up high prices and ensure high profits, while here, in the U.S.S.R., those guilty of such crimes would be sent to a lunatic asylum.

It is easy to see how far Stalin drifted away from what had hitherto been the main stream of Socialist and Marxist thought. What his socialism had in common with the new society, as it had been imagined by Socialists of nearly all shades, was public ownership of the means of production and planning. It differed in the degradation to which it subjected some sections of the community and also in the recrudescence of glaring social inequalities amid the poverty which the revolution inherited from the past. But the root difference between Stalinism and the traditional Socialist outlook lay in their respective attitudes towards the role of force in the transformation of society.

Marxism was, as it were, the illegitimate and rebellious offspring of nineteenth-century liberalism. Bitterly opposed to its parent, it had many a feature in common with it. The prophets of *laisser faire* had deprecated political force, holding that it could play no progressive role in social life. In opposition to liberalism, Marxists stressed those historic instances and situations in which – as in the English and French revolutions, the American War of Independence and the Civil War – force did assist in the progress of nations and classes. But they also held that the limits within which political force could effect changes in the outlook of society were narrow. They held that the fortunes of peoples were shaped primarily by basic economic and social processes; and that, compared with these, force could play only a subordinate role. Much as the Marxist and the Liberal ideals of society differed from one another, both trends shared, in different degrees, the optimism about the future of modern civilization, so characteristic of the nineteenth century. Each of the two trends assumed that the progress of modern society tended more or less spontaneously towards the attainment of its ideal. Marx and Engels expressed their common view in the famous phrase that force is the midwife of every old society pregnant with a new one. The midwife merely helps the baby to leave the mother's womb when the time for that has come. She can do no more. Stalin's view on the role of political force, reflected in his deeds rather than his words, oozes the atmosphere of twentieth-century totalitarianism. Stalin might have paraphrased the old Marxian aphorism: force is no longer the midwife – force is the mother of the new society.

Notes

1 J. Stalin, *Sochineniia* (Moscow, 1946–48), vol. vii, p. 373, speech at the fourteenth congress.
2 Stalin, *Sochineniia*, vol. vii, p. 103.
3 Stalin, *Sochineniia*, vol. vii, pp. 79, 334–8.
4 Stalin, *Problems of Leninism* (Moscow, 1945), p. 221, 'On the Grain Front'.
5 'There are people', he said in July 1928, 'who think that individual farming is at the end of its tether and is not worth supporting. Such people have nothing in common with the line of our party'. Stalin, *Leninism* (London, 1933), vol. ii, p. 131.
6 Stalin, *Problems of Leninism*, p. 267.
7 Stalin, *Problems of Leninism*, p. 293.
8 Stalin, *Problems of Leninism*, p. 318.
9 Stalin, *Problems of Leninism*, p. 325.
10 Stalin, *Sochineniia*, vol. vii, pp. 308, 315.
11 *The Case of Leon Trotsky* (London, 1937), p. 245, and *Bulleten Oppozitsii*, no. 27 (March, 1932).
12 Stalin, *Leninism*, vol. ii, p. 151.
13 Stalin, *Leninism*, vol. ii, p. 153.
14 Stalin, *Leninism*, vol. ii, p. 172.
15 Stalin, *Leninism*, vol. ii, p. 328.
16 To be accurate, the increase was to be by 47 per cent. Stalin himself later admitted to a conference of industrial managers that it was only 25 per cent; and even this figure is doubtful. Cf. *Leninism*, vol. ii, p. 385, and *Problems of Leninism*, p. 351.
17 L. Trotsky, *The Real Situation in Russia* (London, n.d), pp. 64–7; and Stalin, *Problems of Leninism*, 'On the Grain Front', pp. 206–16.
18 Stalin, *Problems of Leninism*, pp. 301 ff.
19 In that critical period the author travelled in Russia and the Ukraine. He remembers a striking account of the collectivization given to him, in a railway carriage on the way from Moscow to Kharkov, by a colonel of the G.P.U. The colonel was completely broken in spirit by his recent experiences in the

countryside. 'I am an old Bolshevik', he said, almost sobbing, 'I worked in the underground against the Tsar and then I fought in the civil war. Did I do all that in order that I should now surround villages with machine-guns and order my men to fire indiscriminately into crowds of peasants? Oh, no, no!'

20 Stalin, *Leninism*, vol. ii, p. 344.

21 Stalin, *Problems of Leninism*, p. 480.

22 Stalin, *Problems of Leninism*, p. 483.

23 Stalin, *Problems of Leninism*, p. 356. To grasp how novel Stalin's words sounded in Russia, when they were spoken, one has to note the extent to which they rehabilitated the Tsarist past. In Stalin's summary of Russian history, Russia invariably appears as the victim of foreign conquerors and oppressors. Hitherto Bolshevik historians and writers specialized in exposing the seamy side of Russian history, in throwing light on the conquest and the oppression of weaker nations by the Tsarist Empire. Stalin gave short shrift to that anti-nationalist conception which had since the revolution been inculcated into the young generation. The most prominent expounder of the anti-nationalist view of Russian history, Professor Pokrovsky, was excommunicated some time later; and his books were banned. The rehabilitation of the nationalist tradition was to reach its climax only in the years of the Second World War.

24 Stalin, *Problems of Leninism*, pp. 326–31.

25 The statement on 'Dizziness with Success' seemed to appeal to the familiar popular belief about the 'good' ruler and his 'bad' advisers. Whether the appeal was effective is another question. The comment of an old Ukrainian peasant, questioned by the author, was roughly this: 'Things were very bad in our collective farm, but have been easier since *Stalin* got over *his* dizziness from success'.

26 Stalin, *Problems of Leninism*, p. 329.

27 Professor F. Koshelev, *Stalinskii Ustav-Osnovnoi Zakon Kolkhoznoi Zhizni* (Moscow, 1947), p. 28.

28 Stalin, *Problems of Leninism*, p. 359.

29 John Scott, *Behind the Urals* (London, 1942), p. 9.

30 When Stalin drew up the balance for the first five-year plan, in January 1933, he claimed that only 93.7 per cent of the plan had been fulfilled. Even this was probably an exaggeration. See his *Problems of Leninism*, pp. 398–402.

31 Stalin, *Problems of Leninism*, p. 406.

32 Syrtsov was the head of the Government of the Russian republic, as distinct from the Government of the U.S.S.R. That had, since Rykov's dismissal, been headed by Molotov.

33 A. Barmine, *One who Survived*, (New York, 1945), p. 264.

34 V. Serge, *Portrait de Staline* (Paris, 1940), pp. 94–5.

35 Stalin, *Problems of Leninism*, pp. 404–6.

36 Stalin, *Problems of Leninism*, pp. 431–5.

37 Stalin, *Problems of Leninism*, p. 484. In actual fact illiteracy was still widespread.

38 Stalin, *Problems of Leninism*, pp. 304–5, 360–1.

39 Stalin, *Problems of Leninism*, p. 354.

40 Stalin, *Problems of Leninism*, p. 369.

41 Stalin initiated that policy in his famous speech on the 'six conditions' for industrialization (23 June 1931). After that he emphatically reasserted it in almost every one of his speeches. At the seventeenth congress in 1934, he decried the equalization of wages and salaries as a 'reactionary, petty-bourgeois absurdity worthy of a primitive sect of ascetics but not of a Socialist

society organized on Marxian lines'. Only 'leftist blockheads . . . idealize the poor as the eternal bulwark of Bolshevism' (*Problems of Leninism*, p. 502).

42 Stalin, *Sochineniia*, vol. vii, p. 376.

43 'The basis of bureaucratic rule is the poverty of society in objects of consumption, with the resulting struggle of each against all. When there is enough goods in a store the purchasers can come whenever they want to. When there is little goods the purchasers are compelled to stand in line. When the lines are very long, it is necessary to appoint a policeman to keep order. Such is the startingpoint of the power of the Soviet bureaucracy. It "knows" who is to get something and who has to wait'. (L. Trotsky, *The Revolution Betrayed* (London, 937), p. 110.

44 *The Essentials of Lenin* (London, 1947), vol. ii, pp. 90–3, 104.

45 K. Marx, *Capital* trans. S. Moore and E. Aveling (London, 1948), vol. i, pp. 740–66.

46 The law was adopted in January 1930 (Stalin, *Leninism*, vol. ii, p. 343). Marx, *Capital*, vol. i, p. 761: 'Thus were the agricultural people first forcibly expropriated from the soil, driven from their homes, turned into vagabonds, and then whipped, branded, tortured by laws grotesquely terrible, into the discipline necessary for the wage system'.

47 Marx, *Capital*, vol. i, p. 766.

48 Stalin, *Leninism*, vol. ii, p. 369.

Reading 6 *The politics of repression revisited*

J. ARCH GETTY

Every national history has its oral tradition. Like folklore, such traditions relate popularly accessible histories without reference to documentary analysis or other tools of the trade of professionally trained historians. Sometimes they are based on self-attesting personal accounts and memoirs, on logical constructs of 'what must have happened', or on simple repetition of seemingly authoritative stories of unknown origin. The ideas that Franklin Roosevelt wanted the Japanese to attack Pearl Harbour, that Adolf Hitler did not know about the Holocaust, or that modern history is manipulated by huge but secret conspiracies (organized by Elders of Zion, Masons, or other secret fraternities) are examples of such traditions. Oral historical traditions are persistent, often surviving in the face of contradictory sources and evidence, because they are simple, comfortable, or tantalizing. Sometimes, of course, they can be true.

Russian history has always provided fertile soil for such folkloric history. The last thousand years are filled with tsars secretly living out their final years as monks, heirs to the throne spirited away from death at the last minute by loyal nannies, and a perhaps inordinate number of secret conspiracies. The obsessive secrecy of the Soviet regime further stimulated the oral tradition. Stories about Stalin have circulated at least since the 1920s and include aspects of his genealogy (he was said to be descended from Georgian or Ossetian princes), personal life (secret wives, amorous ballerinas, and illegitimate children in the Kremlin), and the circumstances of his youth and death. Even at this writing, characterizations of Bolshevism as a Jewish conspiracy are routinely heard even in educated circles in Moscow.[1]

Given Russian cultural traditions, there is nothing particularly unusual about such folklore. What should be surprising is that so much of the oral tradition has found its way into the corpus of scholarly literature. Second-hand personal memoirs, gossip, novels, and lurid accounts by defecting spies eager to earn a living in the West are soberly reviewed in scholarly journals, cited in footnotes, and recommended to graduate students. Fictionalized 'letters of old bolsheviks', political histories with invented Stalin soliloquies, and even dramatic plays are routinely incorporated into academic treatments in ways that would be laughable in other national historical studies.[2]

Glasnost' and the collapse of the Communist Party have put the secretive history of Stalinism on a more evidentially sound footing. Arichives began to open; official and unofficial document collections were published. After some years, detailed empirical studies of important aspects of the phenomenon have begun to appear.[3] Doors and windows are now opening in the former Soviet Union. This essay reevaluates the oral tradition in light of new documentation on two points that have sparked considerable controversy: the assassination of Kirov and the presumed planned origins of the Great Purges. It is too early in our source investigation conclusively to solve these problems; our purpose is rather to compare the traditional views with currently available documentation.

Especially since 1987, new information about political events in the 1930s has been surfacing in the former Soviet Union, and various historians in the West have been claiming vindication for their interpretations. What do we know that we did not know before? First, we have an abundance of gruesome new details. We know that there is human blood splattered on Marshal Tukhachevskii's 'confession'. We know that Zinoviev denounced Kamenev, that Ezhov would not permit Piatakov to execute his own wife, and that M. Riutin never capitulated to his interrogators. In addition, we now have confirmation on several details of Stalin's participation in the repression. We know, for example, that he personally edited the lists of defendants and their statements for the 1936 and 1937 show trials, adding some and removing others. He attended 'confrontations' staged by Ezhov between arrested officials and their accusers. He helped draft the indictments of Marshall Tukhachevskii and his fellow military defendants, chose the composition of their court, and personally ordered death sentences for them. (Indeed he signed numerous death sentences, including a record 3,167 on December 12, 1938.) We also know that Stalin personally blocked attempts to lighten the prison regimen or to allow exiles to return home after completing their sentences, and he sponsored the persecution of his enemies' innocent family members.[4] In the fall of 1937, he approved a plan to summarily shoot tens of thousands of 'anti-Soviet elements' and to establish target figures for the shootings by province.[5] As Stalin privately told Georgi Dmitrov, head of the Comintern, in 1937,

> Whoever tries to break the unity of the socialist state, whoever hopes to separate from it specific parts or nationalities, is a sworn enemy of the state, of the peoples of the USSR. And we will destroy any such enemy, even if he is an old Bolshevik, we will destroy his kin, his family. [We will destroy] anyone who by his actions or thoughts, yes even thoughts, encroaches on the unity of the socialist state.[6]

Russians are still struggling with the myth that Stalin somehow did not know what was happening. For decades, this was part of an oral tradition that was rationalization and consolation for millions who otherwise found it difficult to reconcile their own fates with their admiration of him as a strong leader. Most of the new material seems presented to make two points long accepted in the West: that the terror was widespread and that Stalin had a personal role in it. Virtually all of the latest historical revelations are aimed at illustrating these points and the documents presented seem chosen with this in mind. For us in the West, this is knocking at an open door; there has never been any question about his responsibility for the terror or participation in it from 1937. Nevertheless, the factual material that is coming to light on the preceding period, the 'origins' of the terror, is quite interesting and raises as many questions as it answers.

The Kirov affair

The standard view of Stalinist prepurge politics in the thirties, derived from an oral tradition, runs roughly as follows. At the end of the first Five-Year Plan (1932), a majority of the Politburo favored relaxation and reconciliation with political opponents. Led by Leningrad party chief Serge Kirov, this group of Stalinist 'moderates' opposed Stalin's plans to apply the death penalty to dissident party members. Stalin is believed to have argued in the Politburo for imposition of the death penalty on adherents of the 'Riutin Platform', a document conceived and circulated by rightist Bolshevik M. Riutin. The Kirov faction is said to have blocked this bloody suggestion.[7] Stalin became fearful as the moderates gained strength and as Kirov established a reputation for a softer line. At the Seventeenth Party Congress in 1934, Kirov's optimistic and liberal speech evoked huge ovations. More threatening to Stalin, the delegates to the Congress apparently gave Kirov more votes than Stalin in the pro forma elections to the Central

Committee. A large number of anti-Stalin ballots had to be destroyed and the voting results falsified to avoid embarrassment.[8]

After that, Stalin planned to eliminate the popular Kirov, whose standing made him a direct rival. Stalin ordered the secret police (NKVD) to arrange Kirov's assassination. Leningrad Deputy NKVD Chief Ivan Zaporozhets chose one Leonid Nikolaev, a frustrated and bitter party member, to kill Kirov. Zaporozhets won Nikolaev's trust, gave him a revolver, and helped him stalk his victim by informing him of Kirov's habits. He even secured Nikolaev's release on three occasions when watchful policemen stopped the armed assassin for suspicious behavior. Finally, on December 1, 1934, Zaporozhets arranged for Kirov's bodyguard to be away from his charge in the corridor of Leningrad party headquarters, and Nikolaev fatally shot Kirov outside the latter's office. Stalin, ready for the assassination, quickly traveled to Leningrad with most of the Politburo to supervise the investigation. Knowing in advance of the crime, Stalin had a list of conspirators to hand, consisting of former Leningrad supporters of Zinoviev. Kirov's bodyguard, who probably knew too much, died in a mysterious traffic accident on his way to talk to Stalin. At a personal interview with Stalin, Nikolaev cried out that the Leningrad NKVD had put him up to it. Stalin, angry at this lapse and at Zaporozhet's weak control over Nikolaev, then struck Zaporozhets in the presence of the other politburo members.[9]

Recent revelations, intended to show Stalin's personal participation in the repression, have paradoxically produced documents and factual evidence that disprove or contradict key elements of this story. The traditional understanding of Stalin's motive, means, and opportunity to arrange Kirov's assassination, or indeed his supposed grand plan for terror, can no longer be comfortably reconciled with the sources now available. Indeed, professional historians in Russia writing the latest textbooks on Soviet history now consider that although Stalin certainly made use of the assassination, the question of his complicity is now open. The leading Russian specialists on opposition to Stalin similarly now make no judgment on the matter.[10]

The most important source for much of our speculation about politics in the 1930s was always the 'Letter of an Old Bolshevik'. Purporting to be Bukharin's 1936 reporting of Soviet events to Boris Nicolaevsky in Paris, this document is the origin and first evidence for the belief that Kirov represented some kind of liberal alternative to a hard-line Stalin in the early 1930s. This idea has been used to illustrate Stalin's long-term plan to destroy party opponents and to explain why Stalin found it necessary to organize the assassination of an obstructionist and 'soft' Kirov. Every subsequent account that describes this scenario originates with the 'Letter', which is an oft-cited foundation of the oral tradition.[11]

Some scholars have long questioned the validity of the 'Letter' as a source.[12] With the *glasnost*'-era publication of the memoirs of Bukharin's widow, we find that his conversations with Nicholaevsky were purely official and took place in connection with unsuccessful negotiations to purchase some of Marx's manuscripts.[13] Anna Larina disputes Western misuse of the 'Letter', and concludes that Nicolaevsky must have invented the document for political purposes. With her discrediting of the 'Letter', the original source for an anti-Stalinist, moderate Kirov and for a Stalin opposing him is seriously weakened.

The idea of a soft Kirov was always problematic. Trotsky and the remnants of the Leningrad oppositionists certainly did not regard him as a liberal. Kirov had been Stalin's Leningrad point man during the savagery of collectivization and industrialization; he had supervised the rout of the left and right oppositions in his city. Under his leadership, the Leningrad party destroyed more churches than under either Zinoviev or Zhdanov. The Politburo Commission's examination of the Riutin group did not find any evidence that Stalin demanded their execution in 1932, or that Kirov opposed it.[14]

Kirov's speech to the 1934 Party Congress, often taken as a sign of his liberalism, actually praised the secret police's use of forced labour and ridiculed the opposition.[15] The thunderous applause Kirov received is sometimes used to show that he was more popular than Stalin. But Kirov was identified with Stalin, and the parts of his speech producing general ovations were the parts in which he praised Stalin and abused the opposition. Applause for him and his accomplishments in Leningrad was rare and only polite.[16] Careful scrutiny of Kirov's speeches and writings reveals little difference between them and Stalin's utterances, and Soviet scholars familiar with closed party archives scoff at the notion that Kirov was a moderate, an opponent of Stalin, or the leader of any bloc.[17]

Even if he were not a liberal, perhaps Kirov's popularity worried or threatened Stalin, who feared a rival. But V. M. Molotov, when asked by an interviewer whether Kirov posed a threat or alternative to Stalin, replied contemptuously, 'Kirov? A mere agitator'.[18] It has become part of sovietological lore, nevertheless, that 300 delegates voted against Stalin at the Seventeenth Party Congress in 1934, and that Kirov received many more votes than Stalin.[19] This story originated with the testimony of ballot counting official V. M. Verkhovykh, who said in 1960 that '125 or 123' ('I do not remember exactly') delegates voted against Stalin. He said that the embarrassing ballots were destroyed, and that the other members of the ballot commission knew of the destruction and falsification of the results. (Stalin was then officially reported to have received only three negative votes, of a total of 1,059.) In recently published sections of his memoirs, Anastas Mikoian repeated the rumor that he heard only in the 1950s, although he had been a leader at the 1934 Congress.

Although one of the 1960 special commissions charged with investigating the Kirov assassination looked into the archives, it concluded that 166 delegates simply 'did not take part in the voting'. In 1989, there was *another* investigation into the 1934 voting that found that other surviving members of the ballot counting commission had contradicted Verkhovy-kh's story even back in 1960. They would have known of such a ballot discrepancy, and it was presumably safe for them to reveal the story in the first heyday of anti-Stalinism, but none of the other participants would confirm it. The 1989 investigation concluded that 166 ballots were indeed missing, but because the number of original paper ballots is unknown, 'it is impossible definitely to confirm' how many may have voted against Stalin.[20] The evidence is still inconclusive; Stalin may indeed have regarded Kirov as a dangerous rival.

Olga Shatunovskaia has recently written that the Kirov investigation in the 1960s had uncovered convincing evidence that Stalin was behind the assassination.[21] She also revived the story that hundreds voted against Stalin at the Seventeenth Congress, and claimed that materials from the 1960 investigation have since been removed by Party Control Commission (KPK) personnel in order to change that investigation's conclusion. Yet in 1989, investigators checked the earlier commission's documents against KPK and KGB files and concluded that nothing is missing from the earlier collection. They also found that as a Khrushchev-backed KPK investigator back in 1960, Shatunovskaia had not concluded that anyone had voted against Stalin and at that time agreed with the conclusion that Stalin had not organized the killing; she agreed that Leonid Nikolaev was a lone assassin.[22]

The latest attempt to come to grips with the Kirov assassination was the work of A. Iakovlev's Politburo Commission, which in 1989 appointed an interagency investigative team consisting of personnel from the USSR Procurator's Office, the Military Procuracy, the KGB, and various archival administrations. For two years, this team conducted interviews, reviewed thousands of documents, and attempted to check all possible scenarios; their work has added another fifteen volumes to the thirty-year-old efforts.[23] Like all of the other research efforts organized by the Politburo Commission to probe aspects of the repression for publication in *Izvestiia TsK*, the team's charter was to show Stalin's complicity in the repression. It had little political incentive to let him off the hook; quite the contrary. Nevertheless, members of the working team concluded that 'in this affair, no materials objectively support Stalin's participation or NKVD participation in the organization and carrying out of Kirov's murder'.[24]

The team's report opened some rather large holes in the popular version. According to the oral tradition, Leningrad NKVD Deputy Chief Zaporozhets had approached assassin Nikolaev, put him up to the crime, and provided the weapon and bullets. It now seems that Zaporozhets had not been in Leningrad for months before the killing and that he never met Nikolaev.[25] Nikolaev had owned the revolver in question since 1918 and had registered it legally in 1924 and again in 1930. He had purchased the bullets used in the crime legally, with his registration, back in 1930. Contrary to the popular version, Nikolaev was not detained three times while carrying a gun and following Kirov, and then mysteriously released by the Leningrad NKVD. Actually, he had been stopped only once, on October 15, 1934, and the circumstances at that time were not suspicious. A frustrated apparatchik with delusions of grandeur and lifelong chronic medical problems, Nikolaev wrote in his diary that he wanted to be a great revolutionary terrorist.[26]

The Politburo Commission's team also checked the origins of the rumors that Stalin was behind the crime. Most of them come from NKVD defector Alexander Orlov, whose celebrated *Secret History of Stalin's Crimes* has now been published in the former USSR. Contrary to the oral tradition (and published claims[27]) Orlov turns out not to be a highly placed NKVD general, but rather an ordinary investigator (with the rank of major) serving under an assistant chief of department. Orlov's story that assassin Nikolaev told Stalin the day after the killing that Zaporozhets had recruited him (and that Stalin then struck Zaporozhets) 'does not correspond to reality', according to the team's report. Nikolaev had said no such thing; Zaporozhets did not return to Leningrad until days later. The team concludes that only 'one-sided, superficial, unverified facts, rumors and conjectures' support Stalin complicity.[28] With the collapse of Orlov's always improbable version, much of the folklore of the Kirov murder falls apart.

The new point most incriminating to Stalin is that he was prepared to blame the opposition in the immediate aftermath of the assassination. In the very first days after the crime, Stalin eagerly told several people that the assassin was a Zinovievist, even before arrests of them began.[29] The implication is that he anticipated the crime and was ready with a useful version of the conspiracy. This raises an old problem. Without doubt, Stalin used the Kirov assassination to move against the opposition. But the fact that he was immediately prepared to blame the Zinovievists does not show that he arranged Kirov's death. Indeed, if Stalin arranged the murder (and was as clever as we think he was) would he have been so foolish as to raise suspicion by pushing a prepared list so quickly?

We know that for more than a year before the Kirov assassination, the secret police (OGPU, then NKVD) had infiltrated Leningrad discussion circles, and their reports had convinced Ezhov and others that there was credible OGPU evidence of dangerous underground activity.[30] We also now know that the Leningrad NKVD handed Stalin such anti-Zinoviev agent reports (having to do with the alleged 'Green Lamp' and 'Svoiaki' operations) on December 2, the day after the assassination and the same day that he began telling people that Zinovievists were to blame.[31] Casting about for scapegoats in the wake of the assassination, it did not take Stalin long to fasten onto the former Zinovievists. Even then, the matter was not settled. Although their former followers were being rounded up, *Pravda* announced on December 23, 1934, that there was 'insufficient evidence' to try Zinoviev and Kamenev for the crime.[32]

The 1991 results of the investigating team's work on the Kirov matter were not well received by the Politburo Commission's leadership, which suppressed their publication.[33] Stating that such results do not serve a useful political-historical purpose today, Politburo Commission chairman Iakovlev has accused the working group of following a 'mainly juridical' approach.[34] Iakovlev notes that although the investigating team may be right, questions remain. He raises several points, some of which are indeed still unclear: What was the nature of Kirov's relation to Stalin? How did the assassin know Kirov's route? How did he reach the third floor of the Smolny? Was not Kirov's bodyguard with him at the time of the shooting, and why was the bodyguard killed before Stalin could question him?

Actually, some of these questions have been answered in the former Soviet Union. Anyone with a party card could be admitted to the third floor (Nikolaev had one). Neither the bodyguard nor his closest collaborators expected Kirov to come to Smolny that day; he had telephoned and said he was staying at home. Kirov arrived unexpectedly and ran into the unbalanced, gun-toting assassin, who was in Smolny that day not to ambush Kirov, but to secure a pass to the upcoming city party meeting. The assassin and his victim met by accident in Smolny; Nikolaev was not stalking Kirov.[35]

So the question remains, did Stalin organize the murder of Kirov? We still do not know. Since the beginning of *glasnost'*, the press has contained articles both pro and con. Some view Stalin's guilt as an established fact.[36] Others are more doubtful.[37] The well-known Khruschev-era secret reports on the Kirov assassination have not been released. It would seem to be an easy thing to release or summarize their findings officially if they contained proof one way or the other.

According to the persistent oral tradition, Stalin had organized the assassination; only a few anomalies remained. Now, at least in the former Soviet Union, this assumption is not officially supported. The politburo's team has flatly contradicted it and both textbooks and scholarly articles have retreated from it. Of course, it may be that Stalin really instigated the murder. But the two main written accounts of his supposed machinations, from which all other texts derive, have now been shown to be spurious: Their secondhand stories are inconsistent with known facts about the circumstances of the crime. There was always reasonable doubt about Stalin's participation, and now there is more than before.

A planned terror?

According to the oral tradition, Stalin planned his terror and beginning in late 1934 carried it out in measured but sequential steps. The killing of Kirov led to the 1935 party purges (*chistki*), which in turn led to the condemnation of Zinoviev and Kamenev in 1936. Their show trial led in turn to that of Piatakov and Radek in January, the purge of the Red Army in mid-1937, and finally to the trial of Bukharin and Radek in 1938. According to this view, Stalin knew where he was going from the beginning and proceeded to orchestrate a crescendo of terror.

Of course, it is impossible for us to know conclusively what Stalin thought and when. We must be guided by our inferences from known events. If we look at the political history of the early 1930s, we find that the Stalinist leadership frequently pursued initiatives that seemed to run counter to a repressive policy. Beginning with Stalin's 1931 speech rehabilitating the old intelligentsia, a 'moderate line' extended into 1933 with a Stalin/Molotov telegram releasing large numbers of prisoners and with a decision to reduce planned industrial targets in the Second Five-Year Plan.[38] It continued in 1934 with the readmission and rehabilitation of former oppositionists at the Seventeenth Party Congress and the abolition of bread rationing at the end of that year. Indeed, at Stalin's initiative a special commission of the Politburo was formed in 1934 to look into excessive arrests and other misdeeds of the secret police. Among other things, the commission, of which Stalin and Ezhov were members, drafted a policy statement limiting the punitive rights of the dreaded Special Conferences of the NKVD.[39] The commission's work was abruptly terminated by the assassination of Kirov at the end of the year.[40]

But even after the assassination, the policy endured with the anti-Fascist Popular Fronts, the announcement of the new constitution and a campaign to expand party participation and political education as an alternative to 'administrative measures' or repression. A. A. Zhdanov's name is persistently associated with such 'party revival' moves. His Leningrad organization produced numerous resolutions calling for increased political education and popular participation in party committees. He participated in the 1934 Politburo Commission on excessive arrests and took the lead in calling for the restoration to party membership of those expelled in the 1933–6 party purges; his idea was that errant party members should be trained and nurtured, rather than expelled.[41] In June 1936, Stalin interrupted Ezhov at a Central Committee Plenum to complain about so many party members being expelled:

EZHOV: Comrades, as a result of the verification of party documents, we expelled more than 200,000 members of the party.
STALIN: [interrupts] Very many.

EZHOV: Yes, very many. I will speak about this . . .
STALIN: [interrupts] If we expelled 30,000 . . . [inaudible remark],
   and 600 former Trotskyists and Zinovievists, it would be a bigger
   victory.
EZHOV: More than 200,000 members were expelled. Part of this
   number of party members, as you know, have been arrested.[42]

At about this time, Stalin wrote a letter to regional party secretaries
complaining about their excessive 'repression' of the rank and file.[43]
This led to a national movement to reinstate expelled party members,
on the eve of the Great Terror.

A campaign against bureaucratic practices in regional party organizations also attracted national visibility in 1935, when in a highly publicized
attack, Zhdanov accused the Saratov kraikom of 'dictatorship' and 'repression'. In 1936, the all-union discussion of the draft Constitution and even a
decline in the population of the labor camps occurred.[44] At the February
1937 Central Committee Plenum, Zhdanov gave the keynote speech on
democratizing party organizations, ending bureaucratic repression of 'little
people', and replacing the cooption of party leaders with grass-roots
elections.[45] Indeed, under pressure of this line, contested secret-ballot
party elections were held in 1937.

Terror and antiterror seem to have proceeded simultaneously. A good
example of this ambiguity is the strange story of the fall, rise, and fall of
Avel' Enukidze, Secretary of the Central Executive Committee of Soviets.
As is known, Enukidze was attacked at the June 1935 Plenum of the
Central Committee, when he was denounced by Ezhov for laxity and for
protecting 'enemies' within the service apparatus of the Kremlin. Often
seen as a landmark in the escalation of the terror, the Enukidze Affair
seemed to represent the first political attack on an 'Old Bolshevik' with no
oppositionist past.

Actually, the affair was more complicated. Ezhov did indeed deliver a
blistering attack on Enukidze, complete with 'testimony' from the latter's
arrested subordinates. Ezhov argued that these Kremlin conspirators had
planned to assassinate Stalin as part of a Trotskyist–Zinovievist conspiracy (said to have been an outgrowth of the recent Kirov assassination),
and that Enukidze's lax attitude toward them made him at least negligent.
Secondarily, he accused Enukidze of having used official funds to provide
support to the families of certain Old Bolsheviks exiled by the Stalin
regime. Enukidze defended himself by noting that although there were of
course enemies in his apparatus, the same could be said of all Soviet
agencies, including the NKVD itself. He noted that his personal control
over his employees was neither better nor worse than that of other top
leaders.[46]

More interesting is the plenum's reaction to Ezhov's charges. Ezhov had concluded his remarks by formally proposing Enukidze's expulsion from the party Central Committee. But several of the speakers who followed Ezhov called for sterner penalties. Beria, Shkiriatov, and Akulov, for example, said that the officially proposed and approved expulsion from the Central Committee was not enough; Enukidze should be expelled from the party.[47] NKVD chief Iagoda, who is sometimes seen as being soft on persecution of party officials, called not only for Enukidze's expulsion from the party, but for his arrest and conviction: 'It is necessary to say that Enukidze not only facilitated the enemy, but that objectively he was also a sympathizer with counterrevolutionary terrorists'.[48]

Although it is possible that this was all part of a Stalin game to use others as stalking horses of repression, Stalin and his team seem rather to have been unprepared for this escalation of the attack on Enukidze. For his part, Stalin's comments on the speeches were limited to criticizing Enukidze's use of state funds to aid exiles, noting that Enukidze could have innocently used his own money for this without censure. His interjections never touched on the political side of the accusations, never supported Ezhov's terrorist characterization (or Iagoda's strong remedies), and were, in general, not particularly hostile.[49] L. M. Kaganovich then recounted to the plenum the Politburo's deliberations on proper punishment for Enukidze. He noted that at first Stalin had suggested only removing him from the national TsIK (*Tsentral'nyi Ispolnitel'nyi Komitet*, Central Executive Committee) and sending him to run the TsIK of the Transcaucasus. Then, when the matter seemed more serious (possibly after another Ezhov report to the Politburo), Stalin had agreed to remove Enukidze from the TsIK system altogether and to send him to run a resort in Kislovodsk, concluding that expulsion from the Central Committee was in fact warranted 'to make an example'. Kaganovich took no position on the newly proposed harsher punishments, but his remarks suggested that Ezhov's softer proposal had been thought out ahead of time.[50]

Finally, at the end of the plenum, the matter came to a vote. Ezhov's original, officially approved proposal (to expel Enukidze only from the Central Committee) passed unanimously. Then they voted on 'a second suggestion by a series of speakers, as a supplement', to expel Enukidze from the party. This proposal passed, 'by a majority' in show of hands.[51]

But, oddly enough, Enukidze's surprise expulsion from the party was not the end of the story. Exactly one year later, at the June 1936 Plenum of the Central Committee, the Enukidze affair resurfaced. Molotov, who was chairing the meeting, said that at the beginning of 1936, Enukidze had applied for readmission to the party. That had been too soon for consideration (Stalin interjected: 'That would have been to expel him at one plenum and accept him at the next'.). After Molotov observed that readmitting him would make Enukidze very happy, and after Stalin spoke in favor, the plenum voted to approve his readmission.[52]

In a final contradictory twist, though, Enukidze was never readmitted to the party. Shortly after the June 1936 approval, Enukidze applied for a party card to a primary party organization in Kharkov and was accepted. But two months later, his acceptance was overturned by the Kharkov City Party Organization.[53] The main event between approval of his readmission and rejection of it was Ezhov's ascension to leadership of the secret police. Apparently, Stalin changed his mind once again about Enukidze, and it is possible that Ezhov's new power in the fall of 1936 gave him the possibility to make his original attack stick once and for all. Enukidze was arrested and shot in 1937.

In this atmosphere of contradictory initiatives, consider as well the strange story of the fall of Iu. Piatakov at about the same time.[54] In mid-1936, Stalin decided to bring Zinoviev, Kamenev, and others to trial on capital charges. Even though the defendants included other ex-Trotskyists, Piatakov was appointed to be one of the state's prosecution witnesses (*obvinitel'*). But on August 10, in connection with ongoing searches and interrogations, Iagoda and Ezhov uncovered 'evidence' of Piatakov's connection to 'enemies' and immediately sent it to Stalin. Ezhov then confronted Piatakov on August 11, telling him that because of this compromising material, Stalin had decided to remove him as one of the prosecution's helpers; on the same day, Ezhov drafted an order for Stalin to sign appointing Piatakov chief of the Chirchikstroi construction project.[55] Nevertheless, in the course of the Zinoviev–Kamenev trial, Piatakov was indeed mentioned as a possible conspirator by one of the defendants. But by the time the court transcript was published, Piatakov's name had again disappeared as a culprit.[56] Thus, in the course of one month, Piatakov had gone from trial accuser to construction director to potential trial defendant to a mysterious limbo. Someone had changed his mind more than once.

During this time, a confused and desperate Piatakov hardly displayed moderation or humanism; he told Ezhov that he was willing personally to execute Zinoviev, Kamenev, and even his (Piatakov's) former wife, should they turn out to be guilty! He wrote to Stalin on the same date, pledging his loyalty and repeating his dramatic offer, which Ezhov characterized as 'absurd'.[57]

Stalin did not finally decide on Piatakov's arrest until September 12, when he sanctioned his expulsion from the party and arrest. Even then, as Ezhov was arresting economic managers and grilling Piatakov, Stalin's Central Committee secretariat was ordering Ezhov to release several high-ranking industrial leaders.[58] One hand seemed not to know what the other was doing.

There can be several possible explanations for such zigging and zagging. First, Stalin may simply have been trying to project an image of liberalism to cover his administration of terror. That would certainly have been a wise policy for him, and it is difficult to believe that it is not at least part of the explanation. But several facts mitigate against it as the complete answer.

First, Stalin clearly and publicly associated himself with the hunt for enemies after the February 1937 Plenum of the Central Committee, thus destroying any reputation he might have been building as a liberal. We now know that there was resistance to the growing terror on the parts of some low-level functionaries.[59] Stalin's liberal 1934-7 measures zigging and zagging away from terror would have sent the 'wrong signals' and would have supported those trying to *block* repression. That would seem to be counterproductive to a careful Stalin plan for terror.

Another explanation might be based on the existence of a high-level, antirepression Stalinist faction, variously said to consist of Kirov, Ordzhonikidze, Kuibyshev, Postyshev, and others, that attempted to block the designs of Stalin, Ezhov, Kaganovich, and Molotov. The contradictory twists and turns are thus explained by Stalin probing and retreating in the face of antipolice sentiment in the politburo.[60]

The trouble here is that anti-Ezhov liberals in high places are hard to find before the main onslaught of the terror in mid-1937.[61] As we have seen, Kirov is a poor candidate for moderation. Ordzhonikidze, for his part, tried to defend his own subordinates (particularly industrial managers) against Ezhov's depredations and there are persistent but dubious stories that he tried to intercede for Piatakov.[62] Although his lieutenants invoked his name posthumously with the claim that he had opposed the hunt for enemies in industry,[63] Ordzhonikidze does not seem to have objected to terror in general, including that directed against Zinoviev, Kamenev, and Bukharin, and was in fact asked by Stalin to give the main speech on wrecking in industry to the February 1937 Plenum of the Central Committee.[64]

P. P. Postyshev, who according to the oral tradition stood up at the February Plenum in protest against Ezhov, actually interrupted the latter's February 1937 remarks several times with cries of 'Right!'[65] In fact, he would be expelled from the party a year later for being too fierce in his hunt for enemies in the Ukraine.[66] Similarly, rumors that S. V. Kosior, who would be shot the following year, was some kind of closet Bukharinist turn out to be false: At the February 1937 Plenum, he was one of the most vociferous supporters of the Ezhov line.[67] As of this writing, no evidence has been found for a moderate bloc, the influence of which might explain Stalin's strange zigs and zags on the eve of the *Ezhovshchina*. Evidence from the December 1936 and February 1937 Central Committee plenums suggests that no speaker defended the victims of Ezhov and his NVKD.

We must therefore at least entertain a third possible explanation, that the confused and contradictory evolution of the repression before mid-1937 was the product of indecision and chaos. For example, the decision to destroy N. I. Bukharin also followed strange and contradictory twists and turns. Although Ordzhonikidze may have slowed down the attack on industrial leaders, nobody seems to have opposed the crushing of Bukharin and it is difficult to credit the delays to anyone but Stalin.

Bukharin had not come under official suspicion until August 1936, when Ezhov initiated the process in a letter to Stalin suggesting that former rightists were implicated in the Zinovievist–Trotskyist 'plot'. Ezhov asked Stalin's permission to reinterrogate Uglanov, Riutin, and other rightists already sentenced on other charges. Stalin agreed.[68] During August and September, Ezhov worked diligently to assemble 'evidence' against Bukharin by pressuring former rightists Uglanov, Riutin, Rovinskii, and Kotov. The culmination of his effort was a dramatic confrontation between Bukharin and the already arrested G. Sokol'nikov on September 8 in the presence of Kaganovich, Vyshinski, and Ezhov. The attempt failed, because at the meeting Sokol'nikov denied personal knowledge of Bukharin's participation in the treasonous opposition 'bloc'. The record of the confrontation was sent to Stalin and two days later Vyshinskii announced that there was insufficient evidence to proceed legally against Bukharin. Only Stalin could have decided this, and we have no evidence that anyone was defending Buhkarin.[69]

Ezhov continued to smear the former leader of the rightists. Articles appeared in the press questioning the loyalties and records of both Bukharin and Rykov, and on October 7, 1936, Ezhov sent Stalin the protocol of the interrogation of former rightist M. Tomskii's secretary, who accused Bukharin of being part of a 'counterrevolutionary organization'. In November, several of Bukharin's former editorial colleagues were arrested and interrogated, and on November 23, V. I. Nevskii, former head of the Lenin Library, directly accused Bukharin of leading a 'terrorist center'. Altogether in the last quarter of 1936 and the first month of 1937, Ezhov sent his boss more than sixty anti-Bukharin protocols of interrogations and personal confrontations.[70]

December 4–7, 1936, saw a Central Committee Plenum that approved the upcoming (second) show trial of Piatakov *et al.*, and discussed the question of Bukharin's possible guilt. Ezhov gave a report summarizing the mounting 'evidence' against Bukharin as leader of the 'terrorist plot' along with the Trotskyists.[71] Stalin's role and position at the December Plenum are unclear. During the four days of the plenum, Ezhov arranged several 'confrontations' between Bukharin and his already broken accusers, and continued to send Stalin protocols of damning interrogations every day. Before, during, and after the December 1936 Plenum, Bukharin denied his guilt.[72] Stalin debated Bukharin at the plenum, demanded explanations and recantations from him, and even told the Central Committee members, 'You can shoot [him] if you want, it's up to you'.[73] None of the other speakers questioned the case against Bukharin, and every single speaker

accused him. Nevertheless, *Stalin* ended the meeting by 'abruptly' suggesting only to continue 'verification' and to postpone any decision on
Bukharin.[74]

Between this plenum and the next, in February–March 1937, Ezhov had
forced K. Radek and Piatakov to testify directly against Bukharin, and
perhaps it was the cooperation of such big fish that finally tipped the scales
against Bukharin. In any case, we know that Stalin directly attacked
Bukharin at the February 1937 Plenum. We are told that Stalin 'pressured'
the February Plenum's participants, although given the apparent lack of
opposition to Ezhov the previous December, it is not clear why he should
need to do so. Again, it seems that nobody at the plenum defended
Bukharin and Rykov.[75]

A subcommission, chaired by Anastas Mikoian, was formed at the
February Plenum to decide the fate of Bukharin. According to folklore,
all the committee's participants voted to 'arrest, try, and shoot' Bukharin
and Rykov.[76] Again, the lore is wrong; documents show that the event went
quite differently and showed continued indecision and confusion, even on
Stalin's part. The final protocol of the committee meeting shows that
everyone indeed voted to expel Bukharin and Rykov from the party. Ezhov,
Budennyi, Manuilskii, Shvernik, Kosarev, and Iakir were for shooting them
outright. Postyshev, Shkiriatov, Kosior, Petrovoskii, and Litvinov were for
sending them to trial but forbidding a death sentence. The rest voted 'for
the suggestion of Comrade Stalin', which in the final text is given as: 'to
expel from the party, not to send them to trial, and to refer the matter to
the NKVD for further investigation'.

But what exactly was 'the suggestion of Comrade Stalin'? A careful
comparison of the first and final drafts shows that Stalin's suggestion was
originally quite different. He had at first suggested that Bukharin and
Rykov be expelled from the party, *not* sent to trial, and merely exiled
[*vyslat'*]. This was the 'suggestion of Comrade Stalin' that committee
members supported at the meeting when, after Stalin's remarks, they voted
'tozhe' or 'za predlozhenie Tovarishcha Stalina'. Later, apparently in
Mikoian's hand, the draft was corrected to read 'refer the matter to the
NKVD', instead of simple exile. When was the change made and why?
What did Stalin really say? We still do not know.[77]

Finally, even in the printed final version of the resolution, personally
drafted by Stalin, we find the strange formulation, 'The Central Committee Plenum considers that comrades [!] Bukharin and Rykov deserve to be
immediately expelled from the party and sent to trial. But because, in
contrast to the Trotskyists and Zinovievists, they had not received a
serious party reprimand,' they should simply be expelled and referred to
the NKVD.[78]

Of course, Piatakov and Bukharin were eventually shot, and the decision
to transfer Bukharin and Rykov to the NKVD in March 1937 was an

accusation, if not a final condemnation.[79] There has never been any doubt that once Stalin decided someone was an enemy, he showed no mercy or vacillation. The only question is what he decided and when. He was assuredly cruel, vindictive, and sadistic. At the same time, the evidence actually suggests rather the opposite of any careful plan for terror. There was certainly repression; but there is no evidence of a planned straight line to it. There was, on the other hand, considerable indecision, ad hoc campaigns, false starts, and retreats.

The current state of our knowledge provides few details about the roles of Stalin and others in the mounting repression. In particular, the new information presented permits more than one view of the role of N. I. Ezhov. The first, and easiest, is the traditional one in which Ezhov is merely Stalin's tool with no independent position or initiative. He would receive his deadly instructions orally from Stalin and thereby become (for Stalin) a conveniently visible administrator of repression. Any criticism of repression could be deflected toward Ezhov by Stalin, who could pose as a reluctant follower of the NKVD chief at party meetings and other venues. In the end, Stalin could dispose of his tool quietly when the need had passed. Stalin's devious cruelty and our knowledge of his personal participation in the repression makes this version attractive and plausible.

But the sequence of events presented in the written evidence is also consistent with a second scenario (not mutually exclusive with the first) in which Ezhov pursued initiatives, prepared dossiers, and pushed certain investigations in order to promote his own agenda. Although that agenda was often the same as Stalin's, it may not have been identical. We know, for example, that although Stalin agreed to review a (no doubt grisly) manuscript Ezhov was writing on how opposition inevitably becomes terrorism, he never allowed publication.[80] We also know that in his struggle to undermine Iagoda and take over the NKVD, Ezhov did not get Stalin's final nod until after nearly two years of bickering.[81] Events seem to show that in the cases of Piatakov and Bukharin, Ezhov and others were possibly ahead of Stalin in pushing the need for severity. Maybe Stalin was only playing at being reluctant, making Ezhov 'prove' his (or their) case for a doubting audience of Central Committee 'liberals'. But we have seen that, sadly, no such audience seems to have existed. Especially in the internal secret documents we now know about, Stalin had no need to be coy. Certainly he supported Ezhov at key points in the latter's struggle with Iagoda, at the February 1937 Plenum and afterwards. But at specific points along the way it is not always clear whether Ezhov was actively promoting or simply administering repression.[82]

No one has ever doubted or questioned Stalin's participation in organizing the repression. Even from his published writings, not to mention myriad other sources, we have always known that he was an active organizer of the violence and was the person most responsible for the repression.[83] But much of the new information seems to support revisionist doubts about older interpretations and their source bases. The confirmation is necessarily oblique, because new documents and accompanying commentary have to date been chosen and published to illustrate a different interpretation: the innocence of prominent party victims and Stalin's direct organization of their repression. It may well be that Stalin killed Kirov as part of a bloody long-term plan. On the other hand, the documents we have today do not prove it and unavoidably provide details that support alternative or revisionist views of events.

Given the one-sided nature of discourse in the field, it may perhaps not be gratuitous to point out some of the minor, more technical aspects of the revisionist view of the origins of the terror that are being confirmed by new archival evidence. First, when Stalin said in the fall of 1936 that the NKVD was 'four years behind' in uncovering oppositionist plots, he was indeed referring to the 1932 united oppositionist bloc brokered by Trotsky and I. N. Smirnov, and not to the Riutin platform. The 1932 bloc was, then, the catalytic even in the escalation of Stalinist terror.[84] Second, we also now have confirmtion of the fact that party expulsions in the 1935–7 period (that is, after the Kirov assassination and before the onslaught of the terror) were steadily *decreasing* in number, even after the first show trial of summer 1936 and were not especially directed against oppositionists, 'wreckers', or 'spies'.[85] Third, the January 1938 Central Committee resolution criticizing excessive vigilance and unjust persecutions was directed against regional party machines and their leaders who, like Postyshev, expelled rank-and-file members to divert attention from their own people. It had nothing to do with the NKVD.[86] Finally, it now seems clear that regional (oblast) party 'family circles' were able to protect their own from arrest until 1937,[87] because of their power and ability to direct the fire toward the rank and file.

Certainly confirmation of no such technical point 'proves' the revisionist case. But the growing fund of archival evidence does show that the period preceding the great terror was complicated and contradictory and the questions raised or confirmed by the new materials are persistent.

In all these matters, we must constantly question our sources. The evidence presented is based on sensitive documents long suppressed. It might be objected that documents and archives should not be our main sources for the repression. Indeed, we must consider the possibility that they have been altered or falsified. Fearful, culpable, and powerful officials over the years since 1937 certainly would have reason to take an interest in the paper trail of these crimes, and such people were capable of far more than adjusting the documentary record. Certainly, the record is incomplete and we must maintain a healthy suspicion of all official sources from the 1930s.[88] But simply on the basis of suspicion and without any evidence, it would be rash to decide a priori that the archival record is false. Until and unless independent historians and documentary experts are able to examine all the sensitive documents in their physical form and contexts, the scholarly community is not in a position finally to establish their veracity – or lack of credibility for that matter.[89]

Undoubtedly, many will not be convinced by the appearance of anomalies in the traditional paradigmatic folklore of the Kirov assassination and Stalin's plan for repression. In other areas ranging from agriculture to industry to institutional administration, scholars have noted the patchwork, reactive nature of Stalinist decisions, which often seemed to follow events rather than make them. Although we can recognize his hesitation and bungling on all other issues, we seem to have difficulty accepting them when it comes to terror, even though information on politics in the 1930s seems to permit the parallel thesis that there were strange moments of indecision. It is easier to reject contradictory evidence with the deus ex machina of Stalin's supposed cleverness: All twists and turns, hesitations and contradicctions are thus the result of his incredible deviousness, sadism, or calculating shrewdness. There is really no counter to such ahistorical assertions, except that they are based on faith: the a priori presumption of a plan and the belief that anomalies were intentionally part of it. Such elaborate constructs are unnecessary to explain events; the simplest explanation with the fewest assumptions and consistent with the evidence is usually the best.

We need not turn Stalin into an omniscient and omnipotent demon in order to comprehend his evil. Indeed, making him into a superman diminishes the real horror of the period. Stalin was a cruel but ordinary mortal unable to see the future and with a limited ability to create and control it. He was not a master planner, and studies of all of his other policies before and after the 1930s have shown that he stumbled into everything from collectivization to foreign policy. Stalin's colossal felonies, like most violent crimes everywhere, were of the unplanned erratic kind. His evil, like Eichmann's, was ordinary and of this world; it was banally human and is more horrifying for being so.

Notes

1 In late 1991, the author was told in Moscow that Stalin's father was really Alexander Prlszewski, the Siberian biologist after whom the famous diminutive horse is named.

2 I have discussed this problem in connection with older 'sources' in *Origins of the Great Purges: The Soviet Communist Party Reconsidered, 1933–1938*, New York, 1985, 211–220. For more recent examples of invented dialog, see Anatoli Rybakov, *Children of the Arbat*, trans. by Harold Shukman, Boston, 1988; Anton Antonov-Ovseyenko, *The Time of Stalin: Portrait of Tyranny,* New York, 1980; Mikhail Shatrov, 'Dal'she, dal'she, dal'she', *Znamia*, no. 1, 1988.

A compilation of folklore about Stalin is presented in Iurii Borev, *Staliniada*, Moscow, 1990.

3 See A. V. Afanas'ev, (ed.), *Oni ne molchali*, Moscow, 1991; and A. N. Mertsalov (ed.), *Istoriia i stalinizm*, Moscow, 1991; O. V. Khlevniuk, *1937-i: Stalin, NKVD i sovetskoe obshchestvo*, Moscow, 1992; B. A. Starkov (ed.), *Na koleni ne vstanu*, Moscow, 1992, for examples of serious, evidence-based historical monographs.

4 See the accounts in *Izvestiia TsK KPSS*, no. 4, 1989, 42–73; no. 8, 1989, 78–94; no. 9, 1989, 30–50; and Dmitri Volkogonov, *Triumf i tragediia*, Moscow, 1989, vol. 1, part 2, 310 and passim. The present essay does not use the vast corpus of writings from *publitsisty* (journalists) that has appeared since 1985 in *Moscow News*, *Ogonek*, *Novyi mir*, and other journals. This material is almost always presented without footnotes, documents, or citations and it is impossible to verify the sources of information. Other opinions exist on the question; for works that incorporate such material see Robert C. Tucker, *Stalin in Power: The Revolution from Above, 1928–1941*, New York, 1990, and Robert Conquest, *The Great Terror: Stalin's Purge of the Thirties* (revised edition), Oxford, 1990.

5 'Rasstrel po raznariadke', *Trud*, June 4, 1992, 1. See also 'Iosif Stalin: "Vinovnykh sudit" uskorenno. PRIGOVOR–rasstrel', *Izvestiia*, June 10, 1992, 7.

6 From the personal archive of Comintern specialist F. I. Firsov, based on his archival notes from Dmitrov's diary. The author is deeply grateful to Professor Firsov for sharing his encyclopedic knowledge of repression in the Comintern.

7 See Tucker, *Stalin in Power*, 212, 238–242; Roy Medvedev, *Let History Judge: The Origins and Consequences of Stalinism* (revised edition), New York, 1989, 329–330.

8 For example, Medvedev, *Let History Judge*, 331–332.

9 This scenario of the Kirov affair comes to us almost entirely from two sources: the 1936 'Letter of an Old Bolshevik' (Boris I. Nicolaevsky, *Power and the Soviet Elite: 'The Letter of an Old Bolshevik' and Other Essays*, New York, 1965), and NKVD defector Alexander Orlov's *Secret History of Stalin's Crimes*, New York, 1953. Virtually all versions of the story inside and outside the USSR can be traced to one of these two original presentations.

10 S. V. Kulashov, O. V. Volobuev, E. I. Pivovar, *et al.*, *Nashe otechestvo. chast' II*, Moscow, 1991, 310; Boris A. Starkov, 'Ar'ergardnye boi staroi partiinoi gvardii', in Afanas'ev (ed.), *Oni ne molchali*, 215; Khlevnuik, *1937*, 46.

11 For a recent example of Moscow-based historians quoting such Western stories, see B. A. Starkov, 'Delo Riutina', in Afanas'ev, (ed.), *Oni ne molchali*, 170.

12 Roy A. Medvedev, *Nikolay Buhkarin*, New York, 1980, 115–118; Robert H. McNeal, *Stalin: Man and Ruler*, New York, 1988, 355; Jerry Hough and Merle Fainsod, *How the Soviet Union is Governed*, Cambridge, MA, 1979, 159–60; Getty, *Origins*, 214–216.

13 Anna Larina, *Nezabyvaemoe*, Moscow, 1989, 272–289. Of course, Larina's account, written fifty years after the event, should not be uncritically accepted as gospel on the matter. Still, her evidence supports the mounting criticisms of the 'Letter' made by Western historians.

14 *Izvestiia TsK*, no. 6, 1989, 103–115; no. 3, 1990, 150–178.

15 *XVII s"ezd Vsesoiuznoi Kommunisticheskoi Partii (b) 27 ianvaria–10 fevralia 1934g: stenograficheskii otchet*, Moscow, 1934, 252, 253–259. Leon Trotsky, *The Revolution Betrayed*, New York, 1937, 286; Grigori Tokaev, *Betrayal of an Ideal*, Bloomington, 1955, 241, *Sotsialisticheskii vestnik*, no. 8, April 1934, 19.

16 'Vokrug ubiistva Kirova', *Pravda*, Nov. 4, 1991, 4; and *XVII s"ezd*, 251–259.

17 Personal communications to the author from Boris A. Starkov and Oleg
    Khlevniuk. See also Francesco Benvenuti, 'Kirov in Soviet Politics, 1933–
    1934', Discussion Paper no. 8, Soviet Industrialization Project Series, University
    of Birmingham, 1977. The memoir of one of Kirov's Leningrad co-workers can
    remember nothing from his experience with Kirov that suggests 'liberal' oppo-
    sition to Stalin: See Mikhail Rosliakov, 'Kak eto bylo', Zvezda, no. 7, 1989, 79–
    113.

18 D. Volkogonov, 'Triumf i tragediia', Oktiabr', no. 12, December 1988, 81,
    probably taken from F. Chuev's purported interviews with Molotov (Sto sorok
    besed s Molotovym, Moscow, 1991, 308, 322, 353). Molotov used the work
    massovik to describe Kirov. The authenticity of Chuev's book rests on a series
    of recorded tapes he made with Molotov. The tapes have not been scientifically
    authenticated, and Molotov's general veracity is of course questionable.

19 Various versions of the story give 282, 123, 125, 2–4, 5–6, or 3, as the number
    voting against Stalin. See L. S. Shaumian's 'Na rubezhe pervykh piatiletok. K
    30-letiiu XVII s"ezda partii', Pravda, Feb. 7, 1964, where the number 300 is
    given.

20 Izvestiia TsK, no. 7, 1989, 114–121.

21 O. Shatunovskaia, 'Fal'sifikatsiia', Argumenty i fakty, no. 22, 1990.

22 Izvestiia TsK, no. 7, 1989, 120; 'Vokrug ubiistva Kirova', 4. Shatunovskaia
    claims to have been in close contact with Khrushchev at the time and thus
    presumably could not easily have been pressured to vote against her conscience.

23 We now know that there were at least two investigations in the 1960s: the
    Pel'she Commission and the Shvernik Commission. A. Iakovlev, 'O dekabr'skoi
    tragedii 1934 goda', Pravda, Jan. 28, 1991, p. 3.

24 'Vokrug ubiistva Kirova', 4.

25 This would also explain why Zaporozhets received light punishment for negli-
    gence in the Kirov killing.

26 'Vokrug ubiistva Kirova', 4.

27 See A. Rybakov's introduction in Ogonek, no. 46, 1989.

28 'Vokrug ubiistva Kirova', 4.

29 Izvestiia TsK, no. 7, 1989, 69; Izvestiia TsK, no. 1, 1990, 39. He told this to
    Ezhov, Kosarev (head of the Komsomol), Bukharin (editor of Izvestiia), and
    Mekhlis (editor of Pravda). See Izvestiia TsK, no. 1, 1990, 65–93 for arrests of
    Zinovievists, which began on December 8 and which coincided with random
    shootings of former White Guards, already in prison.

30 See the handling of the case of Ia. S. Tseitlin, former Leningrad Komsomol
    leader, related in Izvestiia TsK, no. 1, 1990, 50.

31 Iakovlev, 'O dekabi'skoi tragedii 1934 goda', 3. Of course, Stalin may have
    ordered preparation of such reports.

32 Pravda, Dec. 23, 1934. A few days later, the regime changed its mind again, and
    Zinoviev and Kamenev were brought to trial the next month.

33 'Vokrug ubiistva Kirova', 4. Iakovlev angrily charged that the investigating
    team had improperly leaked a memo he wrote to them: Iakovlev, 'O dekabr'skoi
    tragedii 1934 goda', 1.

34 Iakovlev wrote that a verdict on the Kirov matter is mainly important as an
    indicator of whether Stalin or socialism was to blame for the terror. 'That is
    why knowing the truth means much more to us than merely satisfying our
    intellectual curiosity. That is why the question continues to retain political
    relevance'. Iakovlev, 'O dekabr'skoi tragedii 1934 goda', 4.

35 Iakovlev, 'O dekabr'skoi tragedii 1934 goda', 4. See Rosliakov ('Kak eto bylo'),

who was a Kirov intimate present that day in Smolny. See also Kirilina, 'Vystrely v Smolnom'.

36 See, for example, Rosliakov, 'Kak eto bylo', 111–113.

37 Anna Kirilina, 'Vystrely v Smolnom', *Rodina*, no. 1, 1989, 33–78.

38 Within the Russian Federation the number of criminal sentences in 1934 was more than 25% lower than the previous year. Verdicts against 'counterrevolutionaries' numbered some 4,300 in 1934, a drop of over 50% from the previous year. Estimates based on P. H. Juviler, *Revolutionary Law and Order*, New York/London, 1976, 50, 52.

39 *Rossiiskii tsentr khraneniia i izucheniia dokumentov noveishei istorii*, fond 17, opis 3 (Politburo), delo 943, list 10 (for Stalin and Ezhov's participation), and f. 17, op. 3, d. 954, l. 38 for the resulting 'polozhenie' dated October 28, 1934. Compare its limited provisions to the more severe statement adopted in April of 1937: f. 17, op. 3, d. 986, l. 24. *RTsKhIDNI* is the recently renamed Central Party Archive (TsPA), Institut Marksizma–Leninizma. Because at this writing it is not clear which archival collections will ultimately be included in *RTsKhIDNI*, and because the following fond, opis, and delo numbers refer to the former *TsPA*, I shall hereafter cite this collection as *RTsKhIDNI* (TsPA).

40 Kulashov *et al.*, *Nashe otechestvo*, 309–10.

41 One of the most famous of these was 'Zadachakh partiino-organizatsionnoi i politiko-vospitatel'noi raboty', *Partiinoe stroitel'stvo*, no. 8, April 1935, 7–16. Its call for nurturing and promoting new cadres, collective leadership of party cells, and increased participation were picked up and discussed around the country. See Smolensk Archive files WKP 322, p. 81, and WKP 89, p. 3. See also David Seibert, 'Andrei Zhdanov and the Politics of Moderation', unpublished PhD. dissertation, University of California, Riverside, 1992.

42 *RTsKhIDNI (TsPA)*, f. 17, op. 2, d. 568, ll. 135–136. Later in this plenum, Stalin spoke specifically on this question. Circumstantial evidence suggests that he was genuinely concerned that too many of the rank and file had been expelled because such large numbers of disaffected former members could become an embittered opposition. See *TsGAOR SSSR*, f. 3316, op. 40, d. 22, for a second-hand TsIK report on Stalin's speech. Perhaps because his soft remarks in 1936 were hard to reconcile with his hard sentiments of the following year, they were removed from the archive. According to the pagination, they once were in *RTsKhIDNI (TsPA)*, f. 17, op. 2, d. 568, ll. 460–472.

43 *RTsKhIDNI (TsPA)*, f. 17, op. 21, d. 409, l. 171.

44 Getty, *Origins*, ch. 4. See J. Arch Getty, 'State and Society Under Stalin: Constitutions and Elections in the 1930s', *Slavic Review*, 50: 1, Spring 1991, 18–35 for a discussion of the importance of the new constitution to these developments. For the decrease in GULAG population, see V. Zemskov, 'Arkhipelag GULAG: glazami pisatelia i statistika', *Argumenty i fakty*, no. 45, 1989.

45 *RTsKhIDNI (TsPA)*, f. 7, op. 2, d. 62, ll. 3–10, and *Pravda*, June 12, 935. See also Zhdanov's mass-circulation pamphlet, *Uroki politicheskikh oshibok Saratovskogo kraikoma*, Moscow, 1935. See also 'The preparation of party organizations for elections to the USSR Supreme Soviet under the new electoral system and the corresponding reorganization of party political work', *Pravda*, Mar. 6, 1937.

46 *RTsKhIDNI (TsPA)*, f. 17, op. 2, d. 542, ll. 55–86 for Ezhov's report; and ll. 125–41 for Enukidze's defense.

47 *RTsKhIDNI (TsPA)*, f. 17, op. 2, d. 542, ll. 87, 07, 120.

48 *RTsKhIDNI (TsPA)*, f. 17, op. 2, d. 542, ll. 175.

49 *RTsKhIDNI (TsPA)*, f. 17, op. 2, d. 542, ll. 165, 170, for example.

50 *RTsKhIDNI (TsPA)*, f. 17, op. 2, d. 547, l. 66.
51 *RTsKhIDNI (TsPA)*, f. 17, op. 2, d. 547, l. 70. Unfortunately, the actual vote was not recorded.
52 *RTsKhIDNI (TsPA)*, f. 17, op. 2, d. 568, ll. 165–8. Again, Stalin's 1936 remarks may have seemed incompatible with his hard line of the following year; his remarks were removed from the archive. Formerly, they were *RTsKhIDNI (TsPA)*, f. 17, op. 2, d. 547, l. 167.
53 *TRsKhIDNI (TsPA)*, f. 17, op. 21, d. 5258. For a Gorbachev-era account of the Enukidze affair, which manages not to mention the strange twists of Enukidze's fate, see *Izvestiia TsK*, no. 7, 1989, 86–93.
54 A Trotskyist in the 1920s, Piatakov had broken with the left opposition and in the 1930s had been working in industry. In mid-1936, he was Ordzhonikidze's Deputy Commissar of Heavy Industry.
55 *Ivestiia TsK*, no. 9, 1989, 36–7. This was another strange appointment if Stalin *planned* to later accuse Piatakov of industrial wrecking, which ultimately he would do two months later. Technically, of course, the appointment of the 'industrial wrecker' Piatakov to head a construction project made Stalin guilty of wrecking, according to the mores of the time.
56 Conquest, *Great Terror*, 102.
57 *Izvestiia TsK*, no. 9, 1989, 36–7.
58 See O. V. Khlevniuk, '1937 god: protivodeistvie repressiiam', in Afanas'ev, (ed.), *Oni ne molchali*, 26–27. Khlevniuk believes that this liberalism took place when Stalin was out of town, but it is difficult to believe that Central Committee Secretariat orders to Ezhov could have been issued without Stalin's initiative or approval.
59 See Afanas'ev, (ed.), *Oni ne molchali*, for cases of resistance and reluctance by some mid- and junior-level procurators, army, and even police officers.
60 Robert Conquest, *The Great Terror: A Reassessment*, New York, 1990, is the best presentation of this view. See especially Chapters 4–6.
61 Later, in June 1937, Central Committee members Piatnitskii and Kaminskii spoke against Ezhov, but by then the terror was in full swing and they were swept away in short order.
62 See Khlevniuk, *1937*, 115–144, although Khlevniuk notes that there is no documentary evidence that Ordzhonikidze tried to save Piatakov. See also *RTsKhIDNI (TsPA)*, f. 17, op. 2, d. 573, l. 33, for Ordzhonikidze's telegram 'completely approving and voting yes' on the question of Piatakov's expulsion from the party in September 1936. Similarly, shortly after Piatakov's execution, Ordzhonkidze told a meeting of his department heads that 'damned Piatakov' had been a real enemy and that they must be continually vigilant: *RTsKhIDNI (TsPA)*, f. 85, op. 29, d. 156, ll. 56–63.
63 *RTsKhIDNI (TsPA)*, f. 17, op. 2, d. 612, tom. 2, l. 39 (Gurevich's speech to the February 1937 Plenum); and Khlevniuk, '1937 god: protivodeistvie repressiiam'.
64 The draft of the speech Ordzhonkidze was preparing to give to the February 1937 Plenum, as chief reporter on wrecking in industry, was approved by Stalin and was in character with the hard line of the times: *KTsKhIDNI (TsPA)*, f. 558, op. 1, d. 3350, ll. 1–16.
65 *RTsKhIDNI (TsPA)*, f. 17, op. 2, d. 612, tom. 2, l. 57. The supposed liberal Postyshev also suggested burning down churches to quell religion (tom. 1, l. 27), and complained that leaders were trying to protect their own against Ezhov's rightful cause. Postyshev did, in fact, say that it was 'strange' that one of his subordinates had 'suddenly' become a Trotskyist in 1934, but

concluded that of course the man had always been an enemy. He was not interrupted by Stalin, as the folklore has it (tom. 2, l. 26).

66 *RTsKhIDNI (TsPA)*, f. 17, op. 2, d. 639, ll. 13–33.

67 See his attacks on Gurevich in *RTsKhIDNI (TsPA)*, f. 17, op. 2, d. 612, tom. 2, l. 39; and on Postyshev (tom. 2, ll. 10–12, 15). His speech to the February Plenum called for a virtual witchhunt against Trotskyists in the Ukraine.

68 It was in connection with this embryonic inquiry that prosecutor Vyshinskii mentioned Bukharin and Rykov at the August show trial.

69 *Izvestiia TsK*, no. 5, 1989, 70–1. The writers of the account in *Izvestiia TsK* call this only a 'maneuver' (p. 72), but do not say why or against whom. That Stalin knew of and approved of the decision not to bring Bukharin and Rykov to trial (although he later claimed to have had doubts) is shown in *RTsKhIDNI (TsPA)*, f. 17, op. 2, d. 575, l. 98.

70 *Izvestiia TsK*, no. 5, 1989, 73–4, no. 2, 1990, 48, no. 5, 1989, 84.

71 *RTsKhIDNI (TsPA)*, f. 17, op. 2, d. 575, ll. 6–68.

72 *RTsKhIDNI (TsPA)*, f. 17, op. 2, d. 575, ll. 69–93.

73 *RTsKhIDNI (TsPA)*, f. 17, op. 2, d. 576, l. 67.

74 *Izvestiia TsK*, no. 5, 1989, 72–7.

75 *Izvestiia TsK*, no. 5, 1989, 77–9. The materials of the February Plenum, including Bukharin's defence, are being published in *Voprosi istorii*, beginning with no. 2–3, 1992, 3–44.

76 See, for example, Roy Medvedev, *Let History Judge*, 367.

77 *Izvestiia TsK*, no. 5, 1989, 81–3. For the originals, see *RTsKhIDNI (TsPA)*, f. 17, op. 2, d. 577, ll. 30–3. It is of course possible that the disrepancy was only a clerical or stenographic error, although this would require confusing 'vyslat' with 'napravit' delo Bukharina-Rkyova v NKVD'. And why did the researchers *Izvestiia TsK* include the contradictory photostat without comment? Could it be that they found their political mandate (to show a straight-line Stalin plan of terror) was inconsistent with the evidence?

78 Indeed, the oral tradition got the entire February Plenum wrong. Although many accounts deal with the plenum only in connection with the terror issue (see, for example, Medvedev, *Let History Judge*, 364–8), the real – and only – argument at the meeting was about Zhdanov's and Kalinin's calls to subject regional party secretaries to secret ballot elections. See the uproar that greeted this suggestion in *RTsKhIDNI (TsPA)*, f. 17, op. 2, d. 62, tom. 1 ll. 10–42. This substantially confirms the earlier speculation in Getty, *Origins*, 137–49.

79 Stalin and Ezhov did not put the question of Bukharin and Rykov's trial and 'physical liquidation' before the Central Committee until June 1937, in the hysteria and savage retribution that followed the fall of the military leaders.

80 *Izvestiia TsK*, no. 5, 1989, 73.

81 For this struggle, see *Izvestiia TsK*, no. 9, 1989, 30–50. Although Stalin sometimes supported Ezhov against Iagoda in 1935 and 1936 (at one point even calling up Iagoda and threatening to 'smash his snout' [*modru nab'em*]), Stalin did not replace him until the fall of 1936.

82 B. A. Starkov writes that at the time of his fall, '[Ezhov's] primary crime, however, consisted in the fact that he had not informed Stalin of his actions'. Stalin's relationship to Ezhov's predecessor Iagoda was equally complex. In March 1936, Iagoda proposed to Stalin that all Trotskyists everywhere – even those convicted already – should be resentenced to five additional years out of hand and that any of them involved in 'terror' should quickly be shot. Stalin referred Iagoda's plan to Vyshinskii for a legal opinion, which came back positive in six days. Although Iagoda was ready to move immediately, it was

nearly two months before Stalin issued an order to this effect. See *Izvestiia TsK*, no. 9, 1989, 35–6.

83 Getty, *Origins*, 8–9, 206.

84 Getty, *Origins*, 119–122; *RTsKhIDNI (TsPA)*, f. 17, op. 2, d. 577, l. 9a.

85 Roughly 264,000 were expelled in 1935, 51,500 in 1936. In both years of 'chistka', only 5.5% of those expelled were accused of oppostion and 0.9% for being 'spies' or having 'connections to spies'. Class–alien origins and personal corruption comprised the overwhelming majority. *RTsKhIDNI (TsPA)*, f. 17, op. 120, d. 278, ll. 2–3.

86 Getty, *Origins*, 185–189; *RTsKhIDNI (TsPA)*, f. 17, op. 2, d. 639.

87 Getty, *Origins*, ch. 6; *RTsKhIDNI (TsPA)*, f. 17, op. 71, d. 34 lists party leaders expelled and arrested in the provinces. Although a few raion secretaries were expelled before 1937, it is difficult to find a single obkom official who fell before that year. But in 1937, the oblast party organizations were suddenly decimated.

88 Getty, *Origins*, 8.

89 We do know, however, that those who have seen, used, and publicized such documents both in the 1960s and 1980s have done so under an official and quite proper mandate to show Stalin's connection with the repression, and would presumably have alerted us to any possibility of documentary fakery. Yet no such claims or suspicions have been voiced by those working with the documents.

Chapter 4 Rationality and irrationality

Reading 7 *A debate on collectivization: was Stalin really necessary?*

J. R. MILLAR AND A. NOVE

Introductory remarks

Jerry F. Hough

In all scholarly fields, there are certain questions or subjects which for a time become the focus of intense interest and study by a disproportionate number of the best minds in the field. In Soviet studies of the last decade, the question that, more than any other, has caught the attention of a generation of scholars and provided the basis for exciting reanalysis and debate has been the nature of the 1920s and the First Five-Year Plan – that is, the origins of the Stalin system and the validity of the basic assumptions of the totalitarian model which embodied our understanding of those origins.

There have been a number of major (and, of course, controversial) attacks upon our fundamental assumptions about the Soviet system. It has been argued that Lenin came to accept NEP as the long-term road to communism rather than a temporary retreat; that Bukharin's program rather than Stalin's represented the logical culmination of Leninism; that 'the revolution from above' of 1928–29 actually had many societal sources; that there was little need for massive renewal of capital stock in the First Five-Year Plan period and that relatively little occurred; that women were perhaps the major 'source of accumulation' during the early industrialization drive; that Lysenko's enshrinement as genetics tsar had little relationship to Marxist ideology other than an *ex post facto* one. All of these propositions have been forcefully advanced – and challenged – by leading scholars of the last decade.[1]

Of all the events of the 1920s and early 1930s, however, none has received more serious reconsideration than the collectivization decision of 1928–29. At the center of attention has been not only the process by which the decision was taken, but, more important, the relationship of the decision to the industrialization drive and 'the Soviet model of economic development'. One of the leading figures in that reconsideration is James R. Millar of the Department of Economics of the University of Illinois (Urbana), and he has been asked to begin this discussion with a summary of the revisionist position as he sees it.[2] The other participant in the debate is one of the most distinguished economists in the history of Soviet studies, Alec Nove of the University of Glasgow. The actual title of the debate is taken from the title of a famous article which he wrote in 1962.[3]

What's wrong with the 'standard story'?

J. R. Millar

There are several possibilities as to what the somewhat elliptical title 'Was Stalin really necessary?' actually means. One is: Was Stalin somehow inevitable? Historians of the Soviet period have almost all tended toward some degree of determinism in answering this question and have suggested that to some extent Stalin represented the culmination of forces set in motion at a much earlier date – say, at the turn of the century. But I am not going to charge Alec Nove with asserting some kind of historical inevitability. I take the title to mean: Was collectivization really necessary? Was it necessary in order to achieve the ends – that is, to achieve the rapid rate of industrialization – that the Soviets, in fact, achieved? As we proceed, I want to change the question from 'Was it necessary?' to 'Was it optimal, given the development objectives of the Soviet leadership?'

In dealing with this question, I could follow one of two strategies. I could attack on a very narrow corridor in hopes of overpowering my adversary with detailed statistics and highly abstruse formulations, or, on the contrary, I could attack broadly – launch a broadside against the standard interpretation for which the answer to the question 'Was Stalin really necessary?' is the culmination. I have elected the latter course – to take a running shot at the overall interpretation of what I am calling the 'standard story' of the role of agriculture in industrialization in the Soviet Union. We shall begin at the beginning, and we shall conclude at the end of the First Five-Year Plan. Along the way, I hope to attack a number of elements of what I consider to be the standard interpretation.

The most convenient recent summary of the standard story can be found in the new textbook by Paul R. Gregory and Robert C. Stuart, *Soviet*

Economic Structure and Performance, which is based on the work of most of the economic historians who studied the Soviet Union in the 1950s and early 1960s.[4] In abbreviated form, the story goes something like this: Once the Bolsheviks had gained control, once the Civil War had come to a close and it became obvious that it would be impossible to establish an economy on the principles underlying War Communism, the New Economy Policy (NEP) was introduced. Yevgeniy Preobrazhenskiy, among others, began to attempt to reconcile himself to the institutions of the New Economic Policy.[5] He noted that the policy established a mixed economy, and he argued that the socialist sector would obviously have to grow more rapidly than the private sector during NEP if the socialist revolution was to have a favorable outcome.

According to the standard story, however, Preobrazenskiy said much more than this. He is said to have claimed the need for very rapid industrialization and to have developed the concept of 'primitive socialist accumulation', which is translated in the standard story to mean 'exploiting the peasants in support of industrialization'. The story goes on to say that Nikolay Bukharin – perhaps the other major theorist of the period[6] – retorted with the argument that if the terms of trade were turned against the peasantry, or if the peasants were taxed heavily in any other way, the peasants would simply withdraw from the market, as they already allegedly had done during the 'scissors crisis' of 1922–24.[7]

Thus, the historical issue is presented as a dilemma. For the purposes of military defense against a possible renewed intervention by the West and for the purposes of establishing socialism in the Soviet Union, it was necessary for the economy to industrialize and modernize rapidly. The means proposed to do it – that is, taxing in one form or another the 80 to 85 percent of the population who were peasants – was said to be not feasible, for the peasantry would withdraw from the market and, doing so, would sabotage the possibility of rapid industrialization.

The standard story then turns from the dilemma of NEP to the grain crisis of 1927–28. Marketings of grain were off sharply at this time, and 'emergency measures' were taken in 1928 to confiscate hoards of grain from the peasantry. These emergency measures were ultimately followed by collectivization. According to the argument, the First Five-Year Plan, which had been approved in 1927, did call for a high rate of industrialization, and, just as had been foreseen, the peasants began – whether for political or economic reasons – to sabotage the hopes of industrialization in Soviet Russia.

Stalin then is said to have thought of something Preobrazhenskiy had not – coercion. He thought of forcing the peasants into the collective farm and thereby depriving them of discretion over the level of sowings and over the share of marketings. The state was therefore able to ensure rapid industrialization at the expense of the peasantry. The story asserts that collectivization *did work* in this sense, that it did permit the extraction or the mobilization of a surplus from the peasantry (grain marketings rose sharply during the First Five-Year Plan), and that this squeeze on the peasantry was a significant factor among the sources of rapid industrialization. Preobrazhenskiy was right, it is said, in terms of where the resources had to come from, but he didn't think of collectivization. Stalin was right *and necessary* because he saw that the extraction of the surplus required coercion, since peasants would not surrender the resources voluntarily, and because he was willing to supply the coercion.

That, briefly, is the standard story, and in many ways it is a neat one – easy to teach and easy to remember. Here was Preobrazhenskiy who had the principles clear as to what was necessary. There was Bukharin who pointed out the fatal flaw in the argument. While in Preobrazhenskiy's presumed view, this left a hopeless situation, Stalin arrived to resolve Preobrazhenskiy's dilemma. Collectivization was a necessary step if the Soviet Union was to achieve the rate of industrialization that it did in the 1930s. If the *only* way to achieve that rate of industrialization was through collectivization – if it was the single means available – the word 'necessary' would acquire the same value, or meaning, as the word optimal. From this it would follow that Stalin himself was also necessary – at least *given* the end. Necessary, but, of course, not necessarily desirable.

This is the standard story. What is wrong with it? The answer is – almost everything. Almost every single proposition, every fundament of the story, is either misleading, false, or wrong-headed.

The first problem with the standard story is that Alexander Erlich's famous article on Preobrazhenskiy contains more of Erlich (and of John Maynard Keynes) than it does of Preobrazhenskiy.[8] Erlich read a great deal more intelligence, consistency, and meaningfulness – particularly contemporary economic meaningfulness – into Preobrazhenskiy's writings than was ever there, and particularly more than was ever there during the time of the industrialization debate itself, for Preobrazhenskiy continued to refine his arguments long after the original debate was over.

Preobrazhenskiy spoke of primitive socialist accumulation, and many mistakenly think that this concept is merely analogous to Marx's primitive capitalist accumulation. (The people who say this have not understood what Marx meant by primitive capitalist accumulation.) What Preobrazhenskiy called for in his discussion of primitive socialist accumulation was simply the New Economic Policy. He says so very clearly in several footnotes and in the text of *The New Economics (Novaya ekonomika)*. His proposal was little more than that the terms of trade be turned against the peasantry as a way of financing industrialization.

The reason for Preobrazhenskiy's proposal was very simple. Given the size of the private sector and the size of the public sector, socialism could succeed in Russia only if the public sector were to grow more rapidly than the private. Otherwise, the country would lapse back into a private economy. He argued for a more rapid public growth, and this required intercepting surplus value created in the private sector and transferring it into the public sector. Preobrazhenskiy also called for 'self-exploitation' by the workers in the public sector. In his view, rapid growth required not just exploitation of the peasants, therefore – the proletariat would also have to make sacrifices to finance industrialization. Preobrazhenskiy made a very important point that people in public finance will recognize: given the fact that the premodern direct taxes associated with the tsarist regime had been abandoned, the most efficient form of taxation was almost certainly some kind of indirect taxation, whether imposed through an indirect sales tax or by turning the terms of trade against the peasantry. On this point Preobrazhenskiy was right in terms of modern fiscal theory, but he was more correct generally than most people have realized, as we shall see.

In this debate, Bukharin argued that the peasants would withdraw from the market in the face of such taxation. There is no evidence at all for his assertion. On the other hand, numerous studies of Russian peasant behavior in the 19th century and early 20th century by Russian scholars (one notable example is A. V. Chayanov[9]) suggest that the peasantry would *not* react in this way. In fairly undeveloped countries, peasants do respond to changes in relative prices rather quickly (usually given a year's lag, of course). Consequently, if the terms of trade turn against a *particular* product, the peasants will quit producing and/or marketing it and transfer their efforts to other products. This is true and well-established. But what happens when the terms of trade *turn as a whole against the peasantry*? They maintain or even increase their production and their marketings (or leave the farm for nonrural employment, but only where it is available). When, for example, the peasant family suffers an adverse change in its economic situation through the addition of an extra unproductive mouth to feed (whether a baby or an invalid doesn't matter), the response is for the working members of the family to work harder.[10] This effort of the family to maintain its standard of living in the face of a general adverse economic change takes place not only when there is the birth of a child, but also when there is a new tax, an across-the-board change in the terms of trade, and so forth. This is true not only of the Russian peasantry, but of every agricultural population for which any investigation has been made. For example, it was true of farmers in the United States during the 1930s. What's more, it was true of the Soviet peasants during the 1922–23 'scissors crisis', for, contrary to a widespread misconception in the profession today, they did not withdraw from the market then.[11]

One of the factors that made many people feel the peasants would withdraw from the market was a fallacious notion of peasant self-sufficiency. The problem is partly that, as W. W. Rostow once entitled an article, 'Marx was a city boy'.[12] So were the Bolsheviks, and so have been most Soviet and Western students of the period. They have not understood that there is no such thing as a self-sufficient peasant household, and there wasn't in Russia in the 1920s. Many have a notion that agriculture receives nothing from industry but a few luxuries like a pair of trousers or sugar. But the peasants also need kerosene, matches, soap, salt, condiments, steel for plows, milling services, and a number of other goods and services that a peasant community cannot produce, or at least can in no way produce efficiently.

Indeed, the peasants often weren't even self-sufficient in agricultural products. We have a false picture of a peasant farmer who produced a full range of agricultural goods and marketed a little bit on the side, but that's not the way it was. In the 1920s as well as in the late 19th century, certain peasants produced grain or industrial crops like cotton or flax for the market, and these peasants had to purchase other farm products from other peasants. There were others – in fact, most peasants – who produced the animal husbandry products, fruit, and vegetables for local or urban markets. The production functions and interdependencies of even the poorest peasants in the country were, therefore, very complicated.

If we turn to the grain crisis of 1928, then the standard story clearly is right in suggesting that this event persuaded many Bolsheviks that the end of the NEP had come – that the New Economic Policy had either served its usefulness or that the peasants had decided to sabotage Bolshevik plans. The Bolsheviks were city boys. They didn't understand the peasants, they didn't like the peasants, and there were an awful lot of peasants. Thus, the Bolsheviks were quite prepared to accept an alarming and sinister explanation for the falloff in grain marketings.

However, if the standard story suggests that Draconian measures were necessary to solve the 1928 grain crisis, then it is wrong. As the late Jerzy Karcz has argued – although this is somewhat more controversial – the grain crisis really was a consequence of unfavorable price policy with respect to grain products. The somewhat neglected Soviet economist of the 1920s, Yuriy Larin, pointed out that the peasants considered their animals, as well as their alcohol, their banks, and when grain prices were low, they put grain in these 'banks'.[13] In fact, an unfavorable price relationship had developed between grain and livestock prices during the 1920s, and simultaneously there had occurred a gradual falloff in the marketings of grain during the period. An adjustment of prices within the agricultural sector might well have solved the grain marketing problems rather easily, but the Bolshevik leadership certainly did not understand this.

The final aspect of the standard story – and the crucial one from the point of view of the argument about the necessity of Stalin – is the belief that Preobrazhenskiy was at least right in suggesting that industrialization would occur at the expense of the peasantry. It is argued that since grain marketings *did* increase and the country *did* industrialize rapidly, industrialization must have been carried out at the expense of the peasants – that is, with resources extracted from them.

Yet, as a Soviet economic historian named Barsov has recently shown, Soviet agriculture did not contribute in any significant measure to industrialization during the First Five-Year Plan. Although Barsov's is a very serious and careful analysis, his conclusions may be questioned in the West because of his (Marxist) methodology.[14] However, as I have shown elsewhere,[15] when his data are reworked according to Western conventions and measured in 1928 prices, the contribution of Soviet agriculture – strictly defined as a Western, non-Marxist economist would define it[16] – *actually turns out to have been negative.* The case seems to be even stronger than Barsov realized. Agriculture was a net recipient of real resources in the First-Five-Year Plan from 1928 through 1932. Far from there being a net flow of resources out of agriculture into the industrial sector, there was a reverse flow – and a reverse flow of some consequence when measured in 1928 prices. What is most surprising of all is that the terms of trade did not turn against agriculture during the First Five-Year Plan. *Prices changed – and significantly so – in favor of the agricultural sector.*

How did this favorable change in the terms of trade occur in the face of the terrible suffering? Why weren't the peasants better off? The favorable change in the terms of trade for the peasantry does not mean that the peasants were better off. It simply means that they were able to pass a portion of the burden placed upon them by collectivization, and by the procurement system erected upon it, onto the urban sector.[17]

What really happened? How did this flow of resources into agriculture take place, and how did people overlook it? In the first place, both the Bolsheviks and Western scholars have focused far too exclusively upon a single crop – grain. This crop may have been the most important from the standpoint of the Bolsheviks, but from the standpoint of the peasantry that wasn't the case. Before collectivization most peasants did not market grain at any time. When they marketed, they marketed animal husbandry products or other products raised on the plot. Grain was a major item marketed by some farms, but it was not the item marketed by the majority of peasant farms.

The focus on grain was one of the factors that led people to think that collectivization was successful, at least initially. While grain marketing did rise substantially, Jerzy Karcz has shown that if one takes livestock losses caused by peasant defiance of collectivization and multiplies this figure times official Soviet feeding norms of the period, one arrives at a surplus of grain for marketing purposes that is greater than the actual increase in grain marketings. That is, the animals that were slaughtered did not eat grain, and this left more grain available for marketing.[18] Of course, it also left less in the way of animal husbandry products to market, so the value of total marketings fell.

In the second place, Stalin's compromise with the peasantry, which left the private plot and the collective-farm market in existence, allowed the peasants to charge very, very high prices to the urban area for the products from their own private plots. If one thinks of exploitation in terms of the total Soviet population – urban and rural – the collective-farm market served as a valve tending to equalize the burden on the two sectors. Peasants on their own private account – their own private purchases and their own private sales – produced a net inflow of material resources during the First Five-Year Plan.

In the third place, people neglected the fact that the state was obliged to invest heavily in the Machine-Tractor Stations and in the state farms in order to compensate for the loss of draft power caused by the slaughter of livestock. The state was obliged not only to produce more tractors than it had intended (and to finance their purchase and delivery to agriculture) but also to import more tractors than had been originally planned.

Thus, resources came into agriculture in the form of capital investment in the Machine-Tractor Stations and the state farms, plus an increased and continuing charge for intermediate inputs such as fuel, lubrication, machine maintenance, and so forth. Material resources also flowed into agriculture in the form of peasant purchases of real products. There was only one subsector of agriculture from which there was a net outflow – the collective farm taken by itself, independent of the Machine-Tractor Stations and the peasant private plots. But this outflow was not sufficient to counterbalance the reverse flows. The fact that analysts have focused on the collective-farm sector alone is one of the reasons for the misunderstanding of this period.

In short, rather than Stalin's collectivization program being necessary to finance industrialization, rapid industrial development actually took place during the First Five-Year Plan without any net accumulation from agriculture – in fact, with a net overflow of resources *to* agriculture. While it might seem striking that the successful Soviet industrialization drive was accompanied by a turning of the terms of trade in favor of agriculture, the same pattern is found in the industrialization of Western countries prior to the 1930s. Throughout the 19th century and the early part of the 20th century, productivity changes everywhere (including in the United States) were occurring predominantly in the industrial sector, not the agricultural. The only way the agricultural sector could survive was for the terms of trade to change gradually in its favor, so that it could share the productivity gains made in the industrial sector. It is only with the development of mechanization, pesticides, herbicides, and hybrids that the possibility of an agriculture-first policy has arisen, and this means only *since* the 1930s.[19]

What there is evidence for in the late 1920s in Soviet agricultural policy is complete incompetence. There is no evidence whatsoever to indicate that the peasants would have withdrawn from the market even had the terms of trade been turned against them, and there is no evidence that the terms of trade even *had* to be turned against them. Collectivization was not necessary for the industrialization drive, and it was not optimal either. It was instead a disaster just like a hurricane or any other natural disaster. Economically, no one gained from collectivization, including those promoting rapid industrial development.

The 'logic' and cost of collectivization

A. Nove

'Was Stalin really necessary?' and 'Was collectivization really necessary?' are not quite the same question, although I agree that they are related. I accept straightaway that there were alternatives to the policy being followed and that in certain respects collectivization was just the disaster that my colleague said it was. But it was very difficult for the Bolsheviks to accept any alternative. There are circumstances in which people who have a particular set of beliefs do not regard a particular practical alternative as a practical alternative. If there is a genuine alternative for me to eat either a cheese sandwich or a ham sandwich, this is not an alternative for a rabbi.

In a review of my book, Alexander Gerschenkron strongly objected to the use of the term 'necessity',[20] and perhaps it can be misleading. Certainly, as my article made clear, it has nothing to do with 'desirability' as I use it, and nothing to do with inevitability. For Poland to survive as an independent state in the 18th century, it was necessary to make major political changes. They were not made, and Poland did not survive as an independent state at that time. Moreover, there are in the world a number of different 'necessities' – or, in Russian, '*zakonomernosti*', a nice word for which there is no easy English translation. There are trends, there are tendencies, which have an inner logic and which work themselves through. But, of course, they can be contradicted by other trends and tendencies, and at various crossing points in the processes of history, it is by no means obvious what the outcome will be. Yet one still can identify a series of regularities, a series of tendencies, which I think makes the word 'necessity' meaningful.

Whatever word is used, the essence of the argument about Stalinism in general rests on the totalitarian logic of the seizure of power by a small socialist minority in an overwhelmingly peasant country. There is the logic of the one-party state, there is the logic of trying to change society from above, which *is* part of the seizure of power by the Bolsheviks in the name of building socialism in a peasant country. There is the logic of the tough, organized bureaucracy which the party *had* to become in order to carry out these changes. There is also involved here the Russian autocratic tradition – a tradition of which Stalin was acutely aware. (He thought that there was a necessity for a substitute tsar and naturally preferred, for good personal reasons, that the mantle be his rather than anybody else's.) All of this was exacerbated by the sense of isolation, the sense of danger, and the consequent need for speed as perceived by Stalin and his cohorts. This is not an excuse, of course, for the *wild* excesses that, in fact, occurred during the First Five-Year Plan in a race that was run much too fast. Still, the felt need for speed really was genuine.

So far as agriculture is concerned, and I happily concentrate on that aspect of the question, we must begin with the fact that peasant attitudes really went back to medieval times. It is interesting to note that the peasant program which the Bolsheviks found it politically convenient to adopt at the time of the revolution included a ban on the purchase and sale of land, a ban on employment of labor, and a gearing of the size of the family holding to the number of people available for work and the number of mouths to feed. This program reflected the pre-Stolypin-reform attitudes which still were dominant in the minds of the peasants,[21] but such attitudes also represented a problem for the Bolsheviks as they contemplated rapid change in the face of what appeared to them to be an obsolete peasant agriculture.

I recall a conversation with a former official who said, 'You know, at the time when we were imposing on the peasants a policy which we knew they didn't like, some of us who knew our history remembered the potato riots under Catherine'. Catherine II had ordered the Russian peasants to grow potatoes, which was, of course, the right thing to do. Peasants, being a lot of conservative dunderheads, refused, whereupon Catherine ordered that any peasants not growing potatoes be whipped. After a while, the peasants, having been whipped, planted potatoes and within a number of years were happily eating them. If the Bolsheviks were convinced that the peasants still were outmoded in their thinking and didn't know what was good for them, then it surely must have seemed as proper for the Bolsheviks as for the tsars to make the peasants do something for their own good.

We must also recognize that the effect of the revolution on agriculture was profoundly reactionary. The commercial estates were largely wrecked and redivided, and many, though not all, of the peasant holdings that were consolidated as a result of the Stolypin reforms were also divided. Back it all went into the three-field medieval system – strips, periodic redistributions in some cases, etc., etc. This was an antique system of agriculture, and everybody, including Chayanov, agreed that it was even inconsistent with efficient small holdings, let alone large-scale production.[22] The Bolsheviks may have overestimated the technical advantages of large-scale agriculture, as Marxists have tended to do in the past, but the extent to which they were wrong was perhaps disguised from them by the fact that the existing arrangements in agriculture were very, very obsolete.

The statement that agriculture was not self-sufficient in the 1920s, if taken literally, is, of course, perfectly true. If, however, the statement seems to imply that there was not a reversion to greater self-sufficiency as a result of the revolution, then obviously the statement is wrong. Jerzy Karcz, Robert Davies, I myself, and others have joined in discussions about the measure of marketings, but in the end I am convinced by the following simple argument. In 1913 – admittedly a very good year – the total of all out-of-the village marketings was something like 21 million tons. Stalin claimed that by 1928–29 they had fallen to 12 million. The difference of 9 million tons equals the level of exports in 1913, and exports in 1926–27 were negligible.[23] Since the size of towns was approximately the same in 1913 and 1926, it seems to me that what, in fact, happened is that the peasants and their animals – and I acknowledge that the focus is on grain alone here – were eating what was once exported. It seems to me that the peasants regarded themselves, quite properly, as beneficiaries of their own acquisition of land and as a result ate better than before the revolution. They *were* eating a potential exportable surplus. There is no doubt whatever that if the economic conditions of a family decline, if an extra mouth exists to feed, people will make an effort to feed it, but there should not be a confusion between production response and selling on the market. What the Bolsheviks were concerned about was marketings. While peasants are not completely self-sufficient, they can at the margin make the decision to shift more toward consumption rather than take produce to the market. Industrial workers are in a different position. If you are working more and producing more ball-bearings, you can't eat them. You *can* eat more cabbage and meat.

One can view primitive socialist accumulation – however defined – as a means of mobilizing agricultural exports to pay for the imports of capital goods from the West. That is just one way of looking at the first stages of industrialization from the vantage point of the Soviet leadership – and not an entirely unrealistic way of looking at it. Now, James Millar very properly says that there were alternative means of getting more marketings, and I'm sure there were. The great problem is – what would the consequences of the alternatives be? It seems that both Bukharin and Preobrazhenskiy did run into a dilemma, for Preobrazhenskiy said more than that there was a need to turn the terms of trade against the peasant. He also said that there is a terrible danger from kulaks. And what on earth is a kulak? A kulak is a prosperous peasant. So long as you have this attitude (which Bukharin at first didn't have, but which even he later came to share, or said that he did), you must base yourself and the health of agriculture on the middle peasant. What is a middle peasant? A moderately unsuccessful one.

So long as all the Bolsheviks, including Bukharin (at least after 1925), agreed that the emergence of a powerful, commercially-minded peasantry was a deadly danger to them, they had closed off one potentially viable alternative. This is my point about rabbis and ham sandwiches. If this alternative – which did exist and which may have been a much healthier one even for accumulation (I'll grant that) – was foreclosed, the Bolsheviks were in a fix. I'll also grant at once (and this is in my book) that their fix was rendered considerably worse by the price policy they adopted in agriculture. The grain crisis of the winter of 1927–28 was due much more to price relationships, which were very unfavorable to grain, than to any other single cause in the short run. That I completely accept. But in the longer run, the general level of productivity of agriculture was limited by the settlement of the revolution. The belief that the successful peasant was a kulak and an enemy prevented what would otherwise have been the natural development of a prosperous, commercially-minded peasant agriculture.

The Bolshevik's range of choice was also limited by their attitude toward the market. The whole price policy of the second half of NEP was inconsistent with the maintenance of any sort of market equilibrium, and a number of persons at the time made this point. However, most of the Bolsheviks (though not Bukharin, I think) followed Preobrazhenskiy in regarding the market as the enemy. They saw no reason to make the adjustments required in order to maintain equilibrium. They would say: 'The markets, the traders, the uncontrolled part of the economy are something we have tolerated since 1921 through dire necessity, but really we ought to fight all this'. Preobrazhenskiy only accepted NEP because there was no alternative. As Bukharin pointed out, he saw a *conflict* between socialist planning and what he called 'the law of value', *i.e.*, the market.[24] This kind of approach awoke responsive chords among the Bolsheviks because they were who they were. This is also part of the pattern we are discussing.

Finally, it should be recognized that, while the solution adopted was partly due to Stalin's personal predilections for violence and to the spirit of enthusiasm of the First Five-Year Plan, the Bolsheviks were the first ever to try such a policy, and they had few guidelines. Western economics at the time was interested in equilibrium and in the explanation for trade cycles. The word 'growth' was never mentioned, and discussion of appropriate investment strategies for development was unheard of. Development economics was born in the West after World War II. I don't want to excuse the absurdities of some of Stalin's policies, because a number of people warned him that they were absurd and were rewarded with prison. But at the very least, we have to admit that had he, in fact, studied Western economists at the time, he would have learned very little that was of the slightest relevance to the problems the Bolsheviks were facing.

Now, what about the role of agriculture as a source of accumulation? This is a difficult question because we have here a distinction between intention and outcome, and we also have the problem of measurement in the wake of a disaster. It is not a source of disagreement that there was a disaster. Indeed, even Stalin would probably agree about that. It was, of course, not intended that one-half of the horses and most of the livestock in the USSR should be slaughtered in three years. It was an appalling situation.

So far as intentions are concerned, it is clear that Stalin and his cohorts were discussing ways and means of mobilizing material and financial resources largely, although not exclusively, from agriculture. The term 'pumping over' (*perekachka*) was widely used in the discussions. When Stalin began his policy of industrializing rapidly in tandem with 'soaking' the peasants, Bukharin called it 'military–feudal exploitation of the peasantry' (this is the language he used in 1928).[25] In the outcome, Stalin *et al.* may have been wrong, but that they *thought* they were soaking and exploiting the peasantry was certainly the case, even though the text of the First Five-Year Plan (an absurd document in this respect) indicated that not only accumulation but also consumption would go up at a fast rate.

So far as outcome is concerned, I think we agree that the agricultural disaster resulting from the slaughter of farm animals and the precipitous decline in farm output completely transformed the situation. It is perfectly true, therefore, that (1) the total amount the Bolsheviks could get out of agriculture was notably less than they expected, and (2) the amount that they had to put in (primarily as the result of the slaughter) was greater than they expected. All this is completely true.

However, I have looked at Barsov and puzzled over the implications of his argument that the burden of industrialization was carried on the shoulders of the working class. I put this argument to one of the Russian émigrés, and he said, 'Oh, my God. *Who starved during this period?*'

What, then, is wrong with the argument that is put forward? Firstly, it all ends in 1932, because Barsov ends his article with 1932. If one carried the analysis on through 1935, one would find a reduction in the investment in agriculture in the years following 1932. Moreover, the free market prices were extremely high in 1932–33 (25–30–35 times higher than the official prices for foodstuffs), which certainly benefited those peasants who were able to get to the nearest town and sell their cabbage or some flour. By 1935 these prices were very sharply reduced, and I strongly suspect that if we had the average prices of these years, they would be much lower than in 1932. Thus, it may very well be that emergency inputs to maintain agricultural production in the wake of the draft-animal disaster were followed by a much more effective mobilization of agricultural products in subsequent years.

Indeed, I think that if the relevant figures were available, they would show that the maximum degree of exploitation of the peasantry – in the sense of pumping resources out of agriculture while providing the minimum returns for people and the minimum of technical inputs – took place from 1948 to 1953. In the late Stalin period the government was still paying for compulsory procurements the same prices or almost the same prices as in 1928, and delivery quotas were higher. The undersupply of inputs to the peasants at the time was appalling.

Secondly, I am much bothered by the argument with respect to the prices of 1928 and the alleged improvement in the terms of trade thereafter. Part of the problem is a suspicion that such improvement is notably weighted by the relatively low prices of industrial inputs into agricultural *production* (e.g., items such as tractors), and that it does not necessarily reflect the kind of prices peasants had to pay for consumer goods. If one looks at Malafeyev's book,[26] for instance, one finds that prices were rising toward the end of the First Five-Year Plan, and always more rapidly for rural areas than for urban areas.

An even greater problem is the fact that this was a time of grave shortage. Precisely by the end of 1932, and even worse in 1933, a number of things could not be bought at any price. For a peasant, trousers were by no means unfavorably priced in relation to the price he was able to get for the cabbage he sold in town, but, most unfortunately, there were no trousers to be had. The price system in 1932–33 was unbelievably complicated, with some goods rationed, others distributed through closed shops which were accessible only to those with special cards, etc., etc. Under those conditions, what on earth did prices mean? I know there is also evidence about the volume of movements of goods, but I am worried about these prices which have to be used as weights. The analysis just doesn't seem to square with the realities of the time.

It does seem to me that figures on food consumption graphically illustrate who actually bore the brunt of the worsening situation. From the accompanying table [Table 7.1], one can see that by 1932 there was a very

Table 7.1 Food consumption, 1928–32 (kilograms per capita)

	Bread and grains	Potatoes	Meat
Urban			
1928	174.4	87.6	51.7
1932	211.3	110.0	16.9
Rural			
1928	250.4	141.1	24.8
1932	214.6	125.0	11.2

Source: Iu. A. Moshkov, *Zernovaia problema v gody sploshnoi kollektivizatsii sel'skogo khoziaistva SSSR – 1929–1933 gg.* (The Grain Problem in the Years of All-Round Collectivization of USSR Agriculture – 1929–1933), Moscow, Izdatel'stvo Moskovskogo Universiteta, 1966, p. 136.

sharp decline in the quality of food consumption in the towns, with the population filling their bellies with more bread and potatoes and eating less of the better food (specifically meat). On the other hand, the rural population ate less of *everything* by 1932, and this was before the famine of 1933. These figures suggest that the burden was not borne primarily by the urban population (although unmistakably a decline in the income of the urban population contributed substantially to the high level of investment in agriculture).

Finally, one should not forget the export of labor from the villages. This was both planned and unplanned, and it was massive. Life in the villages was so miserable, and people were so frightened of being labeled kulaks and arrested, that perhaps up to 10 million of them fled to the construction sites and factories that were being built. I don't quite know how to measure it, but it was an important contribution of agriculture to industrialization. The peasants' arrival helped to depress the per capita consumption figures (and the labor productivity) in the cities, thereby creating the impression that the original urban inhabitants suffered more than they did.

In conclusion, let me repeat once more my belief that the actual collectivization program carried out by Stalin, which was a most dreadful thing, was not inexorably predetermined and that it was not morally justified by the outcome of the industrialization drive of the 1930s. One can say that the events which occurred have a pretty powerful explanation, given the nature of the Bolsheviks, the extent to which other alternatives seemed closed to them, and the extent to which they were ideologically predisposed in certain directions. The survival of the regime, given the Bolsheviks' aims and their rapid industrialization program, required a harsh, autocratic type of regime. Yet, as Roy Medvedev has contended in his book,[27] if there is an inherent logic in a cult of personality, much depends on the nature of the personality. When Stalin was in a position to make arbitrary and personal decisions, he went in for wild excesses, both in economic policy and, of course, in the terror. Not for a moment, and certainly not in my article, did I suggest that this was in any sense necessary. This was Stalin showing the face of an oriental despot and behaving in a manner which only became possible after he had succeeded in getting into power, having shown a more moderate and human face while doing so.

Rejoinders

Mr. Millar

It seems to me that the disagreements between Professor Nove and myself are of two different types. In the first place, our images of the Russian countryside in the 1920s are somewhat different. I don't agree, for instance, that Chayanov's studies demonstrate the antique nature of Russian agriculture. On the contrary, the implication of Chayanov's argument is that peasant agriculture could have survived the Soviet regime, as it had the Tsarist, had it not been for the Bolsheviks' misperceptions of the peasantry.

I also do not agree that the decline in marketings can be attributed simply to increased peasant consumption. The great famine of 1921–22 caused a very sharp reduction in animal stocks, and these had to be rebuilt in 1923–24, naturally at some cost in grain. Moreover, the international grain market was a disaster during the 1920s, particularly during the early part of the 1920s. The international price of grain had fallen precipitously, and the Soviet regime had not established an institution to organize the export of grains in these conditions. (The regime did put together an organization to export flax, and this did help to create the necessary demand to maintain the production and sowings of flax.) It does seem absolutely clear to me that the peasants were not self-sufficient and that a turning of the general terms of trade against them would have increased marketings, not just production.

I might add that I also do not believe that the labor which moved out of agriculture in the First Five-Year Plan should be considered a contribution to industrialization. There is no evidence of a shortage of labor in Soviet Russia of the 1920s and the 1930s, nor any evidence of a need to take extraordinary measures to mobilize labor from the countryside. The experience of most developing countries both before and since the Soviet industrialization drive has been an excessive off-farm flow of population, and this without collectivization or anything like it. The unskilled, uneducated Soviet peasants who poured into the cities at that time were in many ways more of a nuisance than a help.

But much more important than any disagreements between us on interpretation of detailed questions is, I think, a fundamental methodological difference in our approaches. Professor Nove is concerned with explaining how things happened, and he is trying to say that, given the Bolsheviks, given the circumstances they faced, given their understanding of the agricultural situation, given the backwardness of Soviet agriculture, given the world situation – given all these factors, how could anything else have been decided?

It seems to me, therefore, that Professor Nove comes perilously close to a determinist position at times, but I am not concerned with arguing this point. I am trying not only to explain what happened, but to evaluate it as a means–end relation. Professor Nove uses 'necessity' in two senses: first, as a 'tendency that has an inner logic'; second, as something that is needed. It was this latter meaning of 'necessity' that he had in mind when he cited the example, 'For Poland to survive as an independent state in the 18th century, it was necessary to make major political changes'. And it is this latter meaning of 'necessity' that primarily interests me. I don't care whether or not Bukharin or Preobrazhenskiy or Stalin or anyone else considered the various alternatives, for that is irrelevant in *evaluating* the appropriateness (optimality) of collectivization as a means to achieve the goal of rapid industrialization. My interest is in assessing whether collectivization or some similar coercive 'squeezing' of the peasantry was needed for the Soviet rapid industrialization program to succeed.

The essence of my argument is that collectivization could not have been necessary for rapid industrialization for the simple reason that it did not, in fact, contribute net resources to the industrial sector. An analysis in terms of 'surplus' is very confusing to anyone raised in neoclassical economic analysis, for what we are talking about is a *net* surplus, a *net* of the movement of goods flowing out of and into agriculture. We are putting prices on these counterflows and measuring the *net* difference. The approach is akin to measuring an export or an import surplus in a country's foreign trade, and treating agriculture and nonagriculture as though they were different countries. In my opinion, Professor Nove is right about the contribution of capital stocks (in contrast to consumer goods) to the improvement in the terms of trade, but since the argument concerns agriculture vs. nonagriculture, the fact that many of the resources flowing into agriculture were directed toward maintaining production simply buttresses my case.

Our knowledge about the net flow between agriculture and the nonagricultural sector after 1932 is, unfortunately, rather meager. Not only does Barsov's main study stop in that year, but on the basis of an examination of the archives, he says we never will have a definitive understanding of the question because some of the necessary data were not collected.[28] In any case, the 'standard story' has always focused on the First Five-Year Plan, not the Second, and it is already a significant revision of the standard theory to say that the contribution of agriculture was postponed until after 1932. I personally am doubtful that the situation changed much after 1932. So far as the postwar period is concerned, I thought that no one argued that collectivization was beneficial to the industrialization drive over a 15- to 20-year span. Collectivization was supposed to have solved an immediate procurement problem, but at a long-term cost to the economy as a whole. As recent developments in the Soviet Union have shown, so many raw materials for industrial production come out of agriculture that there is no way to discriminate sharply against the agricultural sector without in the end discriminating against overall growth.

In my opinion, we don't really know about the relative suffering produced by collectivization. That is, we don't know how the burden was shared between the agricultural and nonagricultural populations. We just know that both suffered losses in real wages and probably losses in real income. The measure in Nove's Table 1 is not definitive, but I don't disagree with it. It is not relevant to the issue between us.[29] In any case, I certainly never said or meant to imply that the burden was placed primarily on the working class. It fell on both classes. *The crucial point is that so much of this suffering was completely unnecessary and contributed in no way to industrialization.*

In conclusion, let me emphasize one point very strongly. One of the reasons that I have been attacking the standard story is that the question at hand is not merely of historical interest. The standard story has worked its way into the accepted Western developmental literature as 'the Soviet model for economic development'. This model (one famous version is the Ranis and Fei model[30]) describes an experience of industrialization in which very rapid growth is achieved, with the agricultural sector playing a real and substantial role as a source of investment resources. But if this model does not describe the actual Soviet experience – and it doesn't – we are left with the question: How *did* the Soviet Union achieve rapid industrial development? Once we get rid of some simple notion that the Soviets extracted resources out of a particular sector, we may be able to start thinking about this question seriously and to come to some accurate understanding of what the Soviet model for economic development really was.

Mr. Nove

It is, I think, wrong to say that I am arguing for a determinist position so far as the initiation of collectivization is concerned. I have contended that there were powerful objective reasons for a despot to be in a position to act and that there were powerful ideological reasons for him to be suspicious of any agricultural policy that created a strong and independent peasantry.

But almost by definition, a despot has a range of choices. Of course, Stalin had around him a group of people – a stratum of semieducated, tough commissars whom he represented and whose interests on the whole they thought he was defending until he killed half of them – but some of the choices were his own.

I have also emphasized that some aspects of the collectivization program were counterproductive in the literal sense. There is nothing to be gained from taking grain away from starving peasants and then exporting it in order to buy machinery which was then wrecked by former peasants who hadn't been taught how to use it. This kind of thing is completely counterproductive, and obviously it occurred.

I recall listening to a woman who was defending a PhD thesis in Moscow University. In the course of discussion, she said: 'I would regard the Soviet agricultural model not as a model for socialism in agriculture, but at best as a tragic necessity. We must hope that no other socialist country would be compelled to follow that road'. She said it to an audience of 100, none of whom rose to object. 'At best', therefore, 'a necessary tragedy' – and the word 'necessary' in this connection can very well be argued about, for in the end Stalin's course proved so counterproductive with respect both to the agricultural sector and to the aims of the First Five-Year Plan. I agree entirely that there could well have been an unexplored range of possibilities, for example, in the form of increased taxation. It is one of the astonishing features of the 1920s that the taxation on the peasants was always rather low, until it became penal as part of the policy of destroying individual peasant farming.

Yet, it does seem to me that the collectivization decision should be treated with some historical perspective. The policy of rapid tempos – of breaking out of what the pro-Stalin Bolsheviks believed to be the vicious circles that were holding them back – is quite understandable. It is quite logical that they should have tried. Moreover, if one adopts a particular strategy for good or for ill, then along with that strategy inevitably go a number of disadvantages which can be seen as costs of the chosen strategy. Look at the Western war economy and all its bureaucratic deformations. If one assumes that a strategy is rational – which it may not be – the errors and waste with which it is associated also in a paradoxical way have a rationality of their own. In a 'great leap forward' strategy, at least some – though not all – of the waste and deformations, including excesses on the part of overenthusiastic comrades, must be expected.

So far as the burden of the industrialization drive is concerned, I agree, of course, that it was not limited to the peasants. (After all, the high free market prices were paid not by the state but by the urban citizens.) Nevertheless, I continue to worry about any calculation based on 1928 prices. In any other circumstances, the consequences of collectivization

would naturally have included much higher prices of agricultural products simply by reason of the extreme shortages. The use of highly
artificial prices both for outputs and inputs can produce very misleading
results.

The best indicator, I think, is the relative welfare, the relative income, of
different strata of the population. One must study the relativities and
dynamics of peasant and urban incomes during and after collectivization.
At the time of Stalin's death, the difference of income between the urban
worker and any kolkhoz peasant not within very easy reach of the market
was very strongly in favor of the urban worker, whatever way one weighs
the evidence.

If one looks at the post-Stalin statistics, one sees a trend in the direction
of evening out this difference to a very considerable extent. Today, the
difference is much smaller and more the kind one would expect in a society
at the Soviet Union's level of development. A fiscal reflection of this change
is the gigantic budgetary subsidy that is given to maintain the difference
between the quite high purchase prices for meat at the farms and the lower
retail prices for meats in the shops. Instead of a high turnover tax revenue
originating through the resale of agricultural products obtained at low
prices, this particular item of revenue probably is insignificant today.

It is only with such an evening-out of the income difference that one can
say the original Soviet method of socialist construction − if that is the
name to give it − was finally, by stages, abandoned. Industrialization
involving the pressing down of peasant standards − or in a sense, the
exploitation of agriculture − cannot be said to have ended until sometime
in the late 1960s.

A moderator's afterthoughts

Mr. Hough

Few debates have, I think, been so successful as this one in clarifying issues
and advancing our understanding. The debate makes clear that several
quite separate issues have been intertwined in our arguments about the
collectivization phenomenon. The first question is the historical one: Why
did it occur? Clearly this is a question that interests Professor Nove very
much and Professor Millar very little. On this question, Professor Nove's
real protagonists would seem to be those scholars, such as Moshe Lewin
and Stephen Cohen, who see Bukharin's program in the late 1920s as the
true Leninist one and who see NEP as a viable (maybe even natural) long-
term Bolshevik alternative. While Professor Nove obviously believes that
Bukharin's program was economically viable (and even desirable), he
seems to be saying that that program was not politically viable and that

any Bolshevik would have been pushed toward something like collectivization at the end of the 1920s.

The second question is: Who suffered most as a consequence of collectivization? To me, the most important contribution of the debate was to clarify that this question can be quite distinct from the question: Which sector contributed most to industrialization? A regime may willingly or unwillingly invest so much in agricultural mechanization that little 'net surplus' is received from the agricultural sector, but, of course, peasants can't eat tractors. Undoubtedly, the question of relative suffering is partly a metaphysical one (What did groups receive in comparison with what was proper or 'natural' for them to receive?), and undoubtedly any accurate analysis of it would have to be quite subtle and differentiated. Many peasant youths surely rejoiced at the newly-created opportunity to move to city jobs, and those peasants near the cities suffered less than more remote peasants. Cotton farmers fared better than those in the non-black-earth region. Similarly, those workers who became Stakhanovites or who simply took advantage of new programs to raise their skills or even to receive higher education are in a much different category from those who remained unskilled. The gross distinction that may make the most sense is one based on age (the young being seen as beneficiaries in overall terms, the middle-aged and the old as the greatest losers), but in general terms Professor Nove must be right in emphasizing that conditions were not good in the villages. Whatever the relative costs borne by the urban and rural family in statistical terms, the urban family, unlike the peasant, often had an unemployed wife who could go to work in an effort to maintain family standards of living.

The third question – or set of questions – involves the concerns that interest Professor Millar most: Did the suffering of the peasants and workers at least 'buy' a rapid rate of industrial growth for the Soviet Union? Was collectivization or something like it necessary for such growth, at least given the regime's reluctance to seek large-scale foreign investments? If it turns out that, whatever the intentions of the leadership, agriculture did not provide much (if anything) in the way of a net surplus to the industrial sector, what was going on that explains the very high rates of industrial growth? What was the 'real' Soviet model of economic development in the sense of the way in which resources were actually mobilized for the industrialization drive? Professor Millar is surely right in holding that this is a question which deserves a most serious reexamination on the basis of new data. It is a question of vital interest not only to historians of the Soviet period but also to theorists of economic development in general – and to those charged with promoting such development in the Third World.

Notes

1 The propositions are advanced, respectively, in Moshe Lewin, *Lenin's Last Struggle*, New York, Pantheon Books, 1968; Stephen F. Cohen, *Bukharin and the Bolshevik Revolution*, New York, A. A. Knopf, 1973; Sheila Fitzpatrick (Ed.), *The Cultural Revolution in Russia, 1928–1931*, forthcoming; David Granick, *Soviet Metal-Fabrication and Economic Development*, Madison, University of Wisconsin Press, 1967; Gail Warshofsky Lapidus, *Women in Soviet Society*, forthcoming; David Joravsky, *The Lysenko Affair*, Cambridge, Mass., Harvard University Press, 1970.

2 The other two major proponents of a revisionist position in this area are Moshe Lewin and (especially) the late Jerzy F. Karcz. See Moshe Lewin, *Russian Peasants and Soviet Power*, London, George Allen and Unwin, 1968; Jerzy F. Karcz, 'Thoughts on the Grain Problem', *Soviet Studies* (Glasgow), April 1967, pp. 399–435; Jerzy F. Karcz, 'Back on the Grain Front', *Soviet Studies* (Glasgow), October 1970, pp. 262–94; Jerzy F. Karcz, 'From Stalin to Brezhnev: Soviet Agricultural Policy in Historical Perspective', in James R. Millar (Ed.), *The Soviet Rural Community*, Urbana, Ill., University of Illinois Press, 1971, pp. 36–70; James R. Millar, 'Soviet Rapid Development and the Agricultural Surplus Hypothesis', *Soviet Studies*, July 1970, pp. 77–93; James R. Millar, 'Mass Collectivization and the Contribution of Soviet Agriculture to the First Five-Year Plan', *Slavic Review* (Columbus, Ohio), December 1974, pp. 750–66.

3 *Encounter* (London), April 1962, pp. 86–92. The article was republished in Nove's collection, *Economic Rationality and Soviet Politics, or Was Stalin Really Necessary*, New York, Praeger, 1964.

4 New York, Harper & Row, 1974. See esp. Chaps. 2, 3, 4, and 12.

5 Yevgeniy Preobrazhenskiy, *The New Economics*, trans. by Brian Pearce, Oxford, Clarendon Press, 1965.

6 See the very full discussion in Stephen F. Cohen, *Bukharin and the Bolshevik Revolution: A Political Biography, 1883–1938*, New York, Vintage Books, 1975, esp. Chaps. 5 and 6.

7 The 'scissors crisis' was considered a crisis by the Bolsheviks because they expected that the sharp adverse change in the terms of trade that occurred in 1922–23 for agriculture would cause the peasants to cease bringing their products to market, thereby creating great hardships for the urban population. It was apparently Leon Trotsky who first described the situation as the 'scissors crisis'. The phrase was based on the fact that the two indexes which were being used to measure the 'adverse' change in the purchasing power of agricultural income, when portrayed on a graph, crossed each other and thus resembled an open pair of scissors.

   The most recent examination of the original data, of the price indexes, and of the various interpretations put forward by Soviet economists at the time of the crisis shows that the peasants did not in fact withdraw from the market and that there was little reason to suppose that they would have done so subsequently. This study also argues that the data and indexes used in the famous scissors diagram are quite unreliable for measuring changes in the purchasing power of agricultural incomes. See Corinne Ann Guntzel, *Soviet Agricultural Pricing Policy and the Scissors Crisis of 1922–23*, unpublished PhD dissertation, University of Illinois (Urbana), 1972.

8 Alexander Erlich, 'Preobrazenski and the Economics of Soviet Industrialization', *Quarterly Journal of Economics* (Cambridge, Mass.), No. 1, February 1950, pp. 57–88.

9 A. V. Chayanov, *The Theory of Peasant Economy*, ed. by Daniel Thorner, Basile Kerblay, and R. E. F. Smith, Homewood, Ill., Irwin, 1966.

10 This is also true with respect to labor. In the urban sector of the Soviet Union during the 1930s, the real wage fell. What was the response of the urban family? More members of the family entered the work force, and those who already had jobs worked longer hours in an attempt to maintain per capita family consumption.

11 See Guntzel, *Soviet Agricultural Pricing Policy*, esp. Chap. 3. For an example of an unsupported assertion to the contrary, see William L. Blackwell, *The Industrialization of Russia*, New York, Thomas Y. Crowell, 1970, pp. 84–5.

12 W.W. Rostow, 'Marx Was A City Boy, or Why Communism May Fail', *Harper's Magazine* (New York), February 1955, pp. 25–30.

13 Iurii Larin, *Sovetskaia derevnia* (The Soviet Countryside), Moscow, Izdatel'stvo Ekonomicheskaya Zhizn', 1925, p. 217.

14 A. A. Barsov, *Balans stoimostnykh obmenov mezhdu gorodom i derevnei* (The Balance of Value Exchanges Between the City and the Countryside), Moscow, Nauka, 1969; see also his 'Agriculture and the Sources of Socialist Accumulation in the Years of the First Five-Year Plan (1928–1933)', *Istoriia SSSR* (Moscow), No. 3, 1968. For a sympathetic Western confirmation of Barsov's findings see Michael Ellman, 'Did the Agricultural Surplus provide the Resources for the Increase in Investment during the First Five-Year Plan?' *The Economic Journal* (Cambridge, England), December 1975, pp. 844–64.

15 James R. Millar, 'Mass Collectivization . . . ,' supra.

16 In such a definition, a type-of-product distinction is made – that is, the agricultural sector is defined to include enterprises or portions of enterprises producing agricultural products only, and rural enterprises producing nonagricultural products are treated properly as part of the industrial sector. This is in opposition to a simple geographical distinction between urban and rural areas.

17 The terms of trade changed gradually but significantly in favor of American agriculture, for example, during 19th- and early 20th-century US development. This does not mean that American farmers were made better off than American industrial workers as a result. It merely means that the greater productivity gains of the industrial sector were shared in this way with the agricultural sector, where productivity increases were smaller. The real income of farmers remained below that of workers throughout the period. The 'favorable' change in the terms of trade for American agriculture merely helped to keep the gap between the two from widening. See Ralph A. Loomis and Glen T. Barton, 'Productivity of Agriculture, United States, 1870–1958', *Technical Bulletin* (Washington, DC, US Department of Agriculture), No. 1238, April 1961, esp. Table 7 and pp. 28–38.

18 Karcz, 'From Stalin to Brezhnev', in James R. Millar (Ed), The Soviet Rural Community, Urbana, Ill., University of Illinois Press, 1971, pp. 42–46.

19 Loomis and Barton, 'Productivity of Agriculture', *Technical Bulletin* (Washington, DC, US Department of Agriculture), No. 1238, April 1961, esp. pp. 9–11 and pp. 28–9.

20 Review of Nove, *Encounter* (London), April 1962, in *Economic History Review* (Welwyn Garden City, England). No. 3, April 1965, pp. 606–9. Reprinted in Alexander Gerschenkron, *Continuity in History and Other Essays*, Cambridge, Mass., Harvard University Press, 1968, pp. 485–9.

21 The reform introduced by P. A. Stolypin in 1906–11 was intended to break up traditional peasant communal-land tenure and gradually replace it by private ownership of land.

22 See Note 9.

23 The marketing figures are discussed in the two Karcz *Soviet Studies* articles cited in footnote 2 ('Thoughts on the Grain Problem' and 'Back on the Grain Front') and in R. W. Davies, 'A Note on Grain Statistics', *Soviet Studies*, January 1970, pp. 314–29.

24 See the discussion in Alec Nove, 'Some Observations on Bukharin and His Ideas', in S. Abramsky and Beryl J. Williams, Eds., *Essays in Honour of E. H. Carr*, London, The Macmillan Press Ltd, 1974, pp. 183–203.

25 Quoted in V. M. Molotov, 'On Two Fronts', *Bolshevik* (Moscow), Jan. 21, 1930, p. 14. See Cohen, *Bukharin*, New York, Vintage Books, 1975, pp. 306–7.

26 A. Malafeyev, *Istoriia tsenoobrazovaniia v SSSR* (History of Price Formation in the USSR), Moscow, Mysl', 1964, p. 148.

27 Roy A. Medvedev, *Let History Judge: The Origins and Consequences of Stalinism*, ed. by David Joravsky and Georges Haupt, New York, Knopf, 1972.

28 Barsov, *Balans stoimostnykh*, pp. 186–90. However, see his recent article, 'The NEP: The Leveling of Economic Relations between the City and the Countryside', in M. P. Kim, Ed. *Novaia ekonomicheskaia politika* (New Economic Policy), Moscow, Nauka, 1974, where he attempts some analysis of the Second Five-Year Plan period.

29 See note 17 above. The lower real income of American agricultural workers during the 19th century does not imply that industrial growth occurred at the expense of the agricultural sector. The truth is quite the opposite.

30 Gustave Ranis and John C. H. Fei, 'A Theory of Economic Development', *The American Economic Review* (Nashville, Tenn.), September 1961.

Reading 8 *Society, state, and ideology during the First Five-Year Plan*

M. LEWIN

The period 1929–33 is probably one of the most momentous quinquennia in the history of Russia, indeed in modern history. The scholar is astounded by the incredible intensity and scope of the transformation of society, not to speak of the bewildering effect those years had on contemporaries. This was a unique process of state-guided social transformation, for the state did much more than just 'guiding': it substituted itself for society, to become the sole initiator of action and controller of all important spheres of life. The process was thus transformed into one of 'state building', with the whole social structure being, so to speak, sucked into the state mechanism, as if entirely assimilated by it.

The pace and violence of the changes were breathtaking. In a matter of a few years much of the previous social fabric, Tsarist and Soviet, was dispersed and destroyed. With the destruction came the creation of new patterns, which, although they emerged very rapidly, became permanent. The sense of urgency in the whole upheaval is baffling: the pace imposed suggests a race against time, as if those responsible for the country's destinies felt they were running out of history. The appearance of a new social hierarchy in the thirties was a similarly speedy and contradictory affair: the emerging ruling strata were kept in a state of perpetual tension and were several times knocked out and partly destroyed before they were allowed to settle down. Most of the makers of the upheaval were themselves transformed, engulfed, and annihilated in this prolonged Walpurgis night, thus giving to those years the traits of a real 'total drama': nobody was left unharmed, and all the survivors became thoroughly disfigured. This was not surprising. The new world being built was not the better and freer world of the dreamers but a Caliban State. That a progressive ideology, initially intended to enhance human freedom and to create higher forms of community, came to serve a police state is one of the peculiarities of the period and an important phenomenon to study.

Before the plans

The Tsarist heritage

The strictly dramatic point of view would suggest that our study should begin at some idyllic moment before the storm, perhaps 1926. But more prosaic scholarly interests will be better served by starting at about 1922, immediately after the great famine that was the culmination of years of war, revolution, and civil strife. This starting point serves to highlight the fact that the lull between the end of one catastrophe and the onset of a new one (quite different in character) lasted a mere seven years: Russia's body social, shattered in our century by a series of cataclysmic events, has shown an amazing capacity to recover.

The period 1914–21 was unquestionably a demographic earthquake. At the end of it, Russia's population was about thirty million less than would normally have been expected: the shortfall included about sixteen million dead in war and civil war, famine, and epidemics, with the remainder accounted for by the calamities that befell potential parents.[1] These figures are relevant to an understanding of the stresses of the thirties, for the thirty million missing out of the 1923 population contributed to the later serious gaps in the labor force and military manpower.

Before war and revolution, Tsarist Russia had seen a significant advance in industrialization and urbanization, with its cities growing faster than the total population. But the whole urban sector comprised no more than about 18 percent of the population, and the modern industrial sector was even smaller than that: less than one in five of the population lived in towns (most of which were quite small provincial backwaters), and only two in one hundred were employed in manufacturing and mechanical industries, compared to 11.6 in one hundred in the United States.[2] Thus most of the cities were dominated by rather small producers. The educated professional and intellectual segment was also small, and it included more bureaucrats and officers than managers, teachers, scientists, and artists.

Rural Russia was bedeviled by poverty, land hunger, and irritating remnants of the old regime of serfdom, and was in the throes of the social unrest created by the Stolypin reforms. These reforms led to the development of a consolidated smallholder class among the peasantry and to the shattering of the communal system, but the hardship they caused the peasants had painful effects.

Official and educated Russia was notoriously detached and isolated from illiterate and semiliterate rural Russia, though the peasants came to the towns in millions in search of seasonal or full-time employment and formed the bulk of the armed forces. This was a symptom of Russia's 'underdevelopment', and one of the most profound.

The top layers of the Russian social and political structure, some 4 percent of the population, presented an intriguing and complicated pattern. They included the top bureaucracy, considered by some (including Lenin) to be the real rulers of Russia – organized, socially cohesive, and highly instrumental in ensuring the stability of the state. But there was a fundamental weakness: decisions on who was to head the bureaucracy and the government were made by a quite antiquated institution, the imperial court. The court, a product of centuries of absolutism, was incapable of making the most of the talent, growing experience, and skills accumulating among the abler elements of the bureaucracy. An important social prop of the system, the nobility, was a decaying class, heavily dependent on the favors of the Tsar and his officials (themselves part of the top stratum of the nobility), deeply in debt, and constantly losing its lands and its economic and political power.

The entrepreneurial classes, developing before and during the war in the wake of an impressive industrial expansion, came to play an important role, especially during the war, but were still inhibited by their low culture, dependence on state tutelage, and political immaturity.

The civil war

Revolution and civil war brought economic life almost to a standstill and destroyed the old social structure. The landowners, bourgeoisie, top officials and, on the whole, army officers ceased to exist as classes or groups. Death and emigration also carried away much of the middle class – the administrative, managerial, and intellectual talent that Russia had begun to develop and use before the war. The whole modern sector of urbanized and industrialized Russia suffered a severe setback, as becomes obvious from the population figures. The entire population of the country fell from its 1917 level by many millions, but the cities – still only a modest sector in Russia – were particularly badly hit. By 1920, city dwellers had fallen from 19 percent of the population in 1917 to 15 percent. Moscow lost half its population, Petrograd two-thirds.[3]

The social structure of the cities also changed. Moscow and Petrograd population figures for 1920[4] show that the middle classes and small producers – members of the free professions, merchants, artisans, and craftsmen – were depleted, while déclassé elements, such as servants of masters who had fled or been killed, stood almost untouched, and with them the quite indestructible criminal demimonde that could not but thrive on the prevailing conditions of dislocation. Two groups now stood out as strongest in these towns: the working class and the category described as 'state employees' (*sluzhashchie*). In the latter, probably, was a mass of lower Tsarist officials who had flocked into the new Soviet offices, as well as many new recruits from the former privileged classes who, being literate, could get office jobs and some kind of haven. A survey prepared for Lenin[5] claimed that in 1920 a typical Soviet institution would shelter, for every fifteen hundred officials, some nine hundred from the former 'working intelligentsia', two hundred and fifty former workers, and about three hundred former landowners, priests, officers, top managers or 'bourgeois specialists', and high Tsarist officials. All these people got into a lot of trouble in later years; the label of '*byvshie liudi*' (people from the past) turned out to be ineradicable.

The working class, especially the hard core that the Soviet system considered its mainstay, dwindled by more than half. Some six hundred thousand served in the Red Army, one hundred eighty thousand were killed, many went into the state and Party *apparat* and others – some seventy-five thousand – into food squads. Many more returned to their native villages in order to survive, or became déclassé in various ways.[6] Those who remained in the factories were diluted by an influx of 'foreign elements' from other social strata conscipted for labor. This admixture contributed to the general industrial demoralization and unrest an element that, as Soviet writers stated, was 'purely peasant': demands for an end to the forced requisition of grain and cattle and the confiscation of 'peasants' domestic objects' (sic).[7] It was alleged that this was a result of the 'corrupting influence of petty-bourgeois anarchy [stikhiia]' on the working class.

As industry came to a standstill, some three million people were fired in an enormous purge of offices and factories. The state could not employ them and could offer them no rations. They included two hundred sixty thousand industrial workers, 27.7 percent of Vesenkha's (i.e., Supreme Council of the National Economy of the USSR) work force.[8]

The peasantry was the class that survived the upheaval best. It absorbed many of the fleeing city dwellers, quite a number of whom – characteristically for Russia – had not yet severed their connections with their native villages. It is important to note the so-called levelling out (*poravnenie*) of the peasantry. Many of the richer peasants disappeared, or lost part of their farms and economic strength, and many poor peasants received land and, at least for the statistician, moved into the category of the 'middle' peasant.

The Civil War left the cities shattered. Russia became much more rural and smallholding than it had been before the storm – a considerable setback in terms of social and economic development. Significantly, Russia's historical 'heartland' – the most developed and populated central regions – was also badly battered. As Lenin's stronghold, the 'heartland' survived the onslaught of the peripheries, but it was bled white and in great need of a respite to recover from the bleeding.

The New Economic Policy

The respite was provided by the New Economic Policy (NEP), which allowed a limited restoration of private enterprise and reestablished market relations between town and country. This helped restore economic activity to prerevolutionary levels and bring the population figures up to and above those of old Russia. It was the tide of robust peasant fertility that made it possible for the country to recover from the war wounds. The cities also grew, regaining or surpassing the prerevolutionary population level by 1926. Working class numbers were back at, though not above, prewar level by the end of NEP.

Restoration of the country's industrial–administrative stronghold earned the new political system a breathing spell, but without producing any important structural changes that might have overcome Russia's backwardness. If anything, this structure was less developed than the Tsarist one. Eighty-two percent of the population still lived in rural areas, and 77 percent earned a livelihood directly from agriculture; 86.7 percent of the employed population lived on agriculture. This was, in crude terms, the level of development of India or Turkey, though Russia was better equipped in terms of administrative and industrial experience. The social structure that emerged in the NEP period was characterized, first of all, by nationalization of the key sectors of the economy, hence a larger role for the state. A parallel novelty, in the political sphere, was the Party and its leadership. This new factor had important social implications too, as the role, status, and well-being of individuals and groups would increasingly be determined by their place in the state apparatus and the Party, not by wealth or birth. This utterly new and momentous fact was not yet fully perceived, because of the continued existence of private sectors and people with money.

The Party, the new linchpin of the system, was in the process of transformation. The old revolutionary organization of political intellectuals and politically active workers (there were no peasants in the Bolshevik party before the revolution, and not many just after) was steadily being eliminated, and a 'secretarial machinery', reflecting the impact of Civil War and NEP recruits on the social composition of the Party, was coming into the ascendant. The lower and middle ranks of the Party, and to some extent the upper ranks, began to draw in semieducated recruits from the milieus of industrial workers and junior government employees, and this important new pool of officials could not fail to make an imprint on the outlook of the party and to penetrate the higher echelons. For some time to come, the very top Party posts would still be held by the former professional revolutionaries – but it was precisely this category that was continually weakened by dissent and pushed out. A crucial role in the state machinery was played by professional experts, the so-called bourgeois intellectuals, who had acquired their skills before the revolution. Only the few who joined the Party before or during the revolution had the privilege of having the 'bourgeois' stigma removed. Their weight was a tribute to the strength of the pool of professional talent that Tsarist Russia already possessed but had not managed to put to full use. Their important role in restoring industry, organizing the state administration, and teaching Russia's youth was parallel to the role peasants played in restoring the country's livelihood and human stock. They would soon, however, have to play the very different role of scapegoat.

The urban population of NEP Russia was made up of a growing working class (estimated at 4.5 million in 1926–27); an army of unemployed, reaching at least the million mark; and the increasingly large and influential group of government employees (reaching 3.5 million at the same period), partly composed of former Tsarist officials and refugees from the former privileged classes. Some seven hundred thousand artisans and half a million small merchants, mainly self-employed, formed a fairly small supply-and-services private sector. To complete the picture, there was a maze of smaller, picturesque underworld elements; an amazingly large number of 'servants' (339,000), middlemen, and speculators (the heroes of Zoshchenko and Ilf and Petrov[9]); and a very small but immensely creative artistic intelligentsia. As for the Nepmen or 'bourgeoisie' – entrepreneurs and merchants employing hired labor – they constituted only 75,600 people (284,000 together with their families), according to one source.[10] Such figures could be inflated by including the small merchants under the heading of 'bourgeoisie',[11] giving the still unimpressive total of 855,000 people (2,705,000 with families). This shows how small the private sector was, even after the quite inadmissible inclusion, common in the official statistics, of peddlers and people renting out a room in an apartment in the category of 'entrepreneurs'.

An assessment of the taxable earnings of all groups and classes of NEP society made by a special committee of Sovnarkom[12] showed that the category called 'small, semicapitalist entrepreneurs' earned per capita only slightly more than Soviet officials, and even this figure was pushed up by the numerically smaller but richer group of merchants belonging to the 'big bourgeoisie'. Artisans employing hired labor similarly earned per capita slightly more than workers or officials. But it was only the few big entrepreneurs and merchants who earned considerable sums, though these were certainly less impressive after tax. The scope of private entrepreneurial activity under NEP can further be seen from figures on the labor force employed by the bourgeoisie. The bulk of private employment was concentrated in the small, basically craft industries, which had 230,400 workers, while the big capitalist entrepreneurs employed only 67,200 people.[13] One would not quarrel with the Soviet statistician who stated that the NEP bourgeoisie was 'suffering from a wasting disease' (khudosochnaia).[14]

Under NEP, the peasantry was to a great extent left to its own devices, coming into contact with cities through the usual ways of the marketplace and part-time work, and with the state at the time of tax assessment and payment. Grain procurement was another area of contact fraught with potential conflict, but in the heyday of NEP this was still a commercial operation. The peasantry was relatively peaceful and not particularly antisoviet. Nevertheless, the Russian peasants, true to their traditions, distrusted the state and its officials – particularly the tax collector, who was for them the symbol of the state. For the peasant, what was 'state' (kazënnyi) came to be seen as the product of a foreign, soulless, and oppressive force.[15]

The phenomenon of otkhod – seasonal departure of peasants in search of work – reappeared with NEP after a prolonged absence during the Civil War, and grew to a stream of several million otkhodniki per year. This put pressure on the towns and increased their unemployment rate, but helped the peasant family make ends meet and allowed the cities to get the indispensable labor force for many difficult jobs. The otkhodnik, a product of rural overpopulation, occupied an intermediary rung between the farmer and the urban worker or artisan; and in this category, probably, were many of the most literate and competent elements of the peasantry.

The social 'levelling' that the revolution caused in the countryside was not significantly disturbed during the NEP years. The most cautious assessments[16] show 2,300,000 farmhands, but of these only 44 percent – about one million people – worked in the private farms, the rest working for the state or for peasant communities. At the other pole of rural society were the 'rural entrepreneurs' (kulaks), holding 750–760,000 homesteads or about 3.4 percent of all farms. By definition, they were supposed to have prospered through systematic exploitation of hired labor.[17] However, the 'systematic exploitation' was hardly impressive, considering that 750,000 rural entrepreneurs were employing only about a million laborers. The most prosperous peasants, according to a large 1927 survey, had two to three cows and up to ten hectares of sowing area, *for an average family of seven people.*[18] Sovnarkom's taxation committee computed that such an entrepreneur made 239.8 rubles a year for each member of his family, compared to a rural official's 297 rubles. Though the kulak still made twice as much as the middle peasant,[19] Soviet rural 'capitalism' barely existed. The state could curb the richer peasants at will; indeed, it did so in 1928–29, when, under pressure of taxation and forced procurements, this stratum shrank very substantially,[20] and rural 'capitalism' began to melt like wax. In defiance of the official class analysis of the peasantry, the attempt at the end of NEP to identify and squeeze out kulaks immediately had adverse effects on the peasantry and agriculture in general; many 'middle' peasants were badly affected, and their economic activity began to dwindle.[21]

The cultural lag

NEP and its class structure, though quite aptly characterized as a 'mixed economy', was not a mixture of 'socialism' and 'capitalism'. Basically the society and the economy were dominated by the rural sector and small-scale producers and merchants, with a small, highly concentrated and influential large-scale industrial sector, and a state administration employing quite a cohort of officials and putting to good use a smaller administrative and professional stratum.[22] This society was spared such familiar phenomena of underdevelopment as absentee landowning and money-lending classes with a plethora of servants and luxurious, conspicuous spending. But it had its own stigmata of backwardness – a greedy, uneducated, and inefficient officialdom and a maze of offices in which a simple citizen, especially a peasant, felt entirely lost and quite unceremoniously mistreated. 'Bureaucratism' was officially attributed to 'survivals of the past' and was combatted under this heading. Linked to the bureaucratic source of corruption were the 'infected spots' (*gnoiniki*) resulting from unholy alliances of officials (especially in the supply networks) with private merchants on big illegal operations with government goods. The press was full of such stories of large-scale corruption, and now and again the whole leadership of a district or even a republic would be purged for having tolerated or participated in such affairs. NEP thus had its share of venality, crooked business deals, and ways to spend the profits, including nightclubs, *cafés chantants*, gambling dens, and houses of prostitution.

In the background lay discrepancies very menacing to the system's future. There was the disparity between the Party's ideology and aspirations and the frustrating reality of a petty-bourgeois country, aptly described by a recent historian as 'large scale theories versus small scale realities'.[23] As the government, not unnaturally, strove to revive and develop the economy, it allowed the cultural front – mass education and the fight against illiteracy – to trail dangerously: the economic recovery had not yet become a cultural one as well. Although the industrial specialist was relatively well off and the white-collar employee in big industry earned almost twice as much as the worker in the period 1926–29, teachers – lowest on the pay scale, especially in elementary schools – were the most neglected part of the 'intelligentsia' in income and status[24] and earned no more than 45 percent of their prerevolutionary salaries.[25] Investments in 'culture' were lagging heavily behind investments in the economy, and Lunacharskii complained to the Fifteenth Party Congress that he had at his disposal less money for schools than the Tsarist educational system had. Some of the top leadership were painfully aware of the problem. Rykov stated at the same congress that without sufficient cultural advance further economic progress would become blocked.[26]

With the proportion of elementary-school pupils per thousand inhabitants even lower than that in many poorly developed countries – and with lower per capita expenses on culture and average duration of schooling in the countryside and in towns[27] – the current expression 'Asiatic lack of culture' (*asiatskaia beskul'turnost'*) had its justification. 'Vodka is squeezing out culture!' a Party writer exclaimed dramatically,[28] though he still did not admit that it was too early to talk of a 'new culture', let alone a proletarian one. It was one of the peculiarities of Party life that obvious facts about society became distorted in the mirror of Party struggles and ideological juggling. Trotskii had to be attacked for having stated the truth that as long as the 'clutches of dictatorship existed', no new culture would emerge.[29]

The 'clutches of dictatorship' would soon be used to spread popular education, but the higher levels of culture, as well as the bearers of that culture, were to go through serious troubles. The party had made a concerted effort, partly successful, to get more workers and peasants into higher education. In 1926, however, limitations on university entry for white-collar and other nonproletarian social groups were eased, and the university became relatively accessible even to sons of 'alien classes', especially those of the 'bourgeois intelligentsia'.[30] But the NEP world, dominated as it was by the mass peasant background, the rapacious moneymaking Nepman, the sternly ideological Party militant, and the conniving, corrupt state official, did not make for any buoyancy in the intelligentsia and student circles. Vodka was widely used among the moody

Russian educated people; and among student youth in particular there were 'manifestations of despair culminating in suicide' at and after the time when the poet Esenin took his life, and 'mischievous behavior culminating in crime', as Lunacharskii put it.[31]

In contrast to the oversensitive intellectual Oblomovs[32] and talented but gloomy Esenins was the current urban type of the ordinary 'soviet lad' – poorly educated, but dodgy and shrewd, semicynical, and semiparasitic. His collective portrait was sketched by Bukharin as follows: a good drinker and a good fighter who can raise hell and swear like a trooper; a lad who won't work too hard and knows how to look after himself.[33] These 'smart fellows' were products of a semideveloped society, on the border of a static and uninspiring rural world and a corrupting urban (usually small-town) world of petty affairs. They were to flock into the clean and unexacting jobs of lower (and often higher) officialdom, into the supply networks, into the criminal world and – why not? – into jobs as police investigators.

In sum, the cultural deprivation of the NEP population – with its working class crammed into a diminishing living space, its massive illiteracy, its tricksters and Oblomovs, its brilliant top layers and crude and ambitious rulers – gave substance and lent credibility to the fears for the fate of the revolution and the future of the state. The danger of degeneration (*pererozhdenie*) of the Party and its leadership – a cry raised by the Party oppositions – was taken up by Bukharin, though somewhat ambiguously since he himself was still one of the leading official spokesmen: if there was no cultural rise of the masses, no constant influx of workers to universities, degeneration was to be feared, as this would certainly push the leading cadres 'to close in upon themselves, to harden into a separate layer, with a tendency to form a new ruling class'.[34]

Bukharin's suggestions for avoiding such an outcome were clearly insufficient. Speedy and half-baked mass education may tend to make people more vulnerable to propaganda and indoctrination[35] and enhance the grip of the leadership and the controllers, rather than make the leaders more open to the pressure of the masses. This was, in fact, what happened after the shattering of NEP society and its furious reshaping during the subsequent 'revolution from above', when mass schooling and crash courses did not prevent the hardening and self-seclusion of the ruling groups, or an unprecedented degree of alienation of state from society.

The big drive

Ruralization of the cities

The all-out drive for industrialization from 1928 opened a period in which so many things happened simultaneously that one could aptly describe it as the birth pangs of a world. There was, to begin with, a huge population movement, with millions milling around the country, building and rebuilding, flocking to towns, searching for a way out of material and other miseries, and with many ending up in the growing concentration camps. At the same time, a massive cadres formation process was launched, bringing in its wake a hectic restructuring of society – a growing industrial working class, sprawling bureaucracies and offices, managements, a scientific establishment, a new hierarchy of status, privilege, and power, and an ominously growing security and coercion establishment that tried to match the energy of the builders by furiously ferreting out and destroying numerous social categories of the past as well as many of the newly formed groups. In the countryside, it was an upheaval as elemental as a hurricane – the old rural structures and ways of life were shattered to their very roots, with uncountable consequences for society and state alike.

The whole explosion was, once more, damaging for population growth. Population growth did not stop, to be sure, but was certainly slowed down, especially in the countryside, by the collectivization terror and the famine in the southern parts of the country in 1932–33. The rural birthrate fell from 49.1 in 1913 (31.7 in cities) to 42–43 in 1923–24 and, finally, to 32.2 in 1935 (24.6 in cities). Material hardship and the turmoil of collectivization were among the main reasons for this trend[36] and, according to a number of sources, Gosplan expected by 1937 a much greater population than was actually found in the 1937 census.[37] Without entering into the complex problem of how high a price in human lives was paid for Soviet development policies, there is no doubt that, as a result of the internal battles of the Five-Year Plans, the Soviet Union was approaching the war – another terrible bloodletting – with many combat divisions missing.

Industrialization was launched on such a scale that the sudden demand for labor flooded the planners and government offices and for a long time threw the whole machinery out of gear. The peasantry had to provide, at short notice, millions of people for the construction sites and the new cities. This in itself was no problem for the notoriously overpopulated countryside. Peasants were used to the quite unorganized but fairly steady *otkhod*, the seasonal departure for work along well-trodden historical routes. But at first the newly created and shaky *kolkhozy* (collective farms) tried to retain the labor force, fearing the prospect of remaining without the labor indispensable for the still unfamiliar tasks of a collective organization. However, governmental measures and the urge of the peasants to leave the *kolkhozy* soon broke down all impediments.[38] During 1926–39 the cities grew by some thirty million people at least, and their share in population grew from about 18 percent to 24 percent (reminding us that by 1939, 76 percent of the population was still rural). During the First Five-Year Plan alone the cities grew by 44 percent, almost as much as during the whole period 1897–1926, and the salaried labor force (workers and officials) more than doubled, growing from 10.8 to 22.6 million.[39] There is no doubt that the bulk of this growth was made up by peasants. If during the years 1928 and 1929 about one million new migrants came to live in the cities, during the next three years three million came each year. The Moscow and Leningrad regions alone each received 3.5 million new inhabitants during the First Five-Year Plan. In 1931 a staggering figure of 4.1 million peasants joined the city population; and for the years 1929–35 the total was 17.7 million.[40] This does not yet give the whole measure of the mass movements and changes, since in addition to those peasants who came to stay in industry, cities, and construction sites, millions of seasonal *otkhodniki* went, with or without contracts, to build roads, canals, and factories. In the remarkable year of 1931 alone, about seven million *otkhodniki* moved around the country.[41]

In the cities, the inordinate and unanticipated growth transformed a strained housing situation into an appalling one, creating the specifically Soviet (or Stalinist) reality of chronically overcrowded lodgings, with consequent attrition of human relations, strained family life, destruction of privacy and personal life, and various forms of psychological strain. All this provided a propitious hunting ground for the ruthless, the primitive, the blackmailer, the hooligan, and the informer. The courts dealt with an incredible mass of cases testifying to the human destruction caused by this congestion of dwellings. The falling standards of living, the lines outside stores, and the proliferation of speculators suggest the depth of the tensions and hardship. Soon the cumulative results of such conditions were to cause widespread manifestations of neurosis and anomie, culminating in an alarming fall in the birthrate. By 1936, in fact, the big cities experienced a net loss of population, with more children dying than being born, which explains the alarm in government circles and the famous laws against abortion proclaimed in that year.

Once the initial urgent need for labor was satisfied and the authorities realized the damaging effects of the chaotic influx into cities, passports and the *propiska* system of obligatory registration with the local police were introduced (by law at the end of 1932 and in practice during 1933). These were methods of controlling movement of the rural population, especially during the hungry winter of 1932–33, when starving peasants trying to save their lives crawled into the cities without permission. A peasant received a passport only if the authorities were satisfied that he was needed in some employment and the *kolkhoz* was ready to let him go.

It was during those years of mass mobilization that the government and managers acquired the characteristically Soviet habit of shuffling the labor force around like cattle. With their eyes fixed only on their targets, they forgot some elementary human needs. This attitude, which was not born in the camps but predated them, served as a background to the growing camp system of the GPU and the 'reeducation through labor' of its inhabitants.

A single term to characterize the process would be 'ruralization' (*okrest'ianivanie*) of the cities. One of the results of this ruralization was the breakdown of labor discipline, which saddled the state with an enormous problem of educating and disciplining the mass of the crude labor force. The battle against absenteeism, shirking, drinking in factories during working hours, and breaking tools was long, and the Soviet government played no 'humanistic' games in this fight. Very soon, methods such as denial of ration cards, eviction from lodgings, and even penal sentences for undisciplined workers were introduced. The same harshness was applied in the fight against deterioration in the quality of industrial products (*brak*); here the fight was directed not only against workers but also against managers and technicians, and the weapons were special laws put in the hands of the prosecutors.

'Tekuchka'

As traditionally happened in times of stress and catastrophe, peasant Russia was turning into *Rus' brodiazhnaia*, a country of vagrants. Massive and rapid labor turnover (*tekuchka*) was characteristic of the early thirties. The factory labor force, hard pressed by working and living conditions, moved around to find something better, encouraged by real or fictitious differences in pay or food. The workers were often (illegally) lured by promises from the managements of construction sites and enterprises, who were forever anxious to have labor reserves to meet crises of plan fulfillment.

It was all too easy to explain this phenomenon by insisting on the petty-bourgeois character of the new working classes, with its concomitant anarchism, self-seeking, lack of discipline, attachment to property, and slovenliness, to use the morally charged vocabulary of Soviet sources. That it was this same petty-bourgeois mass of parasites which actually built the country is one of the paradoxes of this type of class analysis. Factories and mines in these years were transformed into railway stations — or, as Ordzhonikidze exclaimed in despair — into one huge 'nomadic gypsy camp'.[42] The cost of the turnover was incredible. Before they had managed to learn their job, people had already given their notice or done something in order to get fired.

But more: the same process, and on a large scale, was going on among managers and administrators, specialists and officials. At all levels of the local administration and Party *apparat*, people adopted the habit of leaving in good time, before they were penalized, recalled, brought in for questioning, downgraded, fired, or arrested.[43]

Thus workers, administrators, specialists, officials, party apparatus men, and in great masses, peasants were all moving around and changing jobs, creating unwanted surpluses in some places and dearths in others, losing skills or failing to acquire them, creating streams and floods in which families were destroyed, children lost, and morality dissolved. Social, administrative, industrial, and political structures were all in flux. The mighty dictatorial government found itself, as a result of its impetuous activity during those early years of accelerated industrialization, presiding over a 'quicksand' society.

It is not difficult to imagine the despair of the rulers and their fierce resolution to put an end to this situation and introduce law and order into the chaos. The stern traits of the disciplining effort soon became viciously contorted. That the drive pressed hard on the judiciary – itself 'leaking' like everything else – was a foregone conclusion. The secret police (GPU) was allowed to swell its empire to enormous proportions. Constant purges (*chistki*) – a paradoxical method, not unfamiliar in medicine, of dealing with an illness by injecting the same microbes – were undertaken and contributed considerably to the flux. After the early period of 'proletarianization', two additional strategies were used to stabilize the body social: first, creation and consolidation of a network of supervisors in the form of hierarchies, apparatuses, and elites; and then, from about 1934, the adoption of policies that the sociologist Timasheff[44] described as 'The Great Retreat' – a set of classical measures of social conservatism, law and order strategies complete with a nationalist revival, and efforts to instill values of discipline, patriotism, conformism, authority and orderly careerism. That such a policy should be accompanied by another shattering set of purges, in the later thirties, is one more enigma, amazing even for one who is already well versed in the vagaries of Soviet history and policies.

During the Five-Year Plan frenzy (1928–32), all social groups and classes were in a state of flux and shock, partially or totally 'destructured' and unhinged. One can say that for a short span of time, some years ahead of the happy announcements of the coming of a socialist society, Russian society was indeed 'classless' – all its classes were out of shape, leaving a free field for the state and its institutions, themselves very considerably shaken, to act and grow.

Class warfare

The 'aliens'

Industrialization, collectivization, and the formation of cadres were not the only factors in the shaping of the new social structure. Social policies of a quite complex and often contradictory pattern were factors too. Once can tentatively speak of an initial period of 'proletarianization', which could also be called the 'production' (*produktsionnyi*) period, when workers were given preference and drafted through special mobilizations into universities, schools, and administrations. Parallel to this process went *spetseedstvo* (specialist-baiting), overwhelming emphasis on social origin, and the transformation of academies and universities into 'production brigades'. The frenzied 'proletarianization' often emptied the factories of their most experienced and reliable workers and pushed many of them into a hostile environment of officialdom or, on the basis of social origin or Party loyalty alone, into the stressful situation of being enrolled in institutions of higher learning without appropriate academic preparation.

From 1931, this line began to change. Recruitment of workers to offices was formally forbidden at the end of 1930, and somewhat later university enrollment returned to a basis of some ability and academic preparation. A temporary halt to the cruder forms of *spetseedstvo* also occurred at this time. With the fight for labor discipline in factories, *kolkhozy*, and offices, a new strategy was adopted for instilling stability and productivity, which entailed creating a new and strong layer of bosses. This kind of 'elitist' policy would continue, not without some baffling reversals, throughout the thirties.

That mass terror was permeating all these phases is a well-known fact. The first target of the security 'organs' were those who had belonged to the former privileged classes before the revolution ('class enemies'). Later the terror would be turned against the growing elite itself: most of the top layers in Party and state administrations were to be totally renovated by an influx of new recruits from the universities or the lower ranks of the bureaucracy.

One important factor that ought to be strongly emphasized is that for millions there was upward mobility and social promotion in the midst of the whole upheaval. This statement needs to be qualified. Peasants going to factories could not see it then as promotion – for many, the factories meant a drop in their standard of living and self-respect. But it may have been different for the great number who became officials, however low the rank and bad the pay. For those who went to universities and to responsible jobs, or acquired new skills, the social advance was undeniable and the new possibilities were seized on eagerly.

Urban social groups and classes, freshly formed to a great extent, were obviously not yet stabilized in their new jobs and settings, and it would take some time for the new patterns to solidify. Flux remained part of the social landscape for most of the Stalinist period. No wonder that the state, which turned into a Leviathan and kept extending its domination, met no countervailing forces or checks. The state presided imperiously over the social changes and ruled society – but this does not mean that the influencing and shaping was a one-way affair. Though the mighty state machinery was in no direct way accountable to the masses, the social milieu, however passive and defenseless, might exert an influence not unlike that which the conquered sometimes have on their conquerors. But this is a problem that must be left open for further discussion.

Of all social groups, the most defenseless were those destined for 'liquidation as a class'. This could mean anything from simply being squeezed out of one's business and allowed to hide in some office or factory to imprisonment in camps or shooting. The biggest such group, with more than a million homesteads, was that of the kulaks. 'Dekulakization', which consisted of exiling the kulak families to uninhabited territories (plus some straight prison sentences and shootings), was equivalent in its scale to the uprooting of a small nation. It was an economic disaster, with incalculable long-term effects and insignificant, even ridiculous, immediate gains: officially, one hundred seventy million rubles worth of property (or up to four hundred million, according to a reassessment)[45] were confiscated, that is, between one hundred and seventy and four hundred rubles per household. What meager assistance the *kolkhozy* gained from the destruction of 'rural capitalism'! It is probable that even the uncharitable but unavoidable expenditure on resettlement of these people, after shattering them and thinning out their numbers, cost more.

But kulaks were not the only victims of the 'anticapitalist revolution'. All members of the relatively modest sectors of private activity and initiative under NEP now fell into one of the imprecise categories of 'nonlaboring', 'alien', or 'déclassé element', or were *lishentsy* – deprived of civil rights. In the RSFSR alone, 1,706,025 people or some 3.9 percent of all potential voters were *lishentsy*, and in 1932, 3.5 percent were still on the black list.[46] But these figures probably do not express the full numbers of those who got into trouble by virtue of belonging to one category or another of 'people from the past' listed in the edict that instructed authorities on who should be deprived of the right to vote.[47] The methods of dealing with these groups were not restricted to the quite platonic deprivation of the right to vote. Such deprivation was often followed by denial of lodging, food ration, and medical services,[48] and especially by exile. One of the better known aspects of the antibourgeois campaign was the mass arrest of people supposed to have possessed valuables like gold and silver. Another was a huge purge of 'undesirable persons' from the cities in 1932, just before the introduction of passports.[49]

The 'squeezing out of the private businessman' (*vytesnenie chastnika*) consisted of the eviction of about half a million ex-merchants (1.5 million with families), most of whom were small-timers working without employees. Their shops in the countryside, where most of them operated, were assessed in 1927 as having a capital value of 711 rubles per shop.[50] The effects of this eviction operation, as well as similar action against artisans and craftsmen, were momentous. As merchants closed their shops and went to factories, offices, and camps, there arose a deplorable situation of 'commercial desert', a development the state and cooperative sectors were not equipped to cope with. Even the meager goods available could not be distributed. New shops and commercial organizations were quickly founded to cope with the emergency, but their quality remained lamentable and their numbers insufficient for more than a generation. As the lines outside the stores grew, so did the plague of speculation, black markets, and rackets. The fight against speculation – now counting among its victims many people with impeccable class origins – brought a new mass of new criminal offenses into the overcrowded and overworked courts: personal and mass embezzlements, theft in supply networks, fictitious accounting, illicit dealings in ration cards, and so on.[51] A fiercely repressive law of 7 August 1932 against theft in *kolkhozy* was later broadened to embrace all other sectors and became the state's main weapon for protecting its property. Mass thefts were in fact taking place as the economic situation, especially food supplies, deteriorated. The GPU could help neither in supplying food nor in rooting out theft. The nation, disrespectful toward state property, seemed to have been transformed into a nation of thieves.

The working class

For the development of the working class, some figures can provide a telling picture (Table 1). Growth was phenomenal in the First Five-Year Plan period and still considerable in the second, but slowed almost to a standstill as far as industrial and construction workers were concerned in the years 1937–40 (when the increase was mainly in the 'employees' sector). The growth, as already stated, was based on a mass influx of

Table 1

| | (In thousands) | | | |
	1928	1932	1937	1940
Total employment (workers and employees)	10800	20600	26700	31200
Workers only (total)	6800	14500	17200	20000
Workers in industry	3124	6007	7924	8290
Workers in construction	630	2479	1875	1929
Workers in *sovkhozy* and other state farms	301	1970	1539	1558

Sources: A. B. Mitrofanova, in D. L. Baevskii, ed., *Izmeneniia v chislennosti i sostave sovetskogo rabochego klassa*, M. 1961, p. 220; and same author, in R. P. Dadykin, ed., *Formirovanie i razvitie sovetskogo rabochego klassa* (1917–1961), M. 1964, pp. 55–56.

peasants. But even in the pre-Plan period the peasant influence in the working class had been strong, especially in the Ukrainian mining regions. A survey of industrial labor carried out in 1929 showed that 42.6 percent of the workers were of peasant origin, and 20.6 percent had land in the countryside.[52]

Not unexpectedly, the professional level and educational standards of the crude labor force were extremely low. As late as 1939, when things had largely settled down, only 8.2 percent of the workers had an education of seven grades or more.[53] The working class had also become much younger. It included not only a mass of inexperienced and often bewildered peasants, but also many women new to industrial jobs: by 1936 women constituted 40 percent of the work force.

For the managers, for the state, and especially for the workers themselves, the problems arising from such rapid growth were formidable. At the beginning, many of the newly enrolled peasants experienced cultural and psychological shock, manifested, for example, in drinking, hooliganism, criminal behavior, breaking the expensive and unfamiliar machinery, and 'a colossal growth of industrial traumatism'.[54] The problem of labor turnover has already been discussed. The bewildered administrations sometimes tried to placate the workers and sometimes reacted with 'administrative methods' – a flood of fines, dismissals, and repression.

The constant seesaw of short periods of liberalism and long waves of *'goloe administrirovanie'* (crude administrative methods) was by now firmly embedded in Soviet politics. Mass repression was not, as the party liked to put it, some aberration of local officials, but party policy. The harshness of the methods used against absenteeism can be illustrated by a law of 15 November 1932, supplemented a few months later, prescribing dismissal, denial of food rations, denial of access to food shops, and eviction from lodgings regardless – as the text emphasized – of the time of year.[55] Factory administrations were now allowed to starve people in order to ensure their presence in the factories. A single day of 'unjustified absence' was defined as absenteeism, punishable according to this law (in 1938, twenty minutes' absence or lateness would constitute absenteeism).

The overall strategy, of course, was more complex and included more than sheer repression. Trade unions and Party cells were mobilized to serve the needs of production and the plans, and this was supplemented by inculcating in the managers a taste for the pleasures of power. Tough leadership became the style preached by the Party, with Kaganovich teaching the manager to behave in such a way that 'the earth should tremble when the director walks around the plant'.[56] The NEP 'triangle' of Party, trade unions, and management was abandoned in 1929 and replaced by fierce one-man rule (*edinonachalie*). A further method in the struggle to raise the productivity of labor was the enforcement of piece work; spreading of the pay differential; and promotion and offer of better food and priority in lodging, vacations, and school admission for the outstanding worker (*udarnik*) and his children, and for those who stayed long enough on the job. It never seemed sufficient, however, and the fight against the proponents of new categories of morally reprehensible behavior (castigated by the propaganda as 'flitters', 'idlers', 'disorganizers', 'absentees', and so on) always included those 'indiscriminate mass repressions' that Kaganovich, the chief architect of the strategy, pretended to regret in 1936.[57]

From time to time, almost as an afterthought, an Ordzhonikidze or Kirov would appeal to the managers to stop neglecting their workers and to improve their attitude towards them.[58] But the fact was that once the 'triangle' was gone and the Party and trade union turned their 'face to production', they had to turn their face against the workers.

The peasants

In the countryside, a state of major crisis and warfare existed between the government and the peasants. There was nothing like 'dekulakization' in regard to the workers, even in the heat of the ruthless fight to instill discipline in their ranks, and (except in the prewar period) the most repressive bills gainst labor absenteeism did not abolish the freedom to leave the workplace after giving due notice, though many obstacles were put in the way of doing so. Salaries and social benefits paid out to workers, however meager, nevertheless remained an obligation that the state accepted and fulfilled. In the cities, the government's effort to stem disorder was to some degree bearing fruit, and workers, however sluggish and apathetic many of them might be, did learn trades, improve productivity, and yield to more orderly patterns.

In the countryside, the effects of collectivization were of a different kind. For the peasants it was a revolution, a violent destruction of a system of production and of a life pattern. Although even here, after an initial period of shock lasting, probably, from 1930 to 1934, the peasants acquired some working habits and accepted some routines; long-term phenomena persisted, and some have not been overcome even today.[59]

At the root of the difficulty of the *kolkhoz* system lay the fact that the peasants' previous experience, way of life, and educational level in no way prepared them to accept and run the system that was now being imposed on them. It was this contradiction, a Soviet writer stated, that made imperative the state's interference in[60] – or rather takeover of – all aspects of running the *kolkhoz* system. In addition, the strains caused by forcing on a conservative and mostly illiterate people[61] an abrupt change of age-old life patterns were compounded by an attack on their religion – an act of incredible folly, and quite irrelevant to the problems of *kolkhoz* production. Its futility was demonstrated by the later admission of the head of the antireligious crusade that by the end of the thirties two-thirds of the peasants were still believers.[62]

At the very beginning of the process some leaders honest enough to raise a fuss in public predicted the essence of things to come. S. I. Syrtsov, Premier of the government of the RSFSR, sounded the alarm.[63] There could already be observed, at the beginning of 1930, a dangerous 'explosion of consumerist moods': as the regulators and stimulants of his previous life and production were lost, in fact violently repudiated, the peasant's usual urge to save and accumulate was replaced by an equally strong urge to consume everything (*proedat'*); his usual care and worry about the state of affairs on his farm was replaced by apathy and 'a nihilistic attitude toward production' (*proizvodstvennyi nigilizm*). The peasant was now waiting to be guided, expecting to be told what to do. But the state did not know what to do or how to do it, and its agencies in the countryside were in confusion and disarray.

Loss of interest in production was part of the larger problem of loss of identity and self-respect. In the previous system, the peasant was the master (*khoziain*) on his farm and with this, however poor the farm, went the sense of dignity of a free agent. The new situation deprived the peasants of status and freedom: their main objection to the *kolkhozy* was that they would be 'put on a ration system', which would mean a loss of independence. When this happened the peasants, as we have seen, became eager to get away from the *kolkhoz* into towns – a reaction, among other things, against the phenomenon of 'statization' (*okazënivanie*).[64]

The first steps of *okazënivanie* were not part of a deliberately planned strategy. The government was forced, or felt itself forced, to undertake salvage operations that led it ever deeper into the trap of growing interference in all phases and details of agricultural production and organization. The one big step that can be regarded as strategy was the removal of machinery from the *kolkhozy* to the government MTS (Machine Tractor Stations),[65] but much else in government policy at the beginning had the character of ad hoc reactions.

Because the state's needs in grain and other products were urgent and immediate, it pressed on its officials and local administrations to get what was necessary from the peasants. Quite soon the *kolkhoznik* and *kolkhoz* managements found themselves gagged and at the mercy of an all-powerful network of local officials making searches and seizures, judging, punishing, expelling, and, in particular, arresting freely, making liberal use of the meaningless label of *podkulachnik* (kulak's hireling). Ia. A. Iakovlev, the Commissar for Agriculture, formally protested, apparently, at the Central Committee meeting in July 1931 against what he called the 'mass of anti-kolkhoz actions' by local administrations, saying that the *kolkhoznik* had become 'an object of sheer arbitrariness'. But in the same year one of his

Central Committee colleagues, B. P. Sheboldaev, gave the key to the situation and to the policy of the hardliners who were more powerful than
Iakovlev. The *kolkhozy*, he stated, 'have too little goodwill towards the
interests of the state', and there was no justification for 'idealizing the
kolkhoznik'. The old wisdom of rulers – coercion – had to be resorted to
without qualms.[66] This attitude totally disregarded the interests of the
several million peasants. The concerns of the government were epitomized
in the procurement (*zagotovki*) squeeze, 'that touchstone on which our
strength and weakness and the strength and weakness of our enemy were
tested', as Kaganovich said in a sentence crucial to the understanding of
government strategy and the relations between *kolkhoz* peasantry and the
state.[67] 'The enemy' here were truly legion. Hence the shrill demands
coming from the Central Committee to punish 'without mercy' not only
reluctance to part with grain but also what was called 'a maliciously
careless attitude to work';[68] hence the suggestions to local authorities
that bad work should be called 'kulak sabotage' and that lenience toward
transgressors would be considered as help given to the enemy.

Krylenko's[69] typology of 'contravention of socialist legality' in regard to
peasants and the *kolkhoz* included such 'arbitrary treatment of the peasantry as . . . illegal searches and arrests, confiscations, pre-emption of
property, illegal fines and the like'.[70] The capriciousness of the accusations
of 'sloppily careless work' and sabotage becomes clear when we examine
the kind of 'guidance' the state was giving the *kolkhozy*. Obviously the
local Party committees knew nothing about agriculture in general, and
even less about their pet idea – large-scale agricultural production. Stalin
taught that, since the *kolkhozy* were inexperienced, they had to be run
from above by minute party interference. But as Kirov stated in a moment
of despair and truth: 'I myself, sinful man, don't see clearly in agricultural
matters',[71] – this after having given the most ignorant orders to peasants,
and then ordering or approving mass arrests of those who refused to
comply[72] before discovering that he was on a false track.

The more honest Stalinists were more and more despairing of the state
of affairs and were groping for changes. Kirov, who sometimes seemed
utterly disappointed in 1933, called for change and made an appeal to go
and learn from the *kolkhoznik* – a telling statement of the failure of
government methods. But it was at about the same time that Stalin issued
stern instructions to meddle, in effect, with every detail, because the
kolkhozniki did not know how to run their affairs.[73]

The peasants were fettered and 'bureaucratized', and well knew that
they had lost the independence they had had as producers and citizens
under NEP. There was a whole system of discrimination, amounting to a
special legal and social regime for the *kolkhoz* peasantry. If lack of legally
guaranteed rights was to be the trait of the system in regard to all classes,
the peasant was particularly vulnerable because of the ideological formula

of the regime, which considered him suspect in terms of his class origin, in terms of the inferior status of *kolkhozy*, in terms of the purity of socialism in comparison with state-run institutions. Whereas the worker earned a salary – more or less state controlled, but independent of the total output of the industry or of the industry's efficiency – the *kolkhoznik* was paid from the residual of *kolkhoz* income after the crop had been gathered and the state had taken its share. This income was both insecure and, as was formally acknowledged, insufficient to feed the peasant's family; hence the concession to the peasant allowing him a private plot and a cow (small enough not to make him too happy and forgetful of the *kolkhoz*, but big enough to provide for some of his family's, and the whole country's, essential needs). This allowance, of course, was one of the factors keeping the old peasant alive in the *kolkhoznik*, thereby providing an additional argument for doubting his socialist credentials.

In addition to insecurity of income, the peasants were denied the benefits of social security that the state guaranteed its workers and employees.[74] The peasants were subject to several state corvées – road building, timber hauling and so on – whereas city dwellers had long ago forgotten this remnant of the middle ages. The peasant did not have the freedom of movement, however qualified, that the worker had. His travels were controlled by the passport system and the *propiska* (the document indicating registered place of residence), and also by the law of 17 March 1933 stipulating that a peasant was not allowed to leave the *kolkhoz* without a contract from a prospective employer, duly ratified by the *kolkhoz* management. At about the same time, the USSR Procurator Akulov ordered peasants to be punished by up to six months in prison for not respecting a contract with a state employer. Akulov was reminded by one writer (with unknown results) that introducing criminal law into a basically civil transaction like a labor contract was contrary to the principles of Russian and European labor law.[75] But this was precisely the point: disregarding the interest of 'the state' was all too easily becoming a criminal or, even worse, a political offense. This was one of the attributes of 'Stalinism'.

Here, then, was the system of 'military-feudal' exploitation of the peasantry that Bukharin had fearfully anticipated in 1929, and 'statism' at its purest. A producer (not to say citizen) so strongly fettered and discriminated against could not be efficient. On the contrary, he lost the incentive to exert himself on the job, unless this happened to be his own plot, and became demoralized both as a producer and as a person. 'We are not our own men but the *kolkhoz's*,' the peasants often repeated. This summed up the whole process. Before they had been their own men; now they belonged to the *kolkhoz*, but the *kolkhoz* did not belong to them.

Over the years, slow and not unimportant changes took place within the *kolkhoz* peasantry, such as the emergence of numbers of managers and

administrators who did not exist at all in NEP agriculture. Growing
numbers of tractor drivers made their appearance, as did a sprinkling of
'rural intelligentsia' – but according to a Soviet sociologist, by the end of
the Five-Year Plans this so-called rural intelligentsia was barely distin-
guishable by its level of education from the mass of *kolkhozniki*.[76] The
mass was still composed of peasants, and they were at the bottom of the
social ladder, just as the *muzhik* had been in former times. The only means
of social promotion was to move out. Millions did so whenever they could,
and in so doing probably influenced Soviet society, culture, and the state
much more deeply than is sometimes realized.

The educated and the rulers

'Spetseedstvo'

The so-called intelligentsia is a problem of considerable complexity, and its
story during and after the 'big drive' is crucial for understanding the social
structure that was in the making. Here too we have a state action carried
out with great speed and urgency. The First Five-Year Plan created an
enormous demand for technicians, administrators, and scientists of all
sorts, and the existing training facilities and governmental institutions
were overwhelmed by the task. It is significant that very soon the whole
problem of the 'intelligentsia' became a problem of 'cadres' in the hundreds of thousands and even millions, administered and bureaucratized by
a network of 'departments of cadres', established 'as we go along', as
Ordzhonikidze put it.[77] Improvisation of a social and professional process
of such importance is a trait we keep meeting in this period, not only in the
domain of cadres.

   The attitude toward the intelligentsia in this and previous periods was
shaped by contradictory factors and under changing circumstances. From
the very first days of the regime, the party needed educated people to run
the economy and the state (a dependence that was somehow not anticipated: the party leaders, intellectuals themselves, were busy understanding
'history' and political strategy, not running an economy). However, the
intelligentsia en masse, including the so-called popular (*narodnaia*) intelligentsia, actively opposed Bolshevik takeover, in the massive strikes of late
1917/early 1918. This opposition, in its overt forms, was quite quickly put
down, but the shadow kept hanging over relations between the Party and
the intellectuals.

   With all the disdain for Oblomovs and '*intelligenty*' that Bolsheviks
sometimes encouraged (the notorious 'makhaevite tendencies'), an urgent
need arose to foster respect for members of the intelligentsia. It was not an
easy task. The conundrum can be studied in two statements by Lenin: he

declared on the one hand, 'they must be given work, but they must be carefully watched; commissars should be placed over them and their counterrevolutionary schemes suppressed'; he appealed on the other for respect for culture and those who possessed it, and issued the injunction to 'command less, or rather not to command at all'.[78] That this contradictory attitude would produce zigzags in political tactics and mar relations is obvious. Lenin knew that he could not take a step without experts, and he acknowledged frankly after the Civil War that the Red Army, for example, would not have existed at all without the ex-Tsarist officers who helped create it.[79] But the same was true of the universities, the State Planning Commission (Gosplan), and all the important economic ministries as well. The great dream of preparing 'our own' intelligentsia could not be achieved without the old one cooperating in the job.

NEP settled down to an uneasy acceptance of this situation. The intelligentsia was basically still, at the end of NEP, the 'old' one, non-Bolshevik in its majority. In October 1929 a third of all specialists working in the national economy and a majority of those with higher education were from the old intelligentsia, as were 60 percent of teachers in higher education. The mass of new specialists being prepared under Soviet rule would not just be trained by these instructors, but also undoubtedly politically influenced by them.[80]

The Shakhty affair[81] came as a warning and a demonstration that the 'old' would not have it their way in shaping the profile of the immense mass of new trainees. It opened a period in Soviet history that was not only a tragedy for the old intelligentsia but also amounted to a furious destruction of many cultural values. The hectic creation of instruments for the diffusion of culture – schools, higher schools, universities – was to be accompanied by an unbelievable display of obscurantism and attacks on anything sophisticated or refined. The universities, for example, were almost completely destroyed before a new approach, from about 1934, helped to save them.

During the Shakhty trial and thereafter intellectual circles were panic-stricken and depressed, in a not unjustified expectation of a wave of *spetseedstvo* and mass repressions.[82]

One central idea that the key leaders wanted to 'explain' by the Shakhty trial was that neutrality in politics – that is, toward party policies – could lead to sabotage. This message was now presented in a new way: by a stage production with a recognizable signature on it.

Lenin had earlier been irked by the attitude of educated specialists who claimed noninvolvement in politics as part of a moral and professional ethic. This implied, from Lenin's point of view, that they would work as specialists for the new regime without endorsing it or identifying with its aims. Lenin was prepared to accept this compromise, but Stalin's policies refused any such accommodation. His objective, in common with that of the Inquisition, was to force thinking people to desist from their independent thoughts and moral principles and to identify with a party and with policies felt to be unacceptable or questionable. The most unacceptable was precisely what they were asked to do: to prostrate themselves, to turn their guts out in fervent repentance – or else be declared treasonable. The equation 'doubt = treason' was one of the most deadly tools of the moral and cultural reaction that hit the country at the height of its economic and military construction. Why this presumably optimistic surge of creativity was darkened by such a deeply pessimistic attitude to men and culture is one of the unanswered questions. In any case, the quasi-mystical 'disarm yourself before the Party and repent' was self-defeating. Even the most dedicated and blind follower of the Party line could not prove that he had really never had any doubts.

The singling out of the 'bourgeois intelligentsia' for this treatment was a catastrophe. The country's development could not proceed without the participation of the best professionals, who were badly needed amid the now enormous mass of inexperienced and ignorant newcomers and with the deficit of specialists still growing. Some were mercifully allowed to 'redeem their crimes' – that is, their alleged sabotage – by working 'honestly', inventing or designing in their prison cells or on the site, but with the status of convict. To encourage them to invent machinery and weapons, big salaries and the best food in a hungry country were sometimes given to these men, but at the same time they were kept as prisoners and promised freedom at the price of compliance.

The policy certainly did not have the full approval of all top leaders. Within the framework of a new line initiated in 1931 to stop some of the damage of *spetseedstvo*, Ia. E. Rudzutak explained officially that many lower technicians were too ignorant to be able to distinguish 'wrecking' from the normal professional risk taken by an engineer;[83] but he certainly knew that the problem was not one of 'ignorant technicians'. It was a problem of Party policy throughout, otherwise the excesses of the 'proletarianization' period could not have taken place. There were waves of purges, dismissals, and arrests of 'alien elements' and, in particular, of their children, taking place in universities and institutions. The numerous 'social purges of students' enhanced the anxiety and panic among the intelligentsia and even produced suicides – not to speak of candidates to build the canals.[84] Mass expulsions of students drew a protest from Lunacharskii, who, in a letter to Stalin that was found in the Central Party Archives, considered it unacceptable to persecute sons for the sins of their fathers, especially when the sin was no more than the wrong 'social origin'.[85]

The treatment meted out to old specialists was scarcely beneficial to the rest of the engineers, including the party members, who were not under suspicion. The onslaught on the old engineers hurt the system across the board. Lack of initiative, a tendency to avoid responsibility and hide behind somebody's back, putting the blame on somebody else, and the philosophy that 'it's no business of mine' (*moia khata s kraiu*) came to permeate institutions and whole layers of society.

The intelligent and the less intelligent

The figures on the growth of the 'intelligentsia' during the thirties are staggering. From modest beginnings at the end of NEP it is claimed that there was a leap by 1939 to ten or eleven million employed, amounting to 13–14 percent of the whole population[86] – in itself an important structural change. Numbers of university students grew from 169,000 in 1928–29 to 812,000 in 1940–41, and there was an impressive growth of students in secondary technical schools. In the early years, however, it was not the school system that supplied students for the university and men for professional jobs: in the proletarianization period this was done by mobilization of party members, workers, and peasants through short courses, workers' faculties, *vydvizhenie* (advancement of workers to positions in the apparat or higher education), and so on. In fact, like everything else, the school system was in turmoil during these years, and the quantitative strides were not the whole story. This was especially true of the universities, whose hectic expansion and initially lax admission standards created large numbers of unviable institutions producing graduates whose level of qualification was no higher than that of secondary school. The crash campaign for cadres was costly and to some degree ineffective. Later, measures were taken to stabilize the system and, with the development of secondary schools, mobilizations and discrimination on class grounds ceased. But the effect of such measures on the quality of specialists and officials subsumed under the label of 'intelligentsia' could not be felt quickly. In 1930 a survey of industrial cadres showed that more than half the engineers and technicians in industry were *praktiki* (persons working as engineers and technicians without the appropriate formal training and diplomas) with low education and sometimes without even a crash course. Only 11.4 percent of the engineers and technicians had higher education. The same applied to the whole mass lumped together into the category of 'leading cadres and specialists' in industry at large. A survey taken in 1933 showed that of 861,000 people in this category, some 57 percent had neither higher nor specialized secondary education.[87]

We should examine the general problem of the 'intelligentsia' from yet another angle. The statistical concept used by official publications was faulty and did not express social realities. The term itself hid a set of social policies and a maze of special groups comprising (a) the creative intelligentsia, old and new; (b) the specialists, old and new, covered by the concept of 'engineering and technical workers'; (c) lower officialdom in the various apparats; (d) the higher administration; and (e) the top ruling oligarchy. The last two can be grouped together in the somewhat larger concept of a sociopolitical elite.

This classification makes it clear that the story of the intelligentsia involves more than creating a layer of educated professionals. Hiding or camouflaging the realities of power in statistical or ideological constructions is not an exclusively Soviet phenomenon, but a universal one that takes on different forms in different circumstances. Categories like 'employees' (*sluzhashchie*) or 'intelligentsia' conceal far more than they disclose.

The millions listed as 'intelligentsia' also included an overwhelming majority of officials with little education and a low level of professional skill – three such officials to one educated professional.[88] The lumping together of these unspecialized and poorly educated people with the educated specialists and literati was intended to create the impression of a cultural leap and grossly overstated the true situation. In reality this mass of badly paid officials was an addition to the social structure that did not necessarily elevate it, but, on the contrary, provided a convenient milieu for the spread of irrational and obscurantist tendencies. The category of low officials overlapped only partly with that of *praktiki*, many of whom, although not formally educated, were men of ability. The majority of the low officials were, as a Soviet sociologist put it, quite 'unpromising' (*besperspektivnye*), though many of them filtered through the Party into quite high places in the influential apparats. Many such people were incorporated into the category of Party members listed as 'employees', and they certainly contributed to the moral and cultural decadence of the Party in these years.

Our intention here, it should be said, is not to link degrees of education with moral standards. But we are dealing with a political climate that promoted or appealed to irrational and baser instincts, and that probably received a better response from an inexperienced, uninformed, untrained, and disoriented mass than it would have from the more cultivated, politically alert population.

Exalting this mass that was overcrowding the offices to the glamorous category of 'intelligentsia' was a spurious gesture. The junior officials in any case did not gain much from the policy of promotion and improvement in salary and prestige that was applied to specialists. This policy gained momentum in the process of the fight against wage-levelling (*uravnilovka*). The spread of salaries increased, first among the workers themselves, on the basis of skill and piece-rate norms, and second (at the same time, from 1931 on) when the average salaries of engineers began to grow and to move away from the hitherto privileged norms of industrial workers' earnings. In

August 1931 an important formal step was taken to remove discrimination against the technical intelligentsia: full equality of the technical intelligentsia with industrial workers – including admission of children to higher education, food norms, and rights to sanatoria – was introduced in areas where the industrial workers had had priority. The technical intelligentsia was also given the all-important right to accommodation on equal priority with industrial workers, with the further right – hitherto reserved only for the privileged category of senior officials (*otvetrabotniki*) – of extra space for a study.[89] A year later, a special government committee was created to watch over the construction of housing for engineering and technical workers and scientists.

The position of equality with industrial workers did not last for long, since the status of technical and other specialists continued to rise. During the 'proletarianization' period, the social composition of the university student body had included over 50 percent from the working class, with the 'employee' category falling to 32.8 percent. But in the course of the thirties, class limitations on entrance to universities and the party were removed, and the sons of employees (including specialists) came back in force. In universities, the employee group allegedly rose to 42.2 percent, with the workers dropping back to their position under NEP, 33.9 percent.[90] Obviously sons of workers and peasants were now in the universities in great numbers. But the growing trend in favor of the children of the already educated was unmistakably part of a new scale of values of the policy maker, and of society at large.

From 1934 on, the professional, the specialist, and the administrator would begin to get orderly and guaranteed fixed monthly salaries; and after the quiet removal in 1932 of the *partmaksimum*, which kept salaries of party members at about two hundred fifty to three hundred rubles a month, the gate would be open for the creation of a real pyramid of income and privilege.[91]

The bosses and their 'apparats'

The cadre problem was not just one of getting enough specialists and managers, but of promoting a powerful class of bosses – the *nachal'stvo*, composed of top managers in the enterprises and top administrators in state agencies. The *nachal'stvo*, the state's ruling stratum, was the principal group that the system kept fostering – though we must not forget that in Stalinist terms 'fostering' always meant, even for the most privileged, constant beating.

Nevertheless, the rewards for being admitted to this group were very considerable, especially in a country in a condition of penury, and the power over subordinates was very great. Some privileges – a car, a special pension, separate eating places – were public knowledge. But much was hidden, like the special stores, special warrants, graduated scale of expense accounts, housing privileges, special well-sheltered resorts, and finally the 'sealed envelope' with money over and above the formal salary. All these slowly developed into a formally stratified and quite rigid ladder of importance and power.

The *nachal'stvo* class was born of the principle of one-man direction (*edinonachalie*) as it developed after 1929. The creation of a hierarchical scaffolding of dedicated bosses, held together by discipline, privilege, and power, was a deliberate strategy of social engineering to help stabilize the flux. It was born, therefore, in conditions of stress, mass disorganization, and social warfare, and the bosses were actually asked to see themselves as commanders in a battle. The Party wanted the bosses to be efficient, powerful, harsh, impetuous, and capable of exerting pressure crudely and ruthlessly and getting results 'whatever the cost'. Rudeness (*grubost'*) became a virtue and, more significantly, the boss was endowed with quasi-police power in the workplace: among his prerogatives were fines and dismissals, which meant deprivation of lodging and food, and he had the further resource (even more corrupting) of the local security organs and the public prosecutor. The formation of the despotic manager was actually a process in which not leaders but *rulers* were made. The fact that their own jobs and freedom were quite insecure made the tyrannical traits of their rule probably more rather than less capricious and offensive.[92]

The flood of paper ('bumazhnyi potok')

All the apparats – central and local, party and state – were affected by rapid growth and rapid turnover, purges, low educational and professional standards, and the dysfunctions associated with over-centralization and 'administrative methods'.

Centralization of decision making, coupled with concentration of power, prerogatives, and resources in a few hands at the top, was paralleled by similar tendencies in every single administration. At all levels power went to the top few, and often in the hands of a single boss. We have already discussed this creation of 'small Stalins' in the factories. The phenomenon became all-embracing. But its overall results were only partly calculated and sought for. The policy makers were guided by the idea that in conditions of scarce resources, scarce talent, and not too much commitment in the growing socioeconomic organism, one should concentrate power in fewer, but more competent and reliable, hands. This was reflected in the fostering of the *nachal'stvo*, *edinonachalie*, and, at the summit of the edifice, the 'cult of the individual'. But much of the trend was spontaneous, under the combined impact of policy and those numerous unplanned but tenacious elements, inherent in the bureaucratic world of a dictatorial state, that fitted no strategy and nobody's intentions. These elements might separately be identified as 'deficiencies' by Politburo members, journalists, or inspectors of the apparat; but in fact the 'deficiencies' were so persistent that there was no escape from the conclusion that they amounted to permanent features of the system.

Among them were the 'flood of paper' (*bumazhnyi potok*), the proliferation of officials and offices, and (incredible as it may sound for such a centralized state) multicentrism. A study of Mikoian's commissariat of foreign and internal trade, to take an example, found the whole ministry to be, characteristically, in a state of crisis in 1930. But submergence in details, a flood of 2,500 'papers' a day, and loss of control of essential policy matters and their coordination[93] was not only young Mikoian's problem. Another study[94] of the apparats of local soviet executive committees found the following unpalatable traits: firmly entrenched distrust of lower organs, lack of clarity in the division of functions, multicentrism, parallelism, enormous multiplicity of channels all the way down the line from Moscow to the raions, harassment and pettifogging supervision of the lower level by the higher, and constant delays.[95] Red tape and the bureaucratic style of operation, castigated by the top leaders themselves as 'formalistic paper work' (*kantselarshchina* and *formal'no-bumazhnoe rukovodstvo*), became phenomena from which there was no escape. The leadership and the public alike were bewildered and, in fact, helpless. Stuchka (a leading jurist, theoretician, and Supreme Court judge), for instance, seemed quite astonished to discover what every official knew already, that government departments were engaging in fierce in-fighting: it was real 'class warfare', he said, in which the parties behaved like enemies and genuine competitors.[96] He could only sigh.

The leadership clearly did not understand what was happening or why. Ordzhonikidze, when still head of the commissariat of state inspection, lamented that every time reductions of personnel and financial economies were decreed the result was bigger expenditure and an increase in the number of officials.[97] It was impossible, he went on, to get through the maze of cumbersome and top-heavy apparats and wrench realistic data out of them,[98] and he appealed for a study of the tendency of the apparats to distort government decisions. It was, in fact, an impossible task. Officials formed 'families' and engaged in every kind of mutual protection.

The growing bureaucratic Moloch not only menaced the country but terrified the top leaders as well. They reacted, true to style and tradition, by pressuring and purging the apparats. The general idea was to make the officials feel 'the firm and controlling hand' and, in addition, 'to come down hard on some, as an example to the others' (*bol'no stuknut' kogo sleduet, v primet i nauku drugim)*.[99] As the leadership increased control and terror, 'centralization' was also strengthened and kept breeding more and more of the same phenomena. Facing such pressure from above, officials felt compelled to defend themselves by padding, cover-up, and 'hand in glove' policies – and by redirecting the pressure downwards to get some results.

In this atmosphere, the type that thrived and prospered was precisely the cunning and dodgy character, unscrupulous and conformist, who had learned the hard way the disadvantages of taking any initiative without orders from above. Soon the habit would become second nature, and the system of 'counter-incentives' would mobilize more energies to blocking orders and plans from above than to fulfilling them. Syrtsov, chief of the state machinery of the RSFSR, knew what he was talking about when he commented:

> We bind a man hand and foot with all kinds of agreements; we drive
> him into a bottle, cork it up and put a government stamp on it; and
> then we go round saying: 'Why doesn't this man show any energy or
> any initiative?'[100]

He did not mention terror, but this was obvious. His appeal to solve the problem 'by letting people out of the bottle' led him into trouble the very same year.

Four years later Kaganovich, one of the promoters and practitioners of the method of 'coming down hard', listed the factors responsible for the devastating turnover of personnel in the Party and other apparats: those at the top 'hit from the shoulder', and dismissals and punishments were so frequent that many local party officials, even if highly successful for some time, took it for granted that normality could not last and, in order to avoid catastrophe, decided: better clear out *(nado smyvat'sia)* while the going's good.[101]

The 'logic' of the centralized machinery led to putting the blame only on the lower ranks: if only the oblast committees knew more about their cadres and looked after them better, a Kaganovich would complain. But he could also resort, when necessary, to a broader view: the 'class analysis'. Tsarist officials still in service and all the other 'socially alien, . . . bankrupt, degenerate hangers-on' could be invoked to carry the blame.

These were, in fact, the terms used to guide the mammoth purge of the state apparats ordered by the party in 1929.[102] To purge *(chistit'* or, more lovingly, *podchistit')* became another expression of the current 'art of ruling', and had far-reaching and well-known effects for everyone. The purge of officialdom begun in 1929 dragged on for a full two years, disorganized and disorientated the administrators, dismissed every tenth official who was checked – and then petered out with a decision to stop the whole thing and never return to the method of 'wholesale purges' *(poval'nye chistki)*.[103] As the 160,000 purged officials left (many probably found their way back later) and all the disturbing phenomena remained, including inflation of personnel, the government decreed a new move: not a purge but a 'reduction of personnel', in which a further 153,000 officials were apparently fired in the winter of 1932–33.[104]

This was not going to be the last word. The *chinovnik*, Trotskii thought, was going to swallow the dictatorship of the proletariat if the dictatorship did not swallow him in good time. The prophecy was not quite accurate. The *chinovnik* was 'swallowing' the masses, the state was swallowing those same *chinovniki*, and the proletariat was quite irrelevant to the question. The whole thing was simply the *modus operandi* of a police state, beating the country into a modernity of its own definition and catching some morbid diseases in the process.

Notes

1 F. Lorimer, *The Population of the Soviet Union: History and Prospects* (Geneva, 1946), pp. 38–9, 40.
2 Lorimer, *The Population of the Soviet Union*, p. 22.
3 L. M. Spirin, *Klassy i partii v grazhdanskoi voine v Rossii, 1917–1920* (Moscow, 1968), p. 301.
4 Spirin, *Klassy i partii, 1917–1920*, p. 386.
5 Spirin, *Klassy i partii, 1917–1920*, pp. 386–7. His material is from the Central Party Archives.
6 O. I. Shkaratan, *Problemy sotsial'noi struktury rabochego klassa SSSR* (Moscow, 1970), pp. 351–4.
7 Shkaratan, *Problemy sotsial'noi*, p. 256. He explains these phenomena as well as the oppositions inside the party at that time – notably the Workers' Opposition - as results of vacillations under the pressure of 'spontaneous forces' (*stikhiia*).
8 A. A. Matiugin and D. A. Baevskii (eds), *Izmeneniia v chislennosti i sostave sovetskogo rabochego klassa* (Moscow, 1961), p. 83.
9 Mikhail Zoshchenko (1895–1958), author of many humorous stories of life under NEP; Ilia Ilf and Evgenii Petrov were joint authors of the satirical novels *The Twelve Chairs* (1928) and *The Little Golden Calf* (1931).
10 Computed by Sovnarkom's Committee for the Assessment of the Tax Burden, published in *Statisticheskii spravochnik SSSR za 1928 god* (Moscow, 1929), pp. 42–43, where we also took our figures on the social groups. The figures deal with 'employed' (without their families). The figures are rounded off throughout this paper, since we are interested only in the order of magnitude.
11 I. Magidovich, in *Statisticheskoe obozrenie*, 1928 no. 11, p. 80.
12 *Statisticheskii spravochnik SSSR za 1928 god*, pp. 796–7.
13 A. Ya. Levin, *Sotsial'no-ekonomicheskie uklady v SSSR v period perekhoda ot kapitalizma k sotsializmu: goskapitalizm i chastnyi kapital* (Moscow, 1967), p. 23, for the year 1925–6.
14 Magidovich, in *Statisticheskoe obozrenie*, 1928 no. 11, p. 87. All such figures have to be treated with considerable caution. People were prudent and left undeclared everything they could. But the scope of the capitalist sector is certainly reflected here realistically.

15 The chairman of the agriculture department in Ivanovo–Voznesensk *gubernia*, himself of peasant stock, stated quite clearly: 'The peasant is used to seeing in the government an alien force'. Quoted in M. P. Kim (ed.), *Sovetskaia intelligentsiia: istoriia formirovaniia i rosta* (Moscow, 1968), p. 140.

16 See the excellent paper by V. P. Danilov, 'The rural population of the USSR on the eve of collectivization', *Istoricheskie zapiski*, 1963, no. 74, p. 96.

17 See M. Lewin, 'Who was the Soviet kulak?', *Soviet Studies*, 2, XVIII (1966).

18 Iu. V. Arutiunian, *Sotsial'naia struktura sel'skogo naselenia SSSR* (Moscow, 1971), p. 26.

19 *Stat. spravochnik. SSSR za 1928 god*, p. 42.

20 V. P. Danilov, 'Towards a characterization of the social and political circumstances in the Soviet countryside on the eve of collectivization', *Istoricheskie zapiski*, 1966 no. 79, p. 37; N. A. Ivnitskii, *Klassovaia bor'ba v derevne i likvidatsiia kulachestva kak klassa* (Moscow, 1972), pp. 71, 74.

21 Ivnitskii, *Klassovaiia bor'ba . . . klassa*, p. 65.

22 In 1928 there were only 233,000 specialists with higher education, and among them only about 48,000 engineers. A further 288,000 people had secondary specialized education. See *Trud v SSSR, Statisticheskii sbornik* (Moscow, 1968), pp. 251, 262.

23 R. Pethybridge, *The Social Prelude to Stalinism* (London, 1974), p. 196. The quotation is taken from the title of a chapter in this book.

24 See table in Kim, *Sovetskaia intelligentsiia*, p. 134.

25 Strumilin's computation, quoted in L. Averbakh, *Na putiakh kul'turnoi revoliutsii*, 3rd ed. (Moscow, 1929), p. 72.

26 Rykov and Lunacharskii quoted in Averbakh, *Na putiakh kul'turnoi revoliutsii*, pp. 64 and 68 respectively.

27 Arutiunian, *Sotsial'naia struktura*, p. 38. In 1924 a peasant child would have, on the average, two to three years schooling, children in cities – 3.1 years per child. Such data give a fair picture of the low starting point, in terms of popular education, the regime had to build on.

28 Averbakh, *Na putiakh*, p. 166.

29 Averbakh, *Na putiakh*, pp. 186–7, quoting Trotsky's 'anti-Leninist' opinion from *Literatura i revoliutsiia*.

30 According to Kim (ed.), *Sovetskaia intelligentsiia*, p. 174, workers and peasants occupied half the places in higher educational institutions ('*vuzy*' – rendered as 'universities' in text). The other half – and after 1926 even more – went to 'employees' and 'others' (i.e., children of the propertied classes, past and present).

31 Quoted in M. P. Kim (ed.), *Kul'turnaia revoliutsiia v SSSR, 1917–1965* (Moscow, 1967), p. 95.

32 Oblomov is the hero of a nineteenth-century novel of that title by I. Goncharov – a 'superfluous man' who sinks into idleness and lethargy on his provincial estate.

33 Quoted in Averbakh, *Na putiakh*, p. 121.

34 Averbakh, *Na putiakh*, p. 176.

35 R. Pethybridge, *The Social Prelude to Stalinism*, p. 350; and see his chapter on 'Illiteracy'.

36 M. A. Vyltsan, *Sovetskaia derevnia nakanune velikoi otechestvennoi voiny* (Moscow, 1970), p. 142; Lorimer, *The Population of the Soviet Union: History and Prospects*, p. 112, states that the overall growth rate, 1926–39, was 1.23% a year. This was very high when compared with other countries, but it was much

higher in the USSR itself in 1926 and 1927 as well as, probably, in 1938. Tsarist Russia saw its population grow by 1.74% a year during the period 1897–1914.

37 *Sotsialisticheskoe stroitel'stvo v SSSR* (Moscow 1935), p. xlviii, claims a population of 165,748,400 at the end of 1932, but the 1939 census found only about 5 million inhabitants more. Something must have been very wrong. The 1937 census was disavowed by the government; many statisticians were purged as 'wreckers'.

38 For information on *otkhod* in those years see A. M. Panfilova, *Formirovanie rabochego klassa SSSR v gody pervoi piatiletki* (Moscow, 1964).

39 *Narodnoe khoziaistvo SSSR v 1956 g.* (Moscow 1957), p. 656; Arutiunian, in A. P. Dadykin (ed.), *Formirovanie i razvitie sovetskogo rabochego klassa 1917–1961* (Moscow 1964), pp. 113–15; M. Iu. Pisarev, *Naselenie i trud v SSSR* (Moscow, 1966), p. 68 and passim.

40 M. Ia. Sonin, *Vosproizvodstvo rabochei sily v SSSR i balans truda* (Moscow 1959), p. 143; *Statisticheskii spravochnik SSSR za 1960 g.* (Moscow, 1961), p. 110. It is quite revealing to read Stalin saying in June 1931 (Stalin, *Sochineniia* XIII [Moscow, 1951], p. 53): 'There is no longer any "flight of the peasant to the city" or "spontaneous movement [*samotëk*] of the labor force"'. Soviet scholars had to repeat this outrageous misrepresentation for years. What was really happening was pandemonium – both 'flight' and 'spontaneous movement' as never before.

41 A. V. Kornilov, *Na reshaiushchem etape* (Moscow, 1968), pp. 158–9; Panfilova, *Formirovanie*, p. 80.

42 S. Ordzhonikidze, *Stat'i i rechi* II (Moscow, 1956), pp. 411–12.

43 For some data on this see Ordzhonikidze, *Stat'i i rechi* II pp. 411–12; *Pravda*, 15 November 1931; *Spravochnik partiinogo rabotnika* vypusk 8 (Moscow, 1934), pp. 846–9; *Bol'shevik*, 1934 no. 7, p. 16.

44 Nicholas S. Timasheff, *The Great Retreat. The Growth and Decline of Communism in Russia* (New York: E. P. Dutton and Co., 1946).

45 Ivnitskii, *Klassovaia bor'ba*, p. 242.

46 N. I. Nemakov, *Kommunisticheskaia partiia – organizator massovogo kolkhoznogo dvizheniia (1929–32)*, pp. 159, 168. The category of *lishentsy* was abolished in 1935 (see *Pravda*, 30 December 1935).

47 *Sobranie zakonov i rasporiazhenii raboche-krest'ianskogo pravitel'stva SSSR* 1930, no. 50, art. 524. This is an interesting document in which the sociologist and historian may study the condemned capitalist elements, most of whom never saw much of any 'capital' in their lives.

48 *Sobranie zakonov* 1930, no. 19, art. 212, lists such actions as 'abuses' and forbids them, but this could not have had any effect since the same people could easily be persecuted under other headings.

49 S. Bulatov, in *Sovetskoe gosudarstvo*, 1933 no. 4, p. 71.

50 Data in *Statisticheskoe obozrenie*, 1928 no. 2, p. 80; on capital value per average shop or commercial enterprise, see A. Ia. Levin, *Sotsioekonomicheskie uklady*, p. 125.

51 A full list of offenses that either increased considerably or became the object of a special campaign, and therefore looked particularly ominous, is given in *Sovetskaia Iustitsiia*, 1932, no. 34, p. 13.

52 Shkaratan, *Problemy sotsial'noi struktury*, p. 264.

53 A. Stepanian, in V. S. Semenov, *Klassy, sotsial'nye sloi i gruppy v SSSR* (Moscow, 1968), pp. 20–1.

54 *Sovetskaia Iustitsiia*, 1932, no. 2, p. 15.

55 *Sobranie zakonov* 1932, no. 78, art. 475, and no. 45, art. 244.

56 Quoted in J. Azrael, *Managerial Power and Soviet Politics* (Cambridge, Mass., 1966), pp. 247–8.
57 Kaganovich, in *Bol'shevik*, 1936 no. 13, p. 54.
58 Kirov, *Izbrannye stati'i i rechi* (Moscow, 1957), pp. 700–7.
59 In my article 'Taking Grain', in C. Abramsky (ed.), *Essays in Honour of E. H. Carr* (London, 1974), I describe the mechanism of the procurements and their effect on the development of the *kolkhozy*.
60 Arutiunian, *Sotsial'naia struktura*, p. 158.
61 Arutiunian, *Sotsial'naia struktura*. One quarter of the peasants still could not read in 1939.
62 Iaroslavskii, quoted in Kim (ed.), *Kul'turnaia revoliutsiia*, p. 248.
63 S. Syrtsov, in *Bol'shevik*, 1930 no. 5, pp. 47–9, which is the source of the summary that follows.
64 'Okazënivanie krestian' is the term used by a peasant delegate in *VI s"ezd sovetov*, bulletin, 1931 no. 20, p. 3. He explained that this meant depriving them of the results of their labor, and said that kulaks laughed at the *kolkhozniki* because they were now 'on rations' (*na paike*).
65 Machine Tractor Stations (MTS) were set up in 1929 to consolidate tractor and machinery holdings and service the *kolkhozy*. Later they also assumed functions of political supervision over the *kolkhozy*.
66 A. Ia. Iakovlev, *Voprosy oganizatsii sotsialisticheskogo sel'skogo khoziaistva* (Moscow, 1933), p. 184. Sheboldaev is quoted from *XVII konferentsiia VKP(b), Stenograficheskii otchet* (Moscow, 1932), p. 208.
67 L. Kaganovich, in *Na agrarnom fronte*, 1933 no. 1, p. 40.
68 The Central Committee decision is in *Partiinoe stroitel'stvo*, 1933, no. 5, p. 62. The document illustrates the kind of menacing language the Central Committee was then using.
69 N. V. Krylenko was Commissar of Justice of the RSFSR.
70 *Sovetskaia Iustitsiia*, 1932 nos 5–6, p. 16. The same periodical (1933 no. 15) adds more categories of typical transgressions of the 'crude administrative' variety: forcing the *kolkhoz* to feed all kinds of parasites favored by the raion bosses; imposing illegal corvees; preempting money from the bank accounts of the *kolkhozy*; taking cattle away from them, and so on.
71 S. Krasikov, *Sergei Mironovich Kirov* (Moscow, 1964), p. 176.
72 Summarized from *Sputnik kommunista v derevne*, 1933 no. 2, p. 48.
73 Kirov is quoted from Krasikov, *Sergei Mironovich Kirov*, p. 176; Stalin from *Partiinoe stroitel'stvo*, 1933 no. 5, p. 3.
74 There was even a formal prohibition against creating mutual aid funds from *kolkhoz* resources: it could be done only on the basis of private contributions from the *kolkhozniki* – see *Sputnik kommunista v derevne*, 1933 no. 2, p. 48.
75 *Sotsialisticheskoe zemledelie*, 1933 no. 16–17, p. 9.
76 Arutiunian, *Sotsial'naia struktura*, p. 57.
77 Ordzhonikidze speaking at the Seventeenth Party Conference in 1932, in *Stat'i i rechi* II, p. 340.
78 Quoted in Kim (ed.), *Sovetskaia intelligentsiia*, pp. 48, 56.
79 V. I. Lenin, *Sochineniia*, XL, 5th ed. (Moscow, 1962), pp. 199, 218.
80 Kim (ed.), *Sovetskaia intelligentsiia*, pp. 126–7; S. A. Fediukin, *Velikii oktiabr' i intelligentsia* (Moscow, 1972), p. 377.
81 The Shakhty trial of engineers for wrecking and sabotage was held in May– June 1928.
82 Kim (ed.), *Sovetskaia intelligentsiia*, p. 127, admits that such fears were well

founded, but he puts the blame on 'Makhaevite tendencies' among workers and exempts policy makers from any share in it.

83 *Pravda*, 17 August 1931.

84 Suicides were committed even in such inconspicuous places as Rzhev, where intellectuals could not have been too numerous. The party leadership was disturbed by the phenomenon. See *Smolensk Archives* WKP 55 (document dated July 1930).

85 Kim (ed.), *Sovetskaia intelligentsiia*, pp. 324–5.

86 M. Iu. Pisarev, *Naselenie i trud SSSR* (Moscow, 1966), p. 41.

87 Figures from the 1930 survey are in M. P. Kim (ed.), *Industrializatsiia SSSR 1929–1932* (Moscow, 1970), p. 571; data on the 1933 survey are in *Sotsialisticheskoe stroitel'stvo SSSR* (Moscow, 1935), p. 522.

88 This is an assessment for the year 1937 made by S. L. Seniavskii, *Izmeneniia v sotsial'noi strukture sovetskogo obshchestva 1938–1970* (Moscow, 1973), p. 299. According to him, by 1940 the intelligentsia (in which he includes only specialists with higher or secondary professional education) constituted only 3.3% of the employed population, whereas the 'non-specialized officials' constituted 13.2% of the total employed work force.

89 *Sobranie zakonov* 1931, no. 44, art. 322.

90 Iu. B. Borisov, in Kim (ed.), *Kul'turnaia revoliutsiia*, p. 138. Such figures can be used only as indications of trends; their exactitude is very questionable.

91 V. I. Kuzmin, *Istoricheskii opyt Sovetskoi industrializatsii* (Moscow, 1963), p. 149.

92 The preference for 'crude leadership' does not mean that every manager actually was a despotic type. There certainly were many of the traditional Russian 'paternalist' type and some, a minority, of 'businesslike' frame of mind and style (*delovye*), compromising and conniving. Whatever the typology, their power and privileges were common to the whole category, especially in the more important enterprises and establishments.

93 G. Shklovskii, in *Revoliutsiia prava*, 1930, no. 7, p. 89.

94 Shklovskii, in *Revoliutsiia prava*, 1930, no. 7, p. 89.

95 Shklovskii, in *Revoliutsiia prava*, 1930, no. 7, pp. 59–61.

96 P. I. Stuchka, in *Revoliutsiia prava*, 1930 no. 10, p. 19.

97 Ordzhonikidze, *Stat'i i rechi* II, pp. 228–9.

98 'You can dig there as much as you like, they won't give you exact data'. Ordzhonikidze, *Stat'i i rechi* II, p. 228.

99 These are quotations from P. Postyshev's speech in Kharkov, in *Partiinoe stroitel'stvo*, 1933, no. 5: he was expressing the generally accepted tenets of what was then 'the Bolshevik art of leadership'.

100 Syrtsov, *O nedostatkakh i zadachakh* (Moscow–Leningrad, 1930), p. 15 (speech of February 1930).

101 *Bol'shevik*, 1934 no. 21, p. 12.

102 *KPSS v resoliutsiiakh s"ezdov i konferentsii* II (Moscow, 1957), pp. 541, 546.

103 L. F. Morozov and V. P. Portnov, *Organy partiino-gosudarstvennogo kontrolia 1923–1934* (Moscow, 1964), pp. 139–42.

104 S. Ikonnikov, *Sozdanie i deiatel'nost' obedinënnykh organov TsKK-RKI v 1923–1934 godakh* (Moscow, 1971), p. 212.

SECTION III

LIVING STALINISM

Commentary

Social historians of Russia have rarely been disposed to write 'history with the politics left out,' narrations of everyday life which deprecate or ignore the role of state power, legal frameworks or elite ideologies. If anything, they have been mesmerized by the range and sweep of plans emanating from the minds of 'great men': tsars, ministers, revolutionaries and commissars. 'Top-down' perspectives catalogued turning points, identified conundrums, framed analysis and generally organized the overall shape of events, even in accounts of popular risings such as the 1905 and 1917 revolutions. All this hampered consideration of the activities and inclinations of other parties – subaltern classes, women, the poor and the dispossessed.

This holds true for the social history of the Stalin period. For decades most monographs portrayed the population as the inert receptor of projects designed in the capital and forwarded to the provinces via the regime's 'transmission belts,' the bureaucratic machinery responsible for policy implementation. Only in the past thirty years have new vistas opened up. Stimulated by the general trend towards 'history from below' in the 1960s and 1970s and the work of historians such as Moshe Lewin and Sheila Fitzpatrick, researchers began to change direction. While continuing to stress the importance of actions willed by the centre they reconfigured Stalinism's impact and evolution by exploring how people made sense of their situation, received policy or advanced their own agendas. What has emerged is a more complex, nuanced, and in many ways more puzzling representation: Stalinism as something made 'from below' and 'from above,' by victims and beneficiaries as well as by elites.

Chapter 5: The second revolution and after

During the late 1920s and early 1930s apparently spontaneous risings of peasant women against collectivization engulfed the Russian and Ukrainian countryside, but participants – dubbed irrational and hysterical by Bolshevik observers – were not usually punished under the notorious Article 58 of the Soviet Criminal Code. That fate was reserved for male peasants deemed capable of rational action and overt hostility to socialism. Instead, women were to be dealt with by indoctrination and co-option into officially sanctioned village institutions.

In Lynne Viola's view these remedies were unlikely to meet with much success [Reading 9]. Most women had a lot to lose from collectivization and so their opposition was in fact rationally predicated. Villages buzzed with wild rumours, but even the most extravagant stories reflected real fears: ignorant and overzealous officials did frequently advance madcap schemes of social engineering. In addition, the status of women in rural society depended on the allocation of particular social and economic roles. They raised the children, upheld religion and managed specific agricultural tasks vital to the family's well-being. All this was threatened, whether by central rescript or local initiative.

In Viola's opinion if women were not responding irrationally nor were they behaving hysterically. Spontaneity masked intent, and bab'i bunty assumed forms which might well have been consciously designed to perplex outsiders. Some party leaders were probably aware that there was more to bab'i bunty than met the eye, but depicting them as unpremeditated, irrational events served an important political purpose: it allowed Moscow to minimize the seriousness of the resistance to collectivization and deflect the blame for all that had gone awry onto local agitators.

Many historians would see the women involved in bab'i bunty as passive victims, but Viola's research suggests that they collaborated in making what might be termed 'really existing Stalinism' – that which arose from strife and compromise as against that which was willed. Lewis Siegelbaum also looks at Stalinism from below, but instead analyses the interactions between the regime and one of its most favoured groups [Reading 10]. In August 1935 the Donbass coal miner Aleksei Stakhanov exceeded his output norm fourteenfold, hewing 102 tons in one shift. The party immediately hailed this as a breakthrough, contrasting the qualities he supposedly exemplified – careful planning, rational organization and attention to detail – with the haphazard 'storming' mentality of the First Five-Year Plan's 'shock workers', and his feat quickly became the locus of an officially sponsored drive – Staklanovism – to raise labour productivity.

Siegelbaum interrogates the surface banality of Stakhanovism and postulates the existence of a complex phenomenon riddled with ambiguities. On the one hand Stakhanovism manifested itself as cultural myth, something articulated by the regime for its own purposes. On the other hand reality invaded myth because some workers internalized the movement's prescriptions, thus breathing life into propaganda and ascribing new meanings to the Soviet experience. Feted by the powerful and glorified in the press, a few Stakhanovites acquired the kind of renown enjoyed nowadays by soap opera stars or successful game show contestants. Newsreels displayed images of respectful workers accompanied by dutiful wives receiving cars, refrigerators or the keys to a new apartment, invariably with a party boss in attendance. Siegelbaum believes that these staged events served a number of purposes: showering gifts on individuals celebrated acquisitiveness and reaffirmed the regime's abrogation of egalitarianism, while beneficiaries acted as a goad to others, emblems of what could transpire under socialism and harbingers of a 'higher reality' – the communist utopia of superabundance.

Most, of course, never won glittering prizes or met Stalin, and exhibited relatively high levels of consumption simply by using wages to furnish a room or buy new clothes, but whatever the source of their well-being Siegelbaum represents them as a new, indeterminate sub-group within Soviet society. Frequently young and obviously successful, they could probably count on a wider than normal range of potential marriage partners and a better life for their children. But if some couples inhabited the myth with alacrity and made it their own it remains the case that they were still working class; the movement was never intended to disrupt society or disturb shop-floor hierarchies, although social mobility did occur when Stakhanovites moved into managerial and technical posts during and after the *Ezhovshchina*.

Chapter 6: The purges

Properly speaking, there is no Russian equivalent of the English word *purge*. In Russian the pre-war purges comprise discreet events: show trials of technical specialists between 1928 and 1933; *chistki* in the periods 1928–30 and 1933–35; a *proverka* in 1935; the *obmen* in 1936; and finally the *Ezhovshchina*, which lasted from about 1936–37 to 1938. A ceaseless rumble of persecution accompanied these frightening detonations. Throughout the decade anyone could suddenly be arraigned on charges of wrecking, sabotage, espionage, aiding kulaks, counter-revolutionary activity or plotting to kill a member of the Politburo, and, after torture and summary conviction, be sacked, exiled, hurled into the Gulag or shot. No one knows exactly how many died or languished in prison, but the total runs into many millions.

Whatever the figure the purges cannot be understood simply by reference to actions willed by the centre. Like the witch crazes of medieval and seventeenth-century Europe these were social events. In some way they spoke to the condition of 1930s Russia: for millions to suffer millions had to cooperate, either as active participants or approving onlookers. Why people did so remains an enigma, but we can begin to approach the aetiology of purging by recalling a remark of Isaac Deutscher's:

> Russia had been belated in her historical development. In England serfdom had disappeared by the end of the fourteenth century. Stalin's parents were still serfs. By the standards of British history, the fourteenth and the twen-tieth centuries have, in a sense, met in contemporary Russia. They have met in Stalin.[2]

The point here is that it was not just Stalin who straddled the centuries. Throughout the Great Breakthrough and well into the 1930s not only had most people been raised in a medieval political economy (the village community), they also exhibited a medieval world-view. The Slav lands and the Caucasus teemed with evils we have forgotten. Hobgoblins, demons and infernal spirits permeated physical reality: in secluded glades, by silent trackways, in pools, streams and wells, in unlit barn-lofts or the shadowy corners of rooms lurked everwatchful presences intent on harm. Sometimes they could be avoided or propitiated, and if necessary exposed and thwarted, at least temporarily, for in opposition to darkness stood the forces of light, the saints in heaven whose help could be invoked in times of trouble.

In a bipolar universe, be it fourteenth-century England or early twentieth-century Russia, there are no shades of grey. Coincidence does not exist, nor is anything equivocal, and since nothing happens by accident the price of survival is eternal vigilance. Cows refuse to give milk, crops wither, children die, mine-shafts explode and buildings are struck by lightning because malevolent agents will it so. The second revolution spread this magical culture across the country. Ruralized cities, bustling construction sites and Soviet institutions bulging with people only recently uprooted from the peasantry proved fertile breeding grounds for rumour and speculation. Everywhere the backward half-glance towards the hidden terror jostled secular readings of cause and effect. When projects ran into difficulties, therefore, it was quite natural that fantastic stories of plots, spies, concealed enemies and secret cabals should resonate in society and bewitch the imagination of Stalinist leaders (themselves not too far from the village), and that confession, 'unmasking' and the inquisitorial style should figure so prominently in show trials.

It is with this heritage in mind that we should approach interpretations of the articulation and reception of purging offered by Gábor Rittersporn from Hungary and the Australian Sheila Fitzpatrick, now based in the USA. According to Rittersporn, long before 1941 conspiracy theories had thoroughly drenched the popular mind and saturated governmental practices [Reading 11]. In the early 1930s the regime scapegoated 'former people', but by mid-decade this scenario no longer seemed plausible. Dimly aware that hardship was more than temporary and unable to confront the real causes of failure (incompetence, maladministration and systemic chaos) leaders cast around for new groups to demonize. Since in the realm of theory collectivization and industrialization had strengthened the unity of party and people and liquidated 'antagonistic and exploiting classes', problems were obviously caused by the machinations of alien elements hidden deep within the party-state apparatus. But campaigns to root out 'double dealers,' 'Rightist cliques' or 'Zinovievite–Trotskyite monsters' reinforced hysteria and superstition. Panicked by dire threats emanating from the Kremlin local officials engaged in a frenzied scramble to uncover plots or tried to fob the centre off with lies and obfuscation. In the process they invented enemies, magnified arbitrariness, extended clientism and validated Moscow's belief that officials could not be trusted and that ogres lurked in every corner of the country. In Rittersporn's view a vicious, and in a sense rational, cycle of vigilance, accusation, arrest, torture and confession produced a nightmare world which could credibly be scripted as an omnipresent conspiracy against socialism.

This is not to say that people read the scripts presented to them uncritically or were incapable of finessing the regime's vocabulary. Indeed, Fitzpatrick in her essay on the reception of the *Ezhovshchina* in Voronezh province [Reading 12], contends that, like the women opposed to collectivization earlier in the decade, villagers oscillated between inhabiting and manipulating the official discourse. But in this case she intimates that they seem to have gone much further and attempted to rewrite the meaning of events on their own terms.

In contrast to the great spectacles unfolding in Moscow's Hall of Trades Unions, for the most part local show trials omitted ritual incantations of conspiracies and quasi-supernatural occurrences. Though there were occasional sightings of anti-

Soviet elements deliberately poisoning livestock or laming horses, what Fitzpatrick terms the 'master plot' signalled to the provinces via the national press usually stressed the mundane and the prosaic. Rural courts enthusiastically took up charges levelled at local administrators, but if the regime provided interstices for the utterance of discontent, peasant witnesses conspicuously avoided stock responses (they failed to thank Stalin, for instance, and had little time for allegations of Trotskyism). Instead they raged against abuses of power for personal gain, favouritism towards former kulaks, gross incompetence and gratuitous interference in farm management. Nevertheless, like the witch crazes of earlier centuries, published narratives emphasized bipolar certainties, contrasting virtuous peasants with evil bosses. In addition, Fitzpatrick submits that local show trials probably embodied other features characteristic of the medieval sensibility: for however brief a span, onlookers revelled in carnivalesque reversal, celebrating a world turned upside down in which mice buried cats and peasants killed their tormentors.

Chapter 7: Stalinist culture

As we have seen throughout this book, reading the history of the Stalin period means adjudicating between a series of competing scripts disseminated by the quick and the dead. What reality history possesses was contested by participants while they lived, frozen in the sources and later recontested and reinterpreted (quite literally 're-searched') by historians. 'Soviet Thermidor', 'second revolution', 'revolution from above', 'Great Breakthrough into Socialist Construction', 'the purges,' 'Ezhovshchina', 'Stalinism' – even the words 'Stalin', Stalin period' or 'the Stalin dictatorship' – are attempts to impose meaning on that which could equally be represented as meaningless, or to inscribe cause and effect when mere sequence would answer just as well. Amongst other things history satisfies our craving for patterns and destinations, our urge to disturb the stubborn tranquillity of unadorned chronology and our longing to make the past speak. In the end it is always and everywhere metaphor written over silence.

The turn towards 'history from below' renewed interest in Soviet culture in general, and in particular prompted redefinitions of a metaphor used by both Lenin and Stalin – 'cultural revolution'. In 1978 Fitzpatrick suggested that the Great Breakthrough provided spaces for the release of social tensions brewing since the X party congress. Zealous youngsters impatient with the compromises of the NEP rushed to embrace the new socialist dawn, but though animated by the eschatological rapture evident in many leaders' speeches during the first phase of the industrialization drive they were not always under the centre's control. They purged schools and universities, tossed bourgeois specialists out of research institutes, assailed religion and, declaiming the writings of Marx and Lenin, announced the 'withering away' of money, the family and the law. Thoroughly disconcerted, from about 1931 onwards Stalin decided to call a halt.

Whether she deals with the Civil War, NEP, collectivization, purging or the Stalinist educational system, Fitzpatrick has always challenged crude totalitarian interpretations and emphasized the interaction between central prescription and pressure from below. In consequence, since many academics still find it difficult to accept any approach which appears to shift responsibility away from the Stalin regime for what happened, she has been the target of sustained criticism. But she was not the first to be puzzled by Stalinist cultural policy: as early as 1937 Trotsky had meditated on the decline of revolutionary militancy, and the first Western academic to treat the topic systematically was the American sociologist Nicholas Timasheff.

Writing in 1945, Timasheff characterized Russia's revolution as a vast, three-phase essay in social engineering [Reading 13]. Phase one, lasting from 1917 to 1921 and roughly coterminous with 'War' or 'Military Communism', was the 'Great Experiment' or 'Communist Experiment.' This was followed by a 'Second Socialist Offensive', encompassing planned industrialization and forced collectivization. The third phase, born in 1931–34 and reaching maturity by the end of the Nazi–Soviet War, Timasheff called the 'decline of communism' or 'Great Retreat', a phenomenon which he believed to be akin to the 'return to normalcy' in post-First-World-War Europe and North America. But whereas in the West conservative restabilization occurred relatively quickly, in Russia communist experiment and socialist offensive delayed matters by fifteen years or more.

According to Timasheff, when revolutionaries anywhere try to remake society they must always challenge deep-rooted social institutions. In Russia assaults on the most important of these, the family, started in 1917 and continued into the Second Socialist Offensive. Bolsheviks simplified divorce, decriminalized incest, bigamy, abortion and adultery, and subsequently destroyed marriages via the direction of labour. By 1930 the family was indeed enfeebled, but radical policies had unintended and detrimental effects. Falling birth rates threatened labour supply and military recruitment, lack of parental control bred hooliganism and delinquency, and social confusion and geographical mobility debouched untold multitudes of orphans onto the streets. In response the regime reconsecrated marriage as civic duty, trumpeted the virtues of filial obedience and recriminalized abortion.

In much the same way, tradition drove out radicalism in classrooms and lecture halls. In 1931–32 diatribes against progressive teaching methods started to appear. More drastic counter-reforms soon followed: party leaders unmasked 'left deviationists' in the Commissariat of Enlightenment, designed new curricula, imposed school uniforms and underscored the importance of discipline and authority. By 1945 many schools had abandoned co-education: boys studied subjects that would turn them into good soldiers and workers; girls – soon to be mothers and homemakers – pondered domestic science and childcare.

Treatment of the third institution identified by Timasheff, the Russian Orthodox Church, oscillated between persecution and grudging acceptance, but the Nazi invasion tipped the scales firmly in favour of the latter approach, so much so that by 1944 a Church–state concordat was in the making. If the war were to be won the regime could not afford to alienate potential allies: over the radio priests prayed for a Soviet victory, official organizations arose to foster Church–state links and in 1943, eighteen years after the death of Nikon, Stalin consented to the election of a new Patriarch.

Few people read Timasheff anymore, but his work has influenced almost all subsequent portrayals of Stalinist society: he was the first serious non-Marxist academic to represent cultural policy as a dynamic process arising from the interactions of state, society and ideology, not simply as something willed by party leaders. Fitzpatrick's 'cultural revolution' speaks across the decades to Timasheff's formulations, and even scholars who balk at his schematic approach or refute his chronologies acknowledge an important lexical debt – like several other meta-phors his 'Great Retreat' is embedded in the profession's vocabulary.

Our final metaphor – the 'Big Deal' – comes from one of the most original books on Soviet society to be published in the past half century. If Timasheff treats the 1930s and 1940s as a period of retreat and restabilization, for Vera Dunham the story is much more complex [Reading 14]. Moreover, for her, cultural and social change can best be understood not through decrees, official pronounce-ments or social statistics, but via the plots, allusions and linguistic structures of novels and poetry. Part social history, part literary exegesis and part meditation on Stalinism, her monograph, *In Stalin's Time: Middleclass Values in Soviet Fiction*, reads Soviet pulp fiction as revelatory guide to the interplay of private aspirations, political agendas and public events. For the most part she concentrates on 'high Stalinism', the years 1945 to 1953, but her analysis also reaches back across the entire century and examines the relationship between Bolshevik and pre-revolu-tionary culture.

Dunham displays what she holds to be Stalinism's cultural essence by expound-ing what we might characterize as 'a tale of shifting pronouns'. After 1917 collective imperatives overwhelmed personal inclinations and Bolshevik morality extirpated the individual conscience: in Soviet literature, therefore, Dunham depicts 'we' replacing the Old World's 'I'. During the collectivist optimism of the Great Breakthrough 'we' became ever stronger, but at the same time a new pronoun appeared. As Stalin substituted himself for the party and the purges ripped through society 'He', the Omnipotent Leader, repudiated the collective 'we' and the residual 'I'. According to Dunham yet a third literary shift occurred in the period 1941–45. Because total war forced the regime to cede space to personal concerns 'He' now co-existed with 'thou;' tales of grief, loss of loved ones or dreams of future happiness mingled with panegyrics to Stalin.

Thereafter difficulties arose. In 1946 Andrei Zhdanov, Leningrad's party boss, tried to resurrect 'socialist realism', the official literary doctrine adopted by the First Congress of Soviet Writers in 1934, but Dunham asserts that too much had happened for the *Zhdanovshchina* to have much prospect of success: artless plots featuring positive heroes forever sacrificing themselves on the altar of socialist construction no longer resonated in society, and for several reasons. In the first place, memories of 1917, the Civil War and the Great Breakthrough were fading rapidly. Second, the wartime experience had been so searing that even the 1930s seemed like another world. Finally, and most importantly, she believes that in the late 1940s *meshchanstvo* came into its own.

Meshchanstvo denotes Russia's nineteenth- and twentieth-century lower middle class. Figuratively it signifies philistinism, vulgarity and narrow-minded provincialism. If *meshchanstvo* nearly perished during the Civil War and the cultural revolution, NEP and the Great Retreat provided welcome respites, and in the absence of a second *Ezhovshchina*, avers Dunham, it could flourish more or less unchecked. Henceforward, bureaucrats, engineers, Stakhanovites and their wives – social climbers of all hues – enjoyed relative security of tenure and could indulge their taste for 'chintz and lace-curtain respectability'. Since by the late 1930s regime and *meshchanstvo* had inflected each other, after 1945 the two sides struck a bargain: leaders encouraged acquisitiveness while the *meshchanstvo* eschewed politics. In Dunham's analysis post-war fiction duly recorded this 'Big Deal': 'He' now coexisted with a reconstituted Stalinized 'I', a compound personality synthesized from elements of Russia's pre-revolutionary petty-bourgeois culture and the daydreams of apolitical Bolsheviks and middle-ranking state functionaries.

'I–we' (the 1920s); 'we–He' (the 1930s); 'He–thou' (1941–45); 'He–I' (the post-war years): such, according to Dunham, is the literary trajectory – and therefore the social and spiritual trajectory – of Soviet life and culture.

Notes

1 For some of their most important contributions see S. Fitzpatrick, *The Cultural Front: Power and Culture in Revolutionary Russia* (Ithaca, New York, Cornell University Press, 1992); M. Lewin, *The Making of the Soviet System: Essays in the Social History of Inter-war Russia* (London, *Methuen*, 1985).
2 Reading 5, page 116.
3 Even the NEP is a metaphor, or a least a contested construction. Though the term was in common use after Lenin's speech to the X party congress, Soviet historians disaggregated the NEP into a 'reconstruction' phase lasting from about 1921 to 1925 and a period of 'preparation for socialist construction' running up to collectivization and the First Five-Year Plan. Moreover, in contrast to Western historians they insisted that the NEP ended not in 1927–28 but in 1936, when the 'Stalin constitution' proclaimed the complete liquidation of exploiting and antagonistic classes and the arrival of socialism. Disillusioned contemporaries mocked the NEP as 'New Exploitation of the Proletariat'.

Chapter 5 The Second Revolution and After

Reading 9 *Бабьи Бунты and peasant women's protest during collectivization*

L. VIOLA

Bab'i bunty were an integral part of the rural landscape during the years of wholesale (or сплошная) collectivization. The term could be translated roughly as 'women's riots', yet this translation does not begin to do justice to its specific cultural and historical evocations. 'Бабий' (the adjective) is a colloquial expression for women that refers in particular to country women with country ways. The 'баба' (singular noun) is most often perceived as illiterate, ignorant (in the broader sense of 'некультурная'), superstitious, a rumor-monger, and, in general, given to irrational outbursts of hysteria. The *baba*, might best be seen as a colorful combination of the American 'hag', 'fishwife', and 'woman driver' all rolled into a peasant mold. The element of stereotype is evident. Accordingly, the modifier colors and reinforces the noun that follows. A 'бунт' is a spontaneous, uncontrolled, and uncontrollable explosion of peasant opposition to authority. Not quite a demonstration, it is often aimless (at least in the mind of official observers), generally unpredictable, and always dangerous. A *'babii bunt'*, then, is a women's riot characterized by female hysteria, irrational behavior, unorganized and inarticulate protest, and violent actions.

Such, in any case, were the denotation and connotation of the term as used by Communist Party leaders, local activists, and other observers during collectivization. Rarely, if ever, were *bab'i bunty* described or evaluated in political or ideological terms. The causes of the *bab'i bunty* were generally attributed either to the instigation of agitators, the 'kulaks' and *'podkulachniki'* (kulak henchmen), who supposedly exploited the irrational hysteria of the *baba* for their own counterrevolutionary purposes, or else blamed on the reckless and lawless actions of the cadres who implemented collectivization and had succumbed to 'dizziness from success'. *Bab'i bunty* appear to have been tolerated to a far greater extent than were similar protests led by peasant men. They also seem to have been dealt with less harshly in cases when criminal charges ensued, the women escaping prosecution under the RSFSR penal code article 58 for counterrevolutionary crimes. The *baba* was not perceived as the fairer sex, but as the darker sector of the already dark masses; consequently, like an unruly child or a butting goat, she was often not held responsible for her actions although sometimes subject to reprimand and punishment.

Officials' perceptions of peasant actions are generally based on assumptions about peasant ways and mores. As Daniel Field has demonstrated, however, peasants appear at times to have exploited these official assumptions about themselves for their own ends. Field suggests that peasants manipulated their reputation for naive monarchism as a means of deflecting punishment and as a rationalization for confrontations with officials who, according to peasant claims, were violating the will of the tsar.[1] Although the *baba* was no longer a naive monarchist during the First Five-Year Plan period (despite some cases of a Soviet-style naive monarchism that pitted Stalin and the Central Committee of the Communist Party against local officials after the publication of Stalin's article 'Dizziness from Success'), it may well be that the *bab'i bunty* belied the official perception of peasant women's protest and were neither as irrational nor as hysterical as they appeared to outside observers.

This article is an exploration of the anatomy of the *bab'i bunty* and the protest of peasant women during collectivization. It is an attempt to examine the basis of peasant women's protest, the forms that such protest assumed, and the influence of official perceptions of and government reactions to the women's actions. The article is not intended as a comprehensive treatment of peasant women during collectivization. Nor is it meant to imply that *all* peasant women were opposed to collectivization. Due to the inevitable source problems connected with a topic such as this, the article will necessarily be somewhat impressionistic and the conclusions tentative. It is based on cases of protest in (ethnically) Russian and Ukrainian villages where the *bab'i bunty* occurred; the responses of women to collectivization in Central Asia and in non-Slavic villages are not explored, due to the very different cultural styles of women there and the absence of any overt or exclusively female peasant protest in these areas.

The collectivization of Soviet agriculture gave rise to a massive wave of peasant protest and violence in the countryside during the late 1920s and early 1930s. Peasant unrest began on the eve of wholesale collectivization in 1928 during the implementation of 'extraordinary measures' (i.e., forced requisitions) in state grain procurements. It continued, at varying levels of intensity, to the end of the First Five-Year Plan, by which time wholesale collectivization was basically completed.[2] The largest waves of peasant protest appear to have occurred in the second half of 1929 and in the years 1930–31. In 1929, for example, 30,000 fires were registered in the RSFSR alone and many, if not most, were attributed to arson, or the *krasnyi petukh.*[3] The number of cases of rural mass disturbances prosecuted under article 59^2 of the RSFSR criminal code increased in 1929 from 172 in the first half of the year to 229 in the second half of the year.[4] Although similar statistical data for 1930–31 are more difficult to extract from the sources, there is little doubt that the wave of violence and unrest in those years far surpassed that of the second half of 1929.[5] Peasant violence and protest were an inevitable byproduct of forced grain requisitions, collectivization, and dekulakization and were shaped by the traditional peasant approach to radical politics.

The Communist Party was aware of the dissatisfaction of the peasantry on the eve of and during the collectivization drives of 1930–31. Party concern over the extent of peasant unrest, moreover, appears to have played a significant role in shaping policy. Olga Narkiewicz has concluded that 'it was the fear of a full-scale peasant revolution (whether real or imagined)' that induced the party leadership to pursue the policy of all-out collectivization in the late autumn of 1929.[6] R. W. Davies has linked the March 1930 'retreat' from breakneck collectivization inaugurated by Stalin's 2 March article, 'Dizziness from Success', and the Central Committee decree of 14 March to the widespread peasant unrest of the first months of 1930.[7] This second contention is, in fact, frankly expressed in the later editions of the official history of the Communist Party of the Soviet Union.[8] The party publicly acknowledged the extent and dangers of peasant dissatisfaction in the months following the March retreat and, in particular, at the Sixteenth Congress of the Communist Party in late June and early July of 1930. This acknowledgement was to be the most explicit admission of the extent of the threat to the state posed by peasant unrest during collectivization.

Speakers at the Sixteenth Party Congress noted the key role played by women in the protest against collectivization and the collective farm. Although the extent and intensity of the women's protest were not specified, they were serious enough for Lazar Kaganovich to make the following remark:

> We know that in connection with the excesses [перегибы] in the collective farm movement, women in the countryside in many cases played the most 'advanced' role in the reaction against the collective farm.[9]

A. A. Andreev, the first secretary of the North Caucasus Regional Party Committee, seconded Kaganovich, claiming that women were in the vanguard in the protests and disturbances over collectivization.[10] These claims received concrete substantiation in reports written by workers and officials who served in the countryside during collectivization.[11] The reasons for the 'vanguard' role of peasant women in the protest against collectivization were considered to be the low cultural and political level and backwardness of peasant women, the 'incorrect approach' of rural officials, 'dizzy from success', to the volatile women, and, finally, the exploitation of the women's irrational fears and potential for mass hysteria by the kulak and the omnipresent *podkulachnik.*

The party's response to women's protest against collectivization was different from its response to (male) peasant protest in general, which was usually labeled kulak opposition and dealt with by increasing the level of repression. Instead of repressive measures (although these were not always excluded), the party emphasized a more 'correct approach' to peasant women – an end to the excesses – on the part of rural officials and the need to improve work among women.[12] The importance of work among women, in fact, had been a concern from at least the time of the grain procurement crisis when the potential dangers of female-led opposition to Soviet policy became clear.[13] Work among women basically had two objectives. First, it was held necessary to educate women and expand political indoctrination among them. A second task was drawing more women into active involvement in the political life of the village through participation in the women's delegate meetings, soviet elections, and membership in local soviets and the Communist Party. And, indeed, during the years of collectivization, there was a gradual, but noted improvement in such work as local officials were implored to pay more attention to women and increasing numbers of women were recruited to the party and elected to the boards of local soviets.[14] The state's response and its emphasis on the need to improve work among women were predicated upon the official conception of peasant women's protest as essentially non-political and a function of the ignorance and backwardness of the *baba.*

Nevertheless, the party's efforts were too little and too late. Moreover, and despite periodic waves of party and government expulsions and purges to offset local excesses, the party's contradictory demands of a 'correct approach' to the peasantry and the timely implementation of often brutal policies made it highly unlikely that the rough, civil-war methods of rural officials would be or could be tempered or civilized. Nor could the party mitigate the effect that it perceived the kulak and *podkulachnik* had in sparking women's opposition and the *bab'i bunty.* As a consequence, the party failed to quiet the fears of many peasant women or to prevent the wave of *bab'i bunty* that erupted in the countryside as a reaction to both rumor and reality.

The Communist Party claimed that the underlying basis of women's protest during collectivization was irrational female hysteria unleashed by the 'kulak *agitprop*', or the rumor-mill, and reinforced by the women's *petit bourgeois*, small landholder instincts. It was true that the rumor-mill often played a very important role in sparking *bab'i bunty* and women's protest; it was also true that peasant women's '*petit bourgeois* instincts' played a central role in their opposition to collectivization and the transformation of the life of the village that it entailed. However, the protest engendered by the rumor-mill and by some of the policies of collectivization was not always 'irrational' or the manifestation of a *petit bourgeois* class consciousness.

Rumors about collectivization and the collective farm raged through the countryside. Heated discussions took place in village squares, at the wells, in the cooperative shops, and at the market.[15] At one and the same time, there were tales of the return of the Whites and the *pomeshchiki* (landlords), the coming of Antichrist, Polish *pans*, and the Chinese, the arrival of commissars, Bolsheviks, Communists, and Soviet gendarmes, and impending famine and devastation.[16] Among the rumors were many that struck a particular resonance in the minds and hearts of peasant women. These rumors, broadly speaking, touched upon questions of religion, the family, and everyday life. Some of them assumed fantastic dimensions; others – whether fantastic or not – were sometimes based on actual occurrences.

Rumors concerning the Apocalypse were widespread at this time. During the initial stages of collectivization, there was a wholesale attack on religion and the Church, which, although largely the result of actions of local crusaders and militant atheists, was not officially condemned by Moscow until after March 1930. At this time, churches were closed down and transformed into clubs or offices, church bells were removed, village priests were hounded and imprisoned, and icons were burned. Both the onslaught on religion and the scale of the general offensive on traditional ways of life in the village served to encourage an apocalyptic mindset among the peasantry.

The collective farm became the symbol of the Antichrist on earth. In one village, old women asked, 'Is it true or not? – they say that all who join the collective farm will be signed over to the Antichrist'.[17] On the eve of collectivization, reports from the North Caucasus claimed that a certain personage assuming the identity of Christ was wandering through the villages proclaiming the coming of the Last Judgment. He had in his possession a document from the Virgin Mary calling for everyone to leave the collective farm prior to Judgment Day or else to face the wrath of God. The Christ of the North Caucasus also had a blacklist of collective farmers for use on Judgment Day.[18] When, in the autumn of 1929, the church was closed in the Ukrainian village of Bochkarko, it was claimed that a miraculous light issued from the church and a sign appeared on the cupola, which read: 'Do not join the collective farm or I will smite thee'.[19] In the village of Brusianka (Bazhenskii *raion*, Sverdlovskii *okrug*, in the Urals), tickets to the next world went on sale; they were sold in three classes and prices ranged from 50 kopeks to 2 rubles 50 kopeks.[20]

Peasant women were especially susceptible to rumors about the Apocalypse and Antichrist and to news of events like those described above. The peasant woman was the upholder of religion within the village and household, so it was natural that the attacks on religion and the Church often affected women most acutely. The peasant woman, however, was also said to be particularly responsive to tales of the supernatural. It may be that women's protest sparked by such fantastic rumors was based on a combination of devotion to the faith and superstition. It may also be that tales of the Apocalypse, which forecast an imminent cataclysm in which God destroys the ruling powers of evil and raises the righteous to life in a messianic kingdom, served as a religious justification (either perceived to be real or exploited as a pretext) for peasant resistance to the state or provided a peasant vocabulary of protest.[21] Whether a particular form of peasant protest, a pretext for resistance, or an irrational impulse, peasant women's protest raised by religious rumors and the attack on the Church derived at least in part from legitimate concerns over the fate of the Church and the believers.

There were also rumors that touched upon questions of the family and everyday life and that were especially troubling to peasant women. Some of these rumors were in the realm of the absurd, such as the rumor that spread through the countryside that four thousand young peasant women were to be sent to China to pay for the Far Eastern railroad or the variation of this rumor, which stated that only women weighing over three and one half *puds* (approximately 126 pounds) would be sent to China.[22] Mikhail Sholokhov in the novel *Virgin Soil Upturned* provides another example of rumor in the category of the absurd, most probably a variation of a rumor in actual circulation. Sholokhov writes:

> There was a nun in the village the day before yesterday. . . . She spent the night at Timofei Borshchov's and told them the fowls had been got together so we could send them to town for the townsfolk to make noodle soup with, then we would fix up little chairs for the old women, a special shape, with straw on them, and make them sit on our eggs until they hatched, and any old woman who rebelled would be tied to her chair.[23]

This rumor clearly verged on the fantastic, but it should be noted that it was based on two real grievances that women held during collectivization. These concerned the socialization of domestic livestock – the economic mainstay of a peasant woman's existence – and the introduction of incubators, opposition to which was due either to the fact that their use was predicated on the socialization of poultry or else the perhaps frightening novelty of their appearance.

In addition to these rumors, there were a series of rumors of equally fantastic dimensions, which claimed that collectivization would bring with it the socialization of children, the export of women's hair, communal wife-sharing, and the notorious common blanket under which all collective farmers, both male and female, would sleep.[24] These rumors were of obvious concern to women and, moreover, very possibly were inspired by cases when local officials either attempted to implement similar practices or told peasants that such practices were in the offing. For example, the 25,000er Gorbunevskii, working in the Crimea, announced on 1 March 1930 that his collective farm would become a commune and that all of the peasant children would be socialized. When the parents of the soon-to-be socialized children heard this, they began a massive slaughter of their also soon-to-be socialized livestock, fortunately sparing the children.[25] The RSFSR Commissar of Justice, N. M. Ianson, told of a case involving an 'aesthetic deviation' that may have been the basis of tales of the export of women's hair. According to Ianson, there was a local Communist in the Urals – a former partisan and party member from 1917 or 1918 – who made all the village women cut their hair short. Ianson claimed that the Communist took seriously (and literally) the propaganda centering on the need to create a new life (быт) in the village and to bring the countryside closer to the city. The Communist felt that short hair – as well as the introduction of short skirts – would give the *baba* a more urban look. One *baba* who felt differently, wrote in a letter of complaint, 'he has shamed us for all of our life, only death remains. . . .'[26] Rumors of the common blanket, which were probably the most pervasive of all, also may have derived from one or two cases when local activists discussed the promise of communism. One *Rabkrin* (Workers' and Peasants' Inspectorate) plenipotentiary told women that they would all have to sleep, along with all of the men, under one common blanket.[27] In the North Caucasus, local activists in one village actually went so far as to confiscate all blankets. They told the peasants that henceforth there would be no more individual blankets; all would sleep on a 700 meter-long bed under a 700 meter-long blanket.[28]

Many of these rumors clearly played upon the real fears of peasant women concerning issues of family and everyday life. Moreover, given the enormity of the transformation implemented by the state at this time along with the 'excesses', the horrendously low level of rural officialdom, and the actual occurrence of any number of bizarre instances such as those described above, one can only say with difficulty that peasant women's protest was irrational. One could perhaps claim, as Petro Grigorenko suggests in his memoirs, that women often simply exploited the rumors of the absurd, without really believing them, as a way to attack the collective farm under the guise of irrational, nonpolitical protest and, consequently, as a way to avoid the suppression of resistance by outside forces (armed civilian forces, security troops, or the militia) as might have been the case in an overtly anti-Soviet village uprising.[29] The plausibility of this suggestion will be examined below. For now, it is sufficient to conclude that, whether pretext or actual belief, the rumor-mill struck a deep chord among peasant women who saw many of their most cherished beliefs and domestic interests under attack.

Rumors, however, were not always the spark behind the *bab'i bunty*. Quite often, protest was triggered directly by clearly articulated opposition to the implementation of radical policies. This opposition raises the issue of the *'petit bourgeois* instincts' of peasant women. Such 'instincts', indeed, formed a part of the basis for resistance and figure largely in the rumor-mill, but opposition to policy deriving from so-called *'petit bourgeois'* concerns was often less motivated by 'instinct' than by a set of rational interests, revolving around the family and the domestic economy. For example, peasant women led the protest against attempts to socialize domestic livestock because the domestic livestock was generally the basis and justification of the woman's economic position within the household. Women also protested directly and without recourse to the rumor-mill over issues concerning their children. Once again, the socialization of domestic livestock could be a threat because the loss of a milch cow could very well mean that peasant children would be without milk.[30] In later years, Stalin even admitted how important an issue the loss of a cow had been in provoking women's opposition to the collective farm when he said, 'in the not too distant past, Soviet power had a little misunderstanding with the collective farm women. The issue was cows'.[31] In one village, a *babii bunt* occurred over the proposed closing of a mill. The women's concern here was that, 'we cannot feed our children' if the mill closes down.[32] Some women also objected to the introduction of nurseries. According to Maurice Hindus, the Ukrainian-born American reporter, this was due to the high infant mortality rate in the village. Hindus claimed that there was not a woman in the village that he visited who had not lost a child in infancy, so it was natural that these women were reluctant to entrust their children to the care of others. (This reluctance, moreover, was particularly appropriate, given the experience of caring for socialized livestock.)[33] None of these concerns derived from 'instinct'; rather, they were legitimate and articulate protest against specific policies and practices associated with the initial stages of collectivization.

It is evident that official perceptions of the basis of peasant women's protest were at least in part misconceived and that the *content* of women's protest was rational and based on legitimate concerns. The question that now arises is the extent to which official perceptions about the *form* of women's protest, the *babii bunt*, were accurate?

The *bab'i bunty* were depicted as spontaneous outbursts of mass hysteria marked by indiscriminate violence, disorder, and a cacophony of high-pitched voices all shouting demands at once. Groups of women assembled at the village square became 'milling crowds'. And behind every *babii bunt* could be found a kulak or *podkulachnik* agitator who exploited the ignorant, irrational *babas*. Instead of calmly discussing grievances in an organized, 'cultured' manner, reports describing women's protest claimed, for example, that, at soviet meetings, the women would simply vote against *all* measures of Soviet power regardless of content or that, at secret meetings against the collective farm in March and April 1930, the women (who formed the majority of those in attendance and were the most active participants) would all talk at once with neither chairman or agenda, in an atmosphere of bedlam.[34] Women often physically blocked the carting away of requisitioned grain or the entrances to huts of peasants scheduled to be exiled as kulaks, forcibly took back socialized seed and livestock, and led assaults on officials. The response of officials was frequently to hide or run away and to allow the *bab'i bunty* to take their course until the women ran out of steam – for the most part without recourse to the use of force. In the first half of 1930, the end result was generally the dissolution of the collective farm. The women were seldom held responsible for their actions, thanks to official perceptions of the basis of such actions. The *bab'i bunty* thus accomplished what they set out to accomplish and the state held strong in its perceptions of peasant women's protest.

There is a most illuminating case, rare in its detail, of a *babii bunt* in the Russian village of Belovka in Chistopol canton in the Tatar ASSR in 1929 which perfectly illustrates official perceptions of and reactions to the *bab'i bunty*. The cause of the *babii bunt* in Belovka was a decision made by the local soviet in August 1929 to introduce a five-field system of crop rotation in the village and to carry out a redistribution of peasant lands. Behind the *babii bunt*, according to the description of the case, loomed the 'local kulaks' and, in particular, the insidious figure of one Sergei Fomin, the 'kulak' miller. The case report read:

> As a result of kulak agitation among the *dark, illiterate* [italics mine – L. V.] peasant women, a crowd of 100 people . . . firmly demanded the repeal of the decree on the introduction of the five-field system.

Despite warnings to disperse, the crowd, 'supported by the general din', continued its protest, knocking to the ground and beating a member of the local soviet. At this point, other soviet activists entered the fray and, according to the report, prevented the crowd from realizing its presumed intentions of beating the activist to unconsciousness. The case was brought to the attention of the regional court, which prosecuted the ten most active *babas* and the miller Fomin, who was described as the 'ideological instigator' of the disturbance. Fomin, who was also charged with setting fire to the local soviet secretary's home, was prosecuted separately, according to 'special consideration'. The women, prosecuted under article 59^2 of the criminal code for mass disturbances, were given sentences of imprisonment with strict isolation ranging from two to three years.

The Belovka case was reexamined by the Supreme Court in January 1930, at which time the decision of the regional court was overturned. The Supreme Court held Fomin *exclusively* responsible for the women's actions, describing him as the 'ideological inspiration', the 'ideological leader' [вожак] and maiin 'culprit' in the disturbance. Fomin's 'counter-revolutionary organizational role' in the disturbance was the 'actual root' of the *babii bunt* and, according to the Supreme Court, the regional court had failed to discern this clearly enough. In addition, the Supreme Court accused the local soviet of Belovka of insufficient preliminary preparatory work among women, something that could have mitigated the effects of Fomin's propaganda. Finally, the sentences of the women, all described as illiterate, middle and lower-middle peasants, and representative of the 'most backward part of the peasantry' (i.e., women), were lessened to forced labor within the village for periods ranging from six months to one year. The purpose of the sentences was to serve as a warning and an educational measure and *not* as punishment.[35]

This case is instructive in illuminating official views of and reactions to peasant women's protest. In Belovka, the women were viewed as no more than naive dupes of the local kulaks who served as a figurative battering ram against Soviet power. The local soviet's failure to work among the women and prepare them for the new policy transformed them into ammunition, which the kulak could fire at the Soviet regime. However, the Belovka case may not tell the whole story of the *bab'i bunty.* Petro Grigorenko, in his memoirs, described the *bab'i bunty* as a kind of 'tactic'. The women would initiate opposition to the collective farm or other policies and the men would remain on the sidelines until the local activists attempted to quell the disorder. At that point, the more vulnerable peasant men could safely enter the fray as chivalrous defenders of wives, mothers, and daughters rather than as anti-Soviet *podkulachniki*.[36] Descriptions of *bab'i bunty* by cadres in the field offer confirmation of Grigorenko's findings and appear to belie the official image as presented in the Belovka case.

A riot that occurred in the village of Lebedevka in Kursk at the Buden-nyi collective farm may serve as an example. A 25,000er by the name of Dobychin, serving as a plenipotentiary for collectivization, arrived in the collective farm on 7 March. Dobychin called a meeting of the peasant women and was greeted with cries of 'We do not want a collective farm' and 'You want to derail the *muzhik*'. Dobychin responded, 'We will not hold such types in the collective farm, good riddance. . . . [s]leep it off and you'll see that we will let the *bedniak* [poor peasant] derail him who made you drunk and sent you here'. Dobychin's tactic led to a general uproar and an assault on Dobychin. The women, with one Praskov'ia Avdiushenko in the lead, approached the stage where he stood. Praskov'ia said to Dobychin, 'Ah well, come nearer to us'. With this, she grabbed the worker by his collar and dragged him off the stage. Dobychin somehow managed to escape, but the unrest continued and even escalated when the church watchman's wife began to ring the church bell. With this, all of the peasants entered the fray. They seized their recently socialized livestock and prepared a collective declaration requesting permission to quit the farm. This disturbance, like many others, was not suppressed, but simply ended with the collapse of the collective farm.[37]

A similar situation was described by the worker Zamiatin who was among those workers recruited from the city soviets in early 1930 to work in the local rural soviets. Zamiatin depicted the situation faced by the 25,000er V. Klinov. Zamiatin said that the approach to Klinov's village resembled an 'armed camp'; on his way, he saw a sign nailed to a bridge that read: 'Vas'ka [Klinov] you scum, get out. We will break your legs'. When he arrived, Zamiatin found the village alive with rumors of the approach of a band of riders who were coming to kill all the Communists and collective farmers. In this village, dekulakization had already been implemented but, as happened elsewhere, the kulaks were not yet removed from the village. This omission, according to Zamiatin, had led to the crisis that existed. With Zamiatin's arrival, Klinov set about preparing for the exile of the kulaks. He began by removing the church bell, which traditionally served as tocsin to gather together the peasants in case of emergency. The heads of kulak families were exiled, and all went well until one of the exiled kulaks returned to announce that the other kulaks would soon be coming back to seek vengeance. This led to the decision to exile the families of the exiled kulak heads of households. The announcement of this decision led to an uproar. The peasant women, in an attempt to forestall this action, blocked the entrances of the huts of the kulak families. Several days later, the women also led the opposition to the attempt to cart away the village's grain by blocking the grain warehouse. This led to a *babii bunt*, followed quickly by a general free-for-all in which all the peasants participated in a pitchfork battle. The disturbance was suppressed by the militia, which was called in after all of the peasants had joined the rebellion.[38]

In both of these cases, peasant women were responsible for initiating the resistance and were soon joined by the peasant men in a general village riot. In a classic depiction of a *babii bunt* in a Cossack village in *Virgin Soil Upturned*, the Cossack men stood at the back of the crowd of women urging them on when they attacked the chairman of the local soviet. Here, the women led the attack on the grain warehouse 'with the silent approval of the menfolk at the back'. And while the women were dragging the chairman of the collective farm through the village, the Cossack men broke the locks of the grain warehouse and seized their grain.[39] The women served both as initiators and decoys in this disturbance.

Lev Kopelev has provided yet another description of a *babii bunt*, and one that closely conforms to Grigorenko's hypothesis. Kopelev described a disturbance in a Ukrainian village:

> A 'riot' also broke out in Okhochaya. A crowd of women stormed the kolkhoz [collective farm] stables and barns. They cried, screamed, wailed, demanding their cows and seed back. The men stood a way off, in clusters, sullenly silent. Some of the lads had pitchforks, stakes, axes tucked in their sashes. The terrified granary man ran away; the women tore off the bolts and together with the men began dragging out the bags of seed.[40]

Here, as elsewhere, the *babii bunt* was the first stage in a general peasant riot. Here too the women had specific aims and, whether the riots were intended to dissolve the collective farm, halt dekulakization, or retake socialized seed and livestock, they accomplished their aims.

Women tended to lead the village riots because they were less vulnerable to repression than peasant men. There were even reports of *bab'i bunty* in 1929 when the women brought their children with them into battle or laid down in front of tractors to block collectivization.[41] In the *bab'i bunty*, the men stood to the side. In non-violent protest, the situation was similar. Peasant men frequently allowed their female relatives to express opposition to policy. According to a report of a worker brigade in Tambov, in the Central Black Earth Region, the men did not go to the meetings on collectivization, but sent the women instead. When asked why they did not attend the meetings, the men replied, 'They [the women] are equal now, as they decide so we will agree. . . .'[42] In this way, it was easy for a peasant to claim that he had not joined the collective farm or surrendered his grain because his wife would not let him or threatened him with divorce. The 25,000er Gruzdev was told by one peasant, 'my wife does not want to socialize our cow, so I cannot do this'.[43] One peasant man explained the power of the women in the following way:

> We dared not speak at meetings. If we said anything that the organizers didn't like, they abused us, called us *koolaks*, and even threatened to put us in prison. . . . We let the women do the talking. . . . If the organizer tried to stop them they made such a din that he had to call off the meeting.[44]

It is clear here that at least some peasant men recognized both their own vulnerability and the far greater leverage that peasant women had in speaking out against state policies.

Peasant women were able to get away with a great deal more than their male counterparts in resisting collectivization and the other policies of the times. Force was generally not used to suppress *bab'i bunty*. Furthermore, it would appear that women tended not to be prosecuted under article 58 of the criminal code for counterrevolutionary crimes in cases when opposition to policy led to court actions: in reports of court cases in *Sudebnaia praktika* (supplement to *Sovetskaia iustitsiia*, the organ of the RSFSR People's Commissariat of Justice) in 1930 and 1931, only men appear as defendants in cases prosecuted under article 58. This tendency, along with the infrequent use of force to suppress *bab'i bunty*, was a function of both official images of women's protest as irrational and the fear and inability of rural officials to respond effectively to the type of bedlam created by disgruntled peasant women. And, if actions reveal motives, it is likely that peasant women who rebelled against the policies of collectivization clearly understood how they were perceived and appreciated the power of their 'irrational behavior'.

The *bab'i bunty* that occurred during the years of collectivization were neither as irrational nor as spontaneous as the official accounts tend to conclude. The anatomy of the *bab'i bunty* and the content of peasant women's protest contained several consistent features, which belie the official images. First, the *bab'i bunty* often revealed a relatively high degree of organization and tactics. Following the initial articulation of protest, which could frequently resemble a mob scene, the peasant women would endeavor to disarm local activists or plenipotentiaries by one means or another, sound the church bell to alert the village and mobilize support, and, finally, approach directly the resolution of the problem that had given rise to the protest.[45] Moreover, the women's protest frequently had a specific goal in mind (dissolving the collective farm, seizing socialized seed or livestock, halting grain requisitions or dekulakization, etc.). Second, the women's protest was frequently based upon opposition to specific policies and, whether inspired by seemingly irrational rumors, rumors used as a pretext for resistance, or direct opposition to the implementation of policy, it derived from rational and legitimate concerns and socio-economic interests, which were under attack by the state. Third, peasant women's protest seems to have served as a *comparatively* safe outlet for peasant opposition in general and as a screen to protect the more politically vulnerable male peasants who could not oppose policy as actively or openly without serious consequence but who, nevertheless, could and did either stand silently, and threateningly, in the background or join in the disturbance once protest had escalated to a point where men might enter the fray as defenders of their female relatives. Finally, an important feature distinguished women's protest from protest (generally led by males) officially branded as 'counterrevolutionary'. Many of the counterrevolutionary cases prosecuted under article 58 of the criminal code in late 1929 and early 1930 occurred while the defendants were drunk. Women's protest, on the other hand, appears to have been, with few exceptions, sober and, consequently, perhaps, more rational than male protest.[46]

Several other conclusions about official perceptions of the *bab'i bunty*
and women's protest supplement direct observations on the nature of
peasant women's opposition during collectivization. First of all, the *bab'i
bunty* were very much a part of the traditional peasant approach to
political protest. Peasants rarely resisted the state through organized
political action. Their resistance often assumed the aspect of a spontaneous, disorganized, irrational *bunt*. However, peasant rebellions frequently merely *appeared* irrational to outside observers, who were
powerless to cope with massive explosions of discontent and who, in
the case of the *bab'i bunty*, were reluctant to resort to armed force to
quell riots.[47] The outside observers who wrote about the *bab'i bunty*
tended, in addition, to be city people or, at the very least, of a higher
cultural level than the peasants and, consequently, had a very different
conception of the forms that protest and rebellion were expected to
assume. The rudimentary organization behind the *bab'i bunty* and the
specific grievances articulated in protest were often, in the eyes of outside
observers, overshadowed or impossible to discern against the backdrop of
apparent pandemonium.

Second, and of equal importance, there is a real possibility that the
Communist Party was aware of the true nature and dynamics of the *bab'i
bunty* and women's protest during collectivization. As Field has argued,
the 'myth of the tsar' was as useful to the tsarist government as it was to
the peasantry. It was based on the 'myth of the peasant' and provided the
regime with a rationalization for any problems leading to peasant disturbances.[48] In the Soviet context, the myth of the peasant could serve several
purposes. First, official images of the *bab'i bunty* and peasant women's
protest could be manipulated to minimize the true nature and extent of the
opposition engendered by collectivization. Second, it served a particularly
useful purpose when women's protest engulfed entire villages, including
poor and middle peasant women. In these cases, the party had a ready
rationalization for the contradictions of the class struggle in the village,
for its failure to capture the support of its poor and middle peasant allies
among the peasantry. Finally, particular injustices could be attributed to
officials who, it was said, were violating the essentially correct policy of the
center. In this way, Moscow could, and often did, seek to divert grievances
from the state to local officials, who were frequently used as scapegoats.
Moreover, it is clear that, at least in the months following the March 1930
retreat, peasants also adhered or pretended to adhere to this rationalization, displaying a Soviet-style naive monarchism which pitted rural officials against Stalin and the Central Committee of the Communist Party.[49]

Peasant women played an important role in the protest that consumed
many Russian and Ukrainian villages during the First Five-Year Plan, and
it is important to attempt to understand the nature of this protest and the
state's response to it. Yet, one cannot claim that all women were united, on

the basis of similar interests, in opposition to the collective farm. Dorothy Atkinson has suggested that there were also women (widows, heads of households, wives of seasonal workers) who supported collectivization because of the difficulties of working their land alone and women, mostly young, who were genuinely enthusiastic about collectivization.[50] Furthermore, the general scale of peasant resistance to the state during collectivization should not be exaggerated. Although the exact dimensions of peasant resistance are not known, it is quite clear that the opposing sides in the rural conflicts caused by collectivization were unevenly matched. With the possible exception of the early months of 1930, the state always retained the ability to respond to peasant unrest in an organized fashion with a show of force. And – again with an exception, that of Central Asia – the confrontation between state and peasantry in no way approached the scale of a full-fledged civil war with troop formations and organized national or regional resistance. Despite these qualifications, however, the peasant unrest of these years was of sufficient scale and ferocity to force the state to take notice. And notice it did. The Party admitted that the 'retreat' of 1930 came about as a response to peasant unrest, and Stalin even made note of the opposition of peasant women to the attempt to socialize domestic livestock when, in 1933, he promised a cow for every collective farm household. This was clearly not a retreat from collectivization, but it was a retreat – and a retreat that proved permanent[51] – from many of the most objectionable policies and practices of those times, such as the open attack on the Church, the attempt to socialize domestic livestock, and the unsanctioned 'dizziness' of local cadres who sought to impose upon the peasantry their ideas of socialist construction in the realm of everyday life. It is plausible and logical to suggest that the protest of peasant women played an important role in the amendment of policies and practices in these spheres.

The *bab'i bunty* and the outspoken protest of peasant women do not appear to have continued beyond the First Five-Year Plan. Nevertheless, during the early years of collectivization, the *bab'i bunty* and women's protest proved the most effective form of peasant opposition to the Soviet state. Peasant women played an important role in the resistance to collectivization, defending their interests and demonstrating a degree of organization and conscious political opposition rarely acknowledged.

Notes

1 Daniel Field, *Rebels in the Name of the Tsar*, Boston, 1976, pp. 23, 209–10, 214.
2 By the end of 1931, approximately 60% of peasant households were collectivized. See I. E. Zelenin, 'Kolkhoznoe stroitel'stvo v SSSR v 1931–1932 gg', *Istoriia SSSR*, 1960, no. 6, p. 23.

3 V. P. Danilov, M. P. Kim, and N. V. Tropkin (eds), *Sovetskoe krest'ianstvo. Kratkii ocherk istorii (1917–1970)*, 2nd ed., Moscow, 1973, p. 280.

4 'Doklad o rabote UKK Verkhsuda RSFSR za vtoruiu polovinu 1929 g', *Sudebnaia praktika*, no. 8, 10 June 1930, p. 12.

5 For a rough indication of the scope of peasant unrest in the early part of 1930, see R. W. Davies, *The Socialist Offensive: The Collectivization of Soviet Agriculture, 1929–1930*, Cambridge, MA, 1980, pp. 257–8. According to one Soviet article (which, unfortunately, provides no source), there were 1,678 armed uprisings in the countryside in the period January to March 1930 alone. See B. A. Abramov and T. K. Kocharli, 'Ob oshibkakh v odnoi knige. (Pis'mo v redaktsiiu)', *Voprosy istorii KPSS*, 1975, no. 5, p. 137. In the Lower Volga, there were 165 riots (волынок) in March 1930 and 195 in April 1930 according to V. K. Medvedev, *Krutoi povorot (Iz istorii kollektivizatsii sel'skogo khoziaistva Nizhnego Povolzh'ia)*, Saratov, 1961, p. 119. In the Middle Volga, there were 319 uprisings in the first four months of 1930, as compared to 33 for the same months of 1929 according to F. A. Karevskii, 'Likvidatsiia kulachestva kak klassa v Srednem Povolzh'e', *Istoricheskie zapiski*, vol. 80, 1967, p. 92. And, finally, in Siberia, in the first half of 1930, there were 1000 'registered terrorist acts' according to N. Ia. Gushchin, 'Likvidatsiia kulachestva kak klassa v Sibirskoi derevne', *Sotsial'naia struktura naseleniia Sibiri*, Novosibirsk, 1970, p. 122. Data on 1931 are more scarce, but according to Zelenin, in the spring of 1931, there were open attacks (e.g., arson, destruction of livestock and agricultural equipment, etc.) in 15.8% of all collective farms: see Zelenin, 'Kolkhoznoe stroitel'stvo', p. 31.

6 O. A. Narkiewicz, 'Stalin, War Communism and Collectivization', *Soviet Studies*, vol. 18, no. 1, July 1966, p. 37.

7 Davies, *The Socialist Offensive*, pp. 255–6. For Stalin's article and the Central Committee decree, see I. Stalin, 'Golovokruzhenie ot uspekhov. K voprosam kolkhoznogo dvizheniia', *Sochineniia*, vol. 12, Moscow, 1952, pp. 191–9; and *KPSS v rezoliutsiiakh i resheniiakh s''ezdov, konferentsii i plenumov TsK*, 7th ed., part 2, Moscow, 1953, pp. 548–51.

8 *Istoriia KPSS*, 2nd ed., Moscow, 1962, p. 444; and 3rd ed., Moscow, 1969, p. 405.

9 *XVI s''ezd VKP (b). Stenograficheskii otchet*, Moscow–Leningrad, 1930, p. 70.

10 *XVI s''ezd VKP (b)*, p. 123.

11 For example, M. N. Chernomorskii, 'Rol' rabochikh brigad v bor'be za sploshnuiu kollektivizatsiiu v Tambovskoi derevne', *Materialy po istorii SSSR. Dokumenty po istorii Sovetskogo obshchestva*, fasc. 1, Moscow, 1955, pp. 347–8, 350, 354, 364–6, 369, 375; and examples cited below, pp. 30, 35–7.

12 *XVI s''ezd VKP (b)*, pp. 70, 457. Also see similar statements in *Kollektivizatsiia sel'skogo khoziaistva na Severnom Kavkaze (1927–1937 gg.)*, Krasnodar, 1972, pp. 262–4, 266; and *Zapadnyi oblastnoi komitet VKP (b). Vtoraia oblastnaia partkonferentsiia (5–12 iiunia 1930 g.). Stenograficheskii otchet*, Moscow–Smolensk, 1931, pp. 164–5.

13 To cite just two examples of such concern, at the Fourteenth All-Russian Congress of Soviets in May 1929, a peasant woman activist and delegate from Siberia stressed the need to improve work among women in light of a series of *bab'i bunty* during grain requisitioning. This plea then was echoed by A. V. Artiukhina, the last head of the *Zhenotdel* before its dissolution in 1930, at the Second Session of VTsIK (All-Russian Central Executive Committee of the Soviets), Fourteenth Convocation, in November 1929. Artiukhina warned that if such work was not improved, 'backward' peasant women would not

support collectivization and would be exploited by the kulak. See *XIV Vse-rossiiskii s"ezd sovetov. Stenograficheskii otchet*, Moscow, 1929, Biulleten' no. 3, pp. 11–12; and *II sessiia VTsIK XIV sozyva. Stenograficheskii otchet*, Moscow, 1929, Biulleten' no. 7, pp. 25–8.

14 See, for examples, *Chto nuzhno znat' kazhdomu rabotniku kolkhoza? (Dlia 25000 tov., edushchikh v kolkhozy)*, Moscow, 1930, p. 7; *Derevenskii kommunist*, no. 1, 12 January 1930, p. 32; and M. Kureiko, *25-tysiachniki na kolkhoznoi stroike*, Moscow–Leningrad, 1931, pp. 44–5. For information on the expanding role of women in political life in the countryside, see Dorothy Atkinson, *The End of the Russian Land Commune, 1905–1930*, Stanford, CA, 1983, pp. 367–8; and Ethel Dunn, 'Russian Rural Women', in Dorothy Atkinson, Alexander Dallin, and Gail Warshofsky Lapidus, eds., *Women in Russia*, Stanford, CA, 1977, p. 173.

15 Sadovnikov, 'Shefstvo nad kolkhozom "Revoliutsii"', *Sovetskaia iustitsiia*, no. 6, 28 February 1930, pp. 5–6.

16 These rumors were widespread and have been gleaned from many different sources. See, for examples, TsGAOR (Central State Archive of the October Revolution, Moscow), *f.* 5470, *op.* 14, *d.* 204, *l.* 54 (trade union of chemical workers, *svodka* on the work of Leningrad 25,000ers in the countryside); I. A. Ivanov, 'Pomoshch' leningradskikh rabochikh v kollektivizatsii sel'skogo khoziaistva podshefnykh raionov', *Rabochie Leningrada v bor'be za pobedu sotsializma*, Moscow–Leningrad, 1963, p. 219; N. A. Ivnitskii and D. M. Ezerskii (eds), 'Dvadtsatipiatitysiachniki i ikh rol' v kollektivizatsii sel'skogo khoziaistva v 1930 g', *Materialy po istorii SSSR. Dokumenty po istorii Sovetskogo obshchestva*, fasc. 1, Moscow, 1955, pp. 425–6; and *Sotsialisticheskoe zemledelie*, 31 December 1930, p. 3.

17 L. Berson, *Vesna 1930 goda. Zapiska dvadtsatipiatitysiachnika*, Moscow, 1931, pp. 18–19.

18 TsGAOR, *f.* 5469, *op.* 13, *d.* 123, *ll.* 28–40 (*Dokladnye zapiski* on the activities of metal-workers in the North Caucasus countryside in the fall of 1929; compiled by the metal-workers union).

19 TsGAOR, *f,* 5469, *op.* 13, *d.* 123, *ll.* 78–91 (*Dokladnye zapiski* on the activities of metal-workers in the Ukrainian countryside in the fall of 1929; compiled by the metal-workers union).

20 A. Angarov, 'Sel'sovet i likvidatsiia kulachestva kak klassa', *Bol'shevik*, no. 6, 31 March 1930, p. 25.

21 During the Schism, the Old Believers often expressed protest in similar terms. Moreover, an apocalyptic mindset among peasants seems to be a characteristic response at times of momentous upheaval and transformation. See, for example, Michael Cherniavsky, 'The Old Believers and the New Religion', in Michael Cherniavsky (ed.), *The Structure of Russian History*, New York, 1970, pp. 140–188.

22 Angarov, 'Sel'sovet i likvidatsiia', p. 25.

23 Mikhail Sholokhov, *Virgin Soil Upturned*, tr. by Robert Daglish, vol. 1, Moscow, 1980, p. 176.

24 Berson, *Vesna 1930 goda*, pp. 18–19; *Bastiony revoliutsii. Stranitsy istorii leningradskikh zavodov*, fasc. 3, Leningrad, 1960, p. 241; and see note 16 above.

25 *Trud*, 28 March 1930, p. 3.

26 This local Communist was originally sentenced to six years for his 'aesthetic excess' but later the term was lowered. Ianson claimed he was extremely progressive, given his social conditions. See N. M. Ianson, 'O peregibakh i ikh ispravlenii', *Sovetskaia iustitsiia*, no. 11, 20 April 1930, p. 3; and 'Rech' t.

Iansona na 3-om soveshchanii sudebno-prokurorskikh rabotnikov', *Sovetskaia iustitsiia*, no. 24/25, 10–20 September 1930, pp. 7–8.

27 *Sovetskaia iustitsiia*, no. 13, 10 May 1930, p. 10 (Editorial by P. I. Stuchka).

28 Angarov, 'Sel'sovet i likvidatsiia', p. 21.

29 Petro G. Grigorenko, *Memoirs*, tr. by Thomas P. Whitney, New York, 1982, p. 35.

30 Anna Louise Strong, *The Soviets Conquer Wheat*, New York, 1931, p. 37. It should be noted that Beatrice Farnsworth briefly mentions the rational content of the *bab'i bunty* of collectivization in an essay that appeared as this article was being revised. See her interesting 'Village Women Experience the Revolution', in Abbott Gleason, Peter Kenez, and Richard Stites (eds), *Bolshevik Culture: Experiment and Order in the Russian Revolution*, Bloomington, 1985, p. 254.

31 Stalin, 'Rech' na pervom vsesoiuznom s"ezde kolkhoznikov-udarnikov', *Sochineniia*, vol. 13, p. 252.

32 V. Denisov, *Odin iz dvadtsati piati tysiach*, Krasnoiarsk, 1967, pp. 19–21.

33 Maurice Hindus, *Red Bread*, New York, 1931, p. 14.

34 Berson, *Vesna 1930 goda*, p. 73; S. Leikin, 'Raskulachennyi kulak i ego taktika', *Bol'shevik*, no. 13, 15 July 1930, p. 74; Sadovnikov, 'Shefstvo nad kolkhozom "Revoliutsii"', *Sovetskaia iustitsiia*, no. 6, 28 February 1930, pp. 5–6.

35 'Nepravil'noe vydelenie dela ob ideinom vdokhnovitele massovykh bezporiadkov', *Sudebnaia praktika*, no. 3, 28 February 1930, pp. 11–12.

36 Grigorenko, *Memoirs*, p. 35. Also see Atkinson, *The End of the Russian Land Commune*, pp. 367–8, for support of Grigorenko's conclusion.

37 G. I. Arsenov, *Lebedevka, selo kolkhoznoe*, Kursk, 1964, pp. 43–4.

38 S. Zamiatin, *Burnyi god. Opyt raboty piatitysiachnika v Rudnianskom raione na Nizhnei Volge*, Moscow, 1931, pp. 9–16.

39 Sholokhov, *Virgin Soil Upturned*, vol. 1, pp. 311, 316, 321.

40 Lev Kopelev, *Education of a True Believer*, New York, 1980, p. 188.

41 *II sessiia VTsIK XIV sozyva*, Biulleten' no. 7, p. 28.

42 Chernomorskii, 'Rol' rabochikh brigad', p. 325.

43 Denisov, *Odin iz dvadtsati piati tysiach*, p. 27. It should be noted that in many cases peasant men were sincere about their wives' resistance and that there were reports of divorce and family strife over the collective farm. See Strong, pp. 114–15; and R. Belbei, *Za ili protiv. (Kak rabochii ispravliaet peregiby v derevne)*, Moscow, 1930, p. 50.

44 Hindus, *Red Bread*, pp. 169–70.

45 See the case described in Lynne Viola, 'Notes on the Background of Soviet Collectivization: Metal Worker Brigades in the Countryside, Autumn 1929', *Soviet Studies*, vol. 36, no. 2, April 1984, p. 216, in which the women organizers of a rebellion called upon all women to join the protest or face a fine of three rubles.

46 'Direktiv UKK Verkhsuda RSFSR', *Sudebnaia praktika*, no. 5, 10 April 1930, pp. 4–6.

47 Roberta Manning has analyzed peasant rebellions during the 1905 revolution and its aftermath and has concluded that, 'however spontaneous and chaotic they [riots] might have appeared, they display signs of organization and prior planning and a rudimentary sense of strategy'. See her description of peasant protest in Roberta Thompson Manning, *The Crisis of the Old Order in Russia*, Princeton, 1982, pp. 148–58.

48 Field, *Rebels in the Name of the Tsar*, pp. 2, 213–14.

49 See Lynne Viola, 'The Campaign of the 25,000ers. A Study of the Collectiviza-

tion of Soviet Agriculture, 1929–1931', Ph.D. Dissertation, Princeton University, 1984, chapters 4 and 5.

50 Atkinson, *The End of the Russian Land Commune*, pp. 367–9.

51 As R. W. Davies has demonstrated in *The Soviet Collective Farm*, Cambridge, 1980, the basic shape of collectivized agriculture took form in the years, 1930–31, as a compromise (albeit unbalanced) between the state and the peasantry, between socialist fortress-storming in the village and traditional ways. The state was forced to settle for a program minimum, in which the peasantry was allowed to maintain a private plot, domestic livestock, and limited direct access to the market. After 1930–31, the compromise would be maintained of necessity, and no longer on the basis of peasant protest, by what E. J. Hobsbawm has labeled the 'normal strategy of the traditional peasantry' – passivity – which, he adds, 'is not an ineffective strategy, for it exploits the major assets of the peasantry, its numbers and the impossibility of making it do some things by force for any length of time, and it also utilises a favourable tactical situation, which rests on the fact that no change is what suits a traditional peasantry best'. See E. J. Hobsbawm, 'Peasants and Politics', *Journal of Peasant Studies*, vol. 1, no. 1, October 1973, p. 13. For further information on the shape of collective farming in the 1930s, see Roberta T. Manning, *Government in the Soviet Countryside in the Stalinist Thirties: The Case of Belyi Raion in 1937*, Carl Beck Papers in Russian and East European Studies, no. 301, Pittsburgh, 1984.

Reading 10 *Stakhanovites in the cultural mythology of the 1930s*

L. H. SIEGELBAUM

> One cannot speak to Stakhanovites as a teacher, but as to equals.
> They discuss Tolstoy's style and how it resembles that of Homer.
> P. Romanov, 'Novye liudi'

Traveling in the Donbass in the winter of 1936, Panteleimon Sergeevich Romanov, the author of numerous satirical sketches as well as the massive epic novel *Rus'*, looked out of his chauffer-driven car to see 'sparkling gardens, beautiful stone houses decorated with wood filigree [and] a profusion of cherry, apple and acacia trees'.

'What is this?' he asked the driver.

'Houses for the workers', was the laconic reply. 'Each house has two apartments'.

The car entered the grounds of the Petrovskii mine; and Romanov got out to visit the mine's Stakhanovite room. Inside, he found 'each worker . . . dressed in a good jacket and tie. There was no indication of the former disorder and lack of care in clothing', he wrote. In one corner of the room stood a piano, and flowers seemed to be everywhere. 'Flowers', he noted, 'have an important influence on the psyche. They now occupy an important place in life'. So apparently did classical literature. It was here, in a room set aside for their use, that Stakhanovites were discussing Tolstoy and Homer.

It has been commonplace to dismiss such depictions of life in the Soviet Union of the 1930s as pure fantasy, more in the vein of mythology than reportage. And though it has long been recognized that myths play a significant role in the organization and synthesis of the main ideas of a culture, only recently has Soviet culture been examined from such a standpoint. For a previous generation of Sovietologists, ideology, formalized and conveyed via indoctrination, was of paramount importance. Even while they concluded that many ordinary Soviet citizens responded apathetically and even cynically to such 'ideological bombardment', most Sovietologists confined themselves to studying high politics and the instruments of Soviet power such as the coercive apparatus and agitprop.[1]

This concentration, long dominant in the field, has given way to other interests and approaches. Influenced by developments in anthropology, some scholars have begun to address Stalinist culture and, in particular, its generation of what could be called synthetic folklore. Hence, in recent years, books have appeared on the cult of Lenin, socialist realist novels as anthropological texts, post-Second World War middle-brow fiction, and the Soviet regime's 'rituals of cultural management'.[2] None of these, however, focuses on the 1930s, although Katerina Clark's study of the socialist realist novel treats that decade as central and somewhat special. As she points out, it was in the mid-1930s that Soviet officialdom, having abandoned the 'little man' as the

> cornerstone of the new society, gave full play to *homo extraordinarius*, of whom outstanding Stakhanovites were key examples. From this time on, there were in Stalinist culture . . . two orders of reality, ordinary and extraordinary, and correspondingly, two orders of human being, of time, place and so on. Ordinary reality was considered valuable only as it could be seen to reflect some form, or ideal essence, found in higher-order reality. The distinctions between ordinary reality and fiction lost the crucial importance they have in other philosophical systems.
>
> At this time, as at no other, the boundaries between fiction and fact became blurred. In all areas of public life . . . the difference between fiction and fact, between theater and political event, between literary plot and factual reporting, all became somewhat hazy.[3]

Thus, it is not so much a question of whether the houses Romanov viewed from his car window were really so beautiful and inhabited by workers or whether the miners he encountered actually were comparing the aesthetics of Tolstoy and Homer.[4] Like the Potemkin villages of another age, the scenes described by the Soviet author were intended to portray an ideal or 'higher reality'. The closer, in terms of official ideology, Soviet society got to communism, the more important it became to stress the achievements of the present, soon to be consecrated socialist society.[5] As Stalin asserted at the All-Union conference of Stakhanovites, socialism was not to be construed as 'a certain material equalization of people based on a poor man's standard of living'. It required 'a high productivity of labor, higher than under capitalism', and in this respect, the Stakhanovite movement represented a force for the 'further consolidation of socialism in our country'. At the same time, it was preparing the conditions for the transition from socialism to communism in that it 'contains the first beginnings, still feeble it is true . . . of raising the cultural and technical level of the working class' to that of engineers, technicians, and other mental workers.[6]

However, none of this would have been possible, Stalin asserted, without certain preconditions that made Stakhanovism 'absolutely ripe'. 'First and foremost' among these was 'the radical improvement in the material welfare of the workers'. In what was to become the most frequently cited statement from his speech and something of a motto for the Stakhanovite movement, Stalin proclaimed that 'life has improved, comrades. Life has become more joyous. And when life is joyous, work goes well'.[7] Hence, not only had Stakhanovism opened up the vista of a society in which there would be 'an abundance of products and articles of consumption of all kinds', but it was no less important to demonstrate that such a condition already existed for those workers who, as it were, had earned the right to live prosperously.

To understand this dimension of Soviet cultural mythology, it is therefore necessary to analyze the Stakhanovites' role in the sphere of consumption; for as public-spirited as they were supposed to be, Stakhanovites did not live in the factories. As much as they claimed to love their work and as often as they cited the importance of arriving early for their shifts to check their machines, prepare their tools, and see that they had an adequate supply of raw materials, they were not supposed to sacrifice taking advantage of the abundance of goods and services available to them.

This part of their lives, though not directly connected with material production, grew out of and in turn reinforced the politics of productivity. Almost from the beginning, Stakhanovism contained instructions about how to live as well as how to work. In addition to providing a model for success on the shop floor, it conjured up images of the good life. Indeed, the nexus between work and rest, factory and home was inextricable. Many of the same qualities Stakhanovites were supposed to exhibit in the one sphere – cleanliness, neatness, preparedness, and a keenness for learning – were applicable to the other. Yet as we shall see, the ideal Stakhanovite home and family were not merely adjuncts of the work place.

They were rather symbiotically related. It was not Stakhanovites but their wives who received instruction in home economics. The sexual division of labor in the household, a product of both traditional cultural attitudes and new precepts, thus provided an essential precondition for Stakhanovites' success on the job and the leisure time to pursue officially sanctioned cultural activities.

The idealized Stakhanovite, the purposeful, well-rounded individual, was a particularly well articulated example of the New Soviet Man. This ideological construct, which fundamentally recast the role of the worker in Soviet society, was an important stabilizing factor in a period of great political and social instability. It was also one of the most enduring features of Stakhanovism. Exactly what it consisted of and what relation it bore to Soviet social and cultural reality are the questions to be pursued in this chapter.

I

Before dissecting the cultural mythology of Stakhanovites, we must descend to ordinary reality to assess the material and cultural standards of Soviet industrial workers. Given the paucity of the data and the tremendous variety of circumstances in which workers lived, only a rough approximation of certain general patterns is possible.

Contrary to what had been projected in the First Five-Year Plan, the real wages of Soviet workers fell dramatically after 1928. Estimates of the extent of the decline vary, depending on the indices used, the weight given to market prices as opposed to those of rationed goods, and the impact of the social wage (e.g., health care, pensions).[8] However, there is general agreement that the nadir was reached in 1932–3, after which there was a modest improvement, at least until 1937.

Of course, the composition of the industrial work force of the mid-1930s was very different from what it had been at the outset of rapid industrialization. As many workers were promoted to managerial and technical positions or became full-time party officials, an even larger number of working-class women and peasants of both sexes joined the ranks of industrial workers. The overall secular decline in wages was therefore not experienced as such by all or even a majority of workers throughout the entire period. Moreover, as individual wages dropped, so too did the birth rate among working-class families. Thus, the size of the working-class family shrank, as did the ratio of dependents to wage earners (Table 10.1).

There is no doubt, however, that the living standards of the average working-class family were lower at the end of the First Five-Year Plan than at its outset. Two indices, diet and living space, are revealing in this

Table 10.1 Changing composition of the Soviet working-class family

	1927	1930	1932	1933	1934	1935
Size	4.36	4.02	3.93	3.83	3.77	3.80
Wage earners	1.25	1.32	1.45	1.44	1.44	1.47
Dependents	2.82	2.70	2.49	2.39	2.33	2.33
Ratio of earners to dependents	1:2.26	1:2.05	1:1.72	1:1.66	1:1.62	1:1.59

Sources: For 1927, *Statistika truda*, nos 5–6 (1928):16; for 1930–5, *Rabochii klass v upravlenii gosudarstvom (1926–1937 gg.)* (Moscow: Mysl', 1968), 49.

respect. In Leningrad, where workers' food rations were generally higher than in most other Soviet cities, the average consumption of meat between 1928 and 1933 fell by 72 percent, that of milk by 64 percent, fruit by 63 percent, and butter by 47 percent. In contrast, the consumption of potatoes rose by nearly 20 percent, rye bread by 44 percent, and vegetables by 8 percent.[9] The diet of Moscow workers was similarly altered during these years. Whereas their consumption of meat fell off by an estimated 60 percent and that of dairy products by 50 percent, there was an increase in the quantity of potatoes, cereals, and fish (usually dried) consumed.[10]

As pinched as were the diets of workers in these two cities, the situation in other industrial centers was generally worse. 'No meat, no butter, and almost no sugar or milk . . . only bread and a little cereal grain' was the fare for the riggers of Magnitogorsk during 1932–3, according to John Scott.[11] 'Nothing but black bread, dried fish and tea' was what an American engineer reported that the workers at several steel mills in the Donbass and northern Urals consumed.[12] Unlike a large number of peasants in the Ukraine, not many workers starved, but hunger was widespread.

By 1934, the food crisis had somewhat abated. However, whatever improvement was to occur over the next several years was not, *pace* Stalin, radical. Workers in 1937 were still consuming far fewer meat and dairy products and considerably more potatoes and black bread than in 1928, though the proportion of the diet consisting of the latter item began to fall.[13] Significantly, with the phasing out of rationing, the differentiation between workers receiving higher and lower pay increased. The ratios of per capita consumption of working-class families in the two extreme income categories for the last quarter of 1935 graphically reveal the spread. For meat it was 5.7 to 1; for fruit, 6.7 to 1; and for butter, an incredible 17 to 1.[14]

Housing was a more intractable problem. As with wages, the Five-Year Plan projections for improvements in per capita living space bore no relation to reality. Neither in 1932 nor in 1937 did housing construction reach the levels targeted in respective plans.[15] When one takes into account

the unprecedented and largely unanticipated swelling of the urban population between 1928 and 1932 and, after a slight decline in 1933, the less
spectacular but still prodigious increase during the Second Five-Year Plan,
the full dimensions of the problem are revealed. Per capita living space,
which was a modest 5.65 square meters in 1928, declined to 4.66 square
meters in 1932 and by 1937 had reached a figure of 3.77. According to John
Barber, who cites a variety of statistics to support his assertion, 'All
evidence suggests that workers' living space remained significantly lower
than average as well as sharing in the general decline in size'.[16]

The acute housing shortage produced such phenomena as workers
sleeping in shifts on the same bed, a practice that was widespread in
mining and construction enterprise barracks; railroad stations and even
the factory floor serving as temporary living quarters; and workers'
families being squeezed into corridors and corners, sharing bathrooms,
kitchens, and no doubt much else with other tenants. These conditions
were not particularly new, though they were probably more common in the
1930s. Still, given that most workers had migrated from the countryside,
where living conditions were often more wretched, the absence of comforts
and privacy was not necessarily experienced as deprivation.

Nor by the mid-1930s was it what the privileged stratum of workers
experienced at all. The houses that Romanov described may have been
figments of his imagination, but in many locales quarters were reserved for
families of brigade leaders and leading Stakhanovites that resembled
accommodation for managerial and engineering personnel. Such was the
Busygin housing estate on the outskirts of Gor'kii. And at Magnitogorsk,
according to John Scott, 15 percent of the population, composed of the
families of foremen, brigade leaders, and skilled workers, lived in new
apartments that were equipped with central heating, electricity, and running water.[17]

To this brief summary of workers' material standards must be added a
consideration of their cultural activity and, more generally, the ways in
which they spent their time. Here, the time–budget studies of working-
class families that various Soviet economists periodically conducted are
most useful. What they indicate is a gross disparity between male and
female workers that, far from diminishing, was greater by the mid-1930s
than a decade earlier (Table 10.2).

Although the number of hours spent in productive work was roughly
comparable for men and women throughout this period, the same cannot be
said of time devoted to housework, cultural and educational activities, or,
until 1936, public affairs. The greatest disparity was in housework, where
the ratio of time spent by male and female workers was 1 to 2.8 in 1923–4, 1
to 2.9 in 1930, 1 to 3 in 1932, and 1 to 4.9 in 1936.[18] An examination of the
content of this category suggests that the gap was even wider.

Table 10.2 Time budgets of male and female workers

	1923–4		1930		1932		1936	
	M	F	M	F	M	F	M	F
Productive work	213.3	215.7	179.7	181.8	174	174	183	180
Housework	53.5	150	49.5	143.7	51	153	30	147
Cultural and educational activities	51.3	16.9	53.7	24.9	45	9	33	9
Public affairs	9.0	5.5	27.0	12.0	12	9	3	3
Total	327.1	388.1	309.9	362.4	282	345	249	339

Note: Data represent hours per month. M, male; F, female.
Source: John Barber, 'Notes on the Soviet Working-class Family, 1928–1941' (paper presented at the Second World Congress for Soviet and East European Studies, Garmisch–Partenkirchen, West Germany, September–October, 1980), Tables 1–5.

For working women, the preparation of food was by far the most time-consuming household chore. In 1923–4, it comprised more than half of the 150 hours per month devoted to housework. By 1930, it had dropped to 66 hours (46 percent) but thereafter rose to 72 hours. Time spent looking after children ranked second, averaging between 11 and 15 percent of total housework time, followed by cleaning and repairing clothes, housekeeping, and personal hygiene.[19]

For male workers, personal hygiene ranked first. In 1923–4 it consumed 19 hours per month, or 34 percent of total housework time, rose to 24.6 hours (50 percent) in 1930, and 27 hours (53 percent) in 1932, before falling precipitously to 15 hours (50 percent) in 1936. Time spent on other household chores presents a variegated picture. In the cases of washing and repairing clothes and cleaning and repairing house, the trend was downward; in that of looking after children, it rose between 1923–4 and 1930, only to fall thereafter; and in the preparation of food, it dropped sharply from 14.4 hours in 1923–4 to only 6 hours by 1930 and then rose less steeply, comprising 9 hours per month in both 1932 and 1936.[20] Thus, if one excludes personal hygiene (which, arguably, should not be considered part of housework), the ratios given above are altered as follows: 1 to 3.7 in 1923–4, 1 to 4.5 in 1930, 1 to 5.6 in 1932, and 1 to 8.6 in the Stakhanovite year of 1936.

Why this was so is a question that can be approached from two directions, namely from above and from below. To the extent that the early Bolshevik leadership was committed to the emancipation of women from the narrow confines of the household, that commitment was informed by both normative and instrumental considerations.[21] The former was inherited from the humanistic and egalitarian strains within Europe socialist movements as well as the nineteenth-century Russian intelligentsia's fitful attempts to grapple with the Woman Question. The latter was shaped

more by the recognition that any far-reaching reorganization of Soviet
society along socialist lines would necessarily involve the transformation
of the traditional household and family structures. If the Women's Department (Zhenotdel) of the Central Committee embodied the party's mis-
sionary zeal toward women, then Lenin's condemnation of 'the
backwardness of women, their lack of understanding for the revolutionary
ideals of the man', and early Soviet economists' emphasis on rationalizing
the expenditure of human labor and channeling it into social production
reflected the second orientation.[22]

Both were much in evidence in the 1920s, inspiring educational theories
and policy, literacy and antireligious campaigns, and experimentation in
communal living. However, the impediments to achieving equality both
within the working-class family and outside it remained formidable. They
included the wavering commitment of party leaders, lack of enthusiasm
and even hostility among rank-and-file members, the inadequacy of social
services, the weight of tradition among workers themselves, and, so long as
NEP was extant, limited employment opportunities. Of these, only the last
was to be overcome, as was NEP itself, by the First Five-Year Plan. But
being out of the household for seven hours of wage work did not relieve
women of the burdens of housework. Rather, it intensified them. As Gail
Lapidus explains:

> The exploitation of agriculture to serve industrial expansion, the
> relative neglect of light industry and consumer goods, the under-
> development of the service sector, and the subordination of welfare
> to productivity. . . had far reaching consequences for the role of the
> household in Soviet economic development and for the role of
> women within it. The effects of these patterns was to require the
> household to supply for itself a wide range of services that in other
> societies at comparable levels of development were usually provided
> by the market.[23]

Far-reaching though the consequences would be, they were not necessarily immediate. The fact that men and especially women spent less time
on housework in 1930 than in 1923–4 may signify that there was less food
to prepare. But it could also be correlated with the proliferation of public
catering facilities, laundries, and childcare facilities and the extension of
electrical service in the course of the late 1920s. Inadequate as they were,
and as low a priority as they had, the provision of these services went some
way toward reducing the burdens of housework.

No less significant is the increase in time that both women and men
devoted to cultural and educational activities as well as public affairs. This
may well have been the result of the campaigns the party sponsored in the
1920s as part of its commitment to overcome women's 'backwardness', as
well as a symptom of the Cultural Revolution, then at its height. Much

of the participation in public affairs consisted of passive attendance at meetings usually held in the work place and often during working hours. But approximately one-third of the time working men devoted to this activity was taken up by active party, Komsomol, and trade union responsibilities.[24]

By 1932, however, time devoted to political activities had fallen and was to decline still further by 1936. John Barber is almost certainly correct to see this as a consequence of both the emphasis on production rather than politics in the work place and the 'peasantization' of the work force.[25] Particularly as far as women were concerned, it may also be connected with the increase in time devoted to housework, itself a reflection of social services failing to keep pace with the swelling of the industrial work force.

The downward trend in male participation in cultural and educational activities is slightly more puzzling. To be sure, the lower degree of literacy among peasant migrants and their relative unfamiliarity with cultural outlets such as the theater, the cinema, libraries, and bookstores could account for part of the drop. According to one Soviet study, whereas workers in large cities devoted 5.6 hours per week to reading and attending the theater in 1923–4, such pursuits took up only 4.5 hours in 1936.[26] Nevertheless, one would have expected the expansion of adult education and vocational training courses to have compensated at the least. The solution to the puzzle may lie in the reduction in the number of formal class hours in apprentice school (FZU) courses and the increase after 1933 in the on-the-job component of technical training at the expense of formal classroom instruction.[27] In other words, it is possible that more workers were being trained even while the time required to complete such training was reduced.

It is also possible that the number of workers actually engaged in some form of study under the new scheme has been exaggerated. One writer, commenting on the state of technical minimum courses in Leningrad as of 1936, claimed that enterprise management allocated only half of the ten days per month recommended by Narkomtiazhprom. It was also noted that because of overtime work, 'there is hardly an enterprise where study is not sacrificed'. Average attendance among Leningrad workers in May 1936 was put at 65 percent.[28]

In summary, even as the sexual division of labor was narrowed in industry between the mid-1920s and mid-1930s, it widened in the household. For women, this meant the 'double shift', which left little time and energy for other pursuits. For male workers, the most striking change was their depoliticization and, conversely, an increase in unstructured leisure time. The absence of any systematic data makes it impossible to analyze how such time was spent.[29] Nor is it possible to calculate the amount of leisure time enjoyed by male workers in terms of their skills, occupations, and location or whether they were Stakhanovites. We can, however, explore the ideal–typical dimensions of this question by asking how those whose lives were characterized as joyous were supposed to occupy their nonworking hours.

II

Stalinist Russia, no less than other societies, contained codes of behavior or precepts according to which individual success was judged and rewarded. There were, of course, many paths to success and numerous yardsticks by which it could be measured depending on circumstances and what the authorities considered behavior appropriate to them. During the First Five-Year Plan, the most rewarding path for workers was that taken by outstanding shock workers, many of whom were selected for promotion to the ranks of officialdom.

In subsequent years, these *vydvizhentsy* continued to be the beneficiaries of the regime's solicitude. However, they were not the only ones 'to express an identification with Soviet power, pride in its achievements and the desire that these achievements should be celebrated in an appropriately cultural way'.[30] Many former peasants who had been tempered by the rough-and-tumble conditions in the factories took pride in their achievements, whether such achievements consisted of mere survival, learning a skill, or becoming a relatively privileged shock worker.[31] Having learned how to work according to instructions, they needed instructions on how to live. In less traumatic circumstances, this need could have been fulfilled by the existing core of urbanized proletarians (as, indeed, had been the case in the 1890s and again in the years just before the First World War). But at least in proportional terms, the core had shrunk, and its social weight had diminished. Moreover, the militant class outlook that had been a vital part of the proletariat's revolutionary tradition and identity was distinctly out of favor with the authorities, in both the domestic and, from 1934, the international contexts.

It was not, therefore, proletarian or working-class culture to which uprooted peasants and new workers adapted, but an urban culture that was itself undergoing profound changes.[32] Sensitive foreigners, such as Klaus Mehnert, noticed the differences as early as the winter of 1932. Domestic (*bytovye*) and production communes were no longer sanctioned, their egalitarian practices having become anathema to party leaders. 'The commune, . . . that's a great and beautiful idea', he was told by a former member who had since become 'the first engineer in our works'. 'One day we'll certainly realize it. But everything at the right time. . . . At the moment, . . . the commune is a Utopia, the sum total of petit bourgeois, left-deviation, Trotzki-ist levelling mania.' Asked to justify 'this state of differentiation and the tendency towards egoism which it doubtless inspires', another former communard asserted:

> By unfolding all productive energies, we are coming by way of the principle of output to such an immense increase in production, that one day, this state of shortage of everything, in which we are at present, will be overcome. . . . When once the abundance has been achieved, then . . . things will evolve into Communism quite of their own accord.[33]

This obviously would be a long-term process. In the meantime, the overturning of many revolutionary shibboleths, what N. S. Timasheff referred to as the Great Retreat, continued apace. The Old Bolsheviks and their tradition of self-sacrifice ceased to have validity, their society eventually was disbanded, as was the Society of Former Political Prisoners and Exiles. Rankings, badges, and ratings of all kinds, but especially in the military and in sport, proliferated. 'Higher, farther, and faster' became the new incantations.[34] The cult of the individual hero assumed huge proportions and was crowned by that of the Father of the Peoples, Stalin.

All the while, the image of the heroic worker was undergoing a change. Working to exhaustion and storming in general came to be associated not with communist zeal but with backwardness. Working in a rhythmic manner, studying but also engaging in other pursuits were the characteristics that higher authorities claimed to admire most. As the director of a Urals machine-tool enterprise put it in September 1934:

> Many of us consider that the shock worker is one who works day and night in the shop or factory, who does not crawl out of the shop, and who does not live for other interests except those of production.
>
> It seems to me that it would be more correct to consider a shock worker as someone who works at the factory exactly seven hours, since Soviet power does not permit anyone to work more, who regularly goes to the cinema, visits others, engages in sport and at the same time fulfills all production tasks. Our Soviet shock worker must live in a cultured manner and take advantage of all the good things of life that Soviet power offers him.

To this, Piatakov, presiding over the meeting at which the director spoke, uttered, 'Correct'.[35]

But what were 'the good things of life' and what did living in a cultured manner mean? So long as workers lived on rations in crowded barracks or corners and their leisure time was minimal, these questions were almost irrelevant. Indeed, insofar as being cultured (*kul'turnost'*) was associated with the bourgeoisie and its standards, even to pose such questions was unthinkable. By the mid-1930s, however, the standards had changed, leisure time had expanded for at least some (male) workers, and, as a

result of productivity increases and the expanded application of the progressive piece-rate system, so had their pay packets.

Although we have no firm basis for ascertaining what the material and
cultural expectations of these workers were – except that they were probably greater than they had been four or five years earlier – we do have some
idea of what they were encouraged to seek in these respects. This is
because there exists an array of sources relating to the lives of outstanding
Stakhanovites, or rather the idealized versions of those lives in the form of
speeches, newspaper profiles, and autobiographical accounts published in
book and pamphlet format.

Built around the 'Life is joyous' theme, these sources typically contrast
an arduous and dismal past – sometimes that of tsarist times but also no
more remote than the First Five-Year Plan years – with a brilliant present
and prospects for an even brighter future. They thus constitute a kind of
cultural agenda, one that was shot through with optimism. It bears
repeating that the mythology presented in these accounts bore little relation to the lives of most Soviet workers, Stakhanovites included. Nevertheless, it would be foolish to ignore them for this reason or to deny the
possibility that they had some bearing on ordinary workers' cultural
orientations and aspirations.

To begin with, the acquisition of a room of one's own or, if one were
married and had a family, an apartment was an accomplishment of which
the recipient could be proud. Having spent his first few years in Gor'kii
living in a makeshift wooden barracks, S. A. Faustov, Busygin's rival for
top honors at the Molotov Automobile Works, boasted of his 'beautiful
apartment with all the comforts'. 'If someone had told me that I would be
living in a multi-storey stone building, constructed according to the latest
word in technology, . . . I would have laughed in his face', he wrote.[36] The
contrast between the corner where the Moscow Frunze textile worker, M.
Lysakova, had previously lived and the 'large, airy, warm apartment' she
occupied after becoming a Stakhanovite was at least as great. Another
Stakhanovite textile worker, E. G. Illarionova, confessed to being 'embarrassed' by her apartment, which she described as better than the one in
which the director lived.[37] Where the desire for proper accommodation
went unfulfilled, as in the case of a Leningrad textile mill's best Stakhanovite, the press reminded management of its responsibility.[38]

Personal rewards and the satisfaction derived therefrom were matched
by the celebration of what the nation could now offer its citizens. In place
of ramshackle, jerry-built wooden structures stood 'real palaces' of brick,
stone, and concrete; in place of dark, muddy streets ruled by hooligans,
there were well-lighted, paved thoroughfares filled with automobiles and
trams. Housing was still abysmally scarce, but in Gor'kii there was a
Busygin quarter that was a showplace of worker accommodation, and in
Stalingrad new apartments with flower-bedecked balconies lined the newly

asphalted boulevards. Most basic consumer goods were still in short supply, but at least Gor'kii had its three story department store, 'shimmering with glass'.[39] Brick, asphalt, and glass – these were the building materials of the new cultured life.[40]

So, too, was the possession of scarce consumer goods. 'Now that we have begun to earn decent wages', remarked Diukanov to the All-Union conference of Stakhanovites, 'we want to lead a cultured life. We want bicycles, pianos, phonographs, records, radio sets, and many other articles of culture. But these things are still not to be had in the Donbass. If the party and the government help us, the Donbass will live still better, in a more cultured way'.[41]

The party and government were not slow to respond to this demand, which was also articulated by Central Irmino's party organizer, K. G. Petrov. In early January 1936, when more than 900 Stakhanovite coal miners, engineers, managers, and party officials gathered for a meeting in Stalino, Ordzhonikidze ordered that more than a thousand prizes be distributed to the delegates. The prizes included 50 automobiles (only 12 of which went to Stakhanovites), 25 motorcycles, 500 bicycles, 150 phonographs, 200 hunting rifles, and 150 pocket watches.[42] Individual Stakhanovites in other parts of the country were also favored with gifts. Reference has already been made to the cornucopia of food products presented to the Busygin family. But even more obscure Stakhanovites such as E. M. Fedorova, a garment worker at Leningrad's Red Banner Factory, could suddenly be deluged. From her enterprise, she received a watch; from the district soviet and party *raikom*, a vase, clock, tablecloth, electric samovar, clothes iron, phonograph, and records; from the enterprise party committee, the works of Lenin and Stalin; and from the Leningrad soviet, 122 books.[43]

Most Stakhanovites, however, did not rely solely on the munificence of state, party, and enterprise organizations. With their 'decent' wages, they found themselves able to purchase a range of consumer goods, especially clothing. In this respect no less than in their productivity, they seemed anxious to catch up to and surpass Western norms. As one trade union journal put it, 'Just as they smash the old production norms, so the Stakhanovites surpass the limits of the possibilities of daily life'.[44] To the turner Likhoradov, it was simply a matter of taking advantage of the opportunities provided by the Soviet government to 'live in a cultured way'. 'Why', he asked rhetorically, 'should I not wear a good serge suit [and] smoke good cigarettes?'[45] Were such aspirations compatible with socialist principles? Of course they were. According to one commentator:

> The transition from socialism to communism does not at all mean the gradual (or even any) liquidation of articles of personal consumption. . . . Yesterday's peasant, sleeping on sackcloth draped over

the plankings above the stove, now acquires a bed with springs, good furniture, sheets, tule blankets, curtains, etc.

'This is why', the commentator added, 'Stakhanovites announce with pride their growing prosperity'.[46]

The problem was that not all Stakhanovites knew how to spend their money wisely. This seemed to be particularly the case with young Stakhanovites, whose 'surplus of means often is wasted on dandyism if not on drink'.[47] Thus, the itemization in the press of goods presented to or purchased by model Stakhanovites served an instructional purpose and, in the latter case, illustrated what money could now buy. For example, when a cutting machinist from a mine in Chistiakovo went on a buying spree in November 1935, *Pravda* listed his acquisitions: coats for himself and his wife, several suits, shoes, slippers, and bolts of cloth, as well as a phonograph and records. Another machinist, from the Il'ich mine, was reported to have spent more than 1,300 rubles on coats, trousers, boots, a chest of drawers and other items. For Ivan Antonov, a fitter at Leningrad's Stalin Factory, increased wages were exchanged for a piano, a sofa, a sewing machine, firewood, and felt boots for his two children.[48] Then there was N. I. Slavnikova, a young boring-machine operator who had earned so much that she could not decide what to buy first. As she recounted to the All-Union conference, she turned for advice to her friend Marusia, who had actually earned 500 rubles more than Slavnikova in October 1935. 'What shall we do with all this money?' asked Nina. 'I will buy myself beige shoes for 180 rubles, a silk dress for 200 rubles, and a coat for 700 rubles', was Marusia's reply.[49]

Clothes were not considered articles of culture as such, but they did help to create a cultured appearance. The following description of two young Stakhanovites celebrating the New Year could have come from the society page, were there such an institution in the Soviet press:

> The *brigadir*-welder Vl. Baranov (28, the best Stakhanovite at Elektrozavod) glided across the floor in a slow tango with Shura Ovchinnikova (20, the best Stakhanovite at TsAGI). He was dressed in a black Boston suit that fully accentuated his solidly built figure; she was in a crepe de chine dress and black shoes with white trimming.[50]

Such sophisticates were a long way from the *kolkhozniki*, but even in the villages Stakhanovites could cut a relatively 'advanced' figure, as evidenced by the following *chastushka* recited by Pasha Angelina:

> Oh, thank you dear Lenin,
> Oh, thank you dear Stalin,
> Oh, thank you and thank you again
> For Soviet power.

Knit for me, dear mama
A dress of fine red calico.
With a Stakhanovite I will go strolling,
With a backward one I don't want to.[51]

Clothes, no less than decent accommodation, were important to A. D. Generalova, an automobile worker at the Molotov factory in Gor'kii. In her brief autobiography, which was written 'above all for women to tell them about . . . how I found the path to happiness', she relates how 'several years ago, I lived in barracks and had nothing to wear to go out for a stroll'. All that changed after she became a Stakhanovite and was given a bicycle, a phonograph, and a furnished apartment by the director. 'Now I live in a good apartment, have all the clothes I need, and am a respectable, marriage-able girl'.[52] It must have been with such girls in mind that various trusts advertized in the journal *Stakhanovets* for Lilac, Crimean Rose, and Sweet Pea eau de cologne, toothpaste, and patterns of the latest styles in clothing from Moscow, Leningrad, Paris, London, and Vienna.[53]

A cultured appearance was important, however, not only for marriage-able girls and not only during leisure hours. Shura Martynova, the out-standing female Stakhanovite at Skorokhod, was on her way to work with her husband when she was photographed wearing a fur coat, a feathered hat, and overshoes. A Stakhanovite textile worker, Milovanova, wrote in her factory's newspaper that before leaving for work she made it a practice to clean her shoes, look into the mirror, and carefully arrange her dress. Cleanliness extended to her use of language as well. 'Now I no longer swear', she remarked, 'because I know that for Stakhanovites it is not in character' (*nam stakhanovtsam eto ne k litsu*).[54]

These positive examples were supplemented by criticisms of low stan-dards of dress and organizational efforts to improve the situation. In April 1936, E. Fadeeva, a medal-winning Stakhanovite textile worker, wrote to *Pravda* complaining about the 'untidiness, slovenliness, and lack of culture' exhibited by her fellow workers on the job. This, in her view, displayed a lack of respect toward themselves and their work.[55] The letter sparked a number of meetings at Moscow factories.[56] At the Paris Commune Shoe Factory, the slovenly appearance of many workers, including Stakhano-vites, was decried. Gorshkov, a young bachelor, was described by one of his workmates as coming to work unshaven, in torn pants, and with his belt open ('And he is a Stakhanovite!') Another worker, Naryshkina, was seen shuffling into her shop dirty and disheveled.

This was very much in contrast to the appearance of those attending the meeting at which such denunciations were made. As described by the *Pravda* correspondent, the men were wearing starched white collars and jackets; the female workers were dressed in clean blouses and good skirts, and some were even lightly powdered. 'This too', the correspondent noted, 'is a necessary instrument of the workers that can influence fulfillment of the plan and the quality of production'.[57]

However, managers and engineers had to cooperate and set a good example. One speaker at the meeting criticized management for a shortage of towels, soap, and mirrors in the lavatories. At the Red October Confectionary Factory, female workers resolved to press for an additional restroom so that they could have a manicure every other day.[58] Later that year, turners at the Nevskii Machine Construction Factory in Leningrad lodged a complaint about not having anywhere to change into work clothes. Moreover, they claimed that, far from setting a good example, the engineers were coming to work unshaven and in greasy clothing, 'in the style of workers' (po rabochemu). Such behavior smacked of the misguided petty bourgeois egalitarianism that Stalin had long ago condemned as having nothing to do with socialism. In any case, it was an insult to the 'genuine Stakhanovite', who was characterized as a 'model of cleanliness, tidiness, and culture'.[59]

Finally, the most obvious manifestation of being cultured was partaking in cultural activities. As with production, quantity was very important. To demonstrate that in the year since Stakhanov's record life really had become more joyous, Izvestiia found a plane operator from a Moscow instruments factory who had been to three performances of Evgenii Onegin, two each of Boris Godunov and The Demon, and one each of Carmen and Rigoletto. This same Stakhanovite, Kondrat'ev, also read – everything from Gor'kii's Mother and War and Peace to several of Sholokhov's works. O. P. Chapygina, a Frunze factory worker, also enjoyed the opera and theater. But what was particularly noteworthy was her personal library, which contained 282 books.[60] No less cultured was Aleksandr Ponomarev, the experienced Leningrad fitter who was the subject of a photodisplay that appeared in the Soviet pavilion at the 1937 Paris Exhibition. The camera caught him in several 'characteristic moments' of his 'everyday life', such as reading at home (with a portrait of Stalin gazing down at him from the wall), visiting the Hermitage with his family, and attending the ballet at the Kirov Theater, accompanied by his wife.[61]

These, however, were unusual cases, even in the realm of higher reality. Many Stakhanovites, including those among the outstanding elite, were barely literate. For Stakhanov, Busygin, and others, acquiring culture initially meant being tutored in the Russian language and other subjects before entering one of the industrial academies. D. Kontsedalov, Stakhanov's workmate at Central Irmino, learned how to read together with his wife. 'Every day I learn something new', he wrote to the local Komsomol newspaper. 'This pleases me as much as the first day when I established a record in productivity'.[62]

Thus, if some Stakhanovites were models of cultured individuals, others could be advertized as examples of individuals who had learned to acquire culture. Yet the actual diffusion of culture among Stakhanovites entailed more than finding exemplary individuals. It required bringing culture to workers in the form of new cinemas, libraries, parks, reading circles, group excursions, and so forth.[63] Much of this effort devolved onto the trade unions. Responsible for organizing and operating workers' clubs and 'palaces of culture', the unions' factory committees began to orient their activities especially toward Stakhanovites. Special Stakhanovite rooms, such as the one visited by Romanov, were set up in these establishments. Literacy classes and lectures on such subjects as 'what Stakhanovites should read', personal hygiene, and gardening were organized.[64]

The educational functions of the clubs were supplemented and reinforced by the press. *Stakhanovets*, a journal published by VTsSPS, interspersed reports on Stakhanovites' techniques and the obstacles they faced on the shop floor with pages devoted to history and the natural sciences. Nor were the recreational needs of Stakhanovites ignored. In addition to an informational series on 'noteworthy dates' and a contest that tested readers' knowledge of inventors and inventions, the journal ran a series that told Stakhanovites what to see when they visited Moscow.[65] *Oblast'* newspapers were particularly well placed to guide their readers toward the most appropriate forms of entertainment and recreation. Thus, in its May Day issue, *Magnitogorskii rabochii* published the responses of seventy Stakhanovites to the question of what they intended to do on the holiday. Fifty were going to attend the theater, the cinema, or the circus, twenty-five would be preparing lessons or engaging in various forms of public activity, three were working on 'inventions', and almost all would be reading newspapers and books.[66] It was just such articles that one Stakhanovite asked *Sotsialisticheskii Donbass* (whose coverage of Stakhanovism was otherwise extensive) to print so that 'we can better orient ourselves toward the theater, the cinema and literature'.[67]

Cultured individuals dressing and working in a cultured manner, earning 'decent' wages that enabled them to buy articles of culture, and acquiring a knowledge of culture – this was the idealized picture of Stakhanovites. The picture, however, is incomplete. It excludes the home life of Stakhanovites and the roles that other members of the Stakhanovite family were to play. As international tensions mounted and as struggles within the party and state exploded into the Ezhovshchina, the idealized Stakhanovite family came to assume an importance that could not have been foreseen and that was to endure long after Stakhanovism in the factories had lost much of its significance.

III

The proportional increase in the burden borne by women in the working-class household during the first half of the 1930s coincided with, and was reinforced by, a shift in official Soviet policy toward the family. This shift was neither sudden nor entirely the result of state voluntarism. It occurred as part of a larger process of social integration and stabilization that followed upon the massive social and economic upheavals of the late 1920s and early 1930s.

Although in the course of the First Five-Year Plan, controversies over the proper role of women in a socialist society diminished, the party remained committed, at least in theory, to achieving more than the formal equality of the sexes provided by legislation. Even after the notion of the withering away of the family had been condemned as a leftist deviation and despite the lack of substantial progress in reducing the burdens of housework for women (or educating men to its importance), this ideal persisted in party rhetoric. As an International Women's Day editorial of 1933 put it, 'Our party strives to emancipate women from the material burdens of backward housework by replacing it with communal households, public dining, central washhouses, childcare, etc'.[68]

Thereafter, the emancipatory goal was replaced by an emphasis on the responsibilities of women to the family and the joys derived therefrom. Having been mobilized for production, women would henceforth be mobilized for reproduction. To quote Lapidus again:

> The new orientation, far from devaluing the role of the family, now treated it as a pivotal social institution performing vital functions. It was to serve above all as a model of social order, and for this purpose marital stability was essential. The independence, autonomy and mobility encouraged by earlier legislation were henceforth to be restricted in the interests of preserving a stable and monogamous partnership.[69]

Commenting from enforced exile on the emergent 'cult of the family', Trotsky pointed out that responsibility for maintaining a stable and monogamous partnership varied not only according to sex, but among women of different social strata. In contrast to the '5 percent, maybe 10', who 'build their "hearthstone"' by relying on 'a cook, a telephone for giving orders to the stores [and] an automobile for errands', working women were 'compelled to run to the shops, prepare dinner . . . and carry [their] children on foot from the kindergarten – if, indeed, a kindergarten is available'. 'No socialist labels', he added, 'can conceal the social contrast, which is no less striking than the contrast between the bourgeois lady and the proletarian woman in any country of the West'.[70]

Where, then, did Stakhanovism fit into this picture of 'hypocritical respectability'? There is curiously little information about female Stakhanovites building their hearthstones or raising families. Far from projecting an image of domesticity, female Stakhanovites were impatient to advance in their careers, even if they did so at the expense of homemaking and child rearing. The Skorokhod shoe laster Martynova turned her dining table into a time and motion study base. Using knives and spoons, she went through the production motions while her husband, also a laster, timed her.[71] For Marfa Fomina, the best Stakhanovite at Leningrad's Dzerzhinskii Textile Mill, marriage and raising a family were incompatible with the ambitions of finishing school, increasing the number of machines she tended, and developing her skills as a parachutist. An illiterate country girl until 1932, she now lived in a 'beautiful room', studied, engaged in sport, and did 'interesting things' in the evening. 'Could anyone be as happy as me?' she exulted.[72]

Stakhanovites were noticeably scarce among the working women who testified to the wisdom of the draft decree banning abortions. This was despite the intense propaganda about the advantages Soviet women enjoyed compared with their counterparts in other countries.[73] Indeed, not long before the draft was published, two items appeared in the press underlining the hardships endured by Stakhanovite women who were single parents. One reported the suicide of a *brigadir* at a Kiev spirits factory. According to *Pravda*, her suicide note blamed the enterprise administration for the death of her chronically ill son because it had repeatedly turned down her requests for decent accommodation.[74] Less grim but no less revealing was the self-portrait written by a *brigadir* from the Ordzhonikidze Machine Construction Factory in Moscow. She not only was a Stakhanovite, but as a member of the shop's cultural section helped to arrange for newspaper readings and discussions during rest periods, played the accordian, had recently attended the opera, visited the Tretiakov Gallery and the Lenin Museum, and had ambitions of studying music and pursuing some kind of literary work. All this, however, left her little time to be with her son. Her account of dragging him to her friends on days off or to the baby sitter contrasts strikingly with the ideal family situation of other accounts.[75]

The wives of Stakhanovites led very different lives, and it is with respect to them that we find Stakhanovism and the inculcation of family values intersecting with and reinforcing one another. Initially, these fortunate women were assigned the role of competent helpmates whose example could be emulated by the wives of other workers. 'To your lot', read the assistant director's letter that accompanied the food parcel sent to the Busygins' apartment, 'has fallen the great fortune to be the wife of a man about whom the entire factory is talking. Greeting you, . . . I send a small present and ask you to care for your husband so that he has sufficient rest to repeat his shock work every day'. The good woman replied in kind that she would 'assume responsibility to create conditions at home so that coming from work, he can eat well and rest well and with fresh energy go to the factory to achieve new victories'.[76]

Other Stakhanovites' wives were no less helpful. They closely followed the work of their husbands, inquiring about their results. They promised to create cultured conditions in the home, which meant preparing tasty, nourishing dishes and correctly educating their children.[77] One woman was described by her Stakhanovite husband, a Donbass miner, as 'a real Mikoian' because of her talent at managing the family's food budget. Another was a regular customer at a Leningrad store from which she ordered for home delivery butter, eggs, sardines, and sweet wine. These were all products that, according to *Leningradskaia pravda*, 'count among the ordinary, everyday menus of any worker-Stakhanovite'.[78] And even in the far north, *kolkhoz* women were boasting that, with the earnings of their timber-cutting Stakhanovite husbands, they could afford to place orders with the local ORS to feed and clothe their families properly.[79]

The obvious point was to emphasize to other women that they, too, could lead happy, secure, and comfortable lives if their husbands became Stakhanovites.[80] This image of domestic bliss eventually came to constitute an important theme of the Stakhanovite movement. Stakhanov's description of one of his days off in July 1936 fairly reeks of it. Arising at 9:00 A.M., he had breakfast. While the children went to play and Klavdia, his wife, visited with neighbors, he listened to the radio and read the newspaper. Later, the family decided to drive in their M-1 to the banks of the Donets River. There, they had lunch, went boating, and played volleyball with other miners' families. At home again, Stakhanov wrote out his Russian lessons. Diukanov and his wife dropped by for a visit. After tea, the women 'occupied themselves with their affairs', while the two men played checkers. Then they all went to the local workers' club, where they saw a performance of Pogodin's play *The Aristocrats*.[81]

We should note here a number of attributes of the archetypal Stakhanovite family. Popularity was one. Wherever Stakhanov went – the riverside, the park, the theater, his native village – he reported being surrounded by admiring people. Busygin was so popular that he had a problem deciding where to spend New Year's Eve. So many invitations![82] Sobriety is also evident. The Stakhanovs and Diukanovs drank tea, and the samovar figured prominently in photographs of the apartments of other Stakhanovite families.[83] Finally, the forms of entertainment and recreation, if not exactly elevated, were at least secular and modern – listening to the radio, reading the newspaper, playing volleyball and checkers, going to the theater.

No less interesting is what is left out of Stakhanov's account. We are told that he arose and had breakfast, but not who prepared this or the other meals of the day. While Stakhanov read the newspaper to learn about the new records of cutting-machine operators and the international situation, in which he expressed 'especial interest', Klavdia visited neighbors. Was she also interested in international affairs? What did she read? Could she read? And what were the 'affairs' that she and Diukanova pursued while the men played checkers?

These questions arise because they were raised at the time, not about Stakhanov's wife in particular, but about the wives of other Stakhanovites. They emerged in the rather bizarre but revealing – probably unintentionally revealing – context of an All-Union conference of the wives of commanders of production, that is, heavy-industrial enterprise directors and engineers. More than 1,300 of these worthy ladies – 'housewife-activists' is the way they were described and identified themselves – convened in the Kremlin in May 1936. For three days, they informed one another about and celebrated the good works they had been doing at their respective enterprises. As if to underline the significance of the occasion, all of the highest Soviet dignitaries attended, or at least were photographed on the podium. Forty of the women went away with medals awarded for their initiative in organizing the movement to raise the cultural and living standards of workers and employees in heavy industry.[84]

This movement actually had begun in 1934. Its earliest forms were the beautification of the factory environs (flowers again!) and the improvement of food and service in enterprise cafeterias and conditions in enterprise barracks and dormitories. Though these activities continued to animate the women, it is clear that, with the rise of Stakhanovism, their philanthropy took a new turn. Now Stakhanovites' families would be the main, indeed in many instances the sole, beneficiaries. Evgeniia Vesnik, one of the movement's founders, proudly announced that at the Krivoi Rog metallurgical enterprise she and other women had arranged for a model dormitory for Stakhanovites to be opened. It contained bathrooms, showers, an 'American' laundry, a beauty parlor, and a reading room.[85] Another lady, from Dzerzhinsk, intended while in Moscow to purchase tulle curtains, mirrors, and oil cloth for thirty Stakhanovite rooms in the enterprise dormitory.[86] Others inspected Stakhanovites' apartments and read literary works over tea.[87]

It was the wives and children of Stakhanovites, however, who received the greatest attention. Having in many cases only recently acquired culture themselves, the public-spirited wives of commanders sought to create in their own image cultured women from among Stakhanovite families. They taught them how to read and how to dance, how to crochet, and what to buy. One woman came up with the ingenious idea of giving prizes to the Stakhanovite's wife who kept her house in the best order.[88]

In vain had Nadezhda Krupskaia, a speaker at the conference, worried about these women cutting themselves off from the working class. 'We have found a common language with the wives of Stakhanovites', proclaimed a woman from Tagil in the Urals.[89] No doubt, the recipients of such instruction were glad to speak the same language as the wives of their husbands' bosses. As one woman stated in response to an inquiry from the editor of the Skorokhod factory newspaper, 'We don't want to be left behind. We will work and study to help our husbands build a still brighter future'.[90] The fear of being left behind was probably quite genuine. If, as Trotsky contended, 'one of the very dramatic chapters in the great book of Soviets' will be about ambitious Soviet bureaucrats who abandoned their uncultured spouses, then at least a few pages might be devoted to the fickleness of advanced workers.[91]

IV

Stakhanovites and their wives were thus favored for a number of reasons when it came to receiving instruction. Yet however advanced they were on the shop floor and however quickly they mastered middle-class etiquette, they were still, after all, manual workers. Charity, far from overcoming the inequality between donor and recipient, tended to justify and therefore perpetuate such a relationship.

One wonders, however, about the children. Could it be that a quite different fate was being prepared for them? The evidence is slight but suggestive. In the kindergartens and excursions organized by the charitable wives, Stakhanovites' children were grouped together with those of engineers and technicians.[92] Then there were the children of outstanding Stakhanovites. If little Alesha Martekhov was told by his teacher that as the son of the famous Leningrad Stakhanovite forge operator he had a great responsibility to do well in school, then other Stakhanovites' children eventually could set their sights higher.[93] Take, for instance, the two sons of Aleksandr Ponomarev, who in 1937 were sixteen and ten years old. While the older one was studying to become the captain of oceangoing vessels, little Lev expressed his desire to be a pilot flying polar routes. 'Before the youth of our country, all paths are open!' read the caption beneath their photograph.[94]

Did this mean not only that life would still be more joyous for one's children, but that it would be so because one's children did not have to be workers? Why did the wives of commanders of production consider it appropriate to isolate Stakhanovites' children from those of other workers? And why at the meeting of Stakhanovite miners in Stalino did Sarkisov mention that several of their children were in the process of becoming – or had already become – engineers?[95] Could it have been that, despite claims that Stakhanovites had overcome the gap between mental and manual labor, the instances of role reversal in which they engaged, the privileges they acquired, and the precariousness of being a production engineer or an *intelligent* of whatever specialty, there was no getting around the fact that the standards of status and culture remained largely unchanged?

It is true that at least some Stakhanovites exercised considerable discretionary power in their work and the organization of labor. They could demand the delivery of certain materials and power and order about subordinate and auxiliary workers. However, as Michael Burawoy has pointed out, one can – and in our case, must – distinguish the unification of conception and execution on an individual level from that at the collective or societal level.[96] The former, which does afford a degree of job control, could just as well signify a return to artisanal methods as a harbinger of communism. In any case, status and standards within an individual enterprise or even within the general arena of material production do not necessarily prevail in other spheres of activity. Indeed, it could be argued that so long as material production takes place in certain delimited institutions (industrial enterprises, collective and state farms) and involves only a proportion of the entire able-bodied adult population, cultural standards will be established elsewhere, by those engaged primarily in mental labor.

Role reversal, the idea that Stakhanovites knew more than the professors, may have irked some professors but was nonetheless a phenomenon in which certain astute academicians could take part without sacrificing their positions and could probably even enhance them. Stakhanov and his emulators did not become professors, but were rather in the first instance instructors of their work techniques. In the complex hierarchy of Soviet industry, this put them somewhere between workers of the higher skill grades and low-level technical personnel, or roughly where subforemen and adjusters stood. This was higher than they had been before, but a long way from a shift engineer, factory director, or *glavk* official.

The cultural mythology of this period did not and was not supposed to transform the values of society as a whole. Rather, it was to encourage workers and, in the first instance, Stakhanovites to identify their personal ambitions with those of the nation. Stakhanovites may have helped to revolutionize technique as Stalin claimed, but evidently not relations of production. They had neither risen to the top nor redefined who deserved to be there.

Even in terms of privileges, most Stakhanovites rated no higher than ordinary engineering–technical personnel. The fact that their wages were frequently higher than foremen's salaries, excluding bonuses, was regarded as an anomaly that had to be corrected and eventually was. Scarce consumer goods, tickets to the theater, and trips to their unions' sanatoria were not perquisites that could be obtained for the asking, but came irregularly like the ideal conditions on the shop floor that were conducive to the setting of records. With the exception of complaints by several former engineers who were interviewed as part of the Harvard Interview Project, the evidence overwhelmingly points to the fact that such employees generally enjoyed a higher standard of living than Stakhanovites.[97]

Although that standard was higher, it was not more secure. Even while a niche was being created for Stakhanovites, room was being made farther up the industrial hierarchy. Parallel with and temporarily eclipsing the image of the Stakhanovite worker as the New Soviet Man was the phenomenon of Stakhanovites being promoted to the ranks of lower and even middle management. Like the *vydvizhenchestvo* of the First Five-Year Plan period, this phenomenon was the result of both the prodigious expansion of the white-collar sector and party policy designed to create more accountable white-collar cadres. Such a policy might well have been implicit in the Stakhanovite movement from the outset, but it is apparent neither in the rhetoric nor in the reality of 1935–6. That the promotion of Stakhanovites occurred to the extent that it did can be attributed in large part to the arrests and shake-ups that marked the next two years. It was thus over-determined.

While many Stakhanovite mothers and fathers looked forward to their children making the leap, others had the opportunity to do it themselves. These two developments – of some workers improving their material and cultural standards but remaining workers, and others ceasing to be such – were not peculiar to the late 1930s. Nor were they limited to Soviet society. There was something peculiar, however, about the culture of this period and the behavior it sanctioned that is captured in the following recollection of a former naval officer:

> I would go to the theater . . . and take a seat from where I could watch people coming in. And I could tell by the way they came in who these people were. . . . Now, a Stakhanovite comes in. . . . He is in a curious position. He doesn't really know whether he belongs here. He's been thrown to the top suddenly. But he has an invitation from his plant he carries in his hand and he walks with a self-assured step.[98]

We may therefore conclude by endorsing Jerry Hough's observation that the 'Big Deal' about which Vera Dunham has written so persuasively 'really originated in the 1930s rather than in the 1940s'.[99] That is, beginning in the middle of the Second Five-Year Plan and extending into the years of the Great Purges, the political authorities needed to produce and found 'contented citizens who, in turn, would be eager to pass on the contentment to their children'.[100] We must add, however, that this earlier manifestation of the deal was more democratic than its postwar successor. Far from being restricted to the professional groups – Dunham's 'middle class' – its main targets were industrial workers and, by extension, the more ambitious and accommodating elements among *kolkhoz* peasants.

Nevertheless, both earlier and later manifestations had two things in common. First, the cultural mythology of the latter half of the 1930s was decidedly domestic in orientation and integrative in function. It stressed material acquisitions, thereby stimulating acquisitiveness; it fetishized cleanliness and order; and it virtually banished struggle in favor of 'apolitical conformism'. In all these respects, it prefigured the Big Deal of the late 1940s and early 1950s. Second, although pitched at a lower level of society, the deal of the 1930s involved many of the same people who would be part of the Big Deal of the postwar era. As just indicated, the acquisition of *kul'turnost'* by Stakhanovites prepared them and their children for social advancement, even if higher reality taught them to be content where they were. Dreaming about raising their technical and cultural standards to the level of engineers, some Stakhanovites actually would move into technical positions even before the outbreak of the Great Patriotic War. [. . .]

Notes

1 See Raymond Bauer, Alex Inkeles, and Clyde Kluckhohn, *How the Soviet System Works* (Cambridge, Mass.: Harvard University Press, 1956), 96–113, 138–42; Alex Inkeles and Raymond Bauer, *The Soviet Citizen: Daily Life in a Totalitarian Society* (Cambridge, Mass.: Harvard University Press, 1961), 251–65, 269–72; Merle Fainsod, *How Russia Is Ruled* (Cambridge, Mass.: Harvard University Press, 1965), 594–5.
2 Nina Tumarkin, *Lenin Lives! The Lenin Cult in Soviet Russia* (Cambridge, Mass.: Harvard University Press, 1983); Katerina Clark, *The Soviet Novel: History as Ritual* (Chicago, Ill.: University of Chicago Press, 1981); Vera Dunham, *In Stalin's Time: Middleclass Values in Soviet Fiction* (Cambridge, Cambridge University Press, 1976); and Christel Lane, *The Rites of Rulers: Ritual in Industrial Society – The Soviet Case* (Cambridge, Cambridge University Press, 1981).
3 Clark, *Soviet Novel*, 146–7.
4 Of course, even before the advent of Stakhanovism, some (shock) workers had received separate homes such as those described by Romanov. See, e.g., the letter from such workers at the Chekist mine no. 10 in *Trud*, July 10, 1934.
5 This necessity was not peculiar to the Stalin period. For a penetrating analysis of more recent formulations, see Alfred Evans, Jr, 'The Decline of Developed Socialism? Some Trends in Recent Soviet Ideology', *Soviet Studies*, 38, no. 1 (1986): 1–23.
6 I. V. Stalin *Sochineniia*, ed. Robert H. McNeal (Stanford, Calif.: Hoover Institution, 1967), 1 (XIV), 90.
7 I. V. Stalin *Sochineniia*, 1 (XIV) 91–2.
8 Abram Bergson, *The Structure of Soviet Wages* (Cambridge, Mass.: Harvard University Press, 1944); Janet Chapman, *Real Wages in Soviet Russia since 1928* (Cambridge, Mass.: Harvard University Press, 1963); Naum Jasny, *Soviet Industrialization, 1928–1952* (Chicago, Ill.: University of Chicago Press, 1961).
9 O. I. Shkaratan, 'Material'noe blagosostoianie rabochego klassa SSSR v perekhodnyi period ot kapitalizma k sotsializmu (po materialam Leningrada)', *Istoriia SSSR*, no. 3 (1964): 40; *Rabochii klass v upravlenii gosudarstvom (1926–137 gg.)*, ed. K. V. Gusev and V. Z. Drobizhev (Moscow: Mysl', 1968), 50–1.
10 John Barber 'The Standard of Living of Soviet Industrial Workers, 1928–1941', in *L'Industrialisation de l'URSS dans les années trente*, ed. Charles Bettelheim (Paris: Editions de l'Ecole des hautes études en sciences sociales, 1982), 111–12.
11 John Scott, *Behind the Urals: An American Worker in Russia's City of Steel* (Bloomington: Indiana University Press, 1973), 112.

12 Quoted in Barber, 'Standard of Living', 112.
13 *Rabochii klass v upravlenii*, 51. Workers' consumption of black bread in the first six months of 1936 reportedly declined 33 percent compared with the same period in 1935. See S. Kheinman, 'Uroven' zhizni trudiashchikhsia SSSR', *Planovoe khoziaistvo*, no. 8 (1936): 114.
14 Kheinman, 'Uroven' zhizhni', p. 116.
15 See figures in Barber, 'Standard of Living', 113–14.
16 Barber, 'Standard of Living', 114. In Leningrad, where an additional 200,000 square meters of living space became available to workers in 1931 mainly because of the resettlement of 'nonworking elements' of the population, the figure was 5.5 square meters per worker. Shkaratan, 'Material' noe blagosostoianie', 42.
17 John Scott, *Behind the Urals*, 231–4.
18 John Barber, 'Notes on the Soviet Working-Class Family, 1928–1941' (paper presented at the Second World Congress for Soviet and East European Studies, Garmisch–Partenkirchen, W. Germany, September–October, 1980), Table 2. A time-budget study of more than one thousand working-class families in Leningrad in 1932 revealed that, for every hour that men devoted to housework, women spent 3.3 to 4.3 hours depending on the industry in which they worked and their level of skill. See V. Lebedev-Patreiko, G. Rabinovich, and D. Rodin, *Biudzhet vremeni rabochei sem'i (po materialam Leningradskogo obsledovaniia)* (Leningrad: LNHKKL, 1933), 114.
19 Barber, 'Soviet Working-Class Family', Table 2.
20 Barber, 'Soviet Working-Class Family', Table 2.
21 This distinction is made by Gail W. Lapidus, *Women in Soviet Society* (Berkeley and Los Angeles: University of California Press, 1978), 73–82. Lapidus contrasts both with a third orientation, typified in the writings of Stalin, where utilitarian considerations were paramount.
22 Quoted in Lapidus, *Women*, 74. This is not to imply that Lenin was unconcerned with the plight of women as such or that Zhenotdel activists ignored the general social and economic benefits to be derived from female emancipation.
23 Lapidus, *Women*, 103–4.
24 *Trud v SSSR, 1931 g.* (Moscow: Gosekgiz, 1932), 173.
25 Barber, 'Soviet Working-Class Family', 8.
26 L. A. Gordon, E. V. Kropov, and L. A. Onikov, *Cherty sotsialistiches-kogo obraza zhizni: Byt gorodskikh rabochikh vchera, segodnia, zavtra* (Moscow: Znanie, 1977), 149. The different cultural background and attitudes of peasant migrants may also explain the sharp drop in the amount of time devoted to personal hygiene between 1932 and 1936.
27 According to a joint Central Committee–Sovnarkom decree of September 1933, beginning in 1934 FZU courses were to be reduced from three to four years to six to twelve months, and 80 percent of study time was to be devoted to production. For the impact of the decree on technical training, see A. I. Vdovin and V. Z. Drobizhev, *Rost rabochego klassa SSSR, 1917–1940gg.* (Moscow: Mysl', 1976), 198; L. Al'ter, 'Kul'turno-tekhnicheskii pod''em trudiashchikhsia SSSR', *Planovoe khoziaistvo*, no. 12 (1938): 25–7; I. I. Kuz'minov, *Stakhanovskoe dvizhenie – vysshii etap sotsialisticheskogo sorevnovaniia* (Moscow: Sotsekgiz, 1940), 50; and Sheila Fitzpatrick, *Education and Social Mobility in the Soviet Union, 1921–34* (Cambridge: Cambridge University Press, 1979), 226.
28 V. Kokshin, 'Tehknicheskuiu uchebu na vysshuiu stepen', *NFI*, no. 6 (1936): 12–14. This was the case at the Pervomaisk coal trust, where attendance at

technical minimum courses was reported to be 23 percent and master of socialist labor courses to be 41 percent for the first six months of 1936. *Sotsialisticheskii Donbass* (hereafter *SD*) July 27, 1936).

29 The study cited in note 26 shows that, for workers of both sexes, leisure activities (taking walks, visiting or being visited by friends, engaging in sport, etc.) took up 6.4 hours per week in 1923–4 but 7.9 hours in 1936. No breakdown by sex is given.

30 Fitzpatrick, *Education and Social Mobility,* 253.

31 The intrinsic satisfactions of work, of a job well done, should not be underestimated. As Eric Hobsbawm has written with respect to an earlier transition in Europe and North America, 'The workers themselves provided their employers with a solution to the problem of labour management: by and large, they liked to work and their expectations were remarkably modest. The unskilled or raw immigrants from the countryside were proud of their strength, and came from an environment where hard labour was the criterion of a person's worth'. E. J. Hobsbawm, *The Age of Capital, 1848–1875* (London: Abacus, 1977), 260–1.

32 I am indebted to Diane Koenker for this insight.

33 Klaus Mehnert, *Youth in Soviet Russia,* trans. Michael Davidson (New York: Harcourt, Brace, 1933), 253, 264–5.

34 See the table of the number of people who scaled the five highest peaks in the USSR in 1934 (452) and 1935 (4,263), in *Sotsialisticheskoe stroitel'stvo SSSR* (Moscow: TsUNKhU, 1936), 554. For the substitution of 'physical culture' by 'sport' in the Soviet lexicon and the rapid development of sports clubs and individual athletic competition during these years, see James Riordan, *Sport in Soviet Society* (Cambridge: Cambridge University Press, 1977), 120–52.

35 *Soveshchanie khoziaistvennikov, inzhenerov, tekhnikov, partiinykh i profsoiuznykh rabotnikov tiazheloi promyshlennosti, 20–22 sentiabria, 1934 g. Stenografcheskii otchet* (Moscow: ONTI NKTP SSSR, 1935), 48–9.

36 S. A. Faustov, *Moi rost* (Gor'kii: Gor'kovskoe oblastnoe izdatel'stvo, 1938), 8, 24.

37 *Pravda,* Jan. 11, 1936; *Rabotnitsa,* no. 3 (1936): 9.

38 *I.P,* Oct. 21, 1935.

39 Faustov, *Moi rost* 8; D. N. Vasil'ev, *Moia mechta* (Stalingrad: Kraevoe knigoizd., 1936), 5.

40 In his autobiography, Stakhanov refers to the paved thoroughfares of the Donbass cities and towns he visited with almost comical repetitiveness. See A. G. Stakhanov, *Rasskaz o moei zhizni* (Moscow: Gossotsizd., 1937), 88, 89, 95, 133.

41 *Pervoe Vsesoiuznoe soveshchanie rabochikh i rabotnits-stakhanovtsev, 14–17 noiabria 1935 g., Stenograficheskii otchet* (Moscow: Partizdat, 1935), 30.

42 *Pravda,* Jan. 11, 1936. For the list of gifts and recipients, see *Pervyi usedonetskii slet stakhanovtsev-masterov uglia, 7–10 ianvaria 1936 g. Stalino, Stenograficheskii otchet* (Kiev: Partizdat TsK KP(b)U, 1936), 291–6.

43 *Rabotnitsa,* no. 5 (1936): 2.

44 *Profsoiuznyi rabotnik,* no. 1 (1936): 12.

45 *Pervoe Vsesoiuznoe soveshchanie,* 179.

46 *LP,* June 6, 1936.

47 *Klub,* no. 3 (1936): 8.

48 *Pravda,* Mar. 2, 1936; *Profsoiuznyi rabotnik,* no. 1 (1936): 12. See also *Izvestiia,* Nov. 14, 1936, for an account of a Leningrad Stakhanovite family that spent 1,500 rubles on clothes and linens in one month. For other itemizations, see *Pravda,* Apr. 26, 1936; Mar. 30, 1938.

49 *Pervoe Vsesoiuznoe soveshchanie*, 42–3.
50 *Vechernaia Moskva*, Jan. 2, 1936. On changing styles in clothes among Urals workers during these years, see V. Iu. Krupianskaia, I. R. Budina, N. S. Polishchuk, and N. V. Iukhneva, *Kul'tura i byt gorniakov i metallurgov Nizhnego Tagila (1917–1970)* (Moscow: Nauka, 1974), 236–9.
51 *SD*, Nov. 23, 1936. The occasion was the third congress of Donetsk *oblast'* soviets.
52 A. D. Generalova, *Kak ia stala stakhanovkoi* (Gor'kii: Gor'kovskoe oblastnoe izdatel'stvo, 1938), 3, 14–15.
53 *Stakhanovets*, no. 2 (1937); nos. 1 and 2 (1938).
54 *Rabsel'kor*, no. 1 (1936): 30; no. 11 (1936): 12–13. What a contrast with 1932, when, at the party's Seventeenth Conference, the commissar of light industry was at pains to point out that the outward appearance of Western workers was deceiving. Many did dress neatly, he conceded, but this was at the expense of going hungry. 'Workers abroad take great care about their wardrobe', Liubimov noted, 'in order to conform to the requirements of bourgeois circles. . . . The old jacket is cleaned and pressed every week'. *XVII konferentsiia VKP(b). Ianv.–fev. 1932 g. Stenograficheskii otchet* (Moscow: Partizdat, 1932), 39.
55 *Pravda*, Apr. 20, 1936.
56 And not just in Moscow. See the reports of a meeting at the First of May Factory in Leningrad in *Rabsel'kor*, no. 11 (1936): 13, and the remarks of the Stakhanovite turner Matiunin at a meeting of Stakhanovites and managerial–technical personnel in Khabarovsk in *Tikhookeanskaia zvezda, July 22, 1936*.
57 *Pravda*, Apr. 24, 1936.
58 *Pravda*, Apr. 26, 1936.
59 *LP*, Oct. 26, 1936.
60 *Izvestiia*, Aug. 30, 1936.
61 *Stakhanovets*, no. 12 (1937): 54–6. See also the account of Ivan Antonov, who as a rule did not go to the theater or think about purchasing a summer suit until he became a Stakhanovite, in *Profsoiuznyi rabotnik*, no. 1 (1936): 12.
62 *Marsh udarnykh brigad. Molodezh v gody vosstanovleniia narodnogo khoziaistva i sostialisticheskogo stroitel'stva, 1921–1941 gg. Sbornik dokumentov* (Moscow: Molodaia gvardiia, 1965), 340–1.
63 For increases in the number of such cultural outlets in these years, see *Kul'turnoe stroitel'stvo, SSSR, Statisticheskii sbornik* (Moscow–Leningrad: Gosplanizdat, 1940), 141–204.
64 *Klub*, no. 2 (1936): 8, 10–11, 14–15; no. 3 (1936): 8, 21. Note, incidentally, the term 'palace', which replaced the more humble 'house' of culture around this time.
65 *Stakhanovets*, no. 1 (1937): 56, 60–1; no. 3 (1937): 63; no. 4 (1937): 52–5; no. 6 (1937): 53–6.
66 *Magnitogorskii rabochii*, May 1, 1936. Obviously, each worker was intending to engage in more than one activity.
67 *SD*, May 5, 1936.
68 *ZI*, Mar. 8, 1933.
69 Lapidus, *Women*, 112.
70 Leon Trotsky, *The Revolution Betrayed* (New York: Merit, 1965), 156–7.
71 *Pravda*, Oct. 12, 1935; *LP*, Nov. 14, 1936.
72 *LP*, Oct. 21, 1935; *Profsoiuznyi rabotnik*, no. 2 (1936): 9.
73 For a few exceptions, see *LP*, May 28, June 1, July 30, 1936.
74 *Pravda*, Mar. 6, 1936. see also *Izvestiia*, Mar. 6, 1936.
75 *ZI*, Mar. 8, 1937.

76 Quoted in V. Lel'chuk, 'Aleksei Busygin', in *Novatory, Sbornik* (Moscow: Molodaia gvardiia, 1972), 154. See also *Rabotnitsa*, no. 3 (1936): 3, where housewives were urged 'to help husbands and children become Stakhanovites'.

77 *PS*, no. 13 (1936): 76; *LP*, Oct. 18, 1935. See also the letter from the wives of three Baku Stakhanovites in *Pravda*, Nov. 3, 1935.

78 *Pervyi usedonetskii slet*, 127; *LP*, Nov. 5, 1936.

79 *Za sotsialisticheskii sever* (Kotlas), Feb. 17, 1936.

80 In case anyone missed the point, however, the far northern women asked, 'Why can't your husbands be Stakhanovites, have high wages and purchase new goods?' (*Za sotsialisticheskii sever*, Feb. 17, 1936).

81 Stakhanov, *Rasskaz*, 86. *The Aristocrats*, first performed in January 1935, concerned criminals who were reformed through their labor on the Belomor Canal. *Teatral'naia entsiklopediia*, 5 vols. (Moscow: Sovetskaia Entsiklopediia, 1961), 1:275.

82 *Izvestiia*, Jan. 1, 1936.

83 For such photographs, see *Stakhanovets*, no. 12 (1937):37, 41, 52–4. The theme of alcoholics being cured through instruction in Stakhanovite work techniques and the provision of articles of culture (musical instruments, dominoes, books, newspapers, and flowers) appeared in a number of testimonials. See the speech by I. A. Makarov in *Pervoe Vsesoiuznoe soveshchanie*, 68–9, and *Vsesoiuznoe soveshchanie zhen khoziaistvennikov i inzhenerno-tekhnicheskikh rabotnikov tiazheloi promyshlennosti. Stenograficheskii otchet* (Moscow: NKTP, 1936), 237.

84 *Pravda*, May 14, 1936.

85 *Vsesoiuznoe soveshchanie zhen*, 17.

86 *Vsesoiuznoe soveshchanie zhen*, 58.

87 *Vsesoiuznoe soveshchanie zhen*, 189, 232.

88 *Vsesoiuznoe soveshchanie zhen*, 106–7.

89 *Vsesoiuznoe soveshchanie zhen*, 72.

90 *LP*, July 4, 1936.

91 Trotsky, *Revolution Betrayed*, 156. The phenomenon was already quite well known in the mid-1920s. See the testimony in *The Family in the U.S.S.R.*, ed. Rudolf Schlesinger (London: Routledge & Kegan Paul, 1949), 106–7, 109.

92 *Vsesoiuznoe soveshchanie zhen*, 65, 154. See also the reference to special schools attended by Stakhanovites' children in Harvard Interview Project on the Soviet Social System, Russian Research Center Library, Harvard University, interview no. 1,106, p. 21.

93 *LP*, Oct. 18, 1935.

94 *Stakhanovets*, no. 12 (1937): 53.

95 *Pervyi usedonetskii slet*, 40–1.

96 Michael Burawoy, *The Politics of Production* (London: Verso, 1985), 54, 82.

97 Harvard Project, no. 114, p. 11; no. 388, schedule B10, p. 81; no. 1,497, p. 18.

98 Harvard Project, no. 105, schedule B2, pp. 39–40.

99 Jerry Hough, 'Introduction', in Dunham, *In Stalin's Time*, xiii.

100 Dunham, *In Stalin's Time*, 17.

Chapter 6 The Purges

Reading 11 *The omnipresent conspiracy: on Soviet imagery of politics and social relations in the 1930s*

G. T. RITTERSPORN

In August 1941 a young NKVD officer was taken captive by the Germans. He pretended to be a peasant's son who had studied agronomy and mathematics, before being 'mobilised' to work in the political police in the spring of 1938, at the age of twenty-five. He also pretended to having rendered some services to German intelligence in Riga in 1940. His interrogators were impressed by his willingness to cooperate and to present himself in a favourable light.[1] They were equally impressed by his manifestly sincere conviction that there was hardly any sphere of Soviet society where conspiracies were not present in the 1930s. In some respect the young man was far from being poorly informed. Apparently assigned to the surveillance of Komintern officials and foreign Communists in Moscow, he possessed pertinent information about people who must have been unknown even to police cadres, if they were not specialised in his field.[2]

Nevertheless, the interrogators could not help wondering if he was able to distinguish his undeniable familiarity with certain facts and rumours arising out of the NKVD's obsession with the ubiquity of spies and plotters.[3] Indeed, the young man reported a profusion of conspiracies in educational institutions, enterprises and offices as well as in the highest spheres of government in the 1930s. He even presented a chart of the complicated relations among secret organisations of 'leftist' and 'rightist' groups that included defendants in the show trials, commanders of the army and leading officials of the Komintern and the NKVD.[4] Despite his eagerness to seek the favour of his interrogators, he was ready to enter into dispute with them when they objected to his tendency to see spies in entire ethnic groups, and especially when they reminded him that they knew better who had been working for German intelligence in the Soviet Union: so much that he continued to stick to his opinion concerning an alleged German spy, insisting that he was better informed about the real state of affairs behind the régime's façade.[5]

The young officer's propensity to see a complicated web of conspiracies at the centre of Soviet politics had obviously more than a few things to do

with his training at the NKVD and proceeded from a consciously cultivated spy mania in the secret police. Nevertheless, everthing points to the
assumption that Soviet citizens of the epoch were inclined to lend credit to
the régime's propaganda about the subversive activities of plotters and
foreign agents. Captured officers seemed to believe that there was something behind the accusations against the high command in 1937.[6] At the
start of the war, ordinary citizens were ready to accept the idea that the
'whole of our country is full of spies' and to attribute the disastrous
military situation to 'high treason' and 'wrecking' in leading circles.[7]

In the course of the 1930s, political and even social relations came to be
understood increasingly in terms of conspiratorial intrigues. Plots and
wrecking became central paradigms by which the régime sought to explain
political processes and social conflicts, and official as well as popular
milieux were disposed to suspect the work of subversive machinations
behind the apparently inexplicable turmoil that turned into an unmanageable daily reality and represented a permanent threat to the security of
virtually any Soviet citizen.

It became routine for the Soviet authorities to ascribe the régime's
difficulties to 'subversive' activities of 'conspirators' during the collectivisation and industrialisation drives. Well-publicised show trials were
staged between 1928 and 1931 to demonstrate that the hardships of
the period originated in the 'wrecking' of 'plotters' among managerial
and technical cadres and among members of the scientific and planning
establishments.[8] Anti-saboteur campaigns focused on specialists who
were identified as leftovers of the Old Régime, and when the last show
trial of this wave took place in April 1933, against the background of
famine and intense intra-Party conflict and in the wake of a major crisis
of collectivisation and industrialisation, its defendants were once again
Soviet and foreign engineers.[9]

The identity of the 'wrecker' changed, however, in a matter of less than
four years. A new imagery of the 'enemy' emerged by the early months of
1937 which applied to veteran members of the Party, to high-ranking
officials and to practically all cadres. This imagery could be disregarded
as the propaganda of a completely perverted régime, were it not that it
reflected real problems of the system and something of the way they tended
to be seen in leading circles and by the population, and explained a good
deal of the régime's perversity.

It became increasingly doubtful after the early 1930s that the hardships
the public had to endure were temporary and incidental, and that people
alien to the régime could alone be blamed for them. This fiction seemed all
the more difficult to maintain since it was hardly possible to separate the
adversities of daily life from the operation of governmental mechanisms

which turned out to be unmanageable. The official discourse acknowledged that collectivisation and industrialisation had increased the
'strength and authority' of the Party and state apparatus 'to an unprecedented degree' and that 'everything or almost everything' depended therefore on the way officeholders fulfilled their 'decisive [and] exceptional'
rôle. It had to be admitted, however, that this state of affairs did not
mean that the apparatus worked in a uniform, regular and controllable
manner. Hence strict measures were necessary to ensure the implementation of the Party's 'political line'.[10] This line ceased to be the object of
open contestation by the early years of the decade, but the functioning of
the administration, the attempts by top bodies to regulate it and the
response of the apparatus to such attempts were far from making the
régime's policy clear and unambiguous.

Governmental mechanisms had a strong tendency to work in an unpredictable way and, whatever the 'Party line' happened to be, there was every
chance that it would be altered through the daily operation of the apparatus. Virtually all important decisions about industrial and agricultural
policy or about the screening of Party membership were implemented in
such a manner that the outcome had little to do with the originally
envisaged effects. If officials bothered to carry out major directives, they
concentrated their efforts mainly on producing immediate and spectacular
results which often did not amount to more than the appearance of the
projected changes. Far from improving the work of Party bodies and
rationalising management and production, nation-wide campaigns disorganised the administration and the economy and aggravated social tensions.[11] This phenomenon had nothing to do with alternative programmes
of reform-minded cadres, or oppositional movements within the apparatus.
Officials routinely misused their powers in order to make a show of success,
and in many cases they hardly had a choice, confronted as they were by the
indifference or hostility of the masses, by inadequate resources and by
the prospect of censure, dismissal or penal sanctions if they could not
produce at least the semblance of results or find scapegoats for failures.

The behaviour of officials did not deviate from the norms set by
higher bodies, including the centre, whose incompetent or contradictory
measures, scapegoating of subordinates and 'hostile' elements, and tri-
umphal reports on dubious successes were merely imitated by the apparatus. However sincere Moscow's warnings against abuses and excesses
might have been, insiders had no reason to take them too seriously.
Measures to alleviate tensions in the countryside even included a rather
parsimonious amnesty for some categories of peasants who had been
exiled or imprisoned for their alleged or real resistance to collectivisation, and a symbolic amnesty for officials condemned mainly for their
liberal attitude during the ruthless food procurement drives of 1932 and
1933.[12] But a multitude of instructions and injunctions concerning the

sowing and harvesting campaigns and the delivery of agricultural products showed that there was no illusion in high places about the cooperativeness of the population: if results were to be obtained, it had to be put under pressure by grass-roots cadres who were themselves under the threat of penal sanctions.[13]

Moscow had every reason to issue repeated calls for restraint in the prosecution of petty rural officeholders[14] who were frequently put on trial by higher-ups if something went wrong with farming and food procurements. More often than not, however, the latter acted in the spirit of directives of the Central Committee and the government which pressed for quick results and emphasised the personal responsibility of all cadres for the success of the agricultural campaigns.[15] In the same way, it was vain to enjoin local authorities to moderate their zeal in purging the Party and to refrain from persecuting people merely because of their social origin, if the move came some months after a vigilance drive in the name of the Central Committee which had dispatched lists of 'unmasked' people whose 'guilt' was nothing more in most cases than their social origin or their past.[16] Official spokesmen admitted that wholesale repression discredited the régime and that the authority and efficiency of penal provisions would be compromised if used in an inflated and irregular way.[17] Nevertheless, harsh measures against the masses and junior officials seemed justified by instructions which mobilised the judiciary to 'contribute to the successes' of agriculture, industry and transport and to detect 'hostile' intentions behind failures and professional errors.[18]

A paradoxical situation developed in which the activities of individual officeholders often deviated from or were in conflict with policies decided by the central authorities, yet were in harmony with a general pattern of action that was hardly ever compatible with the political line fixed by the centre. The paradox was intimately related to the contradictory political objectives of the régime: ensuring order among the masses as well as social peace, regular and controllable functioning of the administration and its 'decisive and exceptional' rôle. Maintaining order and the preeminence of the apparatus implied the delegation of large powers and created the danger of transgressions and social tensions. On the other hand, control meant curtailing the authority of officialdom, which tended to encourage popular insubordination, as in the case when Moscow publicly condemned the first excesses of collectivisation and triggered a series of riots.[19] When the top bodies tried to regulate the administration's working, they were in fact trying to do away with the logic which their own actions had established and which inevitably reappeared in the operation of the apparatus. A solution to this problem could hardly be found if the dominant position of the Party and state apparatus in society was to be maintained.

Something had to be done, however, since the activities of officialdom manifestly disorganised the régime and brought a deterioration in its relations with the rest of society. The agricultural administration's habit of furnishing false data made a fiction of economic planning, as did the tendency of industrial management to meet plan targets through manufacturing defective goods, raising prices or refusing to fabricate badly-needed products.[20] There could be no question of running a self-contained and highly centralized apparatus if it refused to cooperate with control agencies and, despite repeated warnings, dismissed officials who had been nominated by top bodies.[21] Not even the appearance of a legal order could be maintained where officials extended their powers, especially when they inflicted unauthorised penalties on the population through local ordinancies incompatible with statute law.[22] And the state's legitimate monopoly on violence was under serious threat when the régime proved unable to define which officials were entitled to carry out arrests, and when regional administrations had to be reminded that the supreme governing body had the prerogative to take the ultimate decision about the execution of death sentences.[23]

There could be no secret about the involvement of ranking cadres and Party veterans in the disorganisation of the system's functioning. Authoritative statements emphasised that officials, often high dignitaries with 'well-known merits in the past', were responsible for the irregular and uncontrollable working of governmental mechanisms, and warned that intractable 'bigwigs' would be demoted, dismissed and punished 'without respect of personalities'.[24] Actions were taken against a number of transgressing officeholders but, instead of looking for the origins of their misdeeds in the administration's working, there was a notable tendency to attribute them to 'criminal' intentions and to the allegedly 'alien' social origin of the culprits.[25] Already, during the collectivisation, excessively harsh measures as well as reluctance to apply such measures were ascribed to 'deviationist' or 'hostile' practices of cadres.[26] In this respect, threats to censure distinguished officials merely for their abuses represented a remarkable innovation. Nevertheless, when it came to singling out a Central Committee member, the propaganda did not dwell on his presumed faults. It highlighted his alleged association with 'class enemies' and called for vigilance against 'kulaks' and 'Trotskyists'.[27]

The persistence and ubiquity of official abuse does not allow one to explain it as a transitory phenomenon, and the tensions it provoked within the régime were more than rivalry between centre and periphery. Even top officials had good reasons to feel insecure in face of charges against unruly 'bigwigs', because malpractice and the ensuing conflicts had broad implications for every echelon, in all agencies and in all branches of the apparatus, just as transgressing officials and their allies were likely to be found everywhere. The interaction of agencies in a huge governmental mechanism, and the wide networks of solidarity among cadres spread abuses throughout the apparatus, and the Party-state itself organised officials in groups and coteries which had members, patrons and associates on different hierarchical levels and in many institutions and localities. Any officeholder was likely to participate in a systematic and organised obstruction of openly uncontested policies, and almost any cross-section of the apparatus behaved like a clandestine political opposition, with the sole aim of securing the careers of the incumbents of responsible positions.

Inclined to equate their career with the strengthening of the régime, officeholders were unlikely to grasp the political implications of this state of affairs, and were not disposed to see the disorganising effect of their activities, especially since they followed a pattern that characterised the working of the highest bodies. Obstruction of the régime's policies was as inseparable from the ordinary functioning of the administration as were periodic attempts to check officialdom, and refusal to submit to control agencies was as necessary in order to remain in responsible positions as it was necessary to ensure the regular and controllable operation of governmental mechanisms. The more it became indispensable to fight official abuse, the more such abuse became an integral part of the everyday realities of the system, and the more difficult it became to recognise its manifestations as results of the ordinary functioning of the régime and its relations with the rest of society. Officialdom saw itself as the best representative of the interests of the working masses. This was not conducive to the realisation that the practices of the administration stemmed from unpopular policies. To admit that uncontrollability and abuses were inseparable from the régime's normal universe would cast doubt on the *raison d'être* of the administration as an agency invested with the prerogative to direct and supervise the system's functioning and its own working. These circumstances made it difficult to avoid attributing the régime's problems to the machinations of people alienated from or hostile to the system.

There was already a remarkable tendency in the 1920s to avoid searching for the origins of the administration's intractability in the fact that it was accountable only to itself. Characteristically, the consequences of this state of affairs were debated mainly in terms of an analogy with the French Revolution, and even oppositionists were reluctant to acknowledge that the system had not evolved according to the promises of October.[28] Besides the scapegoating of 'bourgeois specialists', the late 1920s also saw the criminalisation of fractional activities in the Party, and alleged deviations from the sinuous 'General Line' were identified with a negative stereotype which ended with the top leadership creating the image of an organised 'Right Opposition' which never existed in reality.[29] A succession of Party purges accustomed the membership to suspect wrongdoing by 'class-alien elements',[30] and this certainly helped to strengthen the conviction of cadres that the régime's ills had hardly anything to do with the mode of operation of the apparatus. This conviction must have been shaken by attacks against 'bigwigs, braggarts and petty tyrants' and on 'their disregard for the decisions of higher bodies'.[31] But the 'discovery' in June 1936 of wide-spread 'subversion' by former oppositionists must have reassured officials that the origins of the régime's problems would not be sought in the everyday work of the administration. Very soon, however, the pretexts of 'Trotskyism' or 'sabotage' could also be used to clamp down on cadres who had never belonged to the opposition, and whose eventual 'wrecking' consisted only in their working in accordance with the usual pattern of the apparatus.[32]

Difficult to believe as it seems today, the monstrous accusations of 'subversion', 'high treason' or 'conspiracy' against leading officials were not necessarily incredible in the 1930s, especially for insiders of the admin-istration. They were likely to remember strictures like those of a secret circular of late 1927 that complained about the surfacing of confidential Party and government instructions in foreign capitals shortly after their enactment, a circular that also happened to find its way abroad. At the time the leaking of state secrets was attributed to oppositionists, and apparatchiki might also have known about an unsuccessful attempt to set up an oppositional 'bloc' in 1932. It was this 'bloc' that was referred to when the 'Trotskyist' threat was 'rediscovered'.[33] In all probability it was only from hearsay that most officials could learn something about Trotsky's attempts to mobilise followers in the early 1930s by sending postcards to the USSR.[34] On the other hand, a multitude of official documents and declarations mentioned 'anti-Party' groups of militants who were highly critical of the policies prevailing in the first years of the decade and among whom figured a certain number of leading cadres and former 'deviationists'.[35] In one form or another, insiders were likely to have been acquainted with the call of one of these groups to remove the 'grave-digger of the Revolution', Stalin, or with rumours about the dis-satisfaction of certain delegates of the Seventeenth Party Congress with Stalin and their intention to replace him.[36] And accustomed to reason according to the principle of analogy that was a cornerstone of the period's legal practice,[37] officeholders might be tempted to explain the régime's repressed problems in terms of similar phenomena.

Beyond these circumstances, the credibility of charges against 'wreck-ing' and 'conspiring' officials was certainly reinforced by the experience of those who were involved in the political processes of the 1930s. Many of them would have known about obscure manoeuvres, like an abortive attempt of the secret police in 1933–4 to stage a show trial.[38] They might wonder if similar machinations were behind the manifestly contradictory moves that followed Kirov's murder, when for about three weeks the authorities could not decide if the assassin had acted alone or in concert with a White plot or with the former Left Opposition, and nevertheless ordered the execution of dozens of people on the basis of a law that was promulgated in three versions within a week. Since it was finally decided that the murderer belonged to a 'leftist conspiracy', the mass shootings could not be taken even for retaliation, since their victims had been identified as White Guards. Insiders may have been even more bewildered by the inconsistency of the version implicating the Left Opposition, whose former leaders were originally cleared from suspicion and nonetheless slated for banishment, and ended up at a trial at which they were condemned to heavy prison terms, although they were not found guilty of being involved in the alleged plot.[39]

'Revelations' about 'conspiratory machinations' in high places were not entirely unbelievable for people who had some reason to suspect obscure intrigues among top policy-makers, and the number of such people must have been considerable in an apparatus that experienced notable political turnabouts at the time when organised 'wrecking' was 'discovered' in the Party-stage. Changes in industrial policy could not go unnoticed for cadres who had been accused of 'sabotaging' Stakhanovism, before being officially cleared from suspicion[40] at the moment when 'Trotskyist subversion' became a major theme of the propaganda. A year after the noisy vigilance campaign that followed Kirov's assassination, it was decreed unlawful to discriminate and fire people solely on the grounds of an 'alien' or 'suspect' background and, in a striking departure from past practice, the Central Committee warned that the fact of having concealed one's social origin was not necessarily a sufficient reason for expulsion from the Party.[41] While these moves hardly squared with the drive against 'hidden Trotskyists', officeholders could see an obvious contradiction between the line mobilising merely a hunt for ex-oppositionists, and efforts to draw a profile of the 'enemy' that could apply to everyone answerable for any failure of the administration.

Constantly under the threat of finding themselves cast as scapegoats by those higher up the hierarchy, grassroots cadres were not necessarily reluctant to accept the idea that their superiors acted with ulterior motives. And, increasingly exposed to punishment for any deficiency in their administrations, leading officials were by no means impervious to the reasoning that the actions of unruly subordinates had brought about their misfortunes and that these actions proceeded from harmful intentions. Nevertheless, the metaphors of 'wrecking' and 'conspiracy' denoted more than pervasive suspicion within the apparatus. They expressed something that was well beyond the régime's official self-image: the fact that the political process consisted of behind-the-scenes intrigues to manipulate governmental mechanisms, and potentially unmanageable chain-reactions of manoeuvres and counter-moves with unforeseeable consequences. Ever since the 1920s Soviet politics had been characterised by intricate covert manoeuvring in the highest milieux.[42] But a new situation arose in the wake of collectivisation and industrialisation, when the 'decisive and exceptional' rôle of the administration and the extraordinary breadth of officialdom's responsibilities had a strong tendency to make obscure machinations of the entire apparatus inseparable from the régime's policies.

The only legitimate agency of decision-making and action, the Party-state ensured its predominance through trying to assume the direction of all essential activities of society. The everyday functioning of the administration had an immediate impact on the political process, even if this was by no means clear for those who happened to be involved in the petty intrigues of this or that institution, agency or locality. Irregular and uncontrollable working patterns brought disruptions whose agents were genuinely subversive from the point of view of the régime's quasi-military ideal of order, and the disorganisation and social conflicts their actions brought about represented a real threat to the efficiency, popularity and stability of the system. Attempts to impose control were in fact efforts to do away with politics as it had come to be practiced by the 1930s. The failure of these attempts was an integral part of the political process and liable to appear as the result of 'wrecking' and 'conspiracies', especially since control was entrusted to the very administration whose ills were to be cured and officialdom was not inclined to see these ills in the fact that it was accountable only to itself.

The system's logic appeared in the imagery of 'sabotage' and 'plots', so much so that it is questionable if insiders were able to keep entirely away from rationalising the régime's internal conflicts through the representation of a 'struggle' with 'enemies'. It is beyond reasonable doubt that this imagery was cynically manipulated by top politicians, who directly participated in the fabrication of 'proofs' against high-placed 'plotters',[43] and it is more than probable that a great number of dignitaries imitated their example at lower levels of the hierarchy. But even these people seem to have acted in order to avert something that appeared to them as the threat of potential 'conspiracy', be it in the form of their censure by dissenting militants or their attempted ouster at the Seventeenth Congress, in the form of the sheer existence, even at their places of exile and detention, of old oppositionists,[44] or in that of unpredictable machinations by rivals under the pretext of the 'fight' against 'subversion'.

While Bukharin could not help wondering if the high leadership believed Kamenev's 'monstrous [and] mean accusations' against him, he had no doubt about Kamenev's culpability, and reckoned with the possibility that Tomsky was also 'enmeshed' in his 'plot'.[45] People did know that they were not 'enemies' or 'conspirators'. On the other hand, they knew how disorderly the functioning of the régime was, and they also had information about all sorts of irregularities and abuses. The secretive character of dealings within the Party-state made the position and activities of one's colleagues uncertain, and therefore virtually anything could be supposed about anyone, especially about *a priori* 'suspect' people like former oppositionists. These circumstances must have weighed heavily

when a commission of the Central Committee found convincing statements by detainees against Bukharin and Rykov, and decided 'unanimously' to refer their affair to the secret police because of their alleged
connivance with 'plotters'.[46]

Few members of this commission could have been unaware of the way in
which such confessions were obtained. One of these people, P. P. Postyshev,
was amongst those regional leaders whose apparatus suddenly 'discovered'
that 'terrorist acts' had been in preparation against them at the time of the
Kirov murder by 'counter-revolutionary groups' whose alleged participants
were pressed to admit their 'guilt'.[47] Another member, V. Ya. Chubar',
suspected a 'torrent of slander and intrigues by enemies of the people'
when his turn came in the wake of denunciations he himself had helped to
set in motion.[48] A third participant, R. I. Eikhe, headed a region that had
distinguished itself in the launching of the purge: he too was presumably in
danger after the 'evidence' given by the victims of a show trial.[49] He did
not seem to doubt that people arrested with his sanction were 'real
Trotskyists', even when he was already in the hands of the NKVD, though
he maintained that their confessions against him had been dictated by
'conspiratorial' intentions and that other 'proofs' of his 'guilt' were 'dirty
falsifications' of the interrogators.[50] His conviction was shared by a purged
candidate member of the Politbureau, Ya. E. Rudzutak, who wanted to
inform the Central Committee that 'there is in the NKVD an as yet
unliquidated centre skilfully fabricating cases and forcing innocent people
to admit crimes they did not commit'.[51]

It is hardly surprising if cadres 'discovered' that ' . . . what appeared
. . . before to be occasional shortcomings in the work of the Party apparatus . . . were [in fact] a systematic subversive work conducted over the
years [to achieve] the political corruption of the apparatus . . . [and] its
transformation into a blind instrument . . . '.[52] Everything points to the
assumption that, unable to deny their share of responsibility in measures
contributing to the deterioration of the living conditions of the population, fallen officials were probably sincerely claiming to be ignorant of 'the
behind-the-scenes life' of their 'unmasked' superiors and 'blind executants
of the whole work of wrecking'.[53] Inexplicably contradictory directives
became easily understandable as parts of the 'sabotage' that might be
suspected even behind the overburdening of the courts by the purge.[54]
Omnipresent as it appeared, 'subversion' was imputable to any office-
holder, and since cadres were under heavy pressure to reveal culprits in
their ranks, they did their best to deflect the offensive onto the most
vulnerable: against people whose office or affiliations became *a priori*
'suspicious' in the new conditions and, as usual, against people whose
past or personal relations furnished pretexts to designate them as 'hostile
elements'.[55] Everyone could become 'suspect' virtually for anything, and

the circumstances were ideal for settling old accounts, regardless of the consequences and often perhaps in anticipation of intrigues by rivals.

The manipulation of the purge and its unexpected turns had every chance to appear as the work of 'conspiracies', the more so since there was no difference between the muddled and confusing schemes to single out 'enemies' and the usual machinations of the apparatus. As zealous purgers were no less exposed to arrest than officials reluctant to hunt down 'wreckers', devout implementation of the rather uncertain 'line' was as likely to arouse suspicion as attempts to protect hard-pressed associates. Both tendencies could be detected in the actions of the high leadership, therefore people had good reason to feel reassured that they were following Moscow's policies, even if they happened to deviate from them at any particular moment. The understanding of the struggle against the régime's ills in terms of fighting 'subversion' amounted to taking the problems of the system for their solution. No wonder then that these problems were only aggravated in the wake of the purge. The threat intensified the activity of solidarity networks among cadres whose attempts to save each other reinforced the imagery of omnipresent 'plots'.[56] The overenthusiastic hunt for 'enemies' was often nothing more than the application of policies according to the momentary career interests of officials who purged the institutions under their jurisdiction in order to prove their political trustworthiness.[57] Energetic 'cleansing' could also be taken for 'wrecking', especially after January 1938 when the decimated Central Committee warned that the campaign was distorted by 'hostile' manoeuvres.[58]

There was scarcely any need to convince the population about the existence of 'subversive' activities among higher-ups. Allusions to acts of 'sabotage' by grassroots cadres were already multiplying in letters of complaint from peasants and workers at a time when the propaganda was still concentrating its fire merely on 'hidden Trotskyists'.[59] Routinely comparing their superiors to gendarmes or to the bosses of the Old Régime, and indignant to see that they were often shielded from prosecution by local potentates even when guilty of obviously criminal offenses,[60] ordinary citizens were inclined to suspect the authorities of the basest machinations. The masses were ready to attribute all the hardships of their working and living conditions to premeditated wrongdoing by officeholders, and even to demand the shooting of their 'wrecking' superiors.[61] The show trials seemed to suggest that 'it is impossible to trust Party members', though people could also believe that purged 'conspirators' wanted to 'liberate' peasants and workers.[62] Rumours about intricate scheming among top leaders[63] indicate that the turbulent events of 1936–8 convinced the public that everything was possible in high places. Where people were under constant threat of becoming victims of unpredictable reversals in the struggles between their superiors, and believed every Party member was a police spy, that 'the country is ruled by a small bunch of people',[64] politics could easily be seen in terms of conspiratorial intrigues.

Officialdom was also disposed to see clumsy 'cabals' among the population and was obsessed with its potentially 'hostile' acts. When, in the wake of the first 'revelations' about the 'Trotskyist threat', a group of workers wrote to a regional secretary that Kirov could be murdered only because of people like the managers of their factory, the addressee noted on their letter that it represented 'the enemy's method of discrediting the leadership'.[65] There was a remarkable tendency to look for 'subversive' intentions behind the reluctance of the masses to comply with official orders, especially in the rural world where the judiciary was regularly reminded that even negligent work could conceal 'wrecking' or 'counter-revolutionary' acts.[66] One of the most widespread manifestations of popular unruliness, theft of public property, was also declared a 'counter-revolutionary' crime and ascribed to 'enemies of the people'.[67]

Officialdom felt beleaguered by a hostile population whose unpredictable moves motivated local cadres to impose punishments for the use of 'indecent expressions' by their 'subjects' and to restrict their right to assemble or to enter and leave villages.[68] Received ideas about proletarian virtues prompted questions about the supposedly 'class-alien' origins of 'counter-revolutionary attitudes' among workers, for whom close surveillance was nevertheless strongly recommended in order to prevent their political troublemaking.[69] Kirov's assassination revealed a dark hatred toward high dignitaries: people often rejoiced at the killing and prophesied that others would follow, including that of Stalin.[70] In the following weeks an attempted murder of Stalin was persistently rumoured, so that the public believed that he had died when Kuibyshev's death was announced in a Leningrad theatre.[71] But it was far more than megalomaniac fear that dictated a nation-wide clampdown on 'counter-revolutionary expressions in connection with comrade Kirov's assassination'.[72] The population's respect for the system's most publicised symbol was in question, even ultimately, its loyalty to the state, especially in view of the pervasive war psychosis of the period and apparently frequent manifestations among the masses of a willingness to oppose the régime in case of armed conflict.[73] Simple citizens formed the overwhelming majority of the purge victims, subjected to wholesale repression in an increasingly chaotic and murderous attempt to root out the omnipresent danger of popular insubordination that coalesced with centrally-sponsored drive of the wholesale purge of 'former kulaks, members of anti-Soviet parties, White Guards, gendarmes and officials of tsarist Russia, bandits, returned émigrés, participants of anti-Soviet organisations, churchmen and sectarians [and] recidivist criminals'.[74]

There were many possibilities of 'unmasking enemies' among the masses. Nothing was easier than 'cleansing' *kolkhozes* and enterprises from people of allegedly 'kulak' background or from sons and daughters of 'class-alien elements', though such actions – whose victims were sometimes denounced to the police – could also hit 'disorganisers' of production who had a 'corrupting' effect on work discipline.[75] The number of these 'enemies' could be high since, taking advantage of the disarray of the purged apparatus, peasants worked less and less in the *kolkhoz*, illegally enlarged their household plots and avoided paying taxes and making compulsory food deliveries.[76] As the purge unfolded, workers began to defy cadres under the pretext that they were potential 'wreckers' and more and more often absented themselves from the enterprises.[77] Characteristically, calls intended to mobilise the judiciary to fight these practices pretended that they were encouraged by 'enemies of the people', and stopped short of imputing 'sabotage' to workers.[78]

The purge ended with a mobilisation drive to enforce harsh disciplinary and penal measures against workers and peasants.[79] No wonder then that a poll among wartime refugees showed that they were more likely than other social groups to characterise their work environment as 'hostile' or 'frightening'.[80] No wonder also that the powers-that-be felt threatened by the reaction of the masses who, when the war came, could feel betrayed by 'parasitic' bosses whose determination to save only their own skins seemed to confirm forebodings about the disastrous consequences of 'wrecking' and 'plots' of higher-ups.[81]

The imagery of omnipresent 'subversion' and 'conspiracy' denoted a dark feeling of suspicion and threat among leaders and led. This feeling did not necessarily appear as fear from a specific danger, and the underlying experience of anxiousness varied according to age, personal background and social status.[82] It nevertheless permeated the relationships of social categories to each other and to the régime. As social groups define themselves in their relations to each other and to the state, the representation of ubiquitous 'wrecking' and 'plots' revealed a strong inclination of officialdom and the masses alike to identify themselves as potential victims of impenetrable machinations.

Given the omnipresence of misgovernment and official abuse as well as that of the social tensions and political conflict they were inseparable from, the imagery of ubiquitous 'subversion' was by no means ungrounded. It seems difficult to escape the conclusion that the unpredictable, incomprehensible and treacherous daily reality of the system turned out to be a universe of omnipresent conspiracy. From the point of view of those who were inclined to see concerted action by a monolithic Party-state as the *primum movens* of the period's turmoil, it was natural to attribute every event and every twist and turn of the sinuous political line to the machinations of an all powerful centre and its supreme leader, whereas the work of a multitude of competing forces could be suspected by those who had doubts about the régime's ability to control and regiment everything.

In both cases, the representation of 'wrecking' and 'plots' located a paradigmatic feature of the entire system in merely one or some of its parts. The allegorisation of an ineffable evil that came to possess the life-world of every social category, the projection of the régime's elusively hostile universe in identifiable deeds and agents, tallied with traditional popular beliefs.[83] But such a projection could never have taken the form of 'sabotage' and 'conspiracies' without the régime's unwillingness to explain its problems in terms of the administration's ordinary working and social conflict, and it could hardly ever have had murderous consequences without officialdom's attempt to exorcise the system's ills through the use of an apparatus that happened to provoke and embody them. Collective representations of the omnipresent conspiracy were captive of the everyday reality of a system that became colonised by the Party-state's political practice and discourse.[84]

Notes

The author wishes to express his gratitude to the Alexander von Humboldt Foundation whose generous support made this research possible.

1 Political Archive of the Foreign Office, Bonn (hereafter *PA,AA*) Abteilung Pol. XIII, Akten betreffend GPU-Funktionär Shigunow, pp. 175755, 176008, 176019, 176023, 176026–7.
2 *PA,AA*, Abteilung Pol. XIII, pp. 175760, 175770, 175779, 175796, 175925.
3 *PA,AA*, Abteilung Pol. XIII, p. 176023.
4 *PA,AA*, Abteilung Pol. XIII, pp. 175761–3, 175862, 175885, 175888.
5 *PA,AA*, Abteilung Pol. XIII, pp. 176009, 176022.
6 *PA,AA*, Abteilung Pol. XIII, Allgemeine Akten 12, Teil II, DIX 221: 'Vernehmung . . . ', 23 September 1941, p. 2; Abteilung, Pol. XIII, Allgemeine Akten 14: Document 409, p. 2. See also R. V. Ivanov-Razumnik, *Tiurmy i ssylki* (New York, 1953), p. 277 where, writing during the war, the author evokes 'Tukhachevskii's well-known conspiracy' and T-4908 of the Trotsky Papers about Moscow rumours of the summer of 1937 concerning the 'military plot'. (Quoted with the permission of the Houghton Library.)
7 *PA,AA*, Abteilung Pol. XIII, Allgemeine Akten 13, DIX 322: No. 147, 149, 211, 213; Federal Archive, Koblenz (hereafter *BA*) NS 8, 226, p. 35.
8 K. Bailes, *Technology and Society under Lenin and Stalin* (Princeton, 1978) pp. 69–121; H. H. Schröder, *Industrialisierung und Parteibürokratie in der Sowjetunion* (Berlin, 1988) pp. 216–30.
9 H. Kuromiya, *Stalin's Industrial Revolution* (Cambridge, 1988) pp. 292–4; Bailes, p. 280; Schröder, pp. 317–23.
10 *XVII S'ezd VKP (b)* (Moscow, 1934) pp. 33–5, 48, 532–3, 600–01; *KPSS v rezoliutsiiakh i resheniiakh s'ezdov, konferentsii i plenumov TsK*, vol. V (Moscow, 1971) pp. 152–4, 159–160.
11 J. A. Getty, *Origins of the Great Purges – The Soviet Communist Party*

Reconsidered, 1933–1938 (Cambridge, 1985), pp. 58–91; L. H. Siegelbaum, *Stakhanovism and the Politics of Productivity in the USSR, 1935–1941* (Cambridge, 1988) pp. 99–144; G. T. Rittersporn, *Simplifications staliniennes et complications politiques* (Paris, 1988) pp. 49–69.

12 *Sobranie zakonov i rasporiazhenii Raboche-Krest'ianskogo Pravitel'stva* SSSR part I (hereafter *SZ*) (1934) pp. 465–6, (1935) pp. 613–14, 674–5.

13 *Sovetskaia iustitsiia* (hereafter *Slu*) (1934) No. 8, p. 3, No. 9, p. 25, No. 17, p. 22, (1935) No. 4, p. 17, No. 27, p. 2; *Sotsialisticheskaia zakonnost'/Za sotsialisticheskuiu zakonnost'* (*SZak*) (1934) No. 4, pp. 36, 39–41, No. 5, p. 11, No. 7, p. 37, No. 8, pp. 3, 31–2, No. 9, p. 44, No. 10, pp. 1–2, 28–30, 34, No. 11, pp. 48–9, No. 12, p. 48, (1935) No. 10, p. 64, *Ugolovnyi kodeks RSFSR* (hereafter *UK*) (Moscow, 1937) pp. 132, 138.

14 *Slu* (1934) No. 13, p. 13, (1935) No. 2, p. 2, No. 13, p. 5, No. 31, p. 15 (1936) No. 13, p. 5; *SZak* (1934) No. 10, p. 35 (1935) No. 5, pp. 58–9.

15 Smolensk Archive (hereafter *WKP*), RS, 116/154e8 *WKP* 84, p. 42, *WKP* 176, p. 181, *WKP* 196, pp. 178–80.

16 *Bol'shevik* (hereafter *B*) (1936) No. 13, pp. 9, 12–13, No. 15, pp. 45–8; *Partiinoe stroitel'stvo* (hereafter *PS*) (1936) 8, p. 55, No. 14, pp. 52–3, 15, p. 36; *SZ* (1936) pp. 473–4; 'Ob iskliuchennykh iz partii . . . ', *Pravda* (hereafter *P*) (6 June 1936 p. 3; *116/154e*, pp. 44–9, 79–88.

17 *Slu* (1935) No. 10, pp. 1–2, No. 13, p. 5, No. 25, pp. 2–3, No. 27, p. 2 (1936) No. 6, p. 5, No. 13, p. 13, No. 27, pp. 7–8; *SZak* (1935) No. 5, pp. 7, 9–10, No. 6, pp. 5, 7.

18 *Slu* (1934) No. 19, p. 25 (1935) No. 5, pp. 24–5, No. 36, p. 3; *SZak* (1934) No. 12, p. 51 (1935) No. 2, pp. 59–60. See also note 13.

19 L. Viola, *The Best Sons of the Fatherland – Workers in the Vanguard of Soviet Collectivization* (Oxford, 1987) pp. 123–6.

20 *XVII S'ezd* . . . , pp. 23, 153–4, 267–8, 289; 'O zapasnykh chastiakh . . . '; *P*, 16 June 1937, p. 2, 'O beloi zhesti . . . '; *P*, 17 June 1937, p. 3, 'Planovykh del mastera'; *P*, 1 July 1937, p. 3.

21 *PS* (1935) No. 13, pp. 44–5 (1936) No. 20, pp. 37–8, 47, No. 22, p. 48; *B* (1936) No. 6, pp. 76–7; 'O rabote upolnomochennykh KPK', *P*, 17 March 1936, p. 2.

22 *Vlast' sovetov* (hereafter *VS*) (1936) No. 9, pp. 8–9, No. 11, pp. 37–9, No. 16, pp. 23–4, (1937) No. 10, pp. 16–18; *SZak* (1934) No. 5, p. 11; *Slu* (1934) No. 13, pp. 9–10.

23 *Slu* (1934) No. 13, pp. 9–10, (1935) No. 16, p. 9, (1936) No. 27, p. 17, *SZak* (1934) No. 1, pp. 35–6, No. 5, p. 10, No. 7, p. 36; *WKP* 184, p. 16.

24 *XVII V S'ezd* . . . , p. 34; *KPSS v rezoliutsiiakh* . . . , pp. 152–3, 160.

25 *PS* (1934) No. 13, p. 3, No. 16, p. 48, No. 21, pp. 63–4, No. 22 pp. 3–4, (1935) No. 3, p. 47, No. 14, pp. 45–8.

26 R. W. Davies, *The Socialist Offensive – The Collectivisation of Soviet Agriculture 1929–1930* (London, 1980) p. 330; N. E. Zelenin, 'O nekotorykh "belykh piatnakh" zavershaiushchego etapa sploshnoi kollektivizatsii', *Istoriia SSSR* (1989) No. 2, pp. 11, 13–14; Viola, pp. 128–9.

27 Editorials *P*, June 8 and 16, 1935; *PS* (1935) No. 12, p. 10.

28 T. Kondrateva, *Bolcheviks et Jacobins* (Paris, 1989) pp. 113–70.

29 M. Reiman, *Die Geburt des Stalinismus* (Frankfort, 1979) pp. 42–70; Schröder, pp. 172–9.

30 Cf. the reasons for expulsion during the 1929, 1933 and 1935 purges in Getty, pp. 47, 54, 83; Schröder, pp. 183, 345.

31 'Kommunist i sovetskii zakon', *P*, 1 April 1936 p. 2, editorial, *P*, 9 May 1936.

32 Rittersporn, pp. 103–8, 120–31.

33 Reiman, pp. 244–5. For the 'bloc' see Getty, pp. 119–22; *Id.*, 'Trotsky in Exile: The Founding of the Fourth International', *Soviet Studies* (1986) No. 1, pp. 28–9; P. Broué, 'Trotsky et le bloc des oppositions de 1932' *Cahiers Léon Trotsky* (1980) No. 5, pp. 5–37.
34 Trotsky Papers, T-10248 (quoted by the permission of the Houghton Library).
35 R. W. Davies, 'The Syrtsov-Lominadze Affair', *Soviet Studies* (1981) No. 1, pp. 29–50; Schröder, pp. 320–2.
36 *Izvestiia TsK KPSS* (1989) No. 6, pp. 103–6; *Istoriia KPSS* (Moscow, 1963), p. 486; Schröder, pp. 325–6. For data casting doubt on rumours about the Seventeenth Congress, see *Izvestiia TsK KPSS* (1989) No. 7, pp. 114–21.
37 P. H. Solomon, *Soviet Criminologists and Criminal Policy* (New York, 1978) pp. 22–6.
38 For the relevant documents see *PA*, *AA* Botschaft Moskau, A 14d, Verhaftungen bei Controll Co.; Abt. IV Rußland, R15, Verhaftungen bei Angestellten der Controll Co. m. b. H. in Sowjetrußland and Strafverfolgung, Begnadigung, vol. 4.
39 Getty, *Origins* . . . pp. 209–10; G. T. Rittersporn, 'Soviet Politics in the 1930s', *Studies in Comparative Communism* (1986) No. 2, p. 112.
40 F. Benvenuti, 'Stakhanovism and Stalinism, 1934–38', *CREES Discussion Papers*, Series SIPS, No. 30, pp. 40–7; Siegelbaum, pp. 117–20, 127–35.
41 See note 16.
42 R. Service, *The Bolshevik Party in Revolution* (London, 1979), pp. 175–99; Reiman, pp. 118–71.
43 *Izvestiia TsK KPSS* (1989) No. 4, pp. 49, 51–5; pp. 71, 73–4, 76; No. 8, pp. 91–2; No. 9, pp. 36–9, 42.
44 *Izvestiia TsK KPSS* (1989) No. 5, p. 72; No. 6, pp. 112–15; No. 9, pp. 35–6.
45 See his letter to Voroshilov in D. Volkogonov, 'Triumf i tragediia', *Oktiabr'* (1988) No. 12, pp. 118–19.
46 *Izvestiia TsK KPSS* (1989) No. 5, pp. 79–81, 84.
47 See two documents quoted to this effect in Volkogonov, pp. 52–3.
48 Volkogonov, p. 159.
49 Rittersporn, *Simplifications* . . . , pp. 121–3.
50 Volkogonov, p. 161; *Izvestiia TsK KPSS* (1989) No. 3, p. 141.
51 Volkogonov, pp. 161–2; *Izvestiia TsK KPSS* (1989) No. 3, p. 142. The two editions reproduce this document and Eikhe's letter in slightly different wording.
52 *WKP* 392, pp. 96–7; *WKP* 103, p. 126.
53 *WKP* 109, pp. 67, 72; *WKP* 321, pp. 194–5.
54 *WKP* 103, p. 133, *Slu* (1937) No. 8, pp. 11, 16; No. 23, pp. 37–8.
55 Rittersporn, *Simplifications* . . . , pp. 173–91.
56 'Dela sverdlovskogo obkoma', *P*, 22 May 1937, p. 4; 'K chemu privodit politicheskaia slepota', *P*, 31 May 1937, p. 2; 'Dela krasnoiarskogo kraikoma', *P*, 11 July 1937, p. 2; 'Vragi i ikh pokroviteli', *P*, 17 July 1937, p. 3; *B* (1937) No. 14, pp. 5–8; *PS* (1937) No. 15, pp. 40–3; *WKP* 111, pp. 229, 151–2, 176; *WKP* 163, p. 131, *WKP* 321, p. 165.
57 Rittersporn, *Simplifications* . . . , pp. 191–2.
58 *KPSS v rezoliutsiiakh* . . ., pp. 303–12.
59 *WKP* 195, p. 182; *WKP* 197, pp. 77, 89, 230; *WKP* 355, p. 220.
60 *WKP* 195, pp. 52, 182; *WKP* 197, pp. 77, 89, 230; *WKP* 201, p. 246; *WKP* 355, p. 187.
61 *WKP* 195, pp. 21–3.
62 *WKP* 87, p. 6, *WKP* 199, pp. 46, 55.

63 See e.g. *PA, AA*, Botschaft Moskau, A2c Innere Politik der UdSSR (Verwaltung . . .): the embassy to the Foreign Office, 28 September 1936; Pol. Abt. V. Po. 5 Ukraine, Innere Politik . . . , vol. 1: the Kiev consulate to the embassy, 1 April 1937, pp. 1–2; Botschaft Moskau, A4 Militär- und Marineangelegenheiten, vol. 6: telegrams of the embassy to the Foreign Office, 11 and 12 June 1937; Pol. Abt. V Po. 5 Rußland, Innere Politik . . . , vol. 3; 'Lagebericht', 7 July 1937, p.3, vol. 5: v. Tippelskirch to v. Welck, 10 January 1938; Pol. Abt. V Po. 7 Ministerien, Rußland: v. Tippelskirch to Schliep, 1 August 1938.

64 *WKP* 87, p. 7; *WKP* 199, p. 72.

65 *WKP* 355, p. 114.

66 *Slu* (1934) No. 8, p. 3 (1935) No. 11, p. 33, No. 20, p. 24; *SZak* (1934) No. 4, p. 41, No. 11, p. 48, No. 12, p. 48 (1935) No. 2, p. 63; *UK* pp. 135, 138–9.

67 *SZ* (1932) pp. 583–4; *Slu* (1935) No. 5, pp. 2–3, No. 13, p. 3; *SZak* (1937) p. 3; I. V. Stalin, *Sochineniia*, vol. XIII (Moscow, 1951) pp. 207–12.

68 *Slu* (1935) No. 13, p. 5; *VS* (1936) No. 16, p. 24; *SZak* (1938) No. 3, p. 125, No. 6, p. 12.

69 *WKP* 87, p. 7; *WKP* 109, pp. 19, 21, 36.

70 *WKP* 109, p. 73; *WKP* 252, pp. 37–40; *WKP* 316, pp. 6–7; *WKP* 352, p. 115; *WKP* 415, pp. 22, 132; *RS* 921, pp. 133, 294.

71 *PA, AA*, Abt. IV Ru. Po. No. 3, Rußland, Personalien . . . vol. 5: the Leningrad consulate to the embassy, 26 January 1935.

72 *Slu* (1935) No. 18, p. 10.

73 *RS* 921, pp. 294, 300; *WKP* 199, p. 46; *WKP* 362, p. 340; *PA, AA* Botschaft Moskau, A2 Innerpolitische Verhältnisse . . . vol 8: the Kiev consulate to the embassy, 10 April 1935; Botschaft Moskau A2a, UdSSR Parteiwesen: 'Politischer Bericht', 4 July 1935, pp. 2–3; Botschaft Moskau A24e, Zweifelhafte Persönlichkeiten . . . vol. 2: letter in Russian received on 30 December 1936; Botschaft Moskau, A39b Jahresund Halbjahresberichte . . . Charkow: the consulate to the embassy, 12 January 1937, p. 11 and 10 June 1937, p. 14; *BA*, NS 43, 17, p. 533.

74 For the relevant directive dated July 1937 and stipulating that the 'most hostile . . . [of these] elements' had to be shot while others were to be sentenced to long terms of detention, see *Izvestiia TsK KPSS* (1989) No. 10, pp. 81–2.

75 See e.g. *WKP* 516, pp. 2–77, in particular pp. 12–13, 22, 27, 39, 41, 45, 47, 55, 57.

76 *VS* (1938) No. 10–11, pp. 52–3, editorials, *P*, 17 April and 12 August 1938; *Istoriia KPSS*, t. 4, kniga 2-ia (Moscow, 1971), p. 428; *Istoriia SSSR s drevneishikh vremen do nashikh dnei*, vol. 9 (Moscow, 1971) p. 352.

77 Editorials, *P*, 29 April, 11 May, 24 June, and 14 and 25 August 1937; *SZ* (1937) p. 246; *B* (1937) No. 16, p. 19, No. 19, p. 7.

78 *Slu* (1938) No. 17, pp. 10, 12; *B* (1938) No. 23–4, p. 10; 'Lishit' lodyrei . . . ', *P*, 14 December 1938, p. 3; 'Komandiry proizvodstva i trudovaia distsiplina'. *P*, 25 December 1938, p. 2.

79 Rittersporn, *Simplifications* . . . , pp. 296–8.

80 A. Rossi, *Generational Differences in the Soviet Union* (New York, 1980) pp. 216–19, 228–30.

81 *PA, AA*, Abteilung Pol. XIII, Allgemeine Akten 13, DIX 322: No. 120.

82 R. W. Thurston, 'Fear and Belief in the USSR's "Great Tertor": Response to Arrest 1935–1939', *Slavic Review* (1986) No. 2, pp. 213–34; R. A. Bauer, A. Inkeles, C. Kluckhohn, *How the Soviet System Works* (Cambridge, Mass., 1956) pp. 178–9; A. Inkeles, R. A. Bauer, *The Soviet Citizen* (Cambridge, Mass, 1959), pp. 23, 108, 245; Rossi, pp. 184, 186, 217, 229, 239, 324.

83 M. Lewin, *The Making of the Soviet System: Essays in the Social History of Interwar Russia* (New York, 1985), pp. 275–310.
84 For a similar impact of élite concepts and practices on popular beliefs and behaviour see N. Cohn, *Europe's Inner Demons* (London, 1975) pp. 225–55; R. Kieckfeber, *European Witch Trials* (London, 1976), pp. 73–92.

Reading 12 *How the mice buried the cat: scenes from the Great Purges of 1937 in the Russian provinces*

S. FITZPATRICK

The ground trembled under him, he was feared, he was hated. 'Brigand' was what the population always called him. People learned to go out of their way to avoid him, so as not to catch his eye more often than necessary. They say that even little children ran away screaming when they saw him. And when he disappeared, the whole street breathed a sigh of relief behind their gates.

He enjoyed his notoriety and was proud of it. Showing off the 'education' acquired who knows where, he often pronounced with a grim, self-satisfied smirk: 'Where I go, the grass will not grow for ten years'.

Kochetov behaved toward the citizenry exactly like a conqueror toward the conquered. He exacted tribute and called it 'fines for the state treasury'. . . . And people paid up. People preferred to pay because it was safer than not paying. If anyone dared doubt that, Kochetov himself appeared with his 'activists' – and then the floors shook, dishes rattled and children cried. . . . 'If you don't deliver, I'll dig it out of you like God scooping out a turtle'.

Sovetskaia iustitsiia, no. 20 (1937): 22.

The villainous Kochetov was a small-time Soviet boss in a rural district (*sel'sovet*) in Russia's agricultural heartland. In 1937 he fell victim to the Great Purges that swept the Soviet bureaucracy. Along with his immediate superior, the chairman of the *raion* soviet, he was one of a group of local officials indicted for 'counterrevolutionary' crimes and put on trial in Aleshki, the administrative center of an obscure rural *raion* in the Voronezh region.

The Aleshki trial was one of dozens held in *raion* centers in the Soviet Union in the autumn of 1937.[1] These trials were not products of the normal workings of the judicial system. They were show trials with a

political message. Nineteen thirty-seven was the height of the Great
Purges, in which hundreds of thousands of members of the Soviet Communist elite – party and government officials, industrial managers, military
officers – as well as members of the intellectual elite were arrested and
subsequently sent to labor camps or shot as 'enemies of the people'. In the
notorious Moscow trials of August 1936, January 1937 and March 1938,
Bukharin, Zinoviev and other former leaders of the Soviet Communist
Party astonished the world by confessing that they had long been secret
counterrevolutionaries, wreckers, terrorists, agents of the exiled 'Judas-
Trotsky', and spies for hostile capitalist powers.

But Moscow was a long way from Aleshki, and the Aleshki version of
the Great Purge was both rhetorically and substantively worlds apart from
the Moscow trials that inspired Arthur Koestler's famous novel, *Darkness
at Noon*. The petty bureaucratic tyrants and oppressed citizens we meet in
reports of the Aleshki and other *raion* trials of 1937 could have come
straight from the pages of such nineteenth-century Russian satirists as
Saltykov-Shchedrin and Chekhov, who chronicled the follies and abuses
of local officials and the dreariness of provincial life. These officials are
corrupt, venal, illiterate and almost invariably drunk. They are often
ludicrously ill-equipped for their positions, like the head of the *raion*
sector of animal husbandry who had formerly been a ladies' hairdresser,
or his assistant who had been manager of the local public bathhouse.[2]
They make pompous but only semiliterate speeches full of Soviet mala-
propisms. They invite young female tractor-drivers into their offices and
tell them to strip for 'medical inspection'.[3]

In contrast to the Moscow trials, highly stylized productions involving
fantastic scenarios of conspiracy and treason, the *raion* trials were relatively down-to-earth and straightforward. The former officials on trial in
the *raiony* were described as 'enemies of the people' or under the influence
of 'enemies'. But only rarely were political offenses like espionage or
contacts with the Trotskyists or other party oppositionists suggested in
the *raion* trials; and only in a few cases did the prosecution argue that the
indicted officials had intentionally sabotaged agriculture (by acts like
infecting animals with disease, laming horses and so on) because they
were counterrevolutionaries who wanted a return to capitalism. The
accused officials were encouraged to confess their guilt, as in the Moscow
trials, but in fact they often recanted in court and tried to defend themselves, so that the *raion* trials had little of the sinister, mysterious atmosphere of their Moscow counterparts.

Another important difference between the Moscow show trials and
their provincial counterparts was that in rural *raion* trials the core of
the indictment was not treason and political conspiracy but *exploitation
and abuse of the peasantry* by Communists holding official positions at the
raion and *sel'sovet* levels. These accusations, in contrast to their Moscow

counterparts, were almost always completely plausible. In many instances, what the officials were accused of doing (for example, dictating unrealistic sowing plans or extracting so much grain after the harvest that the peasants went hungry) was simply what their jobs and their superiors required them to do. In other instances, the behavior that was condemned in court (for example, bribe-taking, bullying or forcing through appointments of kolkhoz chairmen against the objections of kolkhozniki) was standard practice for Soviet rural officials in the 1930s.

Finally, a distinctive feature of the rural *raion* trials was that the state's case usually rested largely on the evidence of peasant witnesses. Their passionate and circumstantial testimony in court against former *raion* and *sel'sovet* leaders was generally the dramatic centerpiece of the show trials, which were held in the largest auditorium of the *raion* center before large audiences of kolkhozniki who had been brought in from all over the *raion* for the occasion. This was political theater, no doubt, but it was a participatory political theater in which peasant witnesses and auditors appeared to revel in the humiliation of their former bosses. My title, reflecting the *Schadenfreude* (*zloradstvo*) that seems the dominant mood of the rural *raion* show trials of 1937, is that of a popular eighteenth-century Russian woodcut showing the funeral of a large cat, long believed to represent Peter the Great, whose corpse, firmly tied down, is being carried to the grave by a group of dancing and celebrating mice.[4]

The master plot

If the show trials are to be viewed as theater, we have to ask who was writing the plays. At one level, this question has a simple answer: the texts at our disposal were almost all written by journalists of oblast daily newspapers.[5] The newspapers ran long and detailed reports of local show trials, often including allegedly verbatim reports of particularly exciting testimony and court exchanges; they generally appeared sequentially in three or four issues. These reports belong to the Soviet version of the genre of exposé journalism, generally focused on local bureaucratic abuses or court cases, whose ostensible function of political (moral) instruction was combined with an unacknowledged but unmistakable entertainment function. They tended to be written with verve and literary flair, pouring sarcasm and scorn on the delinquencies and hypocrisy of the 'bureaucrats' who were their most frequent targets. These 'exposé' stories and feuilletons were oases in the desert of the Soviet press in the 1930s, which was otherwise largely devoted to unrelenting and mendacious boosterism of Soviet economic achievements, official communiqués and the publication in full of long speeches by party leaders.

But the journalistic texts were only representations of other 'texts', namely the show trials themselves. While it is unlikely that the *raion* trials were scripted with anything like the same care as the central Moscow trials, they were still very far from spontaneous events. At a minimum, they had had the same kind of detailed advance planning in the oblast prosecutor's office and local NKVD branch that any major criminal trial in the United States would be given by the prosecuting counsel – with the important difference that, in the absence of any significant opposition from defense counsel, the prosecutor's plans were less likely to go awry.[6]

The trials' 'scripts', moreover, were drawn from two additional sources. One was the set of signals from Moscow that provided what I will call the 'master plot'[7] of the rural *raion* show trials of 1937 – that is, the generic model on which local variants were based. The other source, on whose identity I will speculate a little later, provided the detailed information on local abuses and crimes that was used in a particular *raion* trial. Despite the existence of a 'master plot', Moscow's hand in the framing and controlling of local show trials should not be exaggerated. The virtually unanimous failure of local trials to take up the hint that Stalin should be lauded for correcting local abuses, or indeed to mention Stalin at all, provides persuasive evidence of the limitations of Moscow's control.

The word 'signal' had a special meaning in Stalinist discourse. It referred primarily to information about important policy shifts that was transmitted from the center to lower-level officials via a nonbureaucratic channel such as the central party newspaper, *Pravda*. A signal was not the same thing as a law or an administrative order, although it might coexist with an explicit instruction given privately by a superior authority to a subordinate one. It was essentially a message about political mood and current priorities, transmitted in the form of a slogan ('The Five-Year Plan in four years!'), a remark (Stalin's interjection at a conference that 'a son does not answer for his father'), an exemplary story, or – as in the cases we are concerned with – an exemplary or 'show' trial (*pokazatel'nyi sud*) that received national publicity. The reception of signals was treated as an instinctive rather than an intellectual act, and people who were not tuned into the right Communist wave length were likely to miss them.[8] In the case of the flood of rural *raion* show trials in the fall of 1937, the signals came in a series of reports and commentaries in *Pravda* highlighting the mistreatment of peasants by local Communist officials.

The first report – perhaps more of a forerunner than one of the series – concerned a show trial of former party and soviet leaders in Lepel' *raion* in Belorussia that was held in March. The accused were charged with illegally confiscating peasant property as payment for tax arrears, despite the recent law forgiving arrears in the light of the exceptionally poor harvest of 1936. According to *Pravda*'s report, the Lepel' investigation was sparked by letters of complaint from local peasants, and the Belorussian state prosecutor took action on instructions from Andrei Vyshinsky, state prosecutor of the USSR. Peasant witnesses testified at the trial, which was held at the Lepel' municipal theater, and the court had reportedly received dozens of letters from peasants grateful for deliverance from their former oppressors.[9]

Three months later, *Pravda* reported a similar show trial from the Shiriaevo *raion* of Odessa oblast in the Ukraine. There, top *raion* officials had been found guilty of 'outrageous' treatment of kolkhozniki and routine violations of the 1935 Kolkhoz Charter,[10] including illegal confiscation of peasant property, extortion, night-time searches, arbitrary exaction of taxes and of suscriptions to state loans, imposition of impossibly high grain procurement quotas in 1936, and 'insulting behavior' toward kolkhozniki.[11] These crimes had come to the attention of the party's Central Control Commission, which had instructed the Ukrainian state prosecutor to take action. The main evidence against the accused in the Shiriaevo trial came from peasant witnesses, more than thirty of whom were called to testify.[12]

A few weeks later, *Pravda* reported similar show trials in Novominsk, a Cossack *raion* in the Black Sea oblast of Rostov, and in the Danilov *raion* of Iaroslavl oblast. The Novominsk trial featured severe economic exploitation by local officials that had provoked thousands of peasants to leave the collective farms.[13] In the Danilov trial, the *raion* leadership was charged with illegally liquidating the 'New Life' kolkhoz and confiscating all its property when officials were unable to resolve a dispute with kolkhoz members.[14] *Pravda*'s coverage of the Danilov affair was notable for its report that at the end of the trial, after stiff sentences had been handed down, local kolkhozniki sent thanks to Stalin for defending them against their enemies – a signal that seemed to fall on deaf ears.[15]

Early in August, *Pravda* elaborated the message of Shiriaevo and Danilov trials in an editorial warning local officials not to mistreat the peasantry. *Raion* officials had been condoning all kinds of violations of the rights of kolkhozniki, *Pravda* stated. Officials had disposed arbitrarily of kolkhoz land and property, behaving as if it were 'their own private property, their own little kingdom (*votchina*)'; they had even liquidated entire collective farms, as in the Danilov case. This was to forget the golden rule that 'kolkhozniki are the masters of their own kolkhoz'.[16]

Emerging from all this was a master plot on the theme of abuse and exploitation of the collectivized peasantry by Soviet officialdom at the *raion* level that formed the basis for the thirty-odd show trials held in rural *raions* of the Soviet Union in September–October 1937. It may be summarized as follows:

Enemies of the people, linked in a mutual-protection and patronage network, had wormed their way into key positions in the *raion* and used their official positions to plunder the peasantry mercilessly. Because of the officials' stupidity and ignorance of agriculture, their incessant orders and interference had done great harm to the collective farms. The peasants, outraged and indignant, had done their best to resist unlawful demands. They had brought suits and written letters of complaint to higher authorities, but these had often been blocked by the mutual-protection ring. Finally, however, the news of the scandalous behavior of local officials got out, and the guilty parties were brought to justice. The simple people – who demanded the severest punishment for their former oppressors – had triumphed over the officials who had cheated and insulted them.

While it is not possible to establish with certainty who were the 'authors' of variants of the master plot used in specific local show trials, the evidence points strongly to a natural (but perhaps, to Sovietologists, unexpected) source – the local peasantry.

Peasants were inveterate letter-writers, complaining about and denouncing those in immediate authority above them in the 1930s. They wrote to party and government leaders like Stalin and Mikhail Kalinin; they wrote to the highest organs of the Soviet and republican governments; they wrote to oblast party committees, prosecutors' offices and NKVD branches; they wrote to oblast newspapers and central newspapers, especially the mass-circulation peasant newspaper, Kres'ianskaia gazeta. They wrote letters and complaints with or without cause, for good reasons and bad, and they generally sent them outside their own raion, to the oblast center or even to Moscow, because of their belief that the bosses in any given raion would back each other up.[17]

Such peasant complaints often triggered the investigations of official wrongdoing at the raion level that led to the rural raion trials of 1937. Local complaints are mentioned as a stimulus in three out of the four 'model' trials reported in Pravda: in the Lepel' case, Vyshinsky's attention was alerted by 'complaints from the toilers of Lepel' raion';[18] 'complaints from kolkhozniki' are mentioned in the Shiriaevo case;[19] and in Danilov, 'letters of sel'kory' (correspondents from the village) disclosed the abuses of the raion leadership, which consequently did its best to suppress them.[20] Similar references to complaints and petitions from the village abound in the raion show trials that took place in the autumn.[21]

Since the general tenor and substance of the grievances aired by peasant witnesses at the raion show trials of 1937 correspond remarkably closely to those of the peasant letters of complaint received by Krest'ianskaia gazeta at the same period, the hypothesis that the scenarios of rural raion show trials were often directly based on local peasant complaints seems extremely plausible.[22] This raises the intriguing possibility that the peasants who appeared as witnesses in the trials were not only full-fledged actors in this political theater but were also (to pursue the theatrical metaphor) playing themselves.

The defendants

The standard cast of characters under indictment at the rural *raion* trials consisted of the former secretary of the *raion* party committee (the top-ranking official in a *raion*), the chairman of the *raion* soviet (the second-ranking official), the heads of the *raion* agriculture department and sometimes the taxation (finance) and procurement agencies, along with other agricultural officials, and a sprinkling of *sel'sovet* and kolkhoz chairmen.

The typical defendant – and, indeed, the typical Soviet official at *raion* or *sel'sovet* level in the 1930s – was a poorly educated man of peasant origin, probably in his thirties or forties, who was a member of the Communist Party. The senior *raion* officials were likely to have spent a year or so at Soviet party school in addition to their basic primary schooling, and they had usually seen something of a broader world through service in other *raion* centers within the oblast and perhaps its immediate neighbors. *Sel'sovet* and kolkhoz chairmen, by contrast, were lucky to have completed primary education, rarely had job experience outside the *raion*, and seem usually to have been natives of the *sel'sovet* in which they served.[23]

If accusations of participation in 'counterrevolutionary Trotskyite conspiracies' were rare in the rural *raion* trials, this surely reflected the fact that few Communists at this low level of the Soviet bureaucracy had ever had personal contact with an actual member of any Communist opposition group.[24] Nevertheless, it became standard practice in these trials to charge at least the senior defendants with counterrevolutionary crimes, using Article 58 of the Criminal Code – although, interestingly enough, Article 58 does not seem to have been used in any of the 'model' trials reported in *Pravda* in the period March–July 1937.[25] The sentences, accordingly, were more severe in the autumn trials than in the spring, and became still harsher in the course of the autumn. Ten years' imprisonment with confiscation of property was the harshest sentence handed down in any of the 'model' trials, while some defendants got off with as little as six months. In the autumn trials, by contrast, it was usual for two or three of the top-ranking defendants to be sentenced to death while other defendants received eight- to ten-year sentences.[26]

In two instances (the Andreevka trial in the Western oblast and the Aleshki trial in Voronezh oblast), second hearings were held in order to impose stiffer sentences.[27] The Andreevka case is of particular interest because the new Smolensk *obkom* secretary, Korotchenko, had made the mistake of sending a rather boastful message to Stalin *before* the verdict was brought in informing him of the success of the Andreevka trial in educating the peasantry and raising vigilance. Stalin responded the next day with a curt instruction that all the Andreevka 'wreckers' should be

shot, but by that time the court had brought in its verdict sentencing them
to various terms of imprisonment. The oblast prosecutor had to lodge a
protest that resulted in an immediate rehearing of the case, which presumably resulted in death sentences for the accused.[28]

The defendants in the rural *raion* trials were strongly encouraged to
confess their guilt, as in the central Moscow trials, but they were a good
deal less cooperative than their Moscow counterparts, especially where
charges of counterrevolution were concerned.[29] In the Aleshki trial, none
of the main defendants made a confession that was satisfactory from the
prosecutors' standpoint. While the top-ranking defendant (Kolykhmatov,
the *raion* party secretary) had admitted to counterrevolution under pretrial
interrogation, he recanted in court and maintained that he was guilty only
of failing to curb his subordinates' overzealous actions that showed poor
judgment and offended the local population. Seminikhin, the former chairman of the *raion* soviet, was similarly recalcitrant, constantly attacking the
credibility of the witnesses on the grounds that they were venting personal
grievances: 'Every few minutes he would jump up and announce to the
court that the witness was personally antagonistic towards him.' As for
Kochetov, the villainous *sel'sovet* chairman, he stubbornly asserted that
while he might be guilty of abuse of power, he was not guilty of counter-
revolution.[30]

In the Andreevka trial, two defendants persistently denied their guilt for
any counterrevolutionary crimes, even at the retrial held as a result of
Stalin's unpublicized intervention. One of the defendants (K. V. Rumiantsev, the former senior *raion* land-surveyor) was particularly obdurate when
questioned about his role in the *raion*'s decision to merge collective farms
against the will of their members:[31]

> RUMIANTSEV. Not guilty. I didn't know that forced merging was a
>   counterrevolutionary crime.
> PROSECUTOR. Did you know you were committing crimes?
> RUMIANTSEV. I knew I was carrying out the will of the head of
>   the *raion* agriculture department and the party committee.
> PROSECUTOR. That is, consciously carrying out wrecking work.
> RUMIANTSEV. (keeps silent)[32]

The charges

Many of the actions for which officials were indicted in the *raion* trials
were not crimes in the ordinary sense. In some cases officials were clearly
being made scapegoats for local economic disasters. In others they were
being held to account for behavior that was really part of their job
description (as in the Rumiantsev case cited above) or for state policies

that were unpopular with the local peasants. An interesting subset of offenses had to do with treatment of kulaks, a subject on which opinion at village level seemed to be distinctly at odds with Moscow. Overall, the most striking common characteristic of the 'criminal' behaviors attributed to the defendants was that they were harmful to peasants, especially kolkhozniki, and offended the peasants' sense of fairness and propriety.

Abuse of power

The many accusations made by peasant witnesses under this heading are among the most colorful and bitter. Curses, insults, beatings, humiliation, intimidation, and unjustified arrests were described as commonplace in the behavior of rural officials toward peasants. In one trial, an eighty-year-old peasant woman related 'with tears' how the *sel'sovet* chairman beat her husband and dumped him in a wheelbarrow; he died two weeks later as result of his injuries.[33] Another witness described how a *raion* official once made four kolkhoz brigade-leaders climb on the stove and stay there, guarded by the local policeman, for four hours. 'When people asked the kolkhoz chairman . . . why he countenanced this, he said "What could I do? After all, [he] was the boss, he could have made me get onto the stove too"'.[34]

The wild behavior of Radchuk, a *sel'sovet* chairman, was described by many peasant witnesses in the Novgorod *raion* trial. Radchuk's specialty was physical assault and forced entry (connected with various forms of extortion) into the homes of kolkhozniki. One witness described how Radchuk began breaking down the door of her house.

> 'Now', he cried, 'I'll chop down the door with an axe, you just watch'. I took fright, jumped out the window, and ran to the post office to telephone my husband in Novgorod. But when he came home, Radchuk had already gone, and the door was broken down with an axe.[35]

Peasants frequently complained about the imposition of arbitrary fines and money levies (sometimes described as 'taxation' or 'contributions to state loans') by *sel'sovet* authorities. In Shiriaevo, for example, it was said that 'a night brigade' had been organized for the purpose, descending on peasants in dead of night to conduct house searches and take inventories of property that might be seized.[36] From the standpoint of peasant witnesses, this was extortion regardless of whether the money went to the state or to individual officials, but they frequently implied that the latter was the case. It was alleged that in Aleshki Kochetov had imposed fines on kolkhoz members totalling sixty thousand rubles in 1935 and 1936: 'He imposed the fines on any pretext and at his own discretion – for not showing up for work, for not attending literacy classes, for "impolite language", for not having dogs tied up'.[37]

The *raion* soviet chairman indicted in the same trial, Seminikhin, was reportedly even more creative in his fund-raising from the population:

> In 1936, two hundred kolkhozniki recruited for construction work went off from Aleshki to the Far East. They were already on the point of boarding the train when three militiamen appeared, read out a long list of names and took all those on the list off under guard to the *raion* soviet and the offices of the chairman.
>
> 'Aha, tax delinquents!' Seminikhin greeted them. 'You thought you could get away? Pay up and look lively about it. Pay up, or I won't let you out of the office and will not permit you to get on the train. And I'll take your suitcases'.
>
> He posted a militiaman at the door and gave the order to let out only those who showed a receipt for payment.
>
> In this manner, the *raion* soviet chairman 'squeezed' seven hundred rubles of their last savings from the kolkhozniki.[38]

In many areas, kolkhozniki had extremely little money to take, so the main form of extortion was seizure of property. There were many and varied accounts of *sel'sovet* and *raion* officials behaving 'as if in their own little kingdoms' and 'exacting tribute from the population'. One country chairman took four or five kilograms of meat from each calf or pig slaughtered, plus vodka whenever he visited the village.[39] A second

> opened unlimited 'free credit' for himself on products [at the local store]. On occasion, he even roused the manager of the store from his bed at night, demanding immediate issue of vodka and snacks for himself. And when he needed potatoes, he simply sent to the nearest kolkhoz for them with an accompanying note to the person in charge of stores.[40]

Kolkhoz chairmen were also accused of treating kolkhoz property as if it were their own private property, selling buildings and (illegally) leasing land on their own initiative and pocketing the profits.[41]

In Aleshki, *raion* chairman Seminikhin had established a so-called 'auxiliary farm' of the *raion* soviet containing thirty sheds, ten cows, seven horses, and other items commandeered from various parts of the *raion*, feeding his herd with feed taken from the kolkhozy. He was particularly successful in raising pigs, selling pork at the local peasant market as well as earning fifteen hundred rubles by selling pigs to the state procurement agency. The ironic comment going the rounds among the peasants was: 'The *raion* soviet has built up a real kulak farm!'[42]

A more malign variant of extortion than regular, small-scale 'tribute' was to strip a kolkhoznik of *all* his possessions in one swoop. In one case cited in the Shchuche trial, a country chairman, coveting the flourishing kitchen garden of a kolkhoznik, 'abruptly dekulakized him and took away all his property'. When he discovered that the victim's wife had managed to sell some small household items before he could confiscate them, 'he took away the money and behaved so abusively that she was reduced to a state where she was sent to a psychiatric hospital'.[43]

Expulsions and liquidations

Complaints by peasants about their expulsion or forced departure from the kolkhoz were among the most frequent of all peasant grievances, judging both by the 1937 *raion* trials and the letters received at the same period by *Krest'ianskaia gazeta*. This may seem paradoxical, given the peasantry's hostility to collectivization less than a decade earlier. But by this time it had become clear that, as a result of heavy state taxation and other factors, peasant farming outside the kolkhoz was not a viable long-term option. Besides, when a member of a kolkhoz was expelled, he not only lost his share of the kolkhoz assets but also risked losing his private plot and even his house. Expulsion conflicts most frequently arose when members of the kolkhoz departed to work for wages elsewhere, usually leaving wives and families in the village. Departure for wage-work was a traditional cause of struggle between the Russian village commune (of which the kolkhoz was in many respects the heir) and individual peasants. It was often in the peasant's interest to depart, either temporarily or on a long-term basis, but in the village's interest to keep him (that is, retain his labor power and tax-paying capacity). After collectivization, as in the old days of serfdom and post-Emancipation redemption payments, peasants needed permission to depart, which now had to be obtained from both the kolkhoz and the *sel'sovet*. In the narratives of the 1937 *raion* trials, however, the kolkhoznik's right to depart was usually taken as a given, and conflicts over departure were thus represented as struggles between righteous peasants and power-abusing kolkhoz and *sel'sovet* chairmen.

Almost twenty witnesses testified in the Aleshki trial that they had been unjustly expelled from the '*Path to Socialism*' kolkhoz. Among them was Matrena Okuneva, who said:

They expelled me from the kolkhoz because I married a worker on the railways, although I continued to live in Lipiagovka and work in the kolkhoz. I never complained, because I thought that's how it was supposed to be. Soon after that Kachkin and Kabanov [kolkhoz chairman and party organizer respectively] appeared in my yard and demanded that I go to weed the beets. I refused because I considered myself expelled from the kolkhoz. Then Kachkin said that the *sel'sovet* would fine me fifty rubles. . . . They took a man's jacket from me, and Kabanov said: 'Be grateful to us, we could have burned [your house] down, only we took pity on the neighbors'.[44]

Other 'expulsion' cases cited seem essentially to have been cases of unauthorized departures of kolkhozniki who were on the brink of starvation because of the harvest failure of 1936. In the Ostrov trial (Pskov oblast), for example, witnesses stated that more than one thousand households had left collective farms in the *raion* in 1935–1936 because they could not survive on the meager amount of grain the kolkhoz was giving them.[45] In the Nerekhta trial (Iaroslavl oblast), peasants blamed the *raion* leadership for 'mass expulsions and forced departures from the collective farms' at the same period. These witnesses clearly felt that the *raion* bosses, like the old estate-owners in the time of serfdom, owed it to their peasants to help them out in time of trouble. For example, they related with indignation how

> after there was a fire in a kolkhoz and sixteen houses burned down, [the kolkhoz chairman] appealed to accused Begalov [chairman of the *raion* soviet] for help, saying that otherwise the kolkhozniki would all leave. In answer to the request, the accused Begalov said: 'To hell with them, let them go'. As a result, twenty households left the kolkhoz.[46]

The liquidation of an entire collective farm by order of *raion* officials was an extreme (and illegal) action that can best be understood from the peasant standpoint as expulsion of *all* the households that constituted the kolkhoz, resulting in the total loss of all village assets including land. In the case of the 'New Life' kolkhoz in Danilov, *raion* officials followed the formal announcement of liquidation by swiftly confiscating all collective property and animals – and then, adding insult to injury, demanded that the former kolkhozniki immediately pay the heavy tax that was levied on noncollectivized peasants.[47] When the 'Forward' kolkhoz in Kirillovo *raion* was liquidated, its land was distributed among neighboring collective farms in what was officially described as a 'voluntary renunciation'. The *raion* authorities went on to confiscate the kolkhoz's horses, agricultural equipment, stock of seed potatoes, and other collective property. From the standpoint of the kolkhozniki, who had owned this same property as individual households before collectivization, the liquidation of the kolkhoz must have seemed a second and definitive seizure of their assets. No wonder that, as witnesses related, the Kirillovo peasants wept when their kolkhoz was dissolved.[48]

Only one of the reported instances of kolkhoz liquidation came from the fertile Black Earth region of the country, and it occurred several years earlier than the non-Black Earth liquidations. Witnesses at the 1937 trial in

Ivnia *raion* (Kursk oblast), stated that in 1933 – that is, during the famine – the 'Lenin' kolkhoz was liquidated by order of the local Machine-Tractor Station (MTS) and its lands given to the neighboring state farm, despite the fact that twenty-eight of thirty-one households voted against it. As a result of the transfer, the peasants were reduced overnight to the status of landless agricultural laborers working for a wage on the state farm.[49]

In both the Danilov and Kirillovo cases, conflict between local officials and kolkhozniki preceded the liquidation of the kolkhoz. In Kirillovo, it was a violent confrontation over the spring sowing plan in 1936, which the kolkhoz general assembly refused to accept, to the outrage of the *sel'sovet* chairman. The Kirillovo trial narrative implies that liquidation of the kolkhoz was essentially a punitive response by local authorities to the peasants' insubordination. In the narrative of the Danilov trial, however, there are suggestions that the *raion* leadership may have had more venal motives for liquidation, perhaps wanting to get hold of kolkhoz property for their own use or that of their friends.

Agricultural disasters

There was nothing new about blaming Soviet rural officials for harvest failures. The accusations made against officials in the *raion* trials of 1937 differed from earlier charges in one important respect, however: the officials were not being blamed for failing to meet state grain procurements targets, as had frequently happened in the early 1930s. This time, they were being blamed for failing to meet the *peasants'* needs – that is, allowing so little grain to be distributed among kolkhoz households after the harvest that the kolkhozniki were brought to the brink of starvation.

Most charges of this kind related to the exceptionally bad harvest of 1936, whose consequences had been felt most acutely in the spring and summer of 1937 before the next harvest came in.[50] In the Krasnogvardeisk trial, a kolkhoz chairman, Alekseev, admitted that he had brought the kolkhoz to economic ruin and described his reaction.

> In 1936 the kolkhozniki received zero payments per labor-day [that is, no grain was distributed after the harvest]. When I saw it all, I decided to run away from the kolkhoz. I told the chairman of the *raion* soviet, Gornov. He said: 'Get away as fast as you can'.

Alekseev took this friendly advice, but not fast enough (probably because he made the mistake of trying to take his house with him, using kolkhoz horses), and he was arrested, together with Gornov, by the NKVD.[51]

In Ostrov *raion*, as a result of the 1936 harvest failure, average kolkhoz earnings dropped by 20 to 50 percent, it was reported at the Ostrov trial.

But because state grain procurements took precedence over peasant needs, many collective farms cut their payments in kind to members much more drastically, and this was treated as a crime in the 1937 *raion* trials. The indicted officials were held responsible for the departure of large numbers of hungry kolkhozniki who went to work for wages in the towns or the state farms in order to survive.[52]

A number of *raion* trials featured charges from kolkhozniki about inept agricultural instructions from *raion* authorities that had caused hardship to peasants and damaged agricultural productivity. 'Unrealistic sowing plans' figured prominently in these complaints, and, despite the fact that it was part of the *raion* agriculture departments' duty to give orders to the collective farms about what crops to sow and where and when to sow them, the rhetorical conventions of the trials allowed peasant witnesses to speak of such instructions with undisguised resentment and contempt. In the Krasnogvardeisk trial, the testimony of a peasant from 'Thirteen Years of the Red Army' kolkhoz was reported to have 'left an enormous impression on all present at the court':

> [The witness] talked about how kolkhozniki tried to protest against wrecking plans and went specially to Manninen, [head of] the *raion* agriculture department. With contemptuous effrontery, that enemy of the people announced to the kolkhozniki: 'If you go to the oblast to complain about our plans, we will add more'.[53]

Peasant witnesses cited many instances of agriculturally illiterate instructions from the *raion* authorities and MTSs. One kolkhoz, for example, was ordered to turn water-meadow and shrubbed area into plowland, leaving nowhere to pasture cattle. In another kolkhoz, the *raion*'s sowing instructions were predicated on the false assumption that its hayfields covered over two hundred hectares, which according to the peasants was double their actual extent ('Under the heading of hayfield, the wreckers included pastureland for cattle, quicksands, and the private plots of kolkhozniki').[54]

Another kind of agricultural disaster that figured prominently in a few *raion* trials was the large-scale loss of livestock. In the trial of Shchuche *raion* (Voronezh oblast), which lost almost one thousand horses in the first half of 1937, this was attributed to lack of fodder associated with the 1936 harvest failure, compounded by an epidemic that started in a Shchuche horse-breeding state farm and spread rapidly throughout the *raion*. The defendants in Shchuche were charged with gross negligence in the livestock losses, not intentional malice.[55]

In two other cases (the Kresttsy and Sychevka trials), however, officials in *raiony* with heavy livestock losses were accused of intentionally infecting animals with diseases.[56] Of all the charges made in the rural *raion* show trials of 1937, these are the least plausible and most reminiscent of the fantastic accusations of conspiratorial counterrevolutionary sabotage that characterized the Moscow trials of the Great Purges. The director of the Sychevka state farm (a former member of the Social-Revolutionary Party, one of the Bolsheviks' political competitors in 1917) was charged with leading a conspiracy to destroy the farm's livestock, using the prevailing unsanitary conditions as a cover for infecting 80 percent of the animals with diseases. Then, it was alleged, the *raion* veterinarian had done his bit to spread the epidemic throughout the country by sending animals from the infected herd to be shown at the All-Union Agricultural Exhibition in Moscow.[57]

A somewhat similar accusation was made against *raion* leaders in the Porkhov trial, although in this case the actual sabotage had been performed by aggrieved peasants. One of these was a noncollectivized peasant who allegedly poisoned kolkhoz cows and horses with arsenic at the behest of the *raion* party secretary. The other was a former kulak who, working as a kolkhoz stablehand after his return from exile, was said to have intentionally lamed the kolkhoz horses.[58]

Favoritism toward former kulaks

Kulaks (prosperous peasants, regarded by Communists as exploiters of poor peasants and potential capitalists) had been 'liquidated as a class' by the Soviet regime at the beginning of the 1930s. What this meant in practice was that a good proportion of kulaks had been sent to labor camps or deported along with their families to distant areas of the Soviet Union, while others had been expropriated and evicted from their homes without arrest or deportation. Of the former group, some had returned from labor camps to the villages by the late 1930s (though the deportees were still forbidden to return). Of the latter group, many had left the countryside and gone to work in the towns, but some were still living in the area, and a few had even joined the collective farms. Official policy toward the group softened around 1936, when the Stalin Constitution restored full citizenship and voting rights to former kulaks and other old 'class enemies'. In the villages, however, the presence of former kulaks often produced conflicts because of their efforts to recover the property that had been confiscated from them and the new owners' and occupiers' efforts to hang on to it.

Peasant witnesses in the trials made many accusations that officials had done favors for former kulaks, presumably often as a result of bribes. It was said that kulaks had managed to get houses and horses back, that they had been given good jobs in the collective farms, and that, once admitted to the kolkhoz, they had taken revenge on peasants who were Soviet activists.[59] In Borisovka *raion* (Kursk oblast) the prosecutor claimed that in 1936 and the first half of 1937, 75 houses were returned to the kulaks who were their former owners, and 134 kulaks had their voting rights restored.[60] Returning the houses meant that schools, kindergartens, kolkhoz clubs, and other communal institutions had to be evicted, but the *raion* leaders were unmoved by their plight. This was held to be the more offensive since the party secretary, Fedosov, had behaved so brutally toward ordinary peasants in the *raion*: 'Everything was taken from the population down to their socks, but [the *raion* party leaders] returned to the kulaks the property that had been legally confiscated from them'.[61]

When kolkhozniki complained to the Borisovka party leaders about the concessions being made to former kulaks, it was reported that the party leaders 'oriented those present at the meeting toward reconciliation with the class enemies'.[62] This is not surprising, since reconciliation was the party's general line at the time in connection with the promulgation of the new constitution.[63] What is more surprising is that in 1937, without any overt change in the party line and with the constitution still in force, this could be treated in Kursk as a political crime.

Kursk was not the only place where this happened. At the trial in Sychevka *raion*, the two senior *raion* officials were also charged with distorting party policy on kulaks by announcing that it was time to forget about the whole idea of class enemies and make appointments and judgments of individuals on the basis of merit. They had instructed *sel'sovet* chairmen to destroy all the existing lists of kulaks and other persons who had earlier been disenfranchised or subject to other forms of discrimination – a reasonable interpretation, on the face of it, of the spirit of the new constitution. But then they had gone further – probably further than the new party line required, and certainly further than public opinion in Sychevka would stand for – and appointed a landlord's son as director of the school and several former kulaks as kolkhoz chairmen, as well as put former merchants in charge of village co-ops. According to peasant witnesses at the trial, the former kulaks who were appointed as kolkhoz chairmen 'caused enormous damage', 'persecuted Stakhanovites and beat them up', and 'destroyed the horses'.[64]

'Suppression of kolkhoz democracy'

According to the Kolkhoz Charter of 1935, collective farms were self-governing bodies whose chairmen were freely elected at the kolkhoz general meeting. But this was not in practice the way chairmen were selected. The normal custom was for local authorities (the *raion* agriculture department or the local MTS) to nominate a chairman, whom the kolkhozniki then duly 'elected'. In the early 1930s the chairman was often an outsider – a Communist or worker sent out from the towns. But by the second half of the 1930s it was becoming increasingly common for locals (kolkhoz members or peasants from elsewhere in the *sel'sovet*) to be nominated as chairmen. It remains uncertain how seriously the central political leaders meant the charter to be taken with regard to democratic election of kolkhoz chairmen, but it seems clear at any rate that *peasants* wanted this provision taken seriously, and that newspapers were willing to endorse and publicize their complaints.

'Suppression of kolkhoz democracy' was one of the standard charges brought against *raion* officials in the rural show trials of 1937. In the Kazachkin trial in Saratov *krai*, for example, the *raion* authorities were accused of focing a kolkhoz to accept a former *raion* official as chairman despite the protests of the kolkhozniki. This man subsequently robbed the kolkhoz of its assets, proving that the kolkhozniki had been right all along.[65]

Sometimes it was alleged that *raion* or *sel'sovet* authorities applied extreme measures of coercion in conflicts with kolkhozniki over chairmen. The liquidation of the 'New Life' kolkhoz in Danilov *raion* was said to be the result of such a conflict.[66] In the Aleshki trial,

> witnesses I. N. Goltsev and V. A. Mishin related how, when they and other kolkhozniki got up at the general meeting in the 'First of May' kolkhoz and criticized the work of the [kolkhoz] administration, demanding that the kolkhoz chairman be fired for failure to carry out his duties, the *sel'sovet* chairman, Kochetov, disbanded the meeting. Four of the most active kolkhozniki, including the two witnesses, were arrested on the basis of his provocative and false statement.[67]

In reporting the trials, oblast newspapers often played up the democracy theme. The Voronezh newspaper, commenting on the revelations of the Shchuche *raion* trial, added its own editorial flourish:

> Ask any kolkhoznik of the 'Red Bitiug' kolkhoz why they elected Zazadravnykh chairman, and they will answer: 'But we didn't elect him. Kordin [the *sel'sovet* chairman] foisted him on us. We protested and didn't want to accept him, but they made us'. And that is completely true. That was the system there.[68]

Virtuous peasants and evil bosses

In the narratives of the *raion* trials, evil bosses exploit and abuse, and peasants are their victims. The relationship of peasants and bosses was presented in clear antithetical terms; there was scarcely any shading of the stark black-and-white contrast between victimizers and victims.

Rarely if ever did peasant witnesses mention a good boss at the *raion* level – one who, say, interceded for them or understood their problems. By the same token, in only a few instances did the gallery of defendants include a peasant who was not an office-holder of some kind, and in those instances the evil peasant was usually a kulak returned from exile.[69]

These same conventions prevailed in peasant letters of complaint to *Krest'ianskaia gazeta*, no doubt reflecting peasants' general disinclination to look anywhere but on the dark side. In real life, however, the dichotomy between rulers and ruled in the Soviet countryside was by no means so straightforward. In the first place, there was a gulf in real life between the status and powers of the *raion* authorities and those at *sel'sovet* and kolkhoz level. In the second place, *sel'sovet* and kolkhoz chairmen were not far removed from the local peasantry. The majority were local peasants themselves by origin – natives of the *sel'sovet* or even, in the case of many kolkhoz chairmen, of the village. There was considerable turnover in these lower offices; and, as we have seen, peasants were pushing with some success for veto power over appointments of kolkhoz chairman. The kolkhoz chairmen, moreover, were not salaried: they were paid (like other kolkhozniki, albeit more generously) with a proportion of the kolkhoz's harvest and income.

The premise that an impassable divide separated evil rulers from virtuous peasants was dramatized many times in the *raion* trials, and not only by peasant witnesses. For example, in the Shchuche trial, which is unusual in the context of *raion* trials for the defendants' willingness to participate in their own indictment, two defendants gave the following answers when the prosecutor asked why they did not try to recruit peasants and workers into their anti-Soviet activities:

> SEDNEV (plant director). Undoubtedly if they [the workers] had known that I was a Trotskyist wrecker, they would have torn me limb from limb.
> POLIANSKII (MTS director). Well, if I had even hinted of wrecking, they [the peasants] would have beaten me up if I was lucky, but more likely would simply have killed me.[70]

The peasant testimony at the trials presented many vivid images of the local 'masters' taunting peasants with their powerlessness.

> – So you went to VTsIK [that is, laid a complaint with the Russian Republican government in Moscow]! But we are the people in power here. I do what I want.[71]
> – I am a Communist and you don't belong to the party. However much you complain about me, you won't be believed.[72]
> – You should have shot the bastard; you wouldn't have got into any

trouble for it [a *raion* official's comment to a subordinate, who had beaten a peasant].[73]

– If five people croak, that will teach you how to work, you idle bastards [a *raion* official's remark to kolkhozniki during the 1933 famine].[74]

– Grain has to be given to the horses. The kolkhozniki can survive without grain.[75]

– The clever ones left the collective farms long ago, and all that remain are the fools.[76]

Reports of the trials stressed the 'deep hatred' with which peasants spoke of their former oppressors in courtroom testimony.[77] Before and during the trials, newspapers reported, resolutions and petitions came in from neighboring collective farms demanding the death sentence for the accused, who were referred to with such epithets as 'contemptible swine' and 'rotten bastards'.[78] The halls where the trials were held were always described as packed, with the audience listening intently, full of indignation against the accused.

Each evening, crowds of kolkhozniki gather near the school. . . . During the trial, as many as fifty statements indicating new facts of abuse and illegality performed by Seminikhin, Kolykhmatov and the others were personally handed by citizens to the oblast prosecutor, who is attending the trial.[79]

In one of the most dramatic confrontations reported in the press, a peasant witness, Natalia Latysheva, turned on the former leaders of Novgorod *raion* as soon as she took the stand.

LATYSHEVA. Comrade judges! Are these really human beings? They are ogres, swine. (*Movement in the hall, cries of approval, confusion on the bench of the accused.*)
CHAIRMAN. Witness, it is facts that are asked of you.
LATYSHEVA. Forgive me, comrade judges, but when I saw those swine, I couldn't contain myself. And it is a fact that they are scoundrels! . . . There they sit, damn them. The kolkhozniki will never forgive them for what they did.[80]

In Latysheva's story, as in those of many other peasant witnesses in the trials, the district's interference in agriculture (for example, in the giving of sowing plans) was completely unjustified and stupid, since the officials had no idea what they were doing. On Latysheva's kolkhoz, for example, the *raion* had tried to discourage the peasants from developing a stud farm and forced them to grow unprofitable and inappropriate crops. But the kolkhozniki were not to be browbeaten.

LATYSHEVA. We did not give up. We decided to breed trotters. And we did – those enemies of the collective farms did not break our spirit. To the astonishment of all, we built up a horse farm, and now we have twenty-one horses of pure Orel stock. (*Spontaneous applause breaks out in the hall, cries of 'Good for you!' and 'Well done!' are heard.*)

CHAIRMAN. Witness, have you anything more to add?

LATYSHEVA. I have. (*The peasant woman turns to the accused, and stands face to face with the enemies of the people . . .*) All the same, our side won, not yours. We were victorious![81]

Our side won! It would be tempting to end the story on this note of populist triumph. But had the peasant mice really won a significant victory over the oppressor cats? After all, the death of a cat does not change the essential relationship of cats and mice; and in Stalinist Russia the downfall of a Kochetov or even many Kochetovs in 1937 does not seem to have produced any lasting changes in an exploitative system of collectivized agriculture and a rural administrative structure that tended to generate petty local despots. To be sure, 1935–37 was a period of relatively conciliatory state policies toward the peasantry, in contrast to the harsh conflicts of collectivization at the beginning of the decade, but by 1938–39 the screws were being tightened again.

In the woodcut 'The Mice Bury the Cat', as in the real world of the Soviet Union in 1937, it is not at all clear who killed the cat that the mice are so gleefully burying. It is hard to believe that the mice themselves were the killers – that is, that peasants had the political strength to take revenge on corrupt bosses without outside encouragement, or, if they had the strength, that this would have been their chosen form of revenge. It is more plausible, certainly, that the peasant mice should have helped bigger predators locate their prey by writing letters of complaint and denunciation against particularly unpopular cat bosses. But peasant denunciations against local bosses were a constant feature of life; moreover, to say that they were probably used in constructing the show trials is not to say that the show trials could not have been constructed without them.

One thing we can be fairly sure of is that once the cat was dead, the mice danced at the funeral. The *raion* show trials of 1937, it seems, were a kind of Soviet carnival[82] – not just an outing for the local peasants, when they got a trip into the *raion* center where vodka was probably on sale, but a real *prazdnik* in which for a few days the world was turned upside down and mice could taunt and mock cats with impunity. Of course, this was not exactly a Bakhtinian Carnival: the mockery had a sly, malicious, almost corrupt quality that is alien to Bakhtin's notion of popular revelry. But then it is likely that real-life medieval carnivals were always a bit crueler and less innocently joyful than they appear in the retrospective view of twentieth-century intellectuals.

If carnival is the appropriate metaphor for the rural *raion* trials, this throws a disconcerting light on the big show trials in Moscow, and perhaps on the Great Purges as a whole. In the familiar *Darkness at Noon* picture of the Moscow trials, victims such as Nikolai Bukharin – the Marxist theorist whom Lenin called the party's favorite – are revolutionary martyrs, tragically destroyed by the cause to which they have devoted their lives. From within this paradigm it seems inconceivable that anybody could see a similarity between the idealistic intellectual Bukharin and the crude and brutal Kochetov. From the standpoint of peasants, however, was one Communist boss any different from another, except in degree of rank and power? If there was reason to dance at Kochetov's funeral, was there not also reason to dance at the funeral of a Kochetov-writ-large such as Bukharin?

Almost certainly the potential carnival appeal of the Great Purge trials was not lost on Soviet political leaders. We can see signs that efforts were made by Stalin and on his behalf to tap into ordinary people's envious resentment of power and privilege. One of these is *Pravda*'s early report in connection with the Danilov trial that kolkhozniki of the *raion* had sent thanks to Stalin for restoring their kolkhoz (which the *raion* leaders had liquidated) and protecting them from their enemies.[83] Another is Stalin's toast to 'the little people' at a reception for Stakhanovite workers in October, when he said that 'leaders come and go, but the people remains. Only the people is eternal'.[84]

It should have worked. According to the conventional wisdom of historians, Russian peasants have always been 'naive monarchists', eager to believe that if the Tsar only knew of the injustices perpetrated by his nobles and officials, he would come riding to the people's rescue.[85] This 'naive monarchism' of the Russian peasant, many Russian intellectuals believe, lay at the root of the Stalin cult, which allegedly could have developed only in a peasant country.[86]

Remarkably, the 'naive monarchism' ploy failed. Ignoring *Pravda*'s hint, peasant witnesses in later trials did *not* credit Stalin with bringing corrupt lower officials to justice. They did *not* report that he had responded to their letters of complaint or attribute to him any guiding role, and they steadfastly avoided such 'naive monarchist' formulations as 'If Stalin had only known what was going on'. In fact, in reported testimony at the trials there are virtually no references to Stalin at all.

This reticence must surely be understood in terms of the peasants' hostile reaction to collectivization and their strong belief that Stalin personally was the man mainly responsible for their sufferings in the early 1930s.[87] That these attitudes had not disappeared in the mid-1930s is shown by the striking reaction of peasants in the Western oblast to the murder of Sergei Kirov, the Leningrad party leader, in December 1934.

Although Kirov is usually described by historians as a relatively popular leader, peasants evidently regarded his death as a fortunate event (on the general grounds that the mice had one less cat to worry about) that called for rowdy celebration. A ditty that appeared in more than one region of the oblast had as its concluding lines: 'They killed Kirov; we'll kill Stalin' (*Ubili Kirova, ub''em Stalina*).[88]

Could it be, then, that Latysheva's *'Our side won!'* was not so far from the mark after all? Were the mice at the cat's funeral really dancing to Stalin's tune? Or was that their own subversive ditty, 'Ubili Kirova', that they were singing?

Notes

1 This account is based on reports of thirty-five show trials held in rural *raion* centers in the Russian Republic (thirty-two trials), the Ukraine (two trials) and Belorussia (one trial) reported in the regional and central press from March to November 1937. The great majority of trials occurred from August to October 1937, and almost all the reports were published in oblast newspapers.

2 *Krest'ianskaia pravda*. 2 September 1937.

3 *Krest'ianskaia pravda*, 3 September 1937.

4 On the provenance of the woodcut 'The Mice Bury the Cat' see Dianne Ecklund Farrell, 'Medieval Popular Humor in Russian Eighteenth-Century Lubki', *Slavic Review* 50 (Fall 1991): 560–2.

5 Virtually all my sources are newspaper reports of rural *raion* show trials, not court records or memoir accounts. If any court records of the trials have survived in Soviet oblast archives, they have yet to be discovered. The Smolensk Archive (available in the West) includes no court records, though it contains valuable related material, some of which has been analyzed by Roberta Manning in her unpublished article, 'The Case of the Miffed Milk-maid'. In A. I. Solzhenitsyn, *The Gulag Archipelago*, vols. 1–2 (New York, 1973), 419–31, there is an account of one show trial (held in Kady *raion*, Ivanovo oblast) which appears to be based on information from one of the indicted officials or a family member.

6 There were defense counsels in some and conceivably most of the rural *raion* trials (see, for example, the Lepel' trial, as reported in *Pravda*, 13 March 1937) but, as was usual in the Stalin period, their role was limited to asking for a more lenient sentence for their clients.

7 I have borrowed this term from Katerina Clark's discussion of the 'master plot' of Socialist Realism in *The Soviet Novel: History as Ritual* (Chicago, 1981), 5–15.

8 Note that, in accordance with this metaphor, it was also possible for signals to be sent 'from below' and received by the top party and government leadership. The peasant complaints and petitions discussed below fall into this category.

9 *Pravda*, 9–12 March 1937.

10 By 1937 the great majority of Soviet peasants were members of a collective farm (kolkhozniki). The Model Charter of the Agricultural Artel (*Primernyi ustav sel'skokhoziaistvennoi arteli*), approved by the Second Congress of Kolkhoz Shockworkers, was issued as a law by the Soviet government on 17 February 1935. It was in effect the kolkhoz constitution, defining the rights and obliga-tions of kolkhoz members and kolkhozy.

11 TASS dispatch, 'Delo nad byvshimi rukovoditeliami shiriaevskogo raiona', *Pravda*, 16 June 1937.

12 Reports on the Shiriaevo trial appeared in *Pravda*, 15–19 June 1937. Information on the trial also appeared in the national agricultural newspaper, *Sotsialisticheskoe zemledelie*, 18 June 1937 and 21 July 1937, as well as in some oblast papers.

13 See *Pravda*, 2 July 1937 and 5 July 1937.

14 The Danilov case was reported in *Pravda*, 15 July 1937, 29 July 1937, 30 July 1937, and 31 July 1937. More detailed reports also appeared in the local oblast paper, *Severnyi rabochii* (Iaroslavl), in daily installments from 26–30 July 1937.

15 *Pravda*, 31 July 1937.

16 *Pravda*, 3 August 1937.

17 For a more extended discussion of peasant letters see my 'Peasant Letters to *Krest'ianskaia gazeta*, 1938' (Paper presented to the AAASS National Convention, Washington, DC, October 1990).

18 *Pravda*, 9 March 1937. The term 'toilers' covered peasants as well as workers, and other honest wage-earners, but in this case it probably refers to peasants.

19 *Pravda*, 16 June 1937.

20 *Pravda*, 30 July 1937. In the 1920s the term 'sel'kor' was usually reserved for the small group of villagers that had consciously taken on the role of 'the eyes and ears of Soviet power' in the village. By the latter part of the 1930s, however, it was used more broadly to refer to any villager who wrote to a newspaper complaining about or giving information on fellow peasants.

21 In the Andreevsk trial, for example, peasant witnesses mentioned that they had sent a telegram of complaint to the people's commissar of agriculture (*Rabochii put'*, 8 September 1937). In Shchuche the complaint had been sent to the Central Executive Committee of Soviets of the Russian Republic (VTsIK) (*Kommuna*, 6 October 1937). In Aleshki peasant complaints against Kochetov were forwarded to the Central Commission of Soviet Control in Moscow by a sympathetic secretary of a neighboring sel'sovet (*Kommuna*, 1 September 1937).

22 That is, the letters expressing criticism of local bosses that are filed in the newspaper's archive under the heading 'Abuses of power' (Tsentral'nyi gosudarstvennyi arkhiv narodnogo khoziaistva SSSR, f. 396, op. 10–11).

23 For unusually detailed biographical data on defendants see the report of the Krasnogorsk *raion* trial in *Rabochii put'*, 29 August 1937.

24 My sample of thirty-two *raion* trials discloses not a single actual Oppositionist among the defendants. The closest to a serious accusation of Trotskyite conspiracy was in the Shchuche trial (which was also unusual in combining industrial and kolkhoz/agricultural themes and personnel), where one of the defendants, director of a sugar plant, admitted that he had been influenced by a Trotskyite he met after graduating from a party technical school in Moscow in 1928 (*Kommuna*, 3 October 1937). In another trial the former *raion* party secretary was accused of softness on Trotskyites (but not membership of a Trotskyite conspiracy) because he let the director of the local veterinary school, a former Trotskyite, go into hiding to avoid arrest (*Kommuna*, 3 September 1937).

25 In the Lepel' trial the accused were indicted under Art. 196 of the Belorussian Criminal Code (violation of Soviet law and abuse of power), and in the Danilov trial they were accused of destruction of socialist property under the law of 7 August 1932.

26 Sentences were reported for ten of the trials and can be deduced for an

eleventh. See *Krest'ianskaia pravda*, 29 August 1937 (Ostrov), 2 September 1937 (Krasnogvardeisk), and 20 October 1937 (Kirillovo); *Kurskaia pravda*, 4 September 1937 (Borisovka); *Rabochii put'*, 29 August 1937 (Krasnogorsk) and 18 October 1937 (Sychevka); *Kommuna*, 6 September 1937 (Aleshki), and 6 October 1937 (Shchuche); *Moskovskaia kolkhoznaia gazeta*, 3 November 1937 (Malin and Konstantinovo); and footnote 28 below (Andreevka).

27 In the Aleshki trial (Voronezh oblast) in September, only two death sentences were imposed, though the prosecutor asked for four. This verdict, too, was subsequently appealed by the oblast prosecutor, resulting in a retrial in November at which three additional death sentences were imposed (*Kommuna*, 6 September 1937 and 20 November 1937).

28 See coded telegrams from Stalin's personal archive (currently held in the 'Presidential' or 'Kremlin' Archive) recently published in *Izvestiia*, 10 June 1992 (I am indebted to Arch Getty for informing me of this publication); and the report in *Rabochii put'* (Smolensk), 2 September 1937. Surprisingly, although Stalin instructed that an announcement of the defendants' execution should be placed in the local press, *Rabochii put'* reported neither the new sentences imposed by the court after the prosecutor's protest nor the execution of the Andreevka defendants that presumably followed.

29 In his account of the Kady trial (see above, footnote 5), Solzhenitsyn suggests that a defendant's withdrawal of his pre-trial confession unhinged the whole proceedings and even caused the *raion* show trial as a genre to be abandoned. In my sample of *raion* trials, however, recanting in court on earlier admissions was not unusual and did not have a devastating effect on proceedings, since most *raion* cases were built more on peasant testimony than on confession by the accused.

30 *Kommuna*, 29 August 1937, 3 September 1937, and 4 September 1937. For other similar denials and protestations see, for example, the reports of the Borisovka and Danilov cases in *Kurskaia pravda*, 29 August 1937; and *Severnyi rabochii*, 30 July 1937.

31 It is not known whether this Rumiantsev was related to a major political figure in the region, Ivan Petrovich Rumiantsev, long-time first secretary of the Western oblast party committee until his disgrace and disappearance in the Great Purges in the summer of 1937.

32 *Rabochii put'*, 5 September 1937.

33 *Kommuna*, 30 August 1937.

34 *Kommuna*, 4 September 1937.

35 *Krest'ianskaia pravda*, 3 September 1937.

36 *Sotsialisticheskoe zemledelie*, 21 July 1937.

37 *Sovetskaia iustitsiia*, no. 20 (1937): 22.

38 *Sovetskaia iustitsiia*, no. 20 (1937): 24.

39 *Kommuna*, 28 September 1937.

40 *Sovetskaia iustitsiia*, no. 20 (1937): 22.

41 *Krest'ianskaia pravda*, 17 August 1937.

42 *Sovetskaia iustitsiia*, no. 20 (1937): 24; *Kommuna*, 4 September 1937.

43 *Kommuna*, 28 September 1937.

44 *Kommuna*, 2 September 1937.

45 *Krest'ianskaia pravda*, 28 August 1937.

46 *Severnyi rabochii*, 22 September 1937.

47 *Sotsialisticheskoe zemledelie*, 26 July 1937.

48 *Krest'ianskaia pravda*, 20 October 1937.

49 *Kurskaia pravda*, 2 October 1937 and 16 October 1937.

50 In one exceptional case from the Nerekhta *raion* trial, the accusations made against a *raion* soviet chairman included his treatment of peasants during the 1933 famine (*Severnyi rabochii*, 22 September 1937).

51 *Moskovskaia kolkhoznaia gazeta*, 5 October 1937.

52 *Krest'ianskaia pravda*, 28 August 1937.

53 *Krest'ianskaia pravda*, 2 September 1937.

54 *Krest'ianskaia pravda*, 26 August 1937 and 2 September 1937.

55 *Kommuna*, 28 September 1937 and 3 October 1937.

56 On the Kresttsy trial see *Krest'ianskaia pravda*, 28 October 1937. On the Sychevka trial see *Rabochii put'*, 12 September 1937 and 16 October 1937.

57 Roberta Manning, 'The Case of the Miffed Milkmaid', gives a fascinating account, drawn from the Smolensk Archive, of the events in Sychevka leading up to the show trial.

58 *Krest'ianskaia pravda*, 30 July 1937.

59 See, for example, *Sotsialisticheskoe zemledelie*, 26 July 1937, 28 December 1937; *Kurskaia pravda*, 14 October 1937; and *Rabochii put'*, 16 October 1937.

60 This is anomalous because the 1936 Constitution had in fact already restored voting rights to kulaks, priests and other former 'class enemies'.

61 *Kurskaia pravda*, 23 August 1937, 26 August 1937, 29 August 1937, and 2 September 1937.

62 *Kurskaia pravda*, 26 August 1937.

63 For a discussion of the changing policy on class in the 1930s see Sheila Fitzpatrick, 'L'Usage Bolchévique de la "Classe": Marxisme et Construction de l'Identité Individuelle', *Actes de la Recherche en Sciences Sociales*, no. 85 (November 1990); 75–80.

64 *Rabochii put'*, 16 October 1937.

65 *Kommunist*, 14 September 1937.

66 *Severnyi rabochii* 30 July 1937.

67 *Kommuna*, 4 September 1937.

68 *Kommuna*, 4 October 1937.

69 For the exceptions (in the Porkhov, Malin and Zolotukhino trials) see *Krest'ianskaia pravda*, 30 July 1937; *Moskovskaia kolkhoznaia gazeta*, 27 October 1937; and *Kurskaia pravda*, 14 October 1937.

70 *Kommuna*, 3 October 1937.

71 *Kommuna*, 6 October 1937.

72 *Krest'ianskaia pravda*, 27 August 1937.

73 *Kommuna*, 28 September 1937.

74 *Severnyi rabochii*, 22 September 1937.

75 *Krest'ianskaia pravda*, 2 September 1937.

76 *Krest'ianskaia pravda*, 2 September 1937.

77 *Krest'ianskaia pravda*, 2 September 1937.

78 *Krest'ianskaia pravda*, 26 August 1937. See also the report of the Pavlograd trial in *Zvezda* (Dnepropetrovsk), 20 September 1937.

79 *Kommuna*, 4 September 1937.

80 *Krest'ianskaia pravda*, 3 September 1937.

81 *Krest'ianskaia pravda*, 3 September 1937.

82 On carnival see Natalie Zemon Davis, 'The Reasons of Misrule', in her *Society and Culture in Early Modern France* (Stanford, 1975), 99–123; Peter Burke, *Popular Culture in Early Modern Europe* (London, 1978), chap. 7; and Mikhail Bakhtin, *Rabelais and His World*, trans. Hélène Izwolsky (Bloomington, 1984).

83 *Pravda*, 31 July 1937.

84 I. V. Stalin, *Sochineniia*, 14 vols., ed. Robert H. McNeal (Stanford, 1967),

1:254. Although eminently quotable, Stalin's aphorism was not widely quoted and does not appear in any of the *raion* trial reports I have read (though admittedly it came too late for many of the trials).

85 For a skeptical examination of the idea of 'naive monarchism' see Daniel Field, *Rebels in the Name of the Tsar* (Boston, 1976).

86 For a rebuttal of this argument see the comments by the distinguished historian of the Russian peasantry, V. P. Danilov, in *Voprosy istorii*, 1988, no. 12:11.

87 See, for example, OGPU reports of rumors and stories circulating in the countryside in the Smolensk Archive, WKP 166, pp. 216, 399.

88 For one scandalous incident involving this ditty see the Smolensk Archive, WKP 355, pp. 36–9. Note that the Russian verb in the first clause is ambiguous as to person: it could mean either 'They killed Kirov' or 'We killed Kirov'.

Chapter 7 Stalinist Culture

Reading 13 *The family, the school, the church: the pillars of society shaken and re-enforced*

N. S. TIMASHEFF

I

In their attempts to create a new culture, the revolutionists always meet resistance. This resistance is displayed by individuals, but they resist because they have been molded by mighty institutions through which social structure and culture are perpetuated. In modern society these pillars of society are the family, the school, and the Church. From the standpoint of the revolutionists two of them, the family and the Church, are hopeless, for it is their very nature to preserve tradition. But the school might perhaps be transformed into an instrument of cultural revolution.

Hence, for those who are eager to endow a nation with a new culture, a definite program of action follows: they must loosen the family ties; they must destroy or at least weaken the Church; and they must transform the school into an accelerator of cultural revolution. This was the natural program of the Communists while they performed their Great Experiment. [. . .]

The general tendency was to destroy the stable character of marital relations and make marriage as easily soluble as possible. Naturally, marriage was liberated from all bonds with religion: after a certain date, church weddings ceased to be accorded any legal effect. Instead of going to church, the prospective consorts had to apply for 'registration' of their marriage to local boards established for that purpose. Measures were taken to deprive the registration of the character of an impressive ceremony. The boards were usually located in some dark and abject room of an office building, and no words about the significance of marriage were uttered by the officials.

The most drastic change concerned divorce: in contradistinction to the old law which made it so difficult, the decrees of December 17 and 18, 1917, permitted every consort to declare that he wanted his marriage to be canceled. No reasons were to be given to the board. Receiving the application, it had to grant the cancellation immediately if there was mutual consent; if this was not the case, divorce was to be granted by the court, but this was a meaningless formality, since the court had to do it at the request of each consort, even if the other one opposed it. If one of the consorts was absent, he or she was notified by a postcard.

In addition to this, incest, bigamy, and adultery were dropped from the list of criminal offenses. Abortion was explicitly permitted by the decree of November 20, 1920, provided that it was performed by an approved physician in a State hospital. Under these conditions the physician had to accede to requests for abortion even if no valid reasons could be established. Under War Communism, inheritance ceased to exist. [. . .]

The period of the Second Socialist Offensive was characterized by additional efforts to uproot the traditional structure of the family. The labor law of the period made it obligatory to accept any job imposed on the individual, and often husband and wife were assigned work in different towns. To the complaint of a teacher that she was artificially separated from her husband, the Labor Board replied that divorce was easy and that she probably could find another husband in the place of her occupation. In Stalingrad it was decided to create 'socialist suburbs' consisting of houses without apartments for family life, replaced by single rooms, refectories, and nurseries. The plan fell through because nobody but bachelors agreed to live in such suburbs.

The antifamily policy was crowned by partial success: around 1930, on the average, family ties were substantially weaker than they had been before the revolution. But this partial success was more than balanced by a number of detrimental effects unforeseen by the promoters of the Communist Experiment. About 1934, these detrimental effects were found to endanger the very stability of the new society and its capacity to stand the test of war. Let us review these effects.

1. The abuse of the freedom of divorce and abortion resulted in an ominous decrease of the birth rate. No natality figures have ever been published for the crucial years, but in 1937, the population proved to be 13 million behind expectation, so that around 1934, the deficit must already have been large. To what extent this was due to the freedoms just mentioned cannot be established. But the following figures speak for themselves: in 1934, in the medical institutions of the city of Moscow, 57 thousand children were born, but 154 thousand abortions were performed; in 1935, already under changing conditions, the figures were 70 thousand, and 155 thousand. As to divorce, the frequency of which also pushes down the birth rate, the following figures were reported from Moscow: in 1934, in 100 marriages there were 37 divorces, and in the first half of 1935, there were 38.3 divorces.[1]

2. The dissolution of family ties, especially of the parent–child relations, threatened to produce a wholesale dissolution of community ties, with rapidly increasing juvenile delinquency as the main symptom. In 1935, the Soviet papers were full of information and indignation about

the rise of hooliganism, i.e., of crimes in which the sadistic joy of inflicting pain on somebody or destroying something of value was paramount. Everywhere, wrote the papers, gangs invaded workingmen's dwellings, ransacked them, and destroyed or spoiled what they did not take away; if somebody dared to resist, he was mercilessly killed. In trains, the hooligans sang obscene songs; to prolong the fun, they did not permit travelers to alight at their destinations if they had not finished singing. Sometimes the schools were besieged by neglected children; other times gangs beat the teachers and attacked women, or regularly fought against one another.

3. Finally, the magnificent slogans of the liberation of sex and the emancipation of women proved to have worked in favor of the strong and reckless, and against the weak and shy. Millions of girls saw their lives ruined by Don Juans in Communist garb, and millions of children had never known parental homes.

II

The disintegration of the family did not disturb the Communists, since this was precisely what they wanted to achieve, but they were disturbed by quite a few collateral effects of the disorganization. The unfavourable trend of the population figures threatened to undermine both the labor supply and the strength of the nation at arms – for wars to be waged by the next generation. In the specific circumstances of 1934, the waste of human energy in juvenile delinquency, the combat against it, and love affairs, and the accumulation of unfavorable attitudes among the victims of the new family order – or perhaps disorder is the correct word? – could no longer be tolerated: they undermined the strength of the nation for the war which was straight ahead. The unfavorable development had to be stopped, and to achieve this the government had no other choice but to re-enforce that pillar of society which is the family. These were the main lines of development:

1. Contrary to the teachings of the previous years, young people were instructed to consider marriage 'as the most serious affair in life', since in principle it should be a union for life. Statements such as follow, which never could have appeared in the course of the Communist Experiment, now daily adorned the Soviet papers and magazines:

There are people who dare to assert that the Revolution destroys the family; this is entirely wrong: the family is an especially important phase of social relations in socialist society. . . One of the basic rules of Communist morals is that of strengthening the family . . . The right to divorce is not a right to sexual laxity. A poor husband and father cannot be a good citizen. People who abuse the freedom of divorce should be punished.

And actually, in 1935 the Soviet government started to prosecute men for rape who 'changed their wives as gloves', registering a marriage one day and divorce the next. [. . .]

To re-enforce the new ideas, very simple, but probably very effective symbolic means were used. The registration offices ceased to be filthy places. Now, young people found them clean, comfortable, well furnished; the officers became polite, friendly, underlining the seriousness of the act. Marriage certificates started being issued on decent paper, no longer on wrapping paper, as was the case previously. For a small additional sum the newlyweds could receive a marriage certificate designed by artists.[2] Then, in the fall of 1936, wedding rings started being sold in Soviet shops.[3] Since these rings are used in church weddings, this novelty could be interpreted as an invitation, on the part of the government, to have the civil marriage, or registration, re-enforced and made almost indissoluble by the Church.

2. The freedom of divorce was first curtailed and then almost abolished. The first phase appears in the law of June 27, 1936, which introduced a number of inhibitions. It calls for the summoning of both parties when a divorce is to be registered.

Moreover, according to the law of September 28, 1935, the fact of divorce must be marked in the passports and birth certificates of the consorts. Commenting on this regulation, *Izvestia* expressed the hope that before marrying a 'fluttering scoundrel', a girl would ask him to produce his papers and then perhaps renounce the honor of becoming is thirtieth bride.[4]

Finally, the fee for divorce which previously had been rather nominal was substantially raised; instead of three rubles, one had to pay 50 rubles for the first divorce, 150 for the second, and 300 for the third and each subsequent divorce.

The effect of the antidivorce drive may be measured by the following figures: in the course of the second half of the year 1936, the number of divorces in the Ukraine was 10,992, against 35,458 in the second half of 1935;[5] in other words, it decreased more than three times.

The second phase appears in the decree of July 8, 1944.

> Prospective applicants for a divorce will henceforth be obliged to state their reasons and satisfy the courts that these reasons are serious and valid. Both parties must appear personally before a lower court which hears all the evidence and then seeks to determine if it cannot effect a reconciliation. If this is believed impossible, the petition can be carried to a higher court. Witnesses must be heard in both courts. The divorce fees have been raised to 2,000 rubles.

It is probable that the courts, obeying the government's directions, will demand very good reasons and irrefutable evidence to grant a divorce. In consequence, obtaining a divorce in Russia will probably become more difficult than in many states of this country.

Moreover, the decree of July 8, 1944, abolished the institution of 'unregistered marriage' introduced in 1926. Now, only 'registered marriage' is legally recognized; as a corollary, the 'bourgeois' distinction between legitimate and illegitimate children has reappeared in Soviet law. In addition to this, 'the research of paternity' has been explicitly forbidden, so that illegitimate children and their mothers will receive no alimony. Very definitely, this will prove a mighty deterrent to extramarital relations, insofar as girls are concerned.

3. The freedom to dispose of unborn children through abortions no longer exists. Early in 1935, a campaign against abortion was started. Articles began to appear in Soviet papers written by high medical authorities, explaining the harm which abortion, especially repeated abortion, inflicts on women.[6] Praising maternity, these authorities declared that the longing for children had suddenly reappeared among the women of the Soviet Union – a manner of saying that now Stalin wanted them to bear as many children as possible. Trials resulting in severe sentences finished the careers of persons operating clandestine 'abortaria': their very emergence disclosed that, without change in the law, Soviet hosptials no longer performed abortion at the simple request of the pregnant woman. Finally, a draft law prohibiting abortion was published and offered for public discussion. Numerous objections were raised, mainly based on intolerable dwelling conditions. Nevertheless, the law of June 27, 1936, abolished the freedom of abortion which had been considered one of the highest achievements of Communism by many pro-Communists.

Repealing the notorious law of November 20, 1920, the new law prohibited abortion in all cases except where there was danger to life or health of the pregnant woman or danger of hereditary transmission of serious sickness. As in the former law, only medical men were permitted to perform the operation. Pressure exerted on a woman to induce her into abortion was declared a crime punishable by two years in prison. To make more childbearing possible, the law promised a large extension of the network of maternity hospitals, day nurseries, and kindergartens. Maternity grants were increased, and special allowances were promised to mothers of six or more children.[7]

4. The peculiar parent–child relationship which had obtained under the Communist Experiment, and which granted superiority to the children, was reversed to one which is considered normal in the world; once more, children have to recognize the authority of their parents. Obviously, the change could not be effected through legal enactment, and the method of persuasion through propaganda was used exactly in the same manner as it

was used to stabilize marriage. Statements like these could be found almost daily on the pages of the Soviet papers, beginning with the spring of 1935:

> Young people should respect their elders, especially their parents . . . The respect and care of parents is an essential part of the Comsomol morals . . . One must respect and love his parents, even if they are old-fashioned and do not like the Comsomol.[8]

In 1939, the official journal of the Union Prosecutor declared:

> Sound moral ideas must be inculcated into the minds of young persons. They must know that lack of care for their parents is found only among savages and that in every civilized society such conduct is considered dishonest and base.[9]

To corroborate these ideas, the journal cited the laws of Solon and Xenophon's works.

The method of positive demonstration was also used, and Stalin himself found it necessary to set the example. In October, 1935, he paid a visit to his old mother living in Tiflis,[10] and in the detailed accounts of his visit signs of love and respect to the old lady by the leader of the World Proletariat were emphasized. A high degree of intimacy in family relations was displayed through the reproduction of such questions as: how did Stalin's children like the jam made for them by their grandmother. Another day Stalin appeared in one of Moscow's gardens with his children, something he had never done previously. Up to that time, the majority of Soviet citizens did not even know that Stalin had any children.

Gradually, the unlimited freedom granted to young people under the Communist Experiment was curbed. One of the most conspicuous items in the process has been the decree of July 15, 1943, excluding children below the age of sixteen from evening performances in theaters and movies.

To strengthen parental authority, an indirect method has been used in the new inheritance law of March 20, 1945. While previous laws limited possible heirs to direct or adopted descendants, consorts, and needy dependants, the new law broadens this list to include parents, brothers, sisters, and public organizations. Although according to the new law the testator may not deprive his minor children or jobless heirs of their rightful portion, its impact on the family is clear: the greater the freedom to dispose of one's estate, the greater is the authority of the head of the family relating to presumptive heirs.

III

Destruction, then reconstruction; that was the pattern of the activity of the Communist rulers regarding the family. What happened to the second pillar of society, the school? [. . .]

The necessity to stop the school experiment was recognized by the Communist leaders when they saw that the program of industrialization could no longer be pushed forward because of the lack of adequately trained young specialists or even generally educated persons. Already in 1931 and 1932, partial reforms were tried. A resolution of the Central Committee of the Communist Party of September 5, 1931, warned the professors and teachers against the survival of pre-Revolutionary educational methods, and also against the indiscriminate application of the so-called 'progressive' methods. The resolution acknowledged that the Soviet school did not give its graduates sufficient preparation for further study. To meet the demands of the Communist leaders, the Commissariat of Education introduced a new curriculum: history as a special subject reappeared; teaching of the 'social sciences', i.e., the Marxist doctrine was curtailed, as was also the compulsory 'social activity' of the pupils. The schools were separated from production and steered towards their natural function, that of teaching. As usual, a number of persons who had been active in the educational system prior to this reform were declared to be subversive deviators from the Party line and were treated accordingly. The center of the pedagogical thought of the previous period, the Institute of Marxist Pedagogy, was disbanded.

On August 25, 1932, the movement was continued by another resolution of the Central Committee. Some more items of 'progressive education' were abolished. The class period was restored in its dignity as the basic unit of teaching. Principals were ordered to elaborate definite schedules and insist on their application. Teachers were ordered to teach their subjects systematically. These were very natural demands indeed. But does not the necessity of emphasizing them say more than volumes about the state of the schools before their formulation?

Important changes took place also in institutions of higher learning. The decree of September 19, 1932, restored the authority of the professors; they were to give the marks to the stduents, not the Communist cells. Furthermore, it was ordered that only those sufficiently prepared and who had passed the entrance examinations were to be registered as students; that lectures were to be given regularly and according to schedule; that such novelties as the 'brigade method' in examinations be abolished;[11] that theses be written by candidates for degrees; that students be relieved from too much social activity; that when selecting young men to be trained for professorial positions, academic achievements, and no longer zeal in Communist propaganda be the decisive factor. These were sweeping changes indeed, but still in the framework of the Great Experiment. The methods of teaching were improved, but what the student was to be taught still continued to be determined by the Communist doctrine. That no departure from fundamentals was envisaged may be derived from the fact that the resolution of 1931 emphasized the importance of purely Communist education in schools and enjoined the local Party committees to supervise the school system closely, especially the teaching of social sciences. The general spirit of the time was not yet favorable to drastic change.

In 1933, the People's Commissar for Education acknowledged that the 'leftist deviation' in school had been ingrained more deeply in the system of education than first assumed. He enjoined the educators to eliminate the anti-Leninist idea that the school was withering away together with the State.[12] But under the general conditions of The Great Retreat, the gigantic disorder and the unspeakable inefficiency of the school system could no longer be tolerated. A program of drastic reforms was elaborated and then actualized, often with substantial additions, the necessity of which appeared in the course of the cure to which the school system was submitted.

IV

[. . .] To bring back order, measures initiated in 1931 and 1932 were reinforced and expanded. In the fall of 1934, 'stabilized teaching plans and programs' were imposed on elementary and secondary schools, stating how many hours a week should be spent in each class for each subject and what particular topics should be taught. In January, 1935, new rules on pupils' self-government were issued. Self-government was entirely abolished in the four lower grades. Where it remained its purpose was defined as that of helping the teachers to raise the level of school work and discipline. In institutions for higher learning the Young Communist organizations, whose activity had made real study impossible, were prohibited from interfering with the orders of the administration and given the task of improving the conditions of study. In May, 1935, yearly examinations were revived, and the passing from one grade to another was made dependent on success at these examinations. Early in the twentieth century, first the reduction in the number of such examinations and then their complete abolition had been hailed in Russia as a significant victory of progressive ideas in education. Thus, in this respect, the new Soviet school order went back to the late nineteenth century.

The most conspicuous item, however, was the restoration of the uniform, for boys and girls alike, both in elementary and secondary schools. This was even more than returning to 'the good old days', since in Imperial Russia uniforms were unknown on the elementary level.

How responsive the school authorities were to this aspect of the retreat may be seen from the following facts. In September, 1935, the journal of the Commissariat of Education gave a preview of the uniform to be introduced at some later date. Immediately people began discussing – not whether uniforms were desirable – but whether 'electric blue', chosen for the girls in secondary schools, would be becoming; some people thought that this would do very well for girls with rosy cheeks but would not be suitable at all for the pale ones. A few days later it was learned that in many places the local authorities had introduced uniforms of their own invention, without waiting for the final order. The center rebuked the overzealous principals and explained that uniforms could be introduced only gradually. In 1944, in relation to girls, the reform was accentuated: pigtails became the officially recommended style of hair dressing.[13]

It was more difficult, however, to restore discipline. 'In accordance with Stalin's personal desire', experienced Communist leaders were sent to the schools of the great cities where discipline was lowest. They were to instill into the minds of the pupils that they had to be polite and respect the authority of the teachers.[14] The teachers were ordered to supervise the conduct of the pupils and help them get rid of such habits as keeping their hats on in class, or jamming the principal into a corner. Budenny, then a great man, was asked to help. In a letter published in December, 1935, he advised the pupils to be quiet in class, pay attention to their teachers, and prepare their home work carefully: they were to spend their leisure time on 'physical culture', advice becoming a military leader. Only a few years earlier, however, he would have added some advice about studying the Communist doctrine. It was symptomatic that he did not.

All these measures met with partial success only. This is beyond question since in October, 1943, the Commissar of Education said: 'Much remains to be done as to discipline. The slightest sign of rudeness, or disrespect towards elders must be dealt with severely. There is still some reluctance to accept a strong attitude towards laziness and hooliganism'.[15] To uproot disorder, a set of 'Rules of Conduct' for the pupils of elementary and secondary schools was elaborated, containing such admonitions as to study well, obey the principals and the teachers, be respectful regarding them and their parents and all old persons in general, and to respect the honor of the class and the school. In some schools these rules were dictated to the pupils in class, and they were ordered to learn them by heart. About the same time, new rules for the University students were issued defining their duties and the order of study.[16]

In the course of the war, an additional step was taken towards the restoration of the pre-Revolutionary school order. This was the abandonment of coeducation, introduced at the beginning of the Revolution and highly praised at that time as one of the most significant steps leading away from bourgeois society, where the girls are allegedly trained to become housekeepers or mistresses of men 'owning' them. The movement away from coeducation started in Moscow in 1942–3, and in the fall of 1943 became general. Articles published at about that time explained that experience with coeducation had shown that there were physiological and psychological reasons against it, namely, the different mental and physical development of boys and girls. Another object was based on the inevitable division of labor between men and women. A boy must be prepared for service in the Red Army, but a girl is essentially a future mother and must know how to look after her children and bring them up. In the course of the academic year 1944–5, different programs of study for boys and girls were introduced, the boys specializing in technical subjects, while the girls were to be trained in pedagogy, handicrafts, domestic science, personal hygiene, and the care of children.[17]

An equally important feature of the reform program consisted in the abandonment of 'political education'. This was probably one of the greatest sacrifices made by the Communist leaders in the course of momentous years 1934–9, when the nation was being prepared for the inevitable war. Very courageously, the leaders recognized the necessity of the step and acted accordingly. The curtailment of political education in elementary and secondary schools was effected through the resolutions of the Central Committee of the Communist Party of April 22 and 24, 1934. Political education was altogether abolished in the seven lower grades of the school. One hour a week was left in the eighth and ninth grades, and two hours in the tenth grade. [. . .]

V

The curve relating to school policy has been strikingly similar to that regarding the family: after long years of destruction and experimentation, feverish efforts were made to restore the situation which existed at the outbreak of the Revolution or even earlier. What happened to the Church, the third pillar of society? Was it not possible to eliminate it entirely?

Very definitely the Communist leaders thought that this was possible and acted accordingly. Throughout the Communist Experiment and well into the period of The Great Retreat, they applied all the measures they could imagine to destroy the Church. [. . .]

It is almost inconceivable that persecution systematically conducted for long years and using all possible approaches to the positions of the enemy was not crowned by complete success. And still this happened: religion and the churches survived. In 1937, it was established that at least half of the adult population had preserved their faith.[18] It was also established that the attack on religion did not liberate the young people from 'religious prejudice' and transform them into 'convinced and consistent atheists', recognizing nothing but the Marxist doctrine in its official interpretation. On the contrary, the Communists were surprised to learn that those young people who allegedly were converted to atheism were more contaminated by crude superstition and magic beliefs than the believers. Finally, they had to recognize that the persecution of religion bred hostility in large masses of the people towards the Soviet regime.[19] This unpleasant revelation struck them more than once. Up to the late 'thirties, every time they became aware of growing animosity, on the basis of religious persecution, they temporarily mitigated the pressure and prepared a new and, they thought, better plan for the destruction of the enemy. They could do so as long as the situation did not involve a direct threat to their power over Russia. But this time, i.e., in the late 'thirties, was threatened. Under such circumstances continuation of the antireligious policy would have exposed the government to a grave danger. Would it not be possible that, in the struggle to come, a large section of the population, namely those embittered by religious persecution, might remain neutral, perhaps even reach the conclusion that German victory would be a lesser evil compared with continuing religious persecution, and would act accordingly?

This danger loomed the greater since, planning to invade Russia, Hitler tried to find weak points in the Russian structure and assumed that the hostility of religious-minded people to an atheist government could be of great help. Therefore, an exceedingly benevolent attitude was displayed by him towards the Russian Orthodox Church, in marked contrast to his intransigent attitude towards the Roman Catholics and the Protestants. Money was given for the erection of a Russian Orthodox Cathedral in Berlin, and appropriation was made for the repair of nineteen Orthodox churches in Germany. This was merely a symptom, but a stymptom pointing to an extremely dangerous situation.

VI

[. .] On the very day of the outbreak of the war, Acting Patriarch Sergius issued a pastoral letter in which he enjoined the believers to take full part in the patriotic effort. The Church, he declared, always was one with the Nation in periods of crisis and would be the same this time. Neutrality, he said, was insufficient; active participation was mandatory. Foreseeing events in western Russia, he condemned in advance any cooperation with the enemy. This letter was given great publicity. In all the churches of the country special services were held with prayers for victory to the Russian Army. These prayers were repeated very frequently during the months of the war. When news about Polycarp's secession reached Moscow, the Acting Patriarch issued a new pastoral letter and put Polycarp on trial by proxy.

The Soviet government recognized the significance of the patriotic attitude of the Church. Through the agency of the Godless Union it declared: 'If the servants of the Church honestly call upon the believers to fight against Fascism, we must not belittle this fact'. Three months after the outbreak of the war the publication of antireligious journals was discontinued, officially, because of paper shortage. Antireligious museums were closed. Heavy taxes on the churches were substantially reduced. When, in December, 1941, the first Russian offensive started liberating several provinces, the Soviet press expressed indigation about the acts of antireligious vandalism committed by the Germans, namely, the destruction or desecration of churches and sacred objects. Both in 1942 and 1943, the severe curfew prevailing in Moscow was lifted for Easter night.[20] In November, 1942, Metropolitan Nicholas of Kiev was appointed to the governmental commission for investigation of 'crimes committed by the German Fascist invaders.'[21] Never, since 1922, had any clergyman been appointed to any official body.

About the same time a book appeared in Moscow entitled *Truth About Religion in Russia*. In any country but Russia the publication of a similar book would not have astonished anybody. But in contemporary Russia this was a sensation. Had not the rulers of Russia prohibited reprinting the Bible and importing it from foreign countries? And now a beautifully printed and copiously illustrated book on religion appeared, comprising contributions of the highest dignitaries of the Russian Orthodox Church, as well as a number of priests and laymen belonging partly to the cultural *élite* and partly to the rank and file believers. There is reason to believe that the book was printed on the presses of the Militant Godless Union. Together with the already mentioned fact that the Union was ordered to protect religion against illegal interference on the part of local authorities, this was the most challenging and ironical feature of the religious phase of The Great Retreat.

On the occasion of the twenty-fifth anniversary of the October Revolution, Acting Patriarch Sergius 'cordially congratulated Stalin, the God-given leader of the military and cultural forces of the nation'. The next year, congratulations came on the part of Metroplitan Nicholas of Kiev. In the meantime, Stalin used different opportunities to express his gratitude to priests for their outstanding help to the Red Army.[22]

The improvement of the State–Church relationship reached its climax when on September 5, 1943,

> Stalin received Acting Patriarch Sergius, Metropolitan Alexei of Leningrad, and Metropolitan Nicholas of Kiev. During the reception Metropolitan Sergius informed Stalin that leading circles of the Orthodox Church intended to hold a Council of bishops in the very near future and elect a Patriarch. The head of the government expressed his sympathy with the decision and said that the government would not hinder this in any way.[23]

A few days later, nineteen Russian Orthodox bishops convened in Moscow and unanimously elected Sergius Patriarch of Moscow and All Russia. On September 12, he was officially installed. Before separating, the

Council addressed a message to the Soviet government expressing the Church's gratitude for the government's friendly attitude, and another message to all the Church members once more severely condemning all those who would support Hitler and his armies.[24]

Then the Archbishop of York of the Church of England arrived in Moscow to visit the hierarchy of the Russian Orthodox Church, and to invite a Russian Church delegation to come to England.[25] A few years earlier, an attempt of Russian Church dignitaries to have any relations with foreign churchmen would have been condemned almost as an act of treason!

About the same time – more precisely, on October 9, 1943, an order was issued creating a Council for Russian Orthodox Affairs to establish liaison between the Soviet government and the Patriarch of Moscow. On June 30, 1944, another Council was established to conduct the State's relations with the other religious groups represented among the Russian population.

The creation of these councils discloses the emergence of an entirely new situation, namely, that of friendly co-operation between the State and religious bodies, especially the Russian Orthodox Church. This statement may be substantiated by passing in review the types of activity by means of which the Church has helped the nation and the government in the struggle against the invader and then noting the rewards which it has received from the government.

First of all, by constant prayers for victory, the Church sustained and strengthened the morale of the people. Moreover, Sergius wrote several messages to the pastors and churchgoers, calling on them to increase their efforts to aid the Army in the fight against the invader.

Secondly, the Church induced the flock to collect money for direct help to the war effort. A few days before the election, Sergius announced that the Church had contributed more than eight million rubles for the building of the Dmitri Donskoy tank column, and that the priests and laity had also donated millions of rubles for aircraft squadrons and the relief of wounded and orphans.[26]

Thirdly, the Patriarch used the authority of the Church to prohibit collaboration with Hitler in German-occupied provinces. On many occasions he solemnly condemned those bishops and priests who had accepted Hitler's lie that his invasion was a crusade and expressed their admiration for his deeds.

Fourthly, the Patriarch helped stir up the resistance to the Germans in territories which were not Russian, but where the influence of Russia was strong. In an Easter message 'to all Christians of Yugoslavia, Czechslovakia, Greece, and others of the Orthodox faith languishing in Fascist captivity', he said:

> Our Orthodox Church is marching side by side with the people. In all churches of the Soviet Union prayers are offered for victory and

collections are made for needs created by the war. Let the lamp of Orthodoxy burn still more brightly before you. The conscience of every sincere Slav and Greek dictates that he shall seek every way to evade working for Germany. May God strengthen our fraternal union.[27]

In this case Sergius could not but use the radio, controlled by the government. This shows that the government appreciated the support of the Church. A similar situation developed at the All-Slavic Congress which was held in Moscow in the summer of 1943. Metropolitan Nicholas was present, accompanied by six bishops. He gave an address extolling the duty of every Christian to fight the Fascists. Since he could not have appeared without the permission of the government, it is obvious that the latter was eager to use the authority of the Russian Church among the peoples of the Balkan and the Danubian basin. [. . .]

VII

The complicated processes studied in this chapter may be summarized as follows:

1. In the course of the Communist Experiment, great efforts were displayed by the Communists to destroy those pillars of society which are the family, the Church, and the school. The three pillars were actually shaken. Quite a few people used, or more exactly abused the liberty of divorce and abortion; quite a few young persons enjoyed freedom from parental authority. The churches lost approximately half of their flock and had to live in poverty, on the margin of official society. The school ceased to transmit to the younger generation the culture tradition accumulated in the course of centuries.

    But, on the one hand, it appeared that the achievements were only partial and could not be made complete. Too many people proved immune against the propaganda of new family relations and atheism. On the other hand, even the partial successes were more than balanced by detrimental effects unforeseen by the promoters of the Experiment.

2. The fluctuations of the policy aiming at the shaking of the three pillars of society have been almost similar regarding the family and education, but entirely different as to religion. Relating to the family and the school, there was for many years consistent accentuation of pressures, whereas with respect to religion, periods of high pressure have alternated with periods of relative relaxation.

3. Inevitably, the Communists came to the conclusion that the pillars of society shaken by them in the course of the Communist Experiment had to be re-enforced. They reversed their policy relating to [the]

school in 1931, the family in 1934, and the Church in 1939. The trend following these reversals forms one of the most conspicuous features of The Great Retreat.

4. When the necessity for reconstruction became clear to the Communists, they were unable to create new patterns, but directed society towards the revival of pre-Revolutionary institutions. To begin with, this restoration was only partial, but in the course of the war became wholesale. Most conspicuous have been the restoration of fees and the abolition of coeducation in schools, the factual abolition of divorce, and the restoration of the Patriarchate and religious education.

5. Viewed as a whole, the measures composing The Great Retreat in the realm studied in this chapter are comparable with the 'return to normalcy' carried out in the Western world after the First World War: in both cases, it was taken for granted that the normal coincided with that which had existed before the disturbance – war in one case, revolution in the other. It may be assumed that the majority of the Soviet citizens applauded the return of the 'good old times' as whole-heartedly as the Western 'bourgeois' approved the corresponding acts of the governments. The main reason for the hostility of large groups towards the government thus disappeared, and a sacred union against the aggressor could materialize.

Notes

1 *Izvestiia*, July 7, 1935.
2 *Izvestiia*, July 7, 1937; *Krasnaia gazeta*, Nov. 4, 1934.
3 New York *Times*, Nov. 18, 1936.
4 *Izvestiia*, February 12, 1937.
5 New York *Times*, July 11, 1944.
6 *Izvestiia*, June 5, 1935.
7 The second antidivorce law (1944) substantially increased the advantages granted to mothers of numerous children. Honorary titles were granted to mothers of seven or more children.
8 *Komsomolskaia pravda*, June 7 and September 29, 1935; *Pravda*, August 4, 1935.
9 *Sovetskaia iustitsia*, 1939, No. 4.
10 *Izvestiia*, Oct. 23, 1935.
11 In reality, this was a kind of collective examination: questions were offered to a group of students, and a collective reply was completed by them. Naturally, at least one good student was introduced into each group, and his knowledge covered the ignorance of the group.
12 From a speech delivered by the Commissar of Public Education, Bubnov, April 21, 1933.
13 *Izvestiia*, Jan. 8, 1944.
14 *Pravda*, Oct. 30, 1935.

15 New York *Times*, Oct. 17, 1943.
16 *Izvestiia*, Apr. 7, Aug. 10, Dec. 1, 1943.
17 *Isvestiia*, Aug. 8 and 10, 1943; Jan. 8, 1944. On June 21, 1944, all the reforms
    relating to the school order were consolidated in a decree 'On measures aiming
    at the improvement of education in schools.' However, in 1945 the government
    had to emphasize that pupils not having acquired the art of faultless spelling
    could not graduate from schools (*Komsomolskaia pravda* Apr. 29, 1945).
    Teachers who displayed leniency in checking mistakes were severely scolded
    (*Uchitelskaia gazeta*, May 26 and June 2, 1945).
18 N. S. Timasheff, *Religion in Soviet Russia* (New York, 1942), p. 65.
19 Timasheff, *Religion*, p. 97.
20 Timasheff, *Religion*, pp. 136ff. See also New York *Times*, April 25 and 26,
    1943, and April 17, 1944.
21 New York *Times*, Nov. 5, 1942.
22 *Izvestiia*, Nov. 10 and Dec. 29, 1942; Nov. 12, 1943.
23 *Izvestiia*, Sept. 5, 1943.
24 *Izvestiia*, Sept. 12, 1943.
25 The Archbishop's visit to Moscow and his statements relating to it have been
    reported in the New York *Times*, Sept. 15, 19, 23 and 24, Oct. 11, 1943, and
    Apr. 27, 1944.
26 New York *Times*, Sept. 12, 1943.
27 *Soviet War News* (published in London), Apr. 27, 1943.

Reading 14 *New protagonists*

V. S. DUNHAM

Road to life

I stand for that image of a revolutionary for whom the private is
nothing in comparison with the public.[1]

So said a canonized hero of the revolutionary epoch, commemorating an
entire ideology. Revolutionary literature steered the young toward the right
Road to Life.[2] Truth was posited as social truth alone.

In the twenties and thirties, writers who shared the regime's views
conceived man as a receptacle for external, social impulses. Society was
an infinitely more valuable good than man. Collectivism was presented to
the young as the highest value. All behavior was examined from the
standpoint of economic and class environment. Despite the dogmatic
aspect of these views, room was left for exploration. For instance, the
relationship between private and public life was, indeed, considered. But
though the frontier between the spheres was extensively commented on and
even romanticized, the autonomy of the private, of the personal, was
resolutely denied. The public was set up to rule over the private, whose

subordination was justified by a streamlined, if simplistic, view of human nature. Man was the result of social impulses.

This environmental absolutism helped to sort, diagnose, and cure the problems of youth. It also led to the useful notion of cultural lag, and provided a weapon against antisocial manifestations by calling them residual byproducts of the prerevolutionary past. They were called 'residues' or 'birthmarks'. All personal deviations from approved social norms, such as homicide or independent thought, could be seen as just such vestiges. In short, the environment in its economic and class aspects determined all problems. It was made to account for all results, the bad as well as the good.

'The family plus environment is responsible'. In the thirties this casual sequence established itself firmly, and many writers illustrated it with dogged devotion. For example, young criminals in fiction were occasionally permitted a psychological twist, or tragic determinism. Here is one confessing:

> 'I am a thief! . . . I am a recidivist, do you hear? I have been sentenced innumerable times. It's high time they shot me' . . . He knew that his last loneliness would start right away . . . and that he would pay for his dog's life and for his death . . . for all his humiliations and for his hunger and for all the prisons and for his escapes and for his father who was a scoundrel and for his mother who was a whore, for everything, properly and fully.[3]

A scoundrel for a father and a whore for a mother; it went a long way to explain the criminal inclination of their child.

The result of impulses from without, received more or less passively, was not necessarily crime; it might be its opposite. The more common theme, in fact, was the Road to Life of the militant party activist whose heroism was motivated by revulsion against a rotten childhood.

One such hero belongs to the leather-jacket era. His jacket conceals a gun. Tense and devout, he serves in the purist ranks of the secret police. Born in degradation as a calamitous surprise to a prostitute, he spends his childhood in proximity to his mother's trade. The initial trauma is a constant ingredient in his dedication to the party. Because of his rigidity, in the end he can accept neither his own sin, which is for him the loss of sexual virginity, nor the party's sin. He sees this in the advent of the NEP, the great economic compromise of the twenties, a similar loss of virginity. He commits suicide. The genetic trauma, as it were, forces him to do so: fatalism overcomes him, anchored in the private nightmare of his childhood. His public and private purism is an attempt to compensate and atone. The key to this man, open and obvious, lies in his memories:

> Lidov came, not Zavalishin. After him others. At first names, then persons, then a series of them. The dark ones. The blonde ones. And

the one with warts. The one who came yesterday gnashed his teeth. And next door in a dark room . . . slept little white Kolya under a quilt on top of a chest of drawers . . . They shuffled about, struggled, gulped, groaned. Shallow laughter. A sigh. A belch. Silence. He asked. Mother sobbed. Her cheeks under tears puffed up like gingerbread and he understood: keep your mouth shut. It might be that he got used to it all. But feverishly he pitied mama. He shivered under his quilt because of a greedy compassion. During the day mama would go to buy sausage in the tavern. Then he kissed the hollow in her bed, the imprint of her body.[4]

In many novels human steel was forged out of the raw material of abandoned and orphaned children, the civil war victims. They were legion. There were those who were rehabilitated by the new mother: Mother Revolution. Lack of family was as formative a mold as the wrong family.

I know neither mother nor father. I was a waif.[5] A beggar, I slept under fences. I starved and I had no shelter. It was a dog's life. Nothing like yours, you sissies and mamma's boys. But then came Soviet power. And Red Army men picked me up. As a whole detachment, they adopted me. They gave me shoes, gave me clothes, and taught me how to read. But the most important thing, they gave me a human understanding. Through them I have become a bolshevik and I'll remain one till my death. I know what the struggle is all about: it is for us, for us paupers, for the power of the workers.[6]

Out of the condemnation of the family and of the 'unfamily', out of the final funeral of the old world there were born the revolutionary heroes, the promethean men, the canonized champions of the Vita Nuova. They were to be revered for a long time. Determinism notwithstanding, they articulated the grandeur of their own power as did one famous hero of the turbulent early twenties. Fearless and selfless, he leads a doomed guerilla detachment. While lost with his small unit in the wilderness of Siberia, he meditates on his faith in social change.

And Levinson was agitated because the deepest and most important matters preoccupied him. In the overcoming of all this misery and poverty lay the basic meaning of his own life. There would be no Levinson, but some other person, if there did not burn in him a desire, not comparable with any other need, for a new, fine, strong, generous human being. But how could one even talk of a new, generous human being while uncountable millions were forced to live such a primitive and pitiful, such an unspeakably shabby life? . . . And he tried to remember himself in childhood, in early youth. But this was difficult for him. The experiences of recent years, when he had become known to everyone as Levinson who was the leader, were too deeply and solidly ingrained and had become too important to him.

A true hero such as this was predetermined by circumstance, environment, and the ethos of the revolution. Much as there was for a man in the vanguard to think about, he steered clear of introspection most of the time. Yet:

> The only thing he managed to remember was an old family photograph with a puny Jewish boy on it with large naive eyes and wearing a black jacket. He was staring with a surprising, unchildish determination at that spot from where, he was told at the time, a beautiful little bird was supposed to fly out. But the bird did not fly out at all. And he remembered now that he almost burst into tears with disappointment. He had to have many more such disappointments before he became finally convinced that 'that's not the way things ever turn out!' And when he had become really convinced of it, he understood what incalculable harm was inflicted on people by those little birds which were supposed to fly out of somewhere and which many people await all their lives in vain. No, he had no need of them any longer. He had crushed in himself mercilessly this inactive, sweet longing for them. He had crushed everything in himself that he had inherited from those damaged generations, raised on false tales about beautiful little birds! 'To perceive everything the way it is in order to change that which is and to bring about that which ought to be' – this is the most simple and the most taxing wisdom at which Levinson had arrived . . . he felt the swell of extraordinary strength which raised him to unreachable heights and from this towering, earthly, human height he conquered his weaknesses, his own weak body.[7]

Faith in the one and only Road saw at the beckoning end of it the glory of a new and just society. This faith provided the certainty with which the line of demarcation was laid between the private and public spheres. If the two coexisted, they did so in abrasive hostility. The public, much like St. George, kept fervently slaying the private dragon. The model marcher was expected to cleanse himself of personal needs before stepping onto the Road. This was the orthodox mood, which prevailed well into the thirties. And such was the message of one novel of that period which stands out as a canonical version of the bolshevik ethos. It stands out as the towering document of the whole thirties period. The author immortalized himself and the epoch of heroic valor in this semiautobiographical account entitled *The Tempering of Steel* (1934). He glorified the victory of the public over the private so well that hardly any other hero had the impact of his Korchagin.

The novel, as the title implies, deals with a man of steel, an ideal communist. His success has to do with one fact. Unlike his predecessors of the chaotic twenties, he is a man without psychological complexities. A cruel and humiliating prerevolutionary childhood gives him all the hatred necessary for a dedicated service to the revolution. As an adolescent, he goes off to take part in the civil war. The civil war leaves him with a cracked skull and a severely damaged spine, but his spirit is intact. A steellike resilience helps him to recover. At seventeen he becomes a tested communist. In the end, his struggle with death equals his devotion to the cause.

He insisted on unrelaxing effort, and craved the most dangerous assignments either in the Red army or among civilian reconstruction workers. His will to remain in the fighting ranks caused him a spectacular struggle with adversity. Before he was thirty he became paralyzed and lost his sight. And yet this living corpse stayed active. With superhuman discipline, always conscious that self-pity would destroy him, he overcame his own tragedy. He forced himself to become a student of a Red university by correspondence. Later he gathered all his inner resources to become a writer. So he continued to be a paragon of communist service. In his time such giving precluded any kind of taking. Self-sacrificial service to the collective makes vivid the comparison between the kind of heroism required in his era and that of the postwar period. His sacrifice is instructive not so much because he served the collective well but because he lived according to the dominant virtue of his time. The highest then was not wanting anything in return. Sacrifice became its own antithesis by turning into total satisfaction. Such a public man could take nothing in recompense, nothing at any rate resembling an ordinary material or status reward. The building of a new society was the gift he gave and the gift he received, the very same gift.

Not only can such a man afford no 'private' life; it is incomprehensible to him. In his native town, there waits for him a long-suffering, understanding, truly proletarian mother. When, still very young, he returns there briefly, she tactfully puts a question to him. Is he in such a hurry to go back to Kiev because, perhaps, he has found a sweetheart there?

'I only see you, when you get hurt', his mother was saying in a gentle voice, packing into a clean bag her son's poor belongings . . . 'Mother, I swore to myself that I wouldn't have anything to do with girls until we finish off the bourgeois in the whole world. You say it's too long too wait? No, mother dear, the bourgeois cannot hold out for long. There shall be only one republic for all people. And we shall send you – all you hardworking oldsters – to Italy. There is such a warm country on the sea. Mother, there never is any winter there. We shall settle you in bourgeois palaces and you will stretch your poor old bones in the warm sun. And we, we will take off for America to finish off the bourgeoisie there'.[8]

As he had promised his mother, he does not permit himself to fall in love. He holds back, although the opportunities are numerous and women fall in love with him. When he does get married, the arrangement is ideological. Once more, it rests on his givingness. In the early stage of his incurable illness, he meets a girl raised in a stifling lower-middleclass family. She is mousy, oppressed, ideologically 'unawakened'. He transforms her. Korchagin could not very well have married his equal. That would have been too easy. As husband, he considers it his primary duty to start his backward companion on the Road. Only a short time later, prostrate with disease, he offers his wife a divorce, so as not to be a burden to her. Increasingly she has less and less time for him. For she is now strenuously training to become a party member. But, of course, she remains loyal. On his part, it would not occur to him to complain of his loneliness. He takes pride in his wife's new independence. It does not matter to him that she still works as a dishwasher. And the day when this humble woman at last gains admission to the party is a day of greater happiness to him than to her.

There was nothing unclear about the monolithic moral face of those early models. They were, to say the least, one-dimensional. They lived for the Public Purpose. And they themselves lacked differentiation, as myths do. In their case it was the grand myth of the implementation of the revolution. Dying, blind and paralyzed, Korchagin writes:

> I still believe that I shall return into the ranks and that in the attacking columns there also will be my bayonet. I cannot not believe. I have no right to. For ten years the party and the komsomol educated me in the art of resistance and the words of our leader were meant for me.: 'There are no fortifications that the bolsheviks cannot take'. [p. 161].

These men were totally absorbed in fulfilling their faith. It ordained a revulsion against private values as a matter of belief, not celebration. Their attempt to understand themselves was a search without any private intent, largely even without individual psychological awareness. They made their self-analysis – as they did everything else – under the aspect of service to the collective.

Certain articles of faith became even more poignant when enacted with the special revolutionary verve of the new woman, the liberated revolutionary woman. The weight of the patriarchal, autocratic, sex-discriminating tradition in Russia had pressed especially harshly on women. Curiously, the revolution in its own way set up a new disparity between the destiny of revolutionary men and women. It promised woman what she did not have before: equality. But, in return, it set a large and discriminatory 'feminine' price for the promise. It took the family away from the awakened woman, or it tried to do so.

We find one model heroine of days gone by in a famous novel, *Cement*. One of its main themes is the development of the new proletarian woman. The heroine's husband is fighting in the civil war. Meanwhile, the heroine – Dasha Chumalova – learns from bloody experience all the viciousness of the old forms of life. She grows to be a 'conscious' bolshevik. She discovers the new revolutionary morality. In the end she becomes its embodiment.

The husband is a valiant Red soldier. On his return from the front, he proves an equally valiant reconstruction worker. He is a man of energy, willpower, and faith. Yet marital conflict becomes inevitable because he craves for a home and a family. In his absence Dasha has changed a great deal. He watches with apprehension her face 'tired but tense and stern as though she were clenching her teeth'. With mounting irritation, he challenges her:

> 'Tell me, Dasha, how should I take all this? I have been in the army. It was tough. I had no respite and not one minute to think about myself. And now I have come home, to my own house, and for the first time I feel wretched. I don't sleep at night, waiting for you. All this time you haven't slept at home. And I don't know where you are; it's as if I have been pushed into a hole to sit with mice and frogs. We haven't been together for three years'.[9]

Her reply is forthright enough. The change in her signifies a drastic departure from his views. And she is not about to regret the loss of her domestic instinct. Her reply is a clear summary of what the new Soviet woman rejects after the revolution:

> 'Do you want pretty flowers to curl on the windowsills and a bed piled with down pillows? No, Gleb, in the winter I live in an unheated room . . . and I eat in the communal kitchen. You see, I am a free Soviet citizen' [p. 46].

As for him, apart from his atavistic longing for flowers on the windowsill, he considers his wife not so much a free Soviet citizen as his property. When she tells him that in the trying years of their separation, she had known other men, he turns 'blind with rage' and calls her a 'dirty bitch' who has 'laid in the ditch with a lot of tramps'. Controlling herself, she replies with a mixture of sententiousness and hope in the educative power of the revolution:

> 'Don't you see, you can't yet listen to me properly. You are a communist. But you are still an animal. And you need a woman as a slave, a slave to go to bed with. You are a good soldier. But you are a bad communist' [p. 117].

Tainted with the past, this man also feels that it is a mother's duty to care for her child. Dasha's awakening, however, leads her to reject the family and let the state raise her child. When he finds out that Dasha has placed their little girl in a children's home, his first impulse is to retrieve her at once. The liberated woman threatens that he can do it only if he commits himself to caring for the child. Times are hard. Conditions in the children's home are nothing short of appalling. In bright daylight, the father sees the fledglings of the State claw each other for a morsel of food.

'All of them, those poor little creatures, will starve to death, Dashka.
You ought all to be shot for the jobs you are doing'.

Terrified, he wants to know if their own daughter is struggling for survival in the same way. Of all the quarrels between this man and woman, both pressed in different ways against the wall by the revolution, this one is the most revealing:

'And why is Nurka [the child] to be more favored than the others? She too has suffered. But if it weren't for us women, lice and disease would have devoured the children and starvation would have wiped them out'.
'Are you trying to tell me that you have saved Nurka, you and the other noisy women, by doing all this?'
'Yes, comrade Gleb. Exactly. Just like that' [p. 58].

The child dies, in that children's home: not only from malnutrition and disease, but from lack of maternal love. In a scene much discussed from the mid twenties on, the dying child implores the mother:

'I want to be with you – so that you never go away again and so that you should be close – and grapes – I want you and grapes' [p. 313].

True, Dasha weeps, flings herself down on mother earth, and tears it with her nails. Yet she personifies the new morality by making herself free. She dispenses with her child, domesticity, her husband for the sake of her public duty and her part in the making of the new life. She breaks up her marriage because she cannot compromise with a man who does not fully appreciate the formidable and costly equality of the new Soviet woman.

Remembering these famous novels of prewar periods helps to establish a perspective. They were imbued with the bolshevik spirit, and the values of which they spoke were anti-individualistic and 'antifamily'. This was not a comfortable code. With it went a zest for a barren home life, even a complete denial of it. In those faraway days, the style of life of the avant-garde meant more than Spartan sobriety. It was not sober; it was intoxicated by its own harshness. Like revolutionary fervor, however, flamboyant romanticism does not last. The classical heroes and heroines disappeared: not because of attrition alone, nor because at some point the regime had no more use for them. It was rather because they were an oversimplification in the first place. As literary images, they symbolized ideological propositions and not psychological complexities. In the decline of revolutionary heroes, one can see the revenge of human nature on extreme didacticism.

But what happened next? How did the regime handle this decline? The handling turned out to be careful and expedient. The successful early heroes were never openly disavowed, for they were few and precious. Instead, they were relegated to history and their flamboyant romanticism was transformed into a sacred monument. So they were made both obsolete and ineffective. Their shortcomings (or rather 'largecomings'), such as their cosmic revolutionary zeal, were in this way not held against them so much as held against their postwar heirs, who still held the tacitly disavowed beliefs. Much confusion was in store for those who wished to reopen the heroic Road to Life.

It was also seen to lead to a dead end, for the postulates about both the public and the private had started to corrode. The grandiose collective idea of the supremacy of the masses was undercut by the stalinist proposition that only the authorities were able to judge what was what in that sphere. Trespassers landed behind barbed wires. This did not mean that the individual was about to gain autonomy; that continued to be denied. The rulers, however, began to set up guidelines as to how certain features of the public will were to blend with certain manifestations of the individual will. A way was being worked out to close this gap, torn open by revolutionary zeal. So a new answer was found as to why the people should work for the social good. Coercive compliance was being converted into the instrumental.

When did the turning point occur? When did the rulers turn away from the legacy of the proletarian revolution? When did they undertake what amounted to an appeal to middleclass values? Two answers seem possible here. Successful stalinization of the social order, as expressed in Stalin's commentaries on his constitution, prepared the way for the ideological rise of the notion of prosperity. Stalin thus gave, in 1936, all the incentives needed for the conversion of the public into the private.[10] One could see this as no more than a program, or the initial stage of the system's embourgeoisement – embourgeoisement from above, engulfing the party first. It is therefore possible to argue that the real turning point occurred during the war, at a time of catastrophic strain when, inevitably, the pivotal social strata (on whom survival depended) managed to make their demands and expectations known. This could be seen as a demand for embourgeoisement from below.

There is no need to decide which of the turning points is more important: the fusion of goals from above and from below is what really matters.

Stalinist literature itself is more indicative of the postwar period for the study of the Soviet middle class. One reason is that the memory of the revolution was still vivid in the thirties. Moreover, in that terrible period of transition, confusion, and terror, middlebrow fiction ran for cover. Nor had it yet been instructed to broach the soothing, slow, evolutionary (and hypocritical) theme of the blending of public and private purposes: not while Ezhov[11] walked the land, nor during the trials, nor during Stalin's first bloodbath. It is only the very perceptive and independent writer who would think of connecting the bloodbath with the regime's embourgeoisement and express fear and disgust. That perception added only to the list of martyrs. Obviously, middlebrow fiction does not explore much without orders. Subservient as it is, and so quite sluggish, it caught up with the large theme of Soviet middleclass preferences only after the war, only when it was told to do so, and then cautiously, judiciously, with a twist.

Pronouns in transition

> Proletarian poets speak neither of 'I'
> Nor of the individual.
> 'I' for the proletarian poet
> Is the same as an obscenity.[12]

Soviet youth of 1917, engaged in changing the world, reappraised pronouns. In the wake of the revolution, poems glorified the collective 'We'. The 'I' seemed both puny and shameful. The 'collective breast' had won the revolution at home and was now marching triumphantly to conquer the world. The spirit soared to messianic heights.

> We are the countless, awesome legions of Labor.
> We have conquered the spaces of oceans and land,
> With the light of artificial suns we have lit up the cities,
> Our proud souls burn with the fire of revolt.
> We are possessed by turbulent, intoxicating passion,
> Let them shout at us: 'You are the executioners of beauty',
> In the name of our Tomorrow we shall burn Raphael,
> Destroy museums, trample the flowers of art.
> We have thrown off the heavy, crushing legacy,
> We have rejected the myths of wisdom bled white,
> Young girls in the luminous kingdom of the future
> Shall be more beautiful than the Venus of Milo . . .
> Our muscles crave gigantic work,
> Creative pangs seethe in our collective breast,
> With miraculous honey we shall fill the comb to the brim,

For our planet we shall find a new, dazzling path.
We love life, its intoxicating wild ecstasy,
Our spirit is tempered by fierce struggle and suffering.
We are everybody, we are in everything, we are the flame and the victorious
    light,
We are our own Deity, and Judge, and Law.[13]

This poem, composed triumphantly in 1917 by a young proletarian, became a model. Many such 'We' odes were chanted and marched to.

   Pronouns denote relationships. In the loud language of revolution what gives man promethean power is his relationship to society. Actively linked to the common good, man can apotheosize his small individual destiny. He can become sovereign. But the revolutionary ardor subsided and the feel of collectivity changed. Some twenty years later – during Stalin's purges – a typical rhapsody sounded like this:

> For the sake of our happiness
> He marched through all storms.
> He carried our holy banner
> Over our enormous land.
> And fields and factories rose,
> And tribes and people responded
> To the call of the leader
> To face the final battle.
>
> From his eyes, clear and pure,
> We took courage and strength
> Like radiant water from a deep well
> On our fighting road.
> Let us, comrades, sing a song
> About the greatest general,
> The most fearless and strong,
> About Stalin let's sing a song . . .
>
> He gave us forever and ever
> Youth, glory, and power.
> He has lit the clear dawn of spring
> Over our homes.
> Let us sing, comrades, a song
> About the dearest person,
> About our sun, about the truth of nations,
> About Stalin let's sing a song.[14]

'We' poetry had become 'He' poetry. The collective was no longer its own Deity and Judge and Law. It was transformed into grateful recipients of benefits bestowed by Stalin. If the collective still marched, it did so awk-wardly, on its knees.[15]

The revolutionary hero was clearly in trouble. A play written in 1930 deals with a revisionist attitude toward the collective. Small wonder that the play was blacklisted during the years of terror.[16] Its setting is Stalin's war against the peasant during the agricultural revolution. A man and a woman are arguing. He is a party official sent to uncooperative villages where he must enforce grain delivery and punish resisting peasants. The woman, whom he loves, suggests that since the job of executioner goes against his nature, he should refuse it. His confessional answer, shedding light on the fear of self under fear, has a significance to this day, and not only in relation to public Soviet man.

RAEVSKY: The party uses people where it needs them.

OLGA: But people may be guided by personal considerations. They cannot be covered by the word 'party'. The party is people.

RAEVSKY: No.

OLGA: What is it, then?

RAEVSKY: The party is a hoop. It is an iron band which holds people together.

OLGA: Perhaps. But that band sometimes hurts. Not everybody is alike. People are not like small bushes. It's impossible to prune them and make them all even. You are different from –

RAEVSKY: I have thought about it. The band often cuts my flesh. But I cannot live without it.

OLGA: You say incomprehensible things.

RAEVSKY: It is complicated, Olga. There was never a chance to talk about it. Imagine a crowd. A standard crowd with identical people wearing ties of the same color. The crowd moves in one direction and speaks the very same measured words. I do not want to be like them. Sometimes I think with horror that every day I put on the same tie as all of them. But there is a more frightening feeling than that. Imagine, Olga, that the crowd passes by without you. And you are left behind alone with your own thoughts and doubts. And the columns keep on marching by. They repeat their words. They sing their songs. And no one turns toward you and their measured step is merciless. I cannot step out of the column, precisely because there are in me these divergent thoughts and divergent feelings. I cannot go away. I need somebody's shoulder next to mine. I need someone to order me and restrain me. I need the band which holds together the various sides of my I.

OLGA: And what if you are misled?

RAEVSKY: I will go and die with all the others. I have fought for the party. I am its soldier.[17]

The first person singular, uncovered in its weakness, eventually spells this soldier's undoing. It turns out that he takes more than he gives, for his personal needs dwarf his energy. It is also obvious that the party, then as later, had more urgent matters on its agenda than to 'hold together the various sides' of an unsturdy ego. This old believer craved to remain true and ardent. But he was bothersome to stalinism, and was done away with. A more suitable believer was recruited. The revolutionary collective had marched in ecstasy toward a Utopia; but under Stalin the destination was reached. Utopia had come about and it had to be lived in. The party soldier in need of being propped up is at fault because his introvert proclivities induce him to scrutinize his own life at the end of the road. He fails not so much because he whines – anachronistically at that, while he is stalking about shooting recalcitrant peasants – but, rather because he flails about as a self-conscious person, painfully aware of his fragility. And it was against this that Stalin's purges were to be directed: to crush the searching self in the party's rank and file. The revolution required true believers. So did Stalin. The violence of both periods required them. Yet Stalin liquidated an entire generation that had answered the call. Why did they have to go under, for all their exercise of absolute discipline?

The reasons for the purges are many. Stalin's alteration in the nature of obedience helps to explain it in part. No matter how absolute revolutionary obedience had been before Stalin, it had called for consent[18] and it had been anchored in some modicum of reason. This had entered into the relationship between the party leadership and the rank and file, and had formed the basis for identification with the symbol 'We'. Stalin annihilated just that element of reason. The obedience he required – and obtained through terror – bypassed the brain, aiming at lower organs. Obedience turned blind, reflexive, visceral. It blended with professional, military, automatic discipline.

The metamorphosis of pronouns accompanies this shift. The revolutionary collective was made up of persons who entered it eager to give up their individual self for what seemed to be a higher, heroic group-self. Their sacrifice sprang from a conscious decision. Self-abnegation cemented the 'We' experience and launched it at the heights. But the supreme symbol faltered under the pressure of stalinism. 'We' turned into 'He' by becoming personalized. On the shambles of 'We', Stalin's personality turned into a monstrous shibboleth. And by a compensatory logic, as his personalization swelled on top, the depersonalization of the party ranks began from below. All were sucked dry. The group adhesion of bolshevik comrades disintegrated. A subservient flock was now being sorted out under a relentless vertical pressure, with the purpose of compromising relationships among equals. And even this very shrunken sense of self was dropped on each citizen from on high, as the twenty-odd years of verse- and prose-glorias to Stalin indicate. One by one, the subject fell into formation to receive His guidance and benefactions in a posture of adoration. With his survival at stake, any functionary endeavored with zeal to detach his 'I' from the 'They' of his peers. But it remained to be seen whether atomization could last unamended.

To the reasons why the system did not crumble under the war, one more could be added. And the shorthand of popular poetry shows that it withstood because, once more, the pronouns shifted. Consider this one war poem. Poignantly sentimental, it entered immediately into the mass culture, instantly setting a trend. It is Russia's best-known Second World War poem.

> Wait for me and I'll come back
> But wait with all your heart,
> Wait when yellow rains
> Bring gloom,
> Wait when snowstorms rage,
> Wait through summer heat,
> Wait when other men are given up
> By those who turn away,
> Wait when from afar
> Letters come no more,
> Wait when those who wait together
> Grow tired of waiting.
> Wait for me and I'll come back.
> Don't consort with those
> Who know by heart
> That time has come to forget.
> Let my mother and my son
> Believe that I have died,
> Let my friends, grown weary,
> Sit by the fireside
> And drink the bitter wine
> To my memory.
> Wait, and do not hurry, please,
> To drink with them.
> Wait for me and I'll come back
> Defying many deaths.
> He who did not wait for me,
> Let him say t'was luck.
> They'll never know
> Who did not wait
> That in the midst of fire
> It is you who saved me
> Through your waiting.

> Why I survived
> Only you and I will know,
> Simply, you knew how to wait
> As no other knew.[19]

Popular 'Thou' poetry gave strength to, and in turn reflected, wartime patriotism. Official poets were permitted to say what people craved for. Love poetry was ushered in too, to supplement the glorias to Stalin, to blend with them into a soothing mixture. A lyrical discovery of primary loyalties was permitted, because in apocalyptic circumstances it did not clash with Stalin-worship. Concessions were made to keep morale up in the catastrophic phase of the war. Since the revolutionary mythology of public heroism was only a dim irrelevant memory, wartime heroism found inspiration in the fortitude of individual patriots and lovers, one by one. Primary loyalties furthered national solidarity, and the appeal to basic private emotions helped the survival of Soviet society as a whole.

As tragic events succeeded each other like waves, from one phase of war to another and on to peace, over the bones of the twenty million dead, the feeble but stubborn lyrical violin responded with several leading themes. It seemed that even love between man and woman yielded to compassion for the fallen brothers. Mixed with guilt, it pressed for expression. Poets repeated again and again that war could not be forgotten no matter how hard one tried to forget; nor could sorrow for the bereaved mother and orphans. One should not even try. 'Thou' poetry, mournful to begin with, turned to lament. There surfaced also a newly insistent theme, that of trust and faithfulness.

> Should I be accused by my motherland,
> Should foe and friend turn away from me,
> I would not seek strength from metal.
> You would give it to me. If only you
> Would not stop believing in me.[20]

One could hardly be more explicit than that. Strength, dignity, truth, in fact, were now linked with the 'Thou'. One more shift in pronominal use and it was possible that the single personal 'I' was about to stand alone, doing the job all by itself of holding together the divergent sides of an individuality. Curiously, grief, compassion, war as a national experience, all that had turned into lament, managed to encourage the individual stance.

But it was largely by default that the humanization of mass poetry, the rapprochement with the personal needs of a bereaved population, had come about. The government's stringent surveillance over literary output had yielded in the early war years to more urgent and more material priorities. At the end of the war, however, the entrenchment of dolorous lyrics, dramatized by singular pronouns, and populated by private mourners and lovers instead of public party heroes, came under scrutiny.

The regime decided to intercept the spreading lament with a massive barrage of ideological edicts. That was one of the main purposes of zhdanovism. It undertook to cancel personal stocktaking by enforcing, once more, forward-strutting public jubilation. It began to steer the citizens away from the mass graves and on to the postwar Road to Life while also steering, in real life, newly uncountable victims into concentration camps.

As for usable literary models, however, there was little to fall back on. The collective tenets had long since corroded. And the pattern of stalinist, atomized heroism, a contradiction in terms never particularly apt for literary image making, clashed with the people's mourning. Although it was attempted by orthodox writers, the restoration of the clichés of the thirties did not work. For one thing, the pronouns balked. Too much had happened in Soviet society to permit large retroactive movements, even in middlebrow fiction. For many reasons, the first pronoun singular would not give way, so the creation of the postwar public hero became a problem. A poem about the newly required heroism illustrates the predicament. Working loudly with the henceforth tenacious personal pronouns,[21] a model veteran promises his abdication from lament.

> You think
> I'll bring to you
> My tired body.
> No,
> Don't think that.
> That's not the way
> I'll come back.
> We shall return to work,
> To puff tobacco,
> To fill the room with smoke.
> I am not seeking gratitude.
> I offer it myself,
> That's what I want.
> What I had to say to the enemy,
> I have said it.
> Now I want to work.
> I'll cross your threshold
> Not to be consoled
> But to console.
> That which I have done
> On my way to you,
> Is not a favor
> But duty.

> I want to work in the smithy
> And sleep in bed.
> I want to write verses about love.
> In the windy conflagration of war
> There was hardly a choice.
> But it is better to return
> With an empty sleeve
> Than with an empty soul.[22]

On the brink of peace, the regime paid special attention to how the returning soldiers were to be handled. The same orthodox poet keeps repeating:

> Don't pity us,
> Don't invite us to rest.
> We are not at all tired.
> We are impatient to take off!
> We need no respite,
> No quietude.
> Don't flatter us with the title
> 'War veteran'.
> We want to renovate
> Through labor
> Our medals and honors.
> The urge for difficult work
> Cuts into our palm.[23]

This is a blueprint for a postwar hero, rather than a large-scale embodiment. In fact, the embodiment failed to arrive. The problems in the way were pragmatic and political, the most difficult being that the soldier's war sacrifice had to be minimized and that the regime was ambivalent about heroism anyway. Heroic on first hearing only, the loud lines just quoted are so ambiguous as to help deheroization. And the supreme truth was rebroadcast: there was only one hero. Adoration of Stalin blossomed with renewed vigor,[24] affecting positive characters to the core, and undercutting them. This strategy went into top gear, as the following typical vignette demonstrates. Amorously, just before ensnaring him, a stalinesque amazon probes the soul of a young man as positive as circumstances would allow:

[She] 'Tell me, do you have a sacred dream? You know what I mean? A fantastic dream, an almost impossible one, but such that you do not wish to part with it. Do you have one?'
[He] 'I do'. [He meditates.] 'I would like to have a talk with comrade Stalin.'[25]

In another instance, the hagiography of feudalism, which had torn all lateral ties apart, reaches a peak when Stalin personally takes the hand of a deserving servant and leads him across the threshold of death, one of the rare instances when the presence of civilian death in the epoch of zhdanovite jubilation was altogether permitted.[26]

The last phase of stalinism brought forth the search for builders, not avengers, or spokesmen for a new justice for all. Work was extolled, but with a significant modification when compared with the labor the revolutionaries had craved. Instead of asceticism, the model of what became known as 'greedy life' was advertised, satisfactory from a private point of view, with room for leisure, gregariousness, and the chance to write love poems.

The revolutionary 'We' mood was crushed by the cult. Enforcing a break between the surviving comrades, Stalin tolerated only the direct bondage of each subject to the state, personified by him. But to those who were with him, survivors and recruits, he had promised already a thing or two before the war. Prosperity, no less, was in the offing, provided the subjects gave him all that was in them. This largely demagogic happening prefigured the wheeling and dealing after the war. The supreme victor was prepared after the war to reach down and distribute some rewards among his best subjects. This much-heralded munificence shaped the postwar hero's happiness, which, incidentally, was required of him. His giving was now to join with his taking. Even at the formulaic level, private aspirations became a prerequisite for entering the public realm. Nevertheless, the regime did not spell all this out with immediate and unequivocal clarity. It kept the new prerequisites for postwar model citizens, as well as the benefits they were to receive, shrouded in ambiguities.

Truth in trouble

The Russian word *pravda*, from old Slavic through all Slavic recensions, tantalizingly is not altogether synonymous with the cognitive sobriety of the western word '*truth*'. It connects rather with *rectus, dexter, justus*, and has a strong undercurrent of justice and due process before God.[27] The ancient moral meaning was revolutionized by nascent bolshevism into aggression. And truth as retaliatory social justice held the entire bolshevik ideological framework together. But that which was participatory or corporate in this principle began to ring hollow under Stalin's rule, and its didactic travails commenced. The war, in a way, only aggravated them. Sometimes, lightheartedness was evoked to mask slippage in meaning. A wartime elegy for an adolescent subsequently martyred by the Nazis is here made to participate in the cover-up. Here is

how Zoya Kosmodemyanskaya is depicted, before her personal and
national ordeal, in her prewar youthful normalcy:

> Truth has become your very demeanor,
> Your very drive and involuntary gesture
> When you talk with adults, when you play
> with children.
> Like a white cloud in the sky, like
> the trace of an oar
> Your golden youth rushes on.
> And your pioneer truth grows.
> Your komsomol truth matures.
> And you advance with a gait
> flying forward,
> The half-open secret tomorrow
> inside of you
> And above you, like the arch of the sky,
> Shines your bolshevik truth.[28]

Truth, merry and zephyr-like, dances with the girl in pastoral mode. At the
outbreak of war, instead of stalinist ideological verities, the private idyll
was greatly extolled. It was politicized, and charged, like every other
policy, with mobilizing all resources. The lovely pictures were, in essence,
promises for the future, a glimpse towards the postwar Big Deal. In poem
after poem commemorating that June 22, the Messerschmidts swooped
down apocalyptically, not on the collective at work, but on a single bucolic
family, basking in domestic bliss and stalinist prosperity. Just before the
tocsin, a hero cuts his private grass in his private garden. The green around
him sparkles with sweet peas, clover, and wild strawberries. Happiness
culminates in serene domesticity:

> The front garden lies under the windows,
> And in the garden onions grow in rows,
> All this together was his house, his home,
> His cozy comfort, and his tidy life.

The hero is no hermit. On the contrary, generous hospitality enlivens his
rural style. His bare feet at this moment derive sensuous pleasure from the
glistening, freshly washed floors. He is relaxed, unpublic.

> It's pleasant to sit down at one's own table
> In a tight family circle,
> And, leisurely, to eat one's bread,
> And to praise the glorious day.[29]

Torn between the private and the public, Truth – with tidy rows of private onions – became unsteady, subject to thematic fission. Moreover, under looser control, writers became spontaneous enough to let several subtruths slip out. A youth falls on the battle field.

> A boy lived on the edge of the town of Kolpino.
> He was a dreamer. He made up stories.
> They called him a liar.
> He collected the gayest and the saddest of stories.
> They were evoked by casual talk, by a book.
> At night he dreamed that the road
> Thundered, enveloped in dust.
> He dreamed that the cavalry was pursued
> By reddish fire through the rye fields.
> And in the morning he turned to his fantasies –
> Just like that.
> And they accused him of lying.
> This boy despised tin soldiers
> And other merry war games.
> But road ditches seemed to him trenches.
> Such fantasy was held against him also.
> He grew and became a man on this troubled unkind planet.
> And when in the winter of 1941
> He was killed,
> I found in his officer's folder
> A short letter he wrote home.
> And the letter was filled with the same
> Stories made up by a boy.
> But I could not smile.
> The corner of the gray page, tightly filled,
> Was drenched in blood.
> He collected many different stories.
> I chose to believe him.[30] [1945]

A child's imagination creates a truth all its own, honored by the poet who now, during the war, first pleads for his own right to distinguish truth from fantasy without supervision.

For a while, the official dogma sagged altogether under the eidetic images of suffering:

> A man leaned over a body of water
> And suddenly saw that his hair was gray.
> The man was twenty-two years old.[31]

Such national experience stimulated an introspection which did not subside in the transition from war to peace. On the contrary, this other young person also looks at himself:

> A minute hung suspended
> On the thread of time
> And fell. And it flattened out like
> A trace on dry sand.
> It cannot come back. A sand pebble,
> It will now course through time.
> It was a particle of my life.
> I did not let it live.
> I killed it this winter afternoon,
> Spoiled by richly available days.
> I filled the minute with nothing.
> I kept no memory of it.
> A tiny chink in the century,
> I failed to save it.
> Here hangs a new minute.
> I will not give it away.[32] [1946]

A fragment among fragments, this is the most personal. The fretting about the meaning of time implies – in the face of Soviet reality – the vulnerability of life which must be filled, individual minute by individual minute.

The old took stock, heavily, in a melancholy mood. Their sadness and stoicism emerged in personal spasms. One pensive, quietist poem caused grief to its author. The vehemence of the criticism[33] indicated that in the hazardous year of 1947 an important issue had inadvertently been stepped on, and that old beliefs, in a state of coma, were coinciding with the birthpangs of possible substitute thoughts.

> People don't forgive me my errors.
> That's all right. I learn to answer for myself.
> News columns in morning papers
> Do not promise me an easy life.
> Lavish in empty promises,
> Days burn out like moths in the fire.
> There are no kindly signs ahead
> Promising an easy life ahead.
> What do I know about it?
> Only what I read in poetry, perhaps.
> Dry snow twirls and glistens,
> Lights beckon from afar.

Heavy burden of my lot,
You end up by being feather light!
I am older now, my hair more gray,
And if I grieve, forgive me.
Let my burden turn more heavy.
To throw it off is much harder
Than to go on carrying it.[34]

Though alone, this person does not seem to need a collective to hold together the divergent sides of her ego. Hers seems to respond to an internal truth courageously: the truth is somewhat drab, but it is sturdy.

How did the regime handle this shift from the public to the private? The answer could not be a simple one. The difficulties can best be gleaned from the ambivalence toward the war hero himself. He was found sorely wanting as soon as the war ended. With his populist leanings and lyrical meditations, he took too much to lament and hand wringing, so irritating the regime. Doleful self-searching disqualified him for postwar onward-and-upward marching. And the stark fact that mourning was as personal as it was national did not help soften the new political edicts.

The regime's ambivalence toward the mythological legacy of the twenties and thirties, complicated by distrust of the returning soldier, did not make it easy, either, to work out clear directives for functional official postwar heroism. Nevertheless, guidelines were issued soon enough.

Inevitably, new ambiguities emerged with them. The postwar model was charged with keeping a balance in general and with balancing clashing traits in particular. For instance, simplicity and extraordinariness were to blend. A completely simple person, he was to be enraptured by that tidy row or two of private onions. At the same time, he was to perform inspiring deeds in the shop or field. But there too, he was to be a radiant achiever, not a brain-straining recluse. Avoiding any kind of exaggeration, his thinking, whether at home or at work, had to be undercut in favor of dreaming. Yet dreaming was not to go wild. It was to be directed to one main channel: good things.

He was to offer an alternative to the depersonalization of Stalin's subjects. What the regime now advertised was a chance for citizens to express themselves in striving for material things, leading to contentment. Just as effectively, and perhaps more importantly, the hero was to reject the lure of that other threatening alternative, a possible revival, some twenty-five years out of season, of large-scale purist public dreams – the seduction, in other words, of residual bolshevism. The regime tolerated least of all the craving for any kind of sectarianism. And it was prepared to pay the necessary price by controlling a blend of the private with the public. Public efforts were henceforth to be tempered by private aspirations. The new hero was to teach how the mixture worked. A three-page ballad with the unpromising title 'The District Boss Bids Farewell' offers a good set of clues. In it a deserving industrial administrator, fully entitled to his ennobling cardiac trouble, contemplates retirement. 'Somewhat stooped, somewhat tired' he knows he must give up his job because he is 'stricken with severe and deep illness', and he knows just as clearly that 'nothing will help him forget . . . the cement and iron ore' to which he has dedicated all his life. Stooped shoulders harmonize with his heart ailment, a demonstration that he has sacrificed himself to public duty. By inference, a deheroization takes place and in its wake the transfiguration of a value or two. Although, if needs be, he would repeat from the very beginning his 'swift, hard, nomadic life', a curious discomfort stirs in his, yes, in his soul:

> There is only one thing that fills his soul with anguish,
> There is only one thing that he cannot correct.
> Beloved hands he recalls as they cared for him,
> Hurrying, full of sorrow over parting.
> Did they not bid him farewell too often?
> Were the separations not too long?

Even at home, he worked from dawn to dawn. And over his cup of tea, he buried himself in a newspaper.

> Concerned with people, concerned with the Don and Volga,
> It did not occur to him to think about Olga.
> How many were the nights she waited.
> How she blossomed under sparse tenderness.
> It had seemed to him that this was a private matter.
> It did not fit into projects and plans.
> But meanwhile Olga Andreevna turned gray.
> Perhaps, too gray. Perhaps, too early.

With equal anguish, he now feels remorse about his feelings for his children: he had neglected them. Meanwhile, though, the telling line is buried furtively in the text: 'It had seemed to him that this was a private matter'. It was not. He was wrong. Former prescriptions for former heroes, calling for the neglect of the family and of domestic bliss, were no longer in effect. A desired new balance was in the making. Private matters were no longer private at all. They were now subject to inspection. The heart ailment here in part means retribution. The boss has learned the lesson so well that he passes it on to the new generation. Bidding farewell to his subordinates, he confronts a young trade union representative. The young man is entirely positive. Of course, he is nervous. He expects to receive orders from the powerful superior on the proper placement of engineers. Instead, the boss astonishes him by insisting on the crumbling of the wall between the private and the public:

> Quite unexpectedly for such a moment
> The boss asked:
> 'You are married, are you not?'
> And the young man stands amazed.
> He stares at the boss's faded tunic.
> He hears the old stern chief of the district
> Say to him:
> 'Take care of your beloved.'[35]

We now observe that tender care of wife and brood has become the new mandatory element of Truth. This timely new component, however, proved hard to tag on to the standing commitment to public exertion. The fact is that the two did not fuse very well. A model citizen pleased with himself was called upon. Obviously, he could not be smug. He was charged with seeking useful positive self-fulfillment. And the awkward problem of careerism surfaced.

Careerism as a key theme also signalled the regime's shift toward middleclass aspirations. It could not, of course, be too openly proclaimed, but it could not be denied either. This double predicament interfered with the didactic task of fiction. Its young heroes and heroines indicate this in their confusion, as we shall now see.

Young people quarrel

Becoming 'somebody' was desirable. What was the proper way? How could individual social elevation be squared with traditional collectivist ideals? This remained unclear for a while. Some notions were borrowed from the private system of preferences – malleable ones, such as the efflorescence of a 'rounded personality' and 'personal happiness'. They were then grafted on to the primary allegiance to public duty, on to public valor. Their grafting, in part because it was an afterthought, betrayed the strain of keeping up the old catechism. They solved some problems, but also created new ones.

For one thing, if the new prescript for 'personal happiness' was to be understood as a franchise for career satisfaction, it also seemed to be granting a contrasting franchise: seeking happiness in apathy. Initially the limits in either direction were not clearly staked out. Unlike the earlier eras of categorical answers, this turned into a period of questions, uneasy and frequently muted.

For instance, in Yurii Trifonov's widely read *Students*, a young veteran adjusts as best he can to the postwar atmosphere. Although his function in the novel is that of a hero, tellingly, 'Truth' and 'Road' beckon him with not much clarity. And they become altogether obscure if he is going to share them with his girlfriend. So, he asks whether she knows where she is going:

'And what is your goal, Lena?'
    'What goal, Vadik?' she asked softly and with surprise.
    'Of your life!'

She bursts out laughing at his 'loud words'. Embarrassed, he turns silent for a while, for the girl, here as elsewhere, steals the show. It is she who superimposes the visceral aspect of the conflict upon its semantics.

The girl happens to take private singing lessons. The young man wants to know why she does, considering that she studies in a pedagogical institute. She answers that she does not sing for professional reasons.

'What for, then?'
    'For –' Lena turned silent for a second and then uttered with her habitual sententiousness, 'a woman, Vadik, must know everything. She must know how to dress, how to be beautiful, how to sing – you understand.'
    'I understand. So, it follows, that you are studying to become a woman?'
Lena looked at Vadik with silent outrage.

When her outrage subsides, she adds in a conciliatory fashion:

'How can I in two words tell you about all my plans, about my future? What's more I don't trouble my mind over such things. What for? I am only beginning to live . . . Students in olden days eternally argued about something. About the final goal in life, about the supreme good, about all sorts of nonsense. But you and I, why should we start these abstract arguments? I am the same kind of komsomol as you are. We have the same ideology. What can we argue about?'

Not that there is nothing to argue about. His remembrance of the war irritates the girl more than anything. It is noteworthy that only here he takes a strong stand.

'No, excuse me', said Vadik firmly. 'Let me finish. At the front I learned to understand many simple things in a new way. Much deeper. And sometimes I discussed with my comrades our future life, our work, our profession. We discussed what we love, what we dream about. We even talked about our goal in life and, you know, the words were very natural and very simple and sincere. They helped us, they gave us more strength. And now – why is it that now they seem so blatant and naive?'

The girl neither knows nor cares. She dismisses the war and its truth. Thereupon, the poor fellow insists that he simply must find out how she wants to live.

'Well, how do I want to live? I want to live honestly, peacefully, well, happily.' After a pause she added undecidely, 'I want to participate in work.'

'Happily, in the sense of getting married happily?'

'So what? Every woman hopes to get married happily', said Lena, immediately turning haughty, 'You know, today you are terribly boring and unoriginal. You are even, forgive me, somewhat vulgar. Do you want to pick a fight?'

'No', said Vadik, shaking his head, 'I don't want to.'[36]

Where his aspirations seem vague, the girl clearly hopes for a comfortable married life, accented by the songs she will sing to her husband. And she says so plainly. These hopes are carried on the crest of rising mesh-chanstvo. It equips her with a potent weapon: derision of the futility of the intelligentsia's posturing. The tone of the argument, however, matters more than the subject of discord. The young man's insecurity, inarticulate-ness, and embarrassment stand out in marked contrast to the girl's ease, even nonchalance. The language of his insecurity in itself points to the trend of deheroization among postwar young heroes.

Failure to achieve a happy family life began to be frowned upon. This pretty, well-dressed miss with her middleclass ways was *en vogue*. Her aspirations could not be dismissed, nor had the regime any intention of dismissing them: on the contrary. Even if the young man attempts to oppose meshchanstvo by expressing correct ideals, he is shown as some-how losing all the same.

Such quarrels filled many a novel. The scope of the problem becomes clearer if one looks at the mirror image of the dispute in another tale. In this reversed version, it is the woman who stands for public heroism; the man is not sure. The man has just been demobilized. He has been a brave soldier. We find him fatigued, drained. He needs time to take stock and rest. He craves to be left alone. It is as simple as that. And it is not that he finds himself at a loss what to do with his life. Having reached home at last fills him with ecstasy. This is to him a miracle, even if it happens to be shell-shocked Leningrad. He has found his young wife safe and sound. He loves her. He relishes a nest of his own. But her arms turn out soon enough neither warm nor soothing. In fact, whatever else she may be willing to offer, it is not shelter. She begins to throw serious accusations at him. Her demands that he adjust his image of public valor cut him deeply. His self-defensive responses seem reasonable.

'I hope you don't think that I don't understand postwar tasks. You may rest assured that even during the war I knew perfectly well that there will be no respite and that there cannot be any. All that is elementary. But I am speaking of something else. I am speaking of that life on the very brink of which you preach and which you practice . . . You need some sort of super-work which takes away all one's life leaving nothing over.'[37]

He obviously does have in mind her presumptuousness, strain and exaggeration. But she remains adamant and keeps nagging. At one point, he pleads with her:

'Let's be grateful for what we have. In the past they would have said, don't invite the wrath of God. Don't you think . . . of those without a family, without a shelter, of those who have lost their own happiness in the struggle for that of others? And we, we have found ours. Is this not enough?'

For her it is not, and she counters with a weapon that ushered in much ambiguity wherever proper postwar aspirations were debated. She accuses him of smugly reclining on his laurels. Anything but placid, she shouts:

'It's not enough, do you understand, it's not enough! What you are talking about is happiness, but it is small, dried up, as if it were in a tin can. I always wanted something bigger and I want you to get cured of your disease, of your sleepy life.' [p. 33]

Another pair in a much debated novel takes us to the countryside, which suggests less sophistication as well as less confusion in the probing which they undertake. The man in the first tale seems a mixed-up boy; the man in the second worn out by the war, but this one is vigorous and rugged and ambitious. He knows what he wants. His name is Rodion; hers Grunia. He returns a glamorous warrior. But his reception leaves something to be desired. To begin with, his wife had been erroneously notified of his death. She had drowned her sorrow in work, and became famous in agricultural work, a much photographed amazon. But now her reputation is no help to them. They do not see eye to eye. He is eager to get on, but for himself. Her dreams are cut of a different cloth, those of an impeccable party-minded heroine:

'What a wonderful life there will be in about a hundred years. It stops your breath to think what people and science will attain!'

This opening gambit of hers does not enthuse him:

'I also like to dream a bit . . . But I don't like my feet to leave the ground. All right, so you dream for a while. But what sense is there in it? And I think that for us . . . there is no point in guessing what is many years ahead. It's too far for us! . . . Better hang on to what is given us now in our own life! Let's not give it away to anybody! Let's enjoy it to the brim so that our heads swirl!'[38]

He had hoped that his wife would support his ambitions 'for a prosperous life and his own great glory'.[39] But his goals hold little attraction for her. She

> rejected everything he suggested! She wanted him to drop all his plans and to follow her in her footsteps. To place himself under the command of his wife? No, she will never achieve that. [p. 50]

There is no way they can manage together, for he does not even understand her working methods. She works for the good of the state, so much so that she loses interest in the very success of her team and in her own merit badges. And he is greatly perplexed at her commitment to national productivity rather than any interest in winning a medal for herself. Immediately after his return in a nocturnal dialogue, ponderously dedicated to career aspirations (rather than to making love after years of separation), he asks for her support, promising

> 'Only in one year's time . . . here in this very spot you and I will each pin a Gold Star! . . . For the sake of that little star I will do anything!'

She reacts with some dismay.

> 'But does happiness consist really of working and living for rewards? All through the war I didn't even think of rewards. I worked without sparing myself. And didn't you do the same over there?'

He, in turn, finds her reasoning peculiar and retorts:

> 'Pride will move everybody these days! Everybody wants to distinguish himself and to be seen by all! Don't tell me that even now you don't think of rewards!'

He has touched a soft spot. She blushes, gets up, becomes agitated, and burns with the inner fever of true believers, exposed to new pressures. Confused, she clutches the collective dogma:

> 'It is so very much to be awarded the title of Hero of Labor. And if, for instance, one of us receives it, it certainly does not mean that just one person is honored but the whole team, the whole collective farm. Could one person achieve anything without the others? . . . It is exactly the same as the passing red banner which hangs in our administration, that's how it is!'

Rodion does not accept the analogy. He wants his own reward, all of it, and not without a touch of paranoia.

'Oh no! . . . The passing banner is ours today, but tomorrow it may be taken away! The little star I speak about, however, will shine for all your life, for you and no one else! And no one will take it away!'

It's her turn now. She regains her composure, sounding as stern as the revolutionary amazons of yesteryear:

'Well, all right! Suppose you are awarded a Hero's Star. And then what?'
'Then I will earn a second one!'
'And then?'

Naturally, he hesitates. But he assembles his wits and points to the refurbished instrumental incentives: recognition, status, and envy produced in others.

'I will be known everywhere; such glory will make everybody envious! If you can't achieve that, then what's the point in putting all your strength into work, what's the point in killing yourself over it?' [p. 103]

Ritual and reward have not yet come to a proper balance. Medals are not used to *close* an account between the regime and the striving citizen. They symbolize rather an ongoing relationship. Byzantic, they are effective devices in the promulgation of the Big Deal. The purist young woman here is indifferent to them but her stance seems hypocritical to her ambitious husband. When the accusation of hypocrisy surfaces, she must ponder whether to keep moving along her zealously orthodox path or to backtrack.

These quarrels give us one useful hint: nobody wins. In the past, that draw, that open-endedness would have been impossible. But of course, since nobody wins, nobody loses. And what is becoming clearer is the nature of the groping itself: the search for the self more than for The Road and Truth.

It is remarkable that this gray and undistinguished fiction managed to convey that even young lovers ceased to communicate too well. The guiding principles to close debate seemed in disrepair. Youth was confronted with an unprecedented problem. It was expected that they make sacrifices. Even more, it was expected that they be happy. The combination of new efforts remained to be worked out.

Jaded people adjust

A look at an older couple shows that the conflict does not disappear with age nor with language which says one thing and means another. A district party secretary named Dry (Sukhov) is having to contend with the illicit love affair of his second party secretary. The 'second' is married. Petulantly, Comrade Dry orders his subordinate to stop the affair.

'Tell me, how long is this going to continue?'
'What?' asked [the second secretary] unsuccessfully pretending that he did not know what it was all about.
'You know very well. Your wife was here again. She cried. She threatens to write to the regional committee. Are you some sort of a low person without status? The masses must emulate you. And you, you display immoral conduct. It's high time to stop this.'[40]

This interchange between two party officials captures an eidetic image of meshchanstvo mores. The wronged wife weeps, she seeks revenge through denunciation at the regional level. At the same time, Comrade Dry suggests that extramarital relations may be acceptable for lowly folk but not for someone whom the masses must emulate. The gap between language and its merely conventional meaning (what 'masses?' what 'immoral conduct?' what 'emulation?') jumps right out from these few lines. One needs no larger context. For the ways of meshchanstvo permeate every line of the story. And Comrade Dry transforms his own fears into coercion, his own insecurity into deadly formalism.

Ordered by the boss to stop the illicit affair, the 'second' replies quickly:

'I can't. Do with me what you wish. I can't.'
'What kind of an approach is this? What do you mean, you can't? The situation in the district is far from brilliant even without you. All we need is that they should start working us over along this line too. Watch out! You can lose your party card for this sort of thing!' [p. 51]

The inadvertently grotesque here combines with the pathetic. Comrade Dry's philistinism becomes threatening. The cluster of terms such as 'they', 'working over', 'along that line' show how helpless the exposed functionary is against the establishment. The forces that impinge on him are formidable, those of stalinist meschanstvo, bureaucratized and canonized.

This genre picture contains other interesting detail. A charming girl with freckles has meanwhile been hired in Comrade Dry's office as a new clerk. The comrade's own family life is not all that it should be. He is married to a representative of arch-meshchanstvo, exploiting her position as wife of the local boss. In the oppressive provincial summer heat, Comrade Dry feels that he is falling in love with the fresh, uncontaminated, freckled office girl. All of a sudden he begins to understand his 'second'. In frustration, he takes a close look at his wife. Until now her abuse of privilege has not bothered him much. Instead of going shopping like everybody else, she has managers of stores deliver merchandise to the house. She sends the party office chauffeur on constant errands to the regional center. She has an employee of a dressmaking atelier come to her house for fittings. All of this is not legal. Worse, she has brought up her son to be a snooty, spoiled brat. Comrade Dry cannot explain her at all. His inability to do so connects with the fact that the 'birthmark' or 'residue' theory, once used declaratively, no longer explains much. But now at least the good comrade is beginning to be aware of the process involved. He meditates:

> At first she somehow developed a greediness for material affluence. And now that she has attained it, she has developed, God knows why, a need to boast about material success way out of proportion to reality. Doesn't she know that I cannot permit the district committee car to be commandeered for some silly sewing supplies? How has she come to be like that? [p. 53]

That is just the point. Meanwhile, the marital conflict takes on the age-old form. Over the dinner table, in the presence of their small son, two people shout at cross-purposes. The good comrade engages in rhetoric. And the wife fights back. With singular expressiveness, gray everyday language, interspersed with cant, opens up sorry horizons beyond these three sitting under one dining room lamp.

> 'Tell me one thing. Are you a Soviet person or are you not?'
> 'Eat your borsch.'
> 'We have discussed this question with you repeatedly', he contin-ued, 'and I thought you had arrived at appropriate conclusions'.
> 'Conclusions, conclusions!' his wife exploded. 'Stuff is being car-ried to the Evdokimovs every week. And here on account of some miserable two meters of fabric for Petya, I must listen to a long lecture. You don't pay any attention to your son. Are you his father or what?' [p. 54]

The 'second' must be punished because his love-life is in disarray. The wife of the 'first', however, gets away with a great deal more. But she also bears herself self-righteously. You can steamroller a small person, but the hard power of the bosses spreads to their wives and makes corruption. Mouthed by those centaurs, half leaders of the masses and half somnolent philistines, ideological tenets lose all meaning and turn into meancing clichés.

The ending is not without a twist, not without a human note. Comrade Dry turns out to be not so dry after all. He seeks a way out in resignation. To remove temptation from his uninspiring path, he requests the transfer of the freckled office girl. Moreover, he even manages to caress his wife's hair after years of marital estrangement. This startles her. He accompanies this gesture of compassion with muted Chekhovian words:

'Well, what are you looking at me like that for? Let's go on living.'

Shame awakens in him for having used nothing but clichés in his attempts to solve personal problems in a party way. In the end, this impotent, mediocre party official does manage to take a look at himself.

Notes

1 N. Ostrovskii, *Kak zakalialas stal* (The Tempering of Steel) (1934) (Moscow, 1947), p. 189.
2 *Road to Life* is the English title of a film made by N. Ekk, based on a work on education, *Pedagogical Poem* by A. Makarenko, a voluminous account, fictional only in form, of Makarenko's experiences with and efforts on behalf of the *besprizornye*, literally the 'uncared for', lost and abandoned children whom the revolution and civil war had tossed into the vortex of destruction and survival. Many had become criminals. Makarenko, it seems, was successful in rehabilitating some. The commune in which he worked was under the patronage, *mirabile dictu*, of the Cheka. With collectivist fervor, Makarenko rhapsodizes in conclusion: 'And on healthy soil, surrounded by Cheka men, supported every day by their energy, education, and talent, the commune grew into a collective of dazzling beauty, of genuine constructive richness, of lofty socialist culture' (Moscow, 1947), p. 637.
3 Iu. German, 'Aleksei Zhmakin', *Literaturnyi sovremennik*, No. 10, 1937, p. 119.
4 I. Ehrenburg, *Zhizn I Gibel Nikolaia Kurbova* (Life and Death of Nikolai Kurbov) (Berlin, 1923), p. 21.
5 *Besprizornik*, see note 2.
6 N. Ostrovskii, *Kak zakalialas stal*, p. 77.
7 A. Fadeev, *Razgrom* (The Route) (1925) (Moscow, 1947), p. 113–14.
8 N. Ostrovskii, *Kak zakalialas stal*, p. 137. The message of this massively propagated work belongs to the romantic twenties. The book of a true believer, it was used through the thirties as a catechism for the young. One can assume, as the regime's needs were changing, this Sunday school text was offered for edification in the expectation that as the young reader matured, confrontation with life would bring the necessary adjustments.
9 F. Gladkov, *Tsement* (Cement) (1925) (Moscow, 1931), p. 45. There are three versions of this work, as important as it is artistically faulty, over which the author fussed a lot: 1925, 1930, and 1944. The most accomplished is the middle version, cited here. The last is an example of self-inflicted disfigurement. Whatever spark, however primitive, the earlier style possessed was extinguished and all 'naturalistic' detail removed to comply with the heavy prudishness of socialist realism.
10 See N. S. Timasheff's durable *The Great Retreat* (New York, 1946); M. Fainsod's *How Russia is Ruled* (second edition, Cambridge, Mass., 1963), pp. 104–8; and especially B. Moore Jr.'s *Soviet Politics – The Dilemma of Power* (second edition, New York, 1965), chapter 8. 'The Mythology of Status and the New Bureaucracy', pp. 159–88.
11 N. I. Ezhov (1895–1940), one of Stalin's most sinister henchmen, Commissar of Internal Affairs from 1936 to 1938, succeeded by Beria. His name engenders 'ezhovshchina', the synonym for the bloodiest of purges.

12 V. Maiakoskii, 'Piatyi internatsional' (Fifth International), *Sobranie sochinenii*, vol. 3 (Moscow, 1968), p. 72.

13 V. Kirillov, 'My' (We) (1917), *Izbrannie stikhotvoreniia 1917–32* (Moscow, 1933), pp. 15–17.

14 M. Izakvoskii, 'Pesnia o Staline' (1936) (Song about Stalin), *Izbrannie stikhotovreniia* (Moscow, 1941), pp. 157–8.

15 Or worse. Foreshadowing what the collective was to run into during the thirties, N. Tikhonov in his 'Ballada o gvozdiakh' (Ballad about Nails) (1919) sang the iron discipline of a crew of prerevolutionary sailors off on a suicide mission. The praise resounds in the laconic requiem: 'One should make nails out of these people. There would be no tougher nails on earth'. *Stikhi i proza* (Verses and Prose) (Moscow, 1945), p. 94. Stalin took his advice.

16 A militant communist, the playwright V. Kirshon perished in the purges of 1938. In the mid fifties he was 'rehabilitated'.

17 V. Kirshon, 'Khleb' (Bread), *Izbrannoe*, (Moscow, 1958), pp. 192–3.

18 'No fully developed despot, it may be surmised, can content himself with compelling his subjects' assent to policies exclusively rational. Only then may he regard his people as fully subject to his will when he can compel their assent to procedures palpably outrageous and absurd': Ronald Hingley, *The Russian Secret Police* (London, 1970), p. 152.

19 K. Simonov, 'Zhdi menia' (Wait for Me), *Voina* (War) (Moscow, 1944), pp. 54–5.

20 S. Schipachev, untitled, *Den poezii* (Day of Poetry) (Moscow, 1956), p. 38.

21 No less didactic than 'We' poetry, the postwar odes to Soviet valor could not do without the 'We' posture either. But in the emerging pronominal promiscuity, the first pronoun singular had long ceased to be an obscenity.

22 M. Lukonin, 'Pridu k tebe' (I Shall Come to You) (1944), *Antologiia russkoi sovetskoi poezii, 1917–57*, vol. 2 (Moscow, 1957), pp. 443–4.

23 M. Lukonin, 'Prishedshim s voiny' (To Those Who Have Returned from War), *Antologiia russkoi sovetskoi poezii*, pp. 444–5.

24 A. Tvardovsky said this, without dodging responsibility, in a requiem for the darkest times and a tainted generation:

> Just try to find the man who
> Did not praise and glorify him.
> Just try and find him!
> Probably not in vain
> The son of the East
> To the very end
> Fulfilled the traits
> Of his hard,
> Of his cruel,
> Wrongness
> And rightness.
> But who of us is fit to be a judge,
> To decide who is right, who is wrong?
> We speak of people. And people
> Do they not create gods themselves?

'Za daliu dal', (Horizon Beyond Horizon), *Sobranie sochinenii*, vol. 3 (Moscow, 1962), p. 341. Not only did these reminiscences in verse receive the 1961

Lenin prize but the confessional portion containing this extract was, unhingingly to some, first published in *Pravda*.

25 A. Kron, 'Kandidat partii' (Party Candidate), *Novyi mir*, No. 10, 1950, p. 19.

26 The death scene of the party organizer Zernov in A. Gribachev's 'Vesna v "Pobeda"' (Spring in 'Pobeda'), *Znamia*, No. 12, 1948, p. 48. In a visionary revelation, shared by author and hero, Stalin speaks thus:

> 'You have struggled not in vain.
> You have labored not in vain.
> Your last day is your first step into the commune.
> Here comes its dawn.'
> Thus, at dawn
>   in 'Pobeda'
> Zernov, the party organizer,
>   died.

27 Skeptics are advised to consult. A. G. Preobrazhesnskii, *Etimologichskii slovar russkogo iazyka* (Moscow, 1910), vol. 2, p. 121.

28 M. Aliger, 'Zoia,' *Stikhi i poemy* (Moscow, 1944), p. 129.

29 A. Tvardovskii, 'Dom u dorogi' (1942–1946) (House by the Road), *Sobranie sochinenii*, vol. 3 (Moscow, 1967), pp. 12–14.

30 A. Mezhirov, 'Stikhi o malchike' (Verses about a Boy) (1945), *Antologiia russkoi sovetskoi poezii, 1917–57*, vol. 2, pp. 572–3.

31 A. Surkov, untitled (1941), *Pesni groznogo serdtsa* (Songs of a Wrathful Heart) (Iaroslavl, 1944), p. 38.

32 A. Krongauz, 'Minuta' (A Minute) (1946), *Antologiia russkoi sovetskoi poezii, 1917–57*, vol. 2, pp. 621–2.

33 Accused of defeatism by Zhdanov's people, the poetess was defended by K. Simonov, editor of *Novyi mir* at the time. Attacks: S. Tregub, 'Novye stikhi Margarity Aliger,' *Literaturnaia gazeta*, October 26, 1946, and V. Ermilov, 'O partiinosti v literature i ob otvetstvennosti kritiki,' *Literaturnaia gazeta*, April 19, 1947. Defense: K. Simonov, 'Zametki pisatelia,' *Novyi mir*, No. 1, 1947.

34 M. Aliger, untitled, *Novye stikhi* (New Poems), as quoted by K. Simonov in 'Zametki pisatelia,' *Novyi mir*, No. 1, 1947, pp. 167–8.

35 L. Oshanin, 'Nachalnik raiona proshchaetsa s nami' (The District Boss Bids Us Farewell), *Antologiia russkoi sovetskoi poezii, 1917–57*, vol. 2, pp. 273–6.

36 Yu. Trifonov, 'Studenty' (Students), *Novyi mir*, No. 10, 1950, p. 157.

37 A. Chakvoskii, 'Mirnye dni' (Days of Peace), *Zvezda*, No. 10, 1947, p. 22.

38 E. Malzev, 'Ot vsego serdtsa' (From the Heart), *Oktiabr*, No. 9, 1948, p. 22.

39 This novel received the Stalin Prize for 1948. The heroine was at the moment proclaimed impeccable. When zhdanovism came out of joint ahead of Stalin's death, the novel was harshly reevaluated by critics and the heroine was now ranked by some among the most wooden and implausible. The erring husband's assets went up on the fickle market of Soviet morality. We do not care one way or another. In this particular instance, regardless of the reversal of critics, the gap between his and her proclivities marks one kind of oscillation in the constantly shifting adjustments of the Big Deal.

40 S. Antonov, 'Novyi sotrudnik' (New Colleague), *Novyi mir*, No. 3, 1954, p. 51.

Index